D1559829

Otherwise Worlds

BLACK OUTDOORS INNOVATIONS IN THE POETICS OF STUDY
A series edited by J. Kameron Carter and Sarah Jane Cervenak

OTHERWISE WORLDS

Against Settler
Colonialism and
Anti-Blackness

**Tiffany Lethabo King, Jenell Navarro,
and Andrea Smith**

Duke University Press
Durham and London 2020

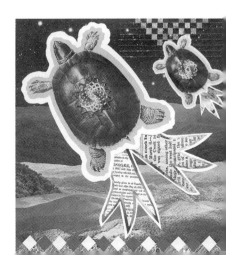

© 2020 Duke University Press
All rights reserved
Printed in the United States of America on acid-free paper ∞
Designed by Aimee C. Harrison
Typeset in Minion Pro and Univers LT Std by Westchester

Library of Congress Cataloging-in-Publication Data

Names: King, Tiffany Lethabo, [date] editor. | Navarro,
Jenell, [date] editor. | Smith, Andrea, [date] editor.
Title: Otherwise worlds : against settler colonialism and
anti-Blackness / Tiffany Lethabo King, Jenell Navarro,
Andrea Smith.
Other titles: Black outdoors.
Description: Durham : Duke University Press, 2020. |
Series: Black outdoors | Includes bibliographical references
and index.
Identifiers: LCCN 2019042304 (print) | LCCN 2019042305
(ebook)
ISBN 9781478007869 (hardcover)
ISBN 9781478008385 (paperback)
ISBN 9781478012023 (ebook)
Subjects: LCSH: Blacks—Study and teaching. | Indians of
North America—Study and teaching. | African Americans—
Relations with Indians. | African Americans—Race identity. |
Indians of North America—Ethnic identity. | Racism. |
Race—Political aspects.
Classification: LCC E98.R28 O84 2020 (print) |
LCC E98.R28 (ebook) | DDC 305.8—dc23
LC record available at https://lccn.loc.gov/2019042304
LC ebook record available at https://lccn.loc.gov/2019042305

Cover art: Kimberly Robertson and Jenell Navarro,
Postcard from an Otherwise World.

We, the editors, have decided to give our proceeds from this book to support the work of Lifted Voices, an organization that works at the intersections of anti-Blackness and settler colonialism.

Lifted Voices is an action-oriented collective committed to defending the lives and rights of Black and Indigenous people, and to combating state violence in all its forms. Their Black and Indigenous membership offers workshops to people of conscience who wish to engage in protest effectively. From direct action 101 to advanced direct action and tactic-specific trainings, the workshops have helped allies around the country realize their visions of protest. Members of the collective also visit elementary schools to talk with young people about social justice work, including transformative justice, Indigenous resistance, prison abolition, and artful protest.

As an abolitionist collective, Lifted Voices also participates in defense committee work, organizing support for people who have been incarcerated for acts of self-defense. This solidarity work with imprisoned people has also involved bail fund drives—including an effort that freed twenty-two detained migrants in the summer of 2019. Lifted Voices believes in transformative justice, community-based accountability, and the need for a world without prisons. They also believe that marginalized people must explore the ways in which we have internalized our oppression and the ways in which we have perpetuated the oppression of others at the behest of white supremacy. They do this without any punitive aim and in the interest of transformation. By building community, building culture, and taking action in defense of ourselves and our lives, we lift our own voices.

For more information or to support the work of Lifted Voices, follow them at https://liftedvoices.org/.

Contents

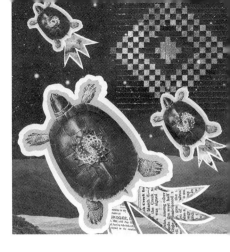

Tiffany Lethabo King, Jenell Navarro & Andrea Smith

Beyond Incommensurability

Toward an Otherwise Stance
on Black and Indigenous Relationality

The relationship between Native genocide and anti-Blackness has been articulated sometimes in terms of presumed solidarity or comparison, such as the notion that Native peoples harbored runaway slaves and that Black fugitives assisted Native peoples in armed struggle against settler encroachment. Sometimes it has been articulated in terms of antagonism, such as the focus on Native peoples who owned slaves and on enslaved or indentured Black people who participated in settler raids on Native nations. Nowadays, it seems to be in terms of incommensurability, which asserts a lack of commonality/relationality between Black and Native folks. This project emerges from us thinking that all of these modes are insufficient. While certainly solidarity, antagonism, and incommensurability are distinct and no one mode of relationality can be presumed, at the same time it is illogical to presume we can talk about any mode without doing it in relationship with one another. If we submit momentarily to the popular position that Black and Native peoples and, by extension, Black and Native politics are at an impasse represented by their incommensurability, then the flip side of being stuck together—or this stuckness—is already a form of relationality. As a result, we think Édouard Glissant's "relation" seems to be a helpful starting point:

> Relation . . . does not act upon prime elements that are separable or reducible. If this were true, it would itself be reduced to some mechanics capable of being taken apart or reproduced. It does not precede itself in its action and presupposes no a priori. It is the boundless effort of the world, to become realized in its totality, that is to evade rest. One does not first enter Relation, as one might enter a religion. One does not first conceive of it the way we have expected to conceive of Being.[1]

It seems that much analysis of the relationship between Indigenous geno-cide/settler colonialism and anti-Blackness tends to be prescriptive in that the analysis presumes a certain prescribed politic—whether it be a call for solidarity in a certain way or a call to reject solidarity. But analysis of re-lationality suggests something *otherwise*—that the relationality between genocide and anti-Blackness is not fixed and easily knowable. In addition, to borrow from Antonio Viego's *Dead Subjects*, there is an imperative in the academy to make Native peoples knowable and to presume that Black peoples are already known.[2] Thus, not surprisingly, the relationship between the two is presumed to be fully representable and it keeps Black and Indig-enous communities in isolation from one another, which is a settler desire/ dream.

Thus, we would prefer an approach that does not presume an "answer" but instead seeks to ask questions about the complexities of this relation, and hence the political possibilities that emerge from asking these questions and engaging in the process of relation. This desire not to presume an an-swer mediates any attempt to trace a genealogy to this conversation with the respective fields of Native studies and Black studies because to tell a story of either field tends to prescribe the outcome of any conversation between the fields. For instance, we could trace the development of Native studies through the influential work of Elizabeth Cook-Lynn's "Who Stole Native Studies" and Winona Stevenson's "'Ethnic' Assimilates 'Indigenous.'"[3] These works argued that Native studies should distance itself from ethnic studies (and presumably from Black studies by extension) because otherwise the field of ethnic studies would relegate Native peoples to a racial minority sta-tus rather than as peoples seeking decolonization. Cook-Lynn and Wheeler contended that engaging Native studies with ethnic studies, postcolonial studies, and so on, which do not share a concern for the liberation of Native peoples, could have the effect of domesticating Native studies into a multi-culturalist project of representation within the academy instead of one that defended Native nations' claims to sovereignty. While there is much to be gained by tracing the genealogy of Native studies through these works, how does this genealogy presume that Black studies (or ethnic studies generally speaking) is fundamentally about articulating a racial minority status? Or we could center the work of Lee Maracle and Roberto Mendoza who argued that Native people and Native studies needed to be in conversation with rad-ical political thought emerging from all sectors of society.[4] Such a genealogy would more easily enable a conversation between Native studies and other fields of thought. At the same time, their work often presumed a more Marxist framework as the point of conversation between Native studies and other fields. Thus, we wonder what might be enabled differently from a conversation that began from different theoretical assumptions? The point here is not to disparage the importance of these works. Rather, it is to say that to delimit the fields of Native studies and Black studies is to delimit the possibilities of conversations between the two. And to have this conversation is to simultaneously open up what the fields of Native studies and Black studies can be.

Similarly, mapping genealogies of Black studies might also work to stifle emergent, lesser known, and otherwise conversations between the two fields. For one, the task of periodizing the field and charting its geographic coordinates is already a contested project. Further, attending to how multiple forms and practices of Black study have turned their scholarly attention to Indigenous peoples might privilege some forms of knowledge production and their political projects over others. The aforementioned project requires a project of its own. For example, Arika Easley-Houser examines antebellum African American print culture (newspapers, political speeches, David Walker's *Appeal*) in order to track the ways African American writers thought and talked about Native Americans in the nineteenth century.[5] Easley-Houser argues that several different political projects, ranging from ones that sought alliances with Native peoples to comparative projects that tried to prove African American superiority to Native peoples and even investigations of Native practices of enslavement, motivated Black nineteenth-century writing on Native peoples.[6] Shortly after founding the Association for the Study of African American Life and History in 1915, Carter G. Woodson authored the article "The Relations of Negroes and Indians in Massachusetts" in 1920 in the *Journal of Negro History*. Throughout the twentieth century there were intermittent attempts on the part of Black individuals and institutions to document and study Black and Native histories and exchanges in America.

During the late 1960s and early 1970s, militant anti-imperialist and anticapitalist activism animated by the Black Power movement in the US and Third World internationalism birthed the first Black studies programs. The strong ties between Black activism and the development of academic departments created fertile ground for conversations between Black and Native scholars and activists. Revisiting Black, Native, and ethnic studies' radical roots encourages a commemoration of histories of solidarity and shared struggle while it also exposes the pressure that universities put on fields like Black studies to "define" itself and distinguish itself from other ethnic studies programs like Native studies. In 1974, Robert Allen wrote about the ways that Black studies and ethnic studies were being "counter-posed" and forced into an "antagonistic relationship" with one another in the academy.[7] While this genealogical approach thus far has limited itself to Black studies in the US, recounting this history helps expose the ways that the settler colonial university worked (and continues) to pit fields like Black and Native studies against one another and prevent generative dialogue.[8]

After the establishment of Black studies departments, a noticeable uptick in scholarship by Black scholars on Black and Native American relations emerged after Jack D. Forbes's book *Africans and Native Americans: The Language of Race and the Evolution of Red-Black Peoples* was published in 1993. In the first decades of the twenty-first century, several Black historians (Sharon Holland; Barbara Krauthamer; Tiya Miles; Celia Naylor; Fay Yarborough) have written books dedicated to the study of Black and Indigenous people in the Southeastern United States. Scholars began to pay particular attention to the practice of slavery among the Five Civilized Tribes. In 2006, Tiya Miles and Sharon Holland coedited the anthology *Crossing Waters, Crossing Worlds: The African Diaspora in Indian Country.* The contributors to the collection used a variety of interdisciplinary methods and rooted their work in primary sources, archival records, and Black and Native literary traditions that told stories of Black and Native relations in North America. *Crossing Waters, Crossing Worlds* emerged around the same time that the emergent field of (white) settler colonial studies was beginning to take shape in Australia and would eventually gain currency in North America.

In the wake of Miles and Holland's *Crossing Waters, Crossing Worlds*, Frank B. Wilderson III authored one of the first interdisciplinary Black studies texts that introduced a theoretical frame for elaborating the complex structural and ontological—political, economic, and libidinal—positions of Black and Native people in the United States. While Wilderson's *Red, White & Black: Cinema and the Structure of US Antagonisms* (2010) represents an important intellectual moment and opening for a discussion of Black and Red relations, the book—and his writings of late—trouble the notion that Black and Indigenous people can be in coalition with one another or even communicate with one another within the terms and parameters of academic and humanist discourse. Calling attention to the problems of humanist frames of interpretation like sovereignty, land, coloniality, and decolonization, Wilderson and Jared Sexton continue to argue for incommensurability. While this political and ontological impasse continues to shape contemporary academic dialogue, Black studies projects in Canada and the Caribbean offer different points of engagement and itineraries for thinking about Black and Indigenous relations.

A Black studies' reading practice that also attends to African diaspora studies as they unfold in the Caribbean and South America has the conceptual space to acknowledge philosophical, literary, and historical traditions that can attend to histories of both enslavement and colonialism. Black and African diaspora scholarship that emerges from the Caribbean and Central and South America directly engages questions of coloniality from theoretical and experiential perspectives. For example, Sylvia Wynter's body of work that traces the "epistemic revolutions" of Western humanism attends to the ways that Blacks (Negroes) and Indigenous (Indios) are made and remade as a perpetual limit point or outside to the boundaries of Man across various colonial formations. Rinaldo Walcott's chapter in this collection draws on this Wynterian tradition in order to elaborate the ways that the Canadian nation-state's project of multiculturalism, which expands to incorporate modes of Indigenous representation into its notion of the human/Man, does so at the expense of Black subjects in Canada. Shona Jackson's book *Creole Indigeneity: Between Myth and Nation in the Caribbean* interrogates the vestiges of humanist violence in the modernist onto-epistemology of labor as a civilizing and modernizing agent for Afro-descended creole subjects in the Caribbean.[9] The Hegelian and colonial holdover that valorizes labor traps Black subjects within limited notions of agency and emancipation as it erases Indigenous subjectivity in Guyana.

Wynter's critique of humanism and its systems of overrepresentation has functioned as a crucial pivot point in Black studies that has enabled some scholars to break up the theoretical impasse presented by Afro-pessimist scholars like Wilderson and Sexton. Wynter's attack on the foundations of humanism itself allow for the emergence of a shared critique to emerge between Black and Native studies. Scholar and coeditor Tiffany Lethabo King, who takes Wynter's lead in her own work and focuses on interrogating the invention of the human, finds that this mode of critique also functions as a space of convergence for the fields of Black and Native studies. Rather than focus on genealogies or origin stories, *Otherwise Worlds* hopes to model practices of reading and listening that create new possibilities for thinking of, caring for, and talking to one another.

One of the conversations that this book emerged from was the Otherwise Worlds conference held in 2015 at UC Riverside. That conference attempted to promote intellectual and political exchange between Native and Black studies by focusing on how the analytics of anti-Black racism intersect with the analytics of settler colonialism. Both Black studies and Native studies have rightfully pointed out the problematics of developing "people of color" or "ethnic studies" projects based on a politics of equivalence (i.e., this racial oppression is like or similar to slavery or Indigenous genocide). However, it is often the case that rejecting a politics of equivalence becomes equated with calls for political or intellectual isolation. Instead, this project proposed to explore the relationality between these forms of racisms and colonialisms as well as explore the political implications of these relationalities.

At the Otherwise Worlds conference, one of the participants, Jared Sexton, talked about the exchange between scholars from Black studies and Native studies as being an exercise in daring to engage and speak to one another as "amateurs" reading in each other's fields. The act of speaking and reading "across" difference without the pretense of knowing, having mastered, or being able to parrot the already accepted assumptions, tenets, and prescribed politics of each discipline produced a space where misreadings and presumptions could surface and be interrogated in earnest. In addition, the willingness to be amateurs enabled us to engage each other as we are, rather than as completely perfected political and intellectual beings such that the only response that becomes enabled is a rejection of readings that lack this perfection. Such an approach also focuses on an ongoing process of continuing engagement rather than a fixation on writing as a final product that can stand for all time.

The Otherwise Worlds conference was an effort toward this kind of continuing engagement that produced generative moments in which participants were forced to slow down, feel the implications of their gaps in knowledge, and acknowledge how a lack of knowledge, attention to, or sustained engagement with each other created moments of impasse and isolation. The initial participants in this conversation included Black and Native scholars, organizers, and cultural workers. Many of the contributors to this collection (Maile Arvin, Ashon Crawley, Marcus Briggs-Cloud, Denise Ferreira da Silva, Chad Benito Infante, Tiffany Lethabo King, Jared Sexton, Andrea Smith, and Rinaldo Walcott,) participated in and or attended the 2015 conference. While in one another's company, attendees of the conference were able to witness the ways that settler colonial and anti-Black violence had been able to mediate Black and Indigenous relations with one another. This violent form of mediation functioned to sequester Indigenous and Black communities, including Black and Indigenous scholars in the academy, in ways that facilitated a lack of contact, missed opportunities for intimacy, and the subsequent production of amateurs that misread and misunderstood one another. To date, the political stakes of issues like the nation, rights, and sovereignty are the contested terrain that continue to create friction between Black and Native communities. This tension becomes particularly acute when discussing the respective politics and platforms of redress as they are articulated by liberal and "leftist" Black and Native activists and movements. For example, Indigenous communities in North America and the Caribbean continue to critique centuries-old Black-led struggles for reparations. Black movements for reparations for slavery continue to elide the fact that reparations, particularly when compensation is configured as land, requires the further consolidation of the US settler nation and affirms its authority to re-distribute wealth and "Native land" as it sees fit.[10] Liberal Black politics that do not call for a redistribution of wealth, land, and resources but simply ask for inclusion in the national body via "civil rights" have also posed a problem for Native communities and their struggles to have treaty rights and Indige-nous self-determination honored. Black politics that do not contest the very existence and idea of the United States present themselves as antagonistic to Indigenous survival and sovereignty. On the other hand, Black abolitionist politics that propose a move away from the very idea of the nation critique Native nations and their movements for sovereignty as overly invested in international, Western, and humanist models of governance that make sur-vival untenable for stateless and nationless Black diasporic peoples. Move-ments for treaty rights and sovereignty that require recognition from and broker deals with the anti-Black US settler nation and international bodies on a nation-to-nation basis undermine the humanity of stateless and nation-less Black descendants of slaves who are not legible on these terms. Thus, conference attendees and participants were able to recognize moments when Native political and intellectual thought centered land, nation, and sovereignty in ways that alienated and could potentially harm Black people. The dialogue that unfolded at the conference also brought to the surface instances in which Black critiques of Native sovereignty conflated Native understandings of the self, community, land, and self-determination with settler epistemologies and ontologies of being, autonomy, and humanity.

While the tension produced by amateur readings of one another's thought was not resolved at the conference, the process and dialogue of talking di-rectly to one another is continued in this collection. While at the Otherwise Worlds conference, we collectively decided that we need to talk to one an-other because Black and Native political projects that seek to grapple with the ongoing legacy and afterlife of slavery, genocide, and colonization by negotiating with violent settler states continue to enact their own forms of betrayal against the Black and Native people "cut out of the deal." Black and Native communities must talk about and come to terms with the reality that Black and Native collectives who negotiate their terms of survival with settler states are forced to compromise the well-being of the other. Further, what we really want to talk to each other about and through is that rather than seeking redress and healing through the settler state, Black and Native people need to think with one another about what healing and redress would look like on otherwise or decolonial and abolitionist terms. Consequently, this collection presumes that is important to have the difficult conversations and to hear things from each other that may sound very critical of the presumptions we deem essential to our intellectual and political projects of survival. The only way for these conflicts to not have the last word is to go through them rather than to avoid them so that otherwise relationalities can emerge.

In this collection, artists, activists, and scholars such as Jenell Navarro, Lindsay Nixon, Se' mana Thompson, J. Kameron Carter, Cedric Sunray, Sandra Harvey, Chris Finley, Kimberly Robertson, and Hotvlkuce Harjo join and extend the conversation in ways that were unanticipated and continue to create generative dislodgings and improvising that require a commitment and process of moving in relation to one another. And this processual approach allows room for polyvocality in the dialogues and readings since every amateur at the table does not need to be an academic. Thus, resisting pretense, we do not deploy this complexity as simply a theoretical exercise but as one that is pivotal for organizing, sustaining, and working toward a "consent not to be a single being."[11] As Fred Moten also asserts in regard to understanding the Black radical tradition, "[it] is not antifoundationalist but improvisatory of foundations."[12] Similarly, the amateur or processual mode of engaging Black and Indigenous relationality also turns toward improvising what the "foundations" of these relations might entail. *Otherwise: something or anything else; something to the contrary.*

Acknowledging the necessity of moving toward something to the contrary, this project recognizes the conceptual limits of knowledge production from within the academy. The very machinations of the academy reproduce liberal thought, politics, and desires. One of the tendencies within the academic industrial complex, especially for those in ethnic studies, is often an imperative to represent one's field or one's "community" in a generally positive manner. Further, there is an additional impulse within disciplines that profess to produce critical social theory to establish that their particular analysis of what they deem the social and attendant radical politics can accord them a form of vanguard status. Even knowledge produced at the very margins of the academy can be folded into (and it sometimes strives for incorporation into) the inventory of products and commodities, like "radical politics," that the university can co-opt and claim, as another engagement of possession, as its own. This anthology remains aware of and vigilant about the ways that the academic industrial complex benefits from and rewards disciplines for carving out unique, irreducible, and incommensurable spaces of knowledge production in order to ensure their value and continued existence within the university.

This tendency to position one's field, ontological position, politics, and modes of knowledge production as incommensurable can inadvertently work in tandem with the need to present one's "community" or field as a benefit-added to the market of ideas within the academic industrial complex. This phenomenon to represent one's field as an added value and commodity form makes sense for the academy where those invested in the academic industrial complex persistently render Native and Black studies illegitimate and under constant attack. At the same time, this approach is generally not all that helpful in terms of promoting healthy organizing since Native and Black communities have both obviously been impacted by five hundred plus years of white supremacy, anti-Black violence, settler colonialism, and genocide. When organizing, we have to create strategies with our communities as they actually are and not in the way we represent them in the academy. Because this project aspires to be more than a "theoretical exercise," the contributors to this anthology both reach outside of the academy and manipulate the protocols of academic knowledge production in order to move into a space of inquiry and engagement that is otherwise. Part of that process of moving into a space of inquiry and engagement that is something new requires squarely addressing racial hostility between Native and Black communities, but not in a blaming way, in order to acknowledge that no community has escaped the violence of white supremacy unscathed. We understand the work of holding space for otherwise listening and engaging between Native and Black studies as processual growing pains. As both fields of study have continued to reshape themselves in distinct ways over the last few decades, we see the constant need for recalibration to address the ongoing practices and logics of anti-Blackness and genocide. Because we position this relationality as inescapably processual where the work of generative recalibration has no presupposed endpoint, we also see these inquiries as meaningful growing pains—pains because these conversations and practices of listening can be difficult and challenging, yet generative and meaningful because they can simultaneously result in relationality building, hope, and joy. The engagement of deeper connections between Black and Native studies/peoples can be indications of the ongoing failures of white supremacy, anti-Blackness, and genocide and lead us to better modes of getting free. *Otherwise: in a different way or manner.*

Furthermore, there tends to be social, political, and cultural capital that is accrued by representing one's community as uniquely as possible. For instance, Native peoples often feel an obligation to represent themselves as the most unique in order to warrant necessary resources. In the ways that Native communities often feel compelled to make unique demands upon the state and be recognized by other oppressed communities, Black people must also establish a unique position, ethos, and orientation to the world. Even as Black abolition and Indigenous decolonization profess to claim a certain ability to resist or evade certain forms of recognition, since as Glen Sean Coulthard has shown that these politics of recognition uphold frameworks of accommodation, mutuality, and reciprocity that attempt to render invisible the crimes of the settler state, there are still claims being made to a certain form of "specialness."[13] While certainly there is distinctness and "specialness," there is also commonality that is part of everyday life in a settler state, or as Christina Sharpe has stated, the "quotidian disaster" of slavery and colonial violence spreads everywhere and the ruptures are ongoing.[14] Therefore, organizing requires us to address our full realities where we have uniqueness, along with commonality, in order to live against the constant disasters of settler colonialism and anti-Blackness. For instance, Native peoples go to stomp dances *and* to the grocery store to assert our many layers of life. Black people are constantly making and remaking forms of life, survivance, and joy in the face of anti-Black violence *and* also make regular trips to the grocery store. We need an otherwise relationality because ordinary folks do not have to be "special" to deserve liberation. *Otherwise: in all ways except the one mentioned.*

Moreover, the inability to really think through these relations negatively impacts Native and Black struggles. For example, Native struggles are not just impaired because of the lack of solidarity with Black struggles. Instead, in some of our experiences with organizing, Native peoples always expected and requested solidarity from Black organizations, and usually received it, but it rarely occurred to Native organizers that they should act in solidarity with Black struggles. The reason was that Native organizers tended to see themselves as disappearing and thus had no capacity to help anyone else. By seeing Native organizers as "disappearing," we ultimately rendered ourselves permanently politically ineffective and powerless. Native people's inability to imagine solidarity with Black organizations was premised on a foundation that ensured that genocide would have the last word, and thus the need for them to reimagine relations with Black liberation differently is necessary, not only because solidarity might be helpful, but because the status quo operates out of a liberation paradigm doomed to fail—another settler desire/dream. It is noteworthy that in Latin America, where Indigenous struggles tend not to operate out of a vanishing paradigm, it is much more common sense that Indigenous peoples do ally with Black struggles.

Black struggles' unique burden to abscond from its position as captive and in some contexts strive for independence as colonized subjects has granted it the capacity to critique racial capitalism, colonial domination, and Indigenous colonization. Global anti-Blackness maps the world as a field in which relations of Black captivity are always at play. While anti-Blackness is certainly a current state of the world, the everyday specificities of anti-Blackness, as well as the modes of resistance to it, need to be attended to in order to assess the living and breathing relations between Black and Indigenous peoples all over the globe and, more specifically, in the Americas. For example, as Charlene Carruthers concludes her book *Unapologetic: A Black, Queer, and Feminist Mandate for Radical Movements*, she poses questions to Black activists about Indigenous people, the land, and the future of their movements:

> There are still deep questions to answer and much work to be done. What claim do Black Americans have to the land Native peoples call Turtle Island? What claim to Indigeneity? Our lineage goes back centuries to slavery and Africa and the Caribbean. Processes of colonization, forced migration, and enslavement have stripped us from our land, and we have always had to fight for it. It is anti-Black to say that after more than three hundred years of labor we have no claim to steward this land. Stewardship, not extractive ownership, should be our North Star.[15]

While Carruthers argues that the movement for Black Lives "must foster transformative conversations among Black folks and Native peoples," must the conversation happen on the terms of liberal discourses like labor?[16] Scholars in Black studies like Michelle Wright and Shona Jackson have critiqued the ways that Hegelian and Marxian notions of labor and laboring are forms of self-actualization that distinguish modern subjects from Indigenous people and animals. The language (of labor) and ontologies (laborer-human) that we have inherited from Western philosophy, as well as socialism and leftist labor movements, contain baggage that posits able-bodied and non-Indigenous workers as contributors to civilization and, therefore, as owners of the land. For example, in the Caribbean and contexts where Black and other racialized people have been able to struggle for and win possession of the "postcolonial" nation-state and the land, Indigenous people continue to struggle to bring attention to their experiences with colonization. Varying notions of Blackness and Black subjectivities necessarily have different relationships with Indigenous peoples and Indigenous struggles. A more sufficiently diasporic approach to Black studies can provide a more nuanced assessment of the asymmetries and contingencies that exist between Black and Native appeals to liberal humanist forms of recognition.

Borrowing from Frank Wilderson's imperative to disappear into Blackness and lose one's human coordinates, it seems that part of the relation is to see how current models of understanding the connections between settler colonialism and anti-Blackness still operate within human coordinates. But it seems that this relation demonstrates that we do not simply look at the connection between two prior givens, but that relation itself helps to constitute Blackness and Indigeneity. Thus, an exploration of Relation requires us to imagine what different kinds of ontological possibilities might exist outside the coordinates of settler, anti-Black ontology. For instance, many of the contributions in this book address the need to tend to nonhuman relationality since there are many ontologies beyond the human scope that constitute "all our relations." Many of the chapters, including those by Andrea Smith, Marcus Briggs-Cloud, Jenell Navarro, Kimberly Robertson, and Lindsay Nixon, incorporate kinship making with nonhuman ancestors and relatives. Thus, the intellectual solidarity this work aims to foster can find its coordinates in Black and Native peoples alongside relations with nonhuman entities such as plant, animal, and star relatives. *Otherwise: in other ways.*

Perhaps one way to think beyond the coordinates of settler, anti-Black modes of being is to actively create otherwise ontologies. Creating the beyond and the otherwise necessarily takes us to Native and Black joy. Many Native and Black artists have led the way in conjuring these productive and beautiful visualities and relations that imagine an existence outside of settler colonialism and the afterlife of slavery. The work of Wendy Red Star in her *Thunder Up Above* series, the mixed media art of Soraya Jean-Louise McElroy titled *Ancestral Alchemy*, musical contributions such as the *Halluci Nation* album by A Tribe Called Red or Amai Kuda and Mı's song "We Can Do It (Dirty Money)," and the visual art of Charmaine Lurch all point to

Indigenous and Black futures—or present futures—to reorder how we live with one another and the world: an otherwise world. Laura Harjo has theorized this more beautiful existence as "radical sovereignty," where we must ask pertinent questions to begin to pull together the future world. For instance, Harjo has moved past traditional geographers' approaches to "scale" by thinking of Indigenous futures as a scale, and "jumping scale" to arrive at a liberatory site/sight. She asks: "How do we imagine futurity and what kind of tools can we apply that invoke radical sovereignty, refuse settler colonial practices, while embracing Indigenous and Mvskoke ways of knowing, that decolonizes how we engage with community to create a trajectory that has a beautiful path to a lush place?"[17] Similarly, Katherine McKittrick writes of how Dionne Brand's poetics reminds her "that the earth is also skin and that a young girl can legitimately take possession of a street, or an entire city, albeit on different terms than we might be familiar with."[18] By considering our human capacity to create and conjure a better world into existence, we have the potentiality to reorder the coordinates of our lives. This in no way erases the historical and present realities of genocide and slavery, but instead seeks to *feel* where we come from to arrive at where we want to be, together. An otherwise world then, feels our histories as Dian Million has argued, in generative ways so that our affective dispositions are part of the liberation paradigm.[19] *Otherwise: if not, or else.*

Moreover, otherwise ontologies could be understood as disruptions in the abjection of Black and Indigenous peoples from the realm of the human. While we realize in very material ways the fact of Black and Indigenous death as expected within the structure of settler colonialism, we also place emphasis on the ways in which our existence as resistance intervenes in these daily expectations. To live an otherwise life, to assert an otherwise being, or to create an otherwise world is to invest in decolonization, as Frantz Fanon has asserted: "Decolonization, which sets out to change the order of the world, is, obviously, a program of complete disorder."[20] And, this disordering, this otherwise-ing if you will, serves to contemplate what further death, devourment, or destruction awaits Native and Black peoples if settler colonialism remains intact. As such, otherwise ontologies are rooted in life, the simple capacity to breathe (Ashon Crawley) and be. But these ontologies do not end here. They strategically employ imagination to flee from the brutal confines of settler colonialism. In keeping with the indeterminacy and fugitivity of this project, the writings in this anthology engage multiple forms: from essays, to zines, to artwork, to recorded conversations, to blogs. These multiple genres seek to engage the imagination in this work by asking such important questions as the following: how do we pull better worlds into existence? How do we carefully tend to relationships between Native and Black communities that lead toward liberation? How do we guarantee an otherwise world for our children and their children?

The Thematics of Otherwise Worlds

The thematics of the collection are titled with Glissant's aforementioned understanding of Relation in mind—especially the notion that Relation is "boundless" and, therefore, "evades rest." While the sections of this book are "Boundless Bodies," "Boundless Ontologies," "Boundless Socialities," and "Boundless Kinship," we acknowledge much overlap throughout many of the distinct pieces, which we see as a thread of possibility for operationalizing boundless Relation.

In order to bring this otherwise collection into the fold of university publishing we have organized the chapters into loose thematic groupings. While we hope that this overview provides the reader with a sense of what conversations we thought were important at the time (the last five years), this attempt to connect, organize, or make certain discussions intelligible to those reading outside of or across the disciplines of Black and Native studies is not intended to be deterministic. We are not providing a road map on how to move through the collection or to give primacy to certain scholarly conversations and their groupings. Instead, we encourage you to read and meander through the collection as you are so moved.

Boundless Bodies

The first thematic in the collection is "Boundless Bodies." In this portion of the book you will find essays that assert various modes of corporeal fugitivity and understandings on how we might free the flesh from the constraints and violence of settler colonialism and anti-Blackness. For example, Ashon Crawley's essay frames the discussion by pointing to an otherwise possibility for bringing Native and Black studies into conversation. Crawley attends to the ways that Hortense Spillers's flesh, Sylvia Wynter's conceptual itineraries, and Alexander Weheliye's reading of Spillers and Wynter trouble "theological and philosophical modalities of thought." Moving with and from the flesh, Crawley provides a breathtaking account of how the flesh's capacity for "vibration" has the potential to unmoor violence and suffering as epistemic points of departure in Black studies. He further contends that an otherwise possibility forces us to be able to challenge the very conceptual categories by which we articulate ourselves and our bodies. As he states, "When we want to imagine *otherwise* possibilities—*otherwise* worlds—we must abolish the very conceptual frame that produces categorical distinction and makes them desirable; we have to abolish the modality of thought that *thinks* categorical distinction as maintainable."

Similarly, Denise Ferreira da Silva's essay carefully contours the process and ethics of "reading the dead" and recognizes the disruptions created by Black feminist poethical labor like Spillers's flesh. Ferreira da Silva's black feminist poethical contribution focuses on the "flesh" and elaborates the ways that poethics break up the spatiotemporality of Western epistemology (separability, sequentiality, determinacy) and philosophy. Using Karl Marx's inability to account for Black and Indigenous land, life, and labor in his theory and law of value as an example, Ferreira da Silva outlines how Black and Indigenous life become unimaginable within Western equations of value. Hence, the assignment of no value to Black and Indigenous life.

Frank Wilderson's and Tiffany Lethabo King's conversation serves as a model of Black study and engages themes of the Black body in pain as an object of study, the field of Native studies, Saidiya Hartman's legacy and circulation within Afro-pessimism, and Wilderson's germinal work *Red, White & Black*. During the conversation, Wilderson discusses his relationship to Native studies and politics as he wrote *Red, White & Black* and how it has changed since then. In the latter half of the conversation, King is forced to contend with Wilderson's change of mind and heart about the potential for the Native's "grammar of suffering" of genocide and the Black's "grammar of suffering "of fungibility to speak to one another. This conversation grapples with the ways intellectual and political investments, as well as disenchantments, shape the way that each scholar approaches the ethical question of honoring Black and Indigenous life. This dialogue also challenges us to speak the "unspeakable" because even when sharp critiques are difficult to hear and may be critiques with which many strongly disagree, they open the possibility of otherwise conversations in the future. All of these works provide a foundation to reframe the lived experiences of Blackness and indigeneity as articulated in the other essays of the book. For instance, while Chris Finley's, Andrea Smith's, and Marcus Briggs-Cloud's essays in this volume speak to the foundational importance of land for Indigenous life, they articulate this importance in an otherwise manner—by not foreclosing what we understand "land" to be.

Boundless Ontologies

The second section of the collection is "Boundless Ontologies," which highlights several essays that focus on the ontological status of Blackness and Indigeneity. For instance, Tiffany Lethabo King's 2016 article "New World Grammars" attempts a conceptual return to conquest. King argues that prior to the advent of white settler colonial studies, Native and Black studies shared the lingua franca of conquest. Conquest as a conceptual and dialogic space enables an interrogation of the violence of genocide and slavery that white settler colonial studies avoids. King argues that Black and Native studies' sustained attention to the anti-Indigenous and anti-Black violence required to make the human grapples with everyday violence and creates the ground for a more ethical encounter between Black and Native scholarly and political projects.

Jared Sexton's 2014 article "The *Vel* of Slavery" takes up settler colonial studies' and Native studies' articulations of injury and loss—loss of land and the political goals of recuperation. Through an interrogation of the political goal and horizon of decolonization and Indigenous sovereignty, Sexton argues that Indigenous and settler colonial studies remain animated by a desire for "resurgence, recovery, and recuperation." Sexton argues that the politics of abolition, specifically "degeneration, decline, and dissolution," pulls away from and radicalizes some of the central claims of decolonization. Black impulses toward abolition lead us to a "baseless" form of politics that assumes "nothing for no one."

Inspired by Wilderson's and Sexton's call to mediate on the ontological status of indigeneity, Andrea Smith contends that slavery cannot be equated with "stolen labor" and similarly that colonization cannot be equated with "stolen land." She argues that the Indigenous marks the creation of the division between the living and the dead or between the human and the nonhuman. Hence, colonization is not simply about stolen land, but about the creation of something called land that can then be stolen. She further suggests that Indigenous genocide works then through a synthesis of operations involving a disappearance of some into Blackness and some into whiteness. The disappearance of Native peoples into Blackness operationally disappears their disappearance, and it functions simultaneously with Indigenous disappearance into whiteness by making a disappearance into whiteness seem like a desirable goal.

Also building on the work of Wilderson, who argues in *Red, White & Black* that there is a "network of connections, transfers, and displacements between a genocided thing and a fungible and accumulated thing," Chad

Benito Infante contends that there is paradigmatic intimacy between Blackness and Indianness through the lens of "the abject non-being of Black and Indian life-in-death that enables the (white) world." While focusing on violence, Infante takes a route less traveled or perhaps even unspeakable for some. In particular, he reworks James Baldwin's notion of "cool fratricide" as a heuristic to read "literary representations of vengeance"—or retributive violence against whiteness—in Black and Indigenous literature. For Infante, the possibility of the death of whiteness becomes a metaphysical bridge between Blackness and Indianness.

J. Kameron Carter similarly takes up the theme of whiteness as about the propertization of the Earth. In conversation with Ashon Crawley, Carter calls for a praxis of political and theological malpractice that challenges the "presumption of the givenness of the state as telos of society or social order." He contends that Blackness, as fundamentally beyond property, and its critique provide the foundation for what he terms Black malpractice, the antidote to settlerism and possibility for the creation of an otherwise world. Thus, while Black studies is often positioned in an orthogonal relationship to settler colonial studies, Carter suggests that the Black radical tradition provides a critical vantage point for decolonization. Thus, while Sexton's and Wilderson's critique of Native studies suggests that a land-centered approach within Native studies requires the speaking subject that depends on anti-Blackness, both Andrea Smith's and J. Kameron Carter's work suggest alternative articulations of land that create different possibilities for Native and Black studies, respectively.

As Winona LaDuke has argued, Indigenous relationship to land is not exclusive, although it is often presumed to be.[21] Consequently, she suggests that Native peoples' connection to land opens the possibility of relationality with all peoples rather than the vantage point by which to invest in an anti-Black quest for humanity. Thus, if Sexton and Wilderson suggest a politics without a demand requiring the loss of human coordinates, and if Silva suggests in this volume a reading of the dead that shows a different articulation of the "human" altogether, Native studies scholars in this volume point to land, not as that which establishes humanity, but as that which reconfigures what that means altogether.

Boundless Socialities

The third section of the book brings together many perspectives on Black and Indigenous sociality. As Fred Moten has argued, the attack on Black lives cannot be separated from the attack on Black *life*—Black sociality in all its vibrant formations. And, as referenced earlier in the collection in the conversation between Wilderson and King, the conversations between Native and Black studies are grounded in the daily realities of conflicts, tensions, and debates between Black and Native communities where our social lives are played out. Thus, this section provides space for "Boundless Socialities" to be written.

Maile Arvin analyzes the connections between anti-Blackness and settler colonialism in the colonization of Polynesia. She notes that anti-Blackness is an ordering logic of colonialism that demarcated Melanesian (Black) from Polynesian (almost white) identity. While this demarcation marks Melanesians as beyond salvation, Arvin notes that Polynesian proximity to whiteness serves the purpose of allowing whiteness to possess Indigeneity and thus lay claim to all that is Indigenous, which includes all forms of Indigenous sociality.

Sandra Harvey elegantly focuses on and parses how the production and surveillance of Black bodies, blood, and Blackness as fixed to slavery emerged alongside of and through Choctaw land allotment policies. Harvey scrutinizes the way that colonial archival power stages modern and "scientific" and cultural knowledge about the body, blood, race, and even language in the very organization of the National Archive's physical structure, the organization and storage of files, and even in the process of conducting interviews. Tracking the way archival power colludes in the emergence of the distinct racial logics of indigeneity and Blackness, Harvey argues that the archives are also complicit in surveilling Black people as attempts to pass out of Blackness or the state of enslavement. Specifically, she shows us that the National Archive, like other state entities, seeks to surveil and suppress Black socialities.

Informed by a similar archive as Harvey, Cedric Sunray reads his own embodiment as well as other white-passing Indigenous people in the context of the identity policing that occurs within the various Indigenous people's tribal politics of "who belongs" as a manifestation of anti-Blackness. Using archival materials from tribal newspapers and interviews that discuss the 2000 census, he tracks the ways that discussions of identity often work to displace nonwhite-passing and Black Indigenous peoples. As with Harvey, Sunray further tracks the anti-Blackness within the federal recognition process, and critiques identity policing within Native communities as essentially an anti-Black project.

However, as Marcus Briggs-Cloud's work suggests, Native communities, while complicit in anti-Blackness, are also constructed through Indigenous cosmologies and epistemologies that deconstruct anti-Blackness as well. He argues that anti-Blackness becomes present within Mvskoke communities at the moment when English becomes the means of communication over the Mvskoke language. Essentially, he argues, it is not possible to be anti-Black within the Mvskoke language. It is not until the English language allows for the possibility that the Earth, as well as some of Earth's peoples, can be understood as property that anti-Blackness can even be intelligible. His work echoes the scholarship of Leanne Simpson, whose work suggests that Indigenous freedom is based less on control of land as it is based on the love of land and all of creation, or what she describes as "connectivity based on the sanctity of the land, the love we have for our families, our language, our way of life. It is relationships based on deep reciprocity, respect, noninterference, self-determination and freedom."[22] Guided by this sense of decolonial love, Briggs-Cloud's essay suggests that Indigenous cosmologies could be a place through which Native peoples can rearticulate their relationship to Blackness that is consistent with precolonial Indigenous values.

Boundless socialities are also visualized in the artwork by Hotvlkuce Harjo. Harjo's generative work on southeastern tattoo revitalization, especially for southeastern women, asserts a Native feminist refusal of societal erasure. Their piece in this collection titled *Mississippian Black Metal Grl on a Friday Night* imagines otherwise ways to uphold traditional tattooing since their images beautifully blur any linear notion of time. Thus, Harjo's representation of time produces images that maintain a present future for southeastern women and their kin.

Boundless Kinship

While the relationship between Native and Black communities can be one of contestation and conflict, several authors and artists point to the otherwise possibilities of relationality between Blackness and Indigeneity. The fourth section of this book, "Boundless Kinship," aims to place essays and artworks together that recognize no restrictions on how Black and Indigenous peoples form kinship with one another. The work of Jenell Navarro and Kimberly Robertson points out the promise of what they term "radical kinship"—a way of realizing otherwise relationality and privileging Indigenous and Black women as conjurers of beauty, joy, and life. By reading relationality in Beyoncé's work, they posit a (re)indigenizing of kinship practices, even those between human and nonhuman subjects. Ultimately, these authors configure the inner and spiritual lives of Black and Indigenous women as a potent source of our fierce and glorious liberation. In tandem, the serigraph included by Robertson titled *Slay* provides a visual reality of Native feminist art and what actually must be "slayed" (settler colonialism, heteropatriarchy, capitalist bullshit) to realize this dream of relationality or radical kinship.

Furthermore, Jenell Navarro and Kimberly Robertson provide an example of how to engage Indigenous and Black activism through art. In collaboration with JusticeLA they created a jailbed beaded in the colors of the four directions to call attention to the disproportionate incarceration of Native peoples in Los Angeles, California, and beyond. There were about fifty jailbeds dropped throughout Los Angeles County on Christmas Eve 2017, many of which called specific attention to the violent incarceration of Black folks as well. Navarro and Robertson's jailbed was dropped in front of the Walt Disney Concert Hall, a site in Los Angeles where Native slaves were once sold on the auction block in Los Angeles. This type of artivism provides a relational antidote to the academic industrial complex and its limiting modes of resistance to the prison system and calls attention to the need to undo all forms of Black and Native confinement in order to make an otherwise world possible.

Working on boundless kinship through art as well, Se'mana Thompson's zine covers from *Queer Indigenous Girl*, Volume 4, and *Black Indigenous Boy*, Volume 2, illustrate what Lindsay Nixon's chapter describes as "speculative visualities," which is an "artistic and aesthetic framework that projects Indigenous life into the future imaginary, subverting the death imaginary ascribed to Indigenous bodies within settler colonial discourse." As Thompson's artworks and Nixon's essay show, Indigenous and Black folks have already experienced the apocalypse, and now we must figure out how to co-ordinate love and kinship back into our lives to reorder all our relations with the entire biosphere. All of these works demonstrate what Michelle Jacob terms a Native feminist "decolonizing praxis" for building a future beyond genocide.[23]

Rinaldo Walcott sees possibilities in articulating the relationship between the colonization of Indigenous peoples and the creation of Black nonpersonhood. He contends that the engagement of Black diaspora studies with Indigenous studies highlights the fact that "the nation-state provides ethno-cultural identities as the basis of an imagined care for the self that always seems to fall short of full human status and expression." This exchange then requires, not the reification of Black and Indigenous identity, but to recognize Indigeneity as a process that can lead to the creation of a *"pure decolonial* project [that] works the ruins of catastrophe to produce more hopeful tales of our present human intimacies and allow[s] the opportunity to reimagine the self anew again." Chris Finley similarly suggests that love and kinship are possible through the creation of what she terms "maroon communities," building on the work of Fred Moten and Stefano Harney. She contends that the insistence on absolute difference in Native, Black, and ethnic studies is at least in part due to the demands of the academic industrial complex, which requires the creation of academic territoriality to sustain itself. She asks, what would have to be abandoned to see not only difference, but togetherness and possibility? Thus, kinship is inclusive in its modes of togetherness when she states, "I'm talking about a deep way of being together. A place where we see the brokenness as a method of relatedness instead of seeking wholeness through comparison and loss."

While again we do not believe any of these authors or artists is attempting to prescribe fixed answers to the ongoings of settler colonialism and anti-Blackness in our world, we do see beautiful gestures of pushing the conversations around Black and Indigenous relations throughout the collection as new turns that hold promise for realizing the otherwise worlds of Black and Indigenous futures—futures realizable in our present lives. Ultimately, we ponder in this collection some of these questions: What can we offer one another to build Relation against all the anti-Black and anti-Indigenous antagonisms on our world? Must we continue to wait to hold space and conversations with one another, or can we just come together as "amateurs"? How can we build Black and Indigenous lifeways that are joyfully unbound and purposefully evade rest/stagnation/fixation? We invite you to continue to add inquiries to this list and think collectively about what an otherwise existence between Black and Indigenous peoples/studies could look like.

Notes

1 Édouard Glissant, *Caribbean Discourse: Selected Essays* (Charlottesville: University of Virginia Press, 1989), 172.

2 Antonio Viego, *Dead Subjects: Toward a Politics of Loss in Latino Studies* (Durham, NC: Duke University Press, 2007).

3 Elizabeth Cook-Lynn, "Who Stole Native American Studies," *Wicazo Sa Review* 12, no. 1 (Spring 1997), and Winona Stevenson, "'Ethnic' Assimilates 'Indigenous': A Study in Intellectual Neocolonialism," *Wicazo Sa Review* 13, no. 1 (1998).

4 Lee Maracle, *I Am Woman: A Native Perspective on Sociology and Feminism* (London: Global Professional Publishing, 1996); Roberto Mendoza, *Look!*

A Nation Is Coming (Philadelphia: National Organization for an American Revolution, 1984).

5 Arika Easley-Houser, "The Indian Image in the Black Mind: Representing Native Americans in Antebellum African American Public Culture," PhD diss., Rutgers University, 2014.

6 Easley-Houser, "Indian Image in the Black Mind."

7 Robert L. Allen, "Politics of the Attack on Black Studies," *Black Scholar* 6, no. 1 (1974): 2–7.

8 The attempts by US universities to pit Black and Native studies against one another and frustrate attempts at interdisciplinary dialogue should be acknowledged, particularly in the face of contemporary celebrations of the field of white settler colonial studies and its new interest in anti-Blackness and settler colonialism. White settler colonial studies has been largely rewarded for its recent interest in comparative and cross-disciplinary work as it attempts to think about Blackness and Indigeneity simultaneously.

9 Shona N. Jackson, *Creole Indigeneity: Between Myth and Nation in the Caribbean* (Minneapolis: University of Minnesota Press, 2012).

10 In the twenty-first century, the movement for reparations led by American Descendants of Slavery (referred to as #ADOS on social media platforms and YouTube) has been reinvigorated. Unlike its predecessor, the National Coalition of Blacks for Reparations in America, which reached its apex in the 1990s, the American Descendants of Slavery movement focuses on the particular plight and justice claims of African Americans (Black people descended from people enslaved in the US rather than all African diasporic descendants of slaves) as citizens who need to be made whole or full US citizens through reparations. According to its founders, Yvette Carnell and Antonio Brown, this twenty-first-century movement for reparations seeks the full inclusion of African Americans into the "wealthiest nation in the world." See "Plantation Dynasties and the Bottom Caste of ADOS," https://www.youtube.com/watch?v=n6m4Pe9j4qw. Rather than a call to bankrupt or undo the nation through reparations—and the redistribution of wealth, land, and resources—the American Descendants of Slavery movement for reparations seeks to share the wealth with the US settler nation.

11 Fred Moten, *Black and Blur*, vol. 1 (Durham, NC: Duke University Press, 2017), Winona Stevenson, "'Ethnic' Assimilates 'Indigenous': A Study in Intellectual Neocolonialism," *Wicazo Sa Review* 13, no. 1 (1998). Stevenson now publishes under the name Winona Wheeler.

12 Moten, *Black and Blur*, 13.

13 Glen Sean Coulthard, *Red Skin, White Masks: Rejecting the Colonial Politics of Recognition* (Minneapolis: University of Minnesota Press, 2014).

14 Christina Sharpe, *In the Wake: On Blackness and Being* (Durham, NC: Duke University Press, 2016), 14.

15 Charlene Carruthers, *Unapologetic: A Black, Queer, and Feminist Mandate for Radical Movements* (New York: Beacon Press, 2018), 136–137.

16 Carruthers, *Unapologetic*, 137.

17 Laura Harjo, *Spiral to the Stars* (Tempe: University of Arizona Press, 2018).

18 Katherine McKittrick, *Demonic Grounds: Black Women and Cartographies of Struggle* (Minneapolis: University of Minnesota Press, 2005), ix.

19 Dian Million, *Therapeutic Nations: Healing in an Age of Indigenous Human Rights* (Tempe: University of Arizona Press, 2013).

20 Frantz Fanon, *The Wretched of the Earth*, preface by Jean-Paul Sartre, trans. Constance Farrington (New York: Grove Press, 1963), 35.

21 Winona LaDuke, *Recovering the Sacred* (Cambridge, MA: South End Press, 2005), 8.

22 Leanne Betasamosake Simpson, *As We Have Always Done: Indigenous Freedom through Radical Resistance* (Minneapolis: University of Minnesota Press, 2017).

23 Michelle M. Jacob, *Yakama Rising: Indigenous Cultural Revitalization, Activism, and Healing* (Tempe: University of Arizona Press, 2013), 109.

BOUNDLESS BODIES

Part I

CHAPTER ONE

Ashon Crawley

Stayed | Freedom | Hallelujah

Walking in the middle of the street, onward to grandmother's house, can get you killed. Walking in a property development in the rain wearing a hoodie while holding Skittles and iced tea can force you unceremoniously toward a violent demise. Showing up at the doorstep in an emergency, with a request for help, can be a murderous event. Listening to loud music in a car with friends can ignite white supremacist logic; it can result in bullet wounds and caskets. Walking down Frederick Douglass Boulevard, "wearing" a gender that is not "yours," can provoke a beating that leads to death. If you whistle, if you stutter, if you're purported to degrade a white woman's honor, you could be lynched; your swelled and mottled flesh could eventually be found in a river named Tallahatchie.

There are more. Why are there so many more? More names? More incidents? The draft of this writing was first written in the midst of protest against Walter Scott's murder. White cop planting evidence, Black cop standing idly by, assisting such a scene. But then there were more. Why also Eric Harris? Why, why, why, we ask?

Fatigue. Worry. The names too numerous, incidents too vulgar to recount here—Black flesh, life in Blackness—speak of life relegated to the zone of vulnerability, life that cannot ascend, life that cannot be assumed to the zone of so-called and so-thought protected. The current theological and philosophic narratives that provide the epistemology of our existence don't tell us how these unsafe lives might actually be lived.

The quotidian, ordinary, everyday nature of these violent incidents should produce within us a restiveness, a restlessness, a desire to exist *otherwise*. It's the violence that is the daily experience of Black flesh, of Black sociality, against which those of us committed to justice must contend. Modes of surveillance will not be the panacea for the end of such interactions. Police wearing cameras will not end such violence. The urgency of our times, times that began *before* the inaugural events of Christopher Columbus's 1492 blue oceanic colonial expansionist mission, demands a thinking about what we might call "*otherwise*" possibilities, *otherwise* inhabitations, *otherwise* worlds. The *otherwise* in all its plentitude vibrates afar off and near, here but also, and, there.

Black flesh knows this truth, the truth about the necessity of *otherwise* possibilities. In the midst of ubiquitous, seemingly unceasing violence, we need: imagination. Black flesh has been theologized about and philosophized on; it has given shape, meaning, and skin to Western epistemologies of identity, humanity, and difference. To have and be flesh, but to be disallowed the chance to be exalted to the station of "Man," to the zone of the citizen, to leave the vestibule: this is the paradox that Alex Weheliye's *Habeas Viscus: Racializing Assemblages, Biopolitics, and Black Feminist Theories of the Human* addresses.[1] It is a book that offers us a vital framework for imagining a world where race—where human life—might be *otherwise* than it is.

As its title suggests, *Habeas Viscus* approaches the topic of Black enfleshment most directly through this writing of Black women, particularly through the writings of famed thinkers Hortense Spillers and Sylvia Wynter. Of Wynter, Weheliye states: "Wynter's large-scale intellectual project, which she has been pursuing in one form or another for the last thirty years, disentangles Man from the human." She does so "in order to use the space of subjects placed beyond the grasp of this domain as a vital point from which to invent hitherto unavailable genres of the human. According to this scheme in western modernity the religious conception of the self gave way to modes of secularized being."[2] This disentanglement, of Man from human, is the dance and play in and as the always irreducible, always open and ongoing, *otherwise* possibility. The Western idea of Man, for Wynter and Weheliye, is a theological-philosophical concept, one grounded in anti-Black and settler colonialist logics. Of Spillers, Weheliye offers that "the flesh is not an abject zone of exclusion that culminates in death but an alternate instantiation of humanity that does not rest on the mirage of western Man as the mirror image of human life as such."[3] Further still, he says, "To have been touched by the flesh, then, is the path to the abolition of Man: this is part of the lesson of our world."[4]

When we want to imagine *otherwise* possibilities—*otherwise* worlds—we must abolish the very conceptual frame that produces categorical distinction and makes them desirable; we have to abolish the modality of thought that *thinks* categorical distinction as maintainable. To attend to anti-Blackness, we must be committed to considering the ways the very concept of Blackness depends upon the theologically and philosophically assigned category about who can and cannot be Man, and therefore human. By delimiting ourselves to the assigned category that produces *and* is produced by the theological-philosophical creation of race-as-difference—we only still ever mine the very terms of order that have already been predetermined.

Accepting racial categories, that is, leaves us interrogating unhelpful questions: Who is, what is, Black, what gets to be, Black? Wynter and Spillers lead us toward *otherwise* frameworks. Following Wynter, who will be, what gets to be, *otherwise* genres of human not relegated by concepts of theological-philosophical knowledge of categorical difference? And following Spillers, who is, what gets to be, flesh? We are contending for otherwise modes of relationality.

Hortense Spillers, in her widely celebrated "Mama's Baby, Papa's Maybe: An American Grammar Book," states: "I would make a distinction in this case between 'body' and 'flesh' and impose that distinction as the central one between captive and liberated subject-positions. In that sense, before the 'body' there is 'flesh,' that zero degree of social conceptualization that does not escape concealment under the brush of discourse or the reflexes of iconography."[5] The flesh is the liberated position and this liberative force is an original, or, in Nathaniel Mackey's words, "previous to situation."[6] What remains to be elaborated in Spillers's conception of flesh is the generalizability of such a claim. Flesh is that which has priority before any theological-philosophical mood or movement befalls it, flesh is before the situation of Christian dogma or what Wynter would describe as the "coloniality of being."[7]

It all comes down to vibration, agitational roughness.

Everything living and dead, everything animate and immobile, vibrates. Vibration is the internal structuring logic of matter. Because everything vibrates, nothing escapes participating in choreographic encounters with the rest of the living world. It's a reality of thermodynamics, of kinesthesia. Everything has a ground state kinesis that cannot be fully evacuated. If everything moves with its own velocity and force, everything sounds out, every object participates in the ceaseless pulse of noisemaking. This embodied refusal to be stilled will have been a gift, the gift of flesh, the gift of *otherwise* possibilities for thinking, for producing, existing. This refusal of stilling has its discordant and harmonic registers, its choreographic-sonic force. And perhaps attention to sound is what Weheliye's *Habeas Viscus* desires most emphatically, the sound of Blackness, of Black flesh.

In 4/4 time—four beats to a measure—the Black Pentecostal church of my youth would sing the song

> I woke up this morning with my mind stayed on freedom
> I woke up this morning with my mind stayed on freedom
> I woke up this morning with my mind stayed on freedom
> Hallelu, hallelu, hallelujah

What interests me most is the ends of the phrases, the *stayed, freedom,* and *hallelujah.* In this short chorus, the words *stayed, freedom,* and *hallelujah* each are emphasized in the performance of the song, singled out through breathed, sung elaboration. The way *we'd* sing it, each word expanded beyond the other: *stayed* takes three beats to the measure, *freedom* four to the measure and *hallelujah* exceeds the borders of the measure, stealing a beat from the preceding, taking all four of its own, and two of the next. *Stayed* remains, like its denotation, within the strictures of its measured elaboration, it remains, abides, and dwells. *Freedom* expands and rubs up against the skin of the measure, fills it out just to, but not exceeding, the point of overwhelming. *Hallelujah* as celebratory, unable to remain stilled, vibrating beyond the borders, unstable in all its Blackpentecostal resonance.

The way Weheliye abides with, meditates on, the thought of Spillers and Wynter produces a similar excess. By considering how they each in their own way trouble the assumptive logics by which we have come to think modern Man, the category of the human, and of racial difference, Weheliye takes up how their meditative thought enfleshes vibratory frequency, a movement that unsettles the assumptive logics and logistics of the known world. Their thought itinerary, their thought as critical performative practice of *otherwise* knowledge production, is the very practice of freedom. This thought, this practice, is the flesh.

In the chorus of "Woke Up This Morning," sometimes the word "freedom" is replaced with the word justice; other times it is replaced by the name Jesus. This replacement is an exchangeability that is not about fungibility nor discardability. Justice does not so much replace as revise and riff upon— offer commentary and enlargement to—the scope of freedom. And the addition and replacement of freedom and justice with Jesus is perhaps a means to assert what Jesus, in Black sacred practice, is supposed to do and mean, is about what capacity Jesus is supposed to carry, the work he set loose into the world. To set at liberty those that are oppressed. To declare the acceptable year of favor and justice.

What these replacements give, with the rhythmic movement from *stayed* to *freedom* to *hallelujah*, is the vibratory force of the flesh, of a zero degree of conceptualization that does not escape because it is itself escape, it is itself liberative. This is the flesh, where the concept that vibrates against the measure is in flux but rooted, each in its capacity to excess. Spillers and Wynter do not so much want to replace one problematic conception of Man, of racialization, of gender, with other strictures that would have us bound. But like the move from *stayed* to *freedom* to *hallelujah*, their works would have us move otherwise, their works would have us critique through elaboration, offering up the concepts to melismatic rupture.

Flesh resonates everywhere. In the Bible, John announced the coming of the Lord thusly: "In the beginning was the Word, and the Word was with God, and the Word was God. . . . And the Word was made flesh, and dwelt among us" (John 1:1, 14a). And in the 2014 documentary *Dreams Are Colder Than Death*, Spillers says "the flesh gives empathy"—the flesh, in other words, gives us the capacity to feel and share in concern with others.[8] The flesh is grounded in sociality, is antiphonal, is perpetually reaching outward to establish relation. What I would like to consider is how this reaching for relation opposes a concept of enclosed, individual embodiment; what I would like to consider is how Spillers's account of the flesh is apposite but in tension with John's Word.

What we find in Spillers is the articulation of the *otherwise* than theological-philosophical argument, an *otherwise* claim about flesh, of which Black female flesh is what most forcefully articulates what liberative positionality is or can be. Spillers undoes the relation of flesh to a particular religious tradition by considering it as the ground of being, by theorizing it as the plural event of Blackness. Blackness—through the flesh—would bear the trace of what in Western thought is called "the religious" without being reducible to any one tradition. Spillers makes us consider how the flesh is not in the first instance Christian; the flesh is available to Islam, it is available to Ifa and Santeria, the flesh is available to Black disbelievers.

The flesh is the ground from which life emerges. The flesh is not reducible to Blackness—but Blackness, Black life, Black sociality, vibration, verve, ongoing movement and restiveness are irreducible in the flesh. Blackness finds its emergence in the resistance, the movement, of the flesh. For Spillers to argue in favor of the flesh, the flesh as liberatory, is for her to disrupt theology-philosophy as a modality of thought. She implies the disruptive potentiality Blackness poses for epistemological delimitation of thought that produces and is produced by what Wynter so forcefully elaborates in her essays as western Man. Such Man is the coloniality of being/power/truth/freedom.[9] Spillers and Wynter work in the plural space of *otherwise* possibility to think *otherwise* worlds of relationality, *otherwise* modalities for existence.

Spillers radicalizes John by mobilizing him to the level of a specific generality. Rather than flesh being made from word, from logos that precedes, flesh is that which stands before any such possibility for words to name, claim, shame. Spillers demonstrates how the flesh instead becomes word, through violent encounter, through theological-philosophical adjudication. What our language sees and calls, language that is infused with the logics of white supremacist ideology, are not bodies but words, confused conceptions that create Man.

What if the flesh was made word, was made to be constrained by the sign, the symbol. As word, it is that which always fails to fully capture the uncapturable liberatory vibration of the flesh, it is that which had to be transformed through theology and philosophy in order to produce the sense, the coherence, of Western epistemologies.

All we have is metaphor. Each word, phrase, and statement merely approaches concepts we would seek to name or claim. All we have is the capacity for metaphor as irreducible relationality, of objects being with other objects, of ideas and concepts forming through relation. Metaphor is excess, excess that is constitutive of otherwise possibilities. Metaphor is excess that precedes any movement or nomination toward word, toward phrase, toward statement. This excess, as metaphor, is the grounds for thinking Black life, life that constantly escapes into the zone of relation, life that refuses to leave excess as grounding. It is why Black dance, vibration, good vibration and movement, is found at the moment, at the site, of disruptive noise in Baltimore. What else would cause folks to dance, to make a metaphoric statement that exceeds the bounds of sense? Music and dance, sound and choreography, are metaphors, are the performed excess of something heard, something, in the flesh, felt—some vibration or movement—that performance seeks to discover continually. Music and dance, sound and choreography, approach that which was felt, approach that excess pulse and rhythm that remained. Like ceaseless misunderstood tears after a dream. Words only gain their meaning by relation, by what precedes and comes after. Words await excess to establish connection. It is this generative opacity of excess that Spillers and Wynter both elaborate.

Such that *stayed, freedom,* and *hallelujah* enunciate the failure of words as enclosed object. Such that *stayed, freedom,* and *hallelujah* each gain through vibration, through resonance, through running up under, rubbing up against and exceeding the enclosure of musicked measure. Black flesh knows something of the truth of elaboration and elongation, about expanding within loopholes of retreat, about movement and vibration against the strictures of cramped time and space.

To privilege the flesh is to consider the *otherwise* possibility of relationality as not grounded in our capacity to endure suffering. There is something that exceeds the totalizing force of seemingly ceaseless violence, some excessive force that was already in us, in us as flesh, that refuses to be suppressed. What to make of the various modalities of violence that befall flesh, the violence of police and militarization, the violence of Middle Passage and Indigenous genocide?

And what to make of the theological-philosophical modality of Western thought that produces categorical distinction such that we are supposed to think Indigeneity apart from and in contradistinction to Blackness; that we are to think the irreconcilability of Black suffering and settler colonialism? Is there a way to think otherwise than violence befalling community as the grounds and basis to think relation, to think community itself?

Perhaps this, the practice of otherwise possibility, is grounded in what Le-anne Betasamosake Simpson might say is the practice of doing *as we have always done*.[10] And perhaps the way to think the relation of Blackness to Indigeneity is to think about what we have always done, been, and what we have available that allows us to think connection. To do as we always have done is to mark the fact that otherwise possibility is not tending toward a future that is to come but is the marking of the practices that we have and do and carry with care and love for one another against the imposition of settler colonial violence, the violence that is coarticulated with anti-Blackness to produce the modern crisis of racialization, the theft of ground and air, and the strangulation of life possibilities. To do as we have always done is to practice what Betasamosake Simpson calls refusal: "refusing colonial domination, refusing heteropatriarchy, and refusing to be tamed by whiteness or the academy."[11]

I have been moved by Betasamosake Simpson's writing about refusal because it gives me another way to think about the practices that emerge from otherwise existence against what Mark Rifkin discusses under the term "settler time."[12] What Rifkin does in his work is to force an exploration of what he calls "two modes of Indigenous critique," that he says are "the insistence that Native people be recognized as contemporary or modern (rather than seen as anachronistic, stunted, or vestigial) and the refusal to pursue non-Native recognition on the basis that it is part of the colonizing interpellation of Indigenous peoples into settler forms and dynamics."[13] I find a similar critique in and as Black study, the desire to think about the flourishing of Black life that does not think Blackness as contemporary or modern, and also is the refusal to think Blackness within the bounds of the given epistemological line of Western thought. Settler time is the temporality of anti-Blackness and we each seek ways otherwise, modes of relation and siblinghood that allow us to practice gentleness and kindness and white supremacism.

And if the ceaseless pulse of violence is the epistemological frame by which modernity enacts itself, empowers and revises itself, if unending violence is the enclosure and logic of modernity's operation, to ground otherwise possibilities for relationality in the very violence incalculable and insufferable that happens to us is to adhere to the logic, is to adhere to the epistemological enclosure and frame, to the musicked measure and rhythmic pulse, of Western theological-philosophical thought. Weheliye's *Habeas Viscus* attempts to get us there, attempts to think Spillers and Wynter together to produce an *otherwise* meditation on the concept, on an *otherwise* genre, of humanity.

This is not to deny that Black suffering, that suffering in Black, exists. I began this meditation with a listing of spectacular events leaving out the many, many more that have gone unremarked, though they are remarkable in their pervasiveness. Rather, this is to question the limits of thinking relationality through suffering as a logic and organizing principle. It is that we still feel, love, have joy, eat good food, smoke and drink liquor and party, it is that we still dream dreams, have visions of *otherwise* possibilities, tap into imaginative resources that make these experiences of Black life in the flesh so acutely sensed, perceived.

Such that even numbness to our times is a means to producing the fleshliness of existence, an *otherwise* feeling of skin and bone and muscle and sinew that draws us into and out of worlds. Even in our numbness is a means to withdraw to the mystery of interiority to allow feeling to flow freely, as if numbness becomes the womb for gestational temporal pause, a shield to allow the ongoing emergence for thinking—and in such thinking, producing—*otherwise* worlds.

Womanist theologian Delores Williams offers the following critique of Black Theology and the place of suffering: "The black experience assumes that the suffering characteristic of the African-American community has resulted only from the horizontal encounter between blacks and whites. The wilderness experience suggests that this characteristic suffering has also resulted from black women's oppression in society and from the exploitation of black women in family contexts."[14] What Williams detects, what Williams discovers, is that the very concept of suffering needs a Blackqueer intervention, one that takes and engages a feminist and womanist hermeneutic. What she outlines and elaborates upon is the way Black suffering centers the wounding and injury of male desire for propertied relations, how Black suffering is normatively grounded in a heteropatriarchal means of thinking the world, thinking the individual, of thinking modern Man.

With the proliferation of violence against transwomen of color, with Black women being the fastest growing prison population, with media blackouts regarding police violence against Black women—in the forms of sexual assault and murder—it becomes important for us to produce justice work that isn't masculinist at its core. This would be work that does not produce suffering, articulated by dominant narratives, as the point of coherence and convergence, as the practice of displacement from one's proper role as citizen, as subject, as aspiring to be Man. And this because suffering, the kind Williams critiques, would remain the zone of male lament regarding displacement, attempting to crowd out other voices because of the individuating nature of the very concept. Articulating Black suffering this way interrupts Black patriarchy from assuming the "rightful" place in the Black community. Black suffering would then come to share strong resemblances to what Daniel Patrick Moynihan's report would call the "tangle of pathology" of Black social life.[15] This elaboration of suffering would then come to share strong resemblances to nationalisms that are about the "rightful" place of Man with women and children behind and supporting such a masculinist, heteropatriarchal ordering.

What Williams discovered but left for us to elaborate are the ways Black suffering as categorical distinction could not accommodate the materiality of reality of the whole of people called Black, how it was always already a delimitation of thought. What if suffering were not the point of departure, what if we did not utilize the epistemology of male injury outlined by Delores Williams, what if we produced—perhaps in the way of Jack Halberstam—failure as an art, as aesthetic practice, to think and conceive otherwise relationality? Perhaps our capacity for relationality otherwise remains unthinkable, a relationality not based on what violence can do, how it does befall us, but a relationality that privileges the discarded remains, the excesses, of aesthetics. This would be a relationality that exists at the limits of knowledge, as perhaps Denise Ferreira da Silva would say.[16]

Let's meet in the zone of *otherwise* possibilities, what Delores Williams calls the "wilderness," what might be considered—following Sylviane Diouf[17]—the secret place of marronage. Timothy James Lockley says of Maroons that they "set out to form independent communities that were self-sufficient and that could exist outside of the systems of government created by Europeans in the Americas" and that these spaces were at times where Africans and Natives, Blacks, and indigenes came together in the service of producing otherwise sociality.[18] "At precisely the moment citizen-subjects were emerging in metropolitan centers, the plantation zone gave rise to an ecological practice closely linked to *marronage*, a process through which human agents found ways to interact with nonhuman forces and in so doing resisted the order of the plantation."[19] Such coming together through emergent *otherwise* forms of personhood, in the wilderness, in swamps, in *otherwise* landscapes that had their attendant soundscapes, would be a critique of Western theological-philosophical Man, would come to include otherwise possibilities for relationality not just between these otherwise modes of personhood but otherwise relations to land itself, a critical intervention into what would come to be normative relations to the ecological and the necessity of displacement, of settler colonialist logics and logistics.

"Autonomy was at the heart of their project and exile the means to realize it," Diouf writes. "The need for foolproof concealment, the exploitation of their natural environment, and their stealth raids on farms and plantations were at the very core of their lives. Secrecy and the particular ecology of their refuges forced them to devise specific ways to occupy the land and to hide within it."[20] Marronage is the practice of intellectual possibility otherwise.

And it is there where *stayed, freedom,* and *hallelujah* sound in and out, produce resonance. It is there where *stayed, freedom,* and *hallelujah* lose their religiocultural specificity not in the cause of dilution but in the production of dispersing the sonic force, the liberating enfleshment such sounds, such sentiments generate. It is in the zone of the openness, the space of vulnerability, that must be protected.

Weheliye states that "the flesh provides the ground, the loophole of retreat, the liminal space, and the archipelago for those revolutions that will have occurred but remain largely imperceptible within Man's political and critical idioms."[21] It is this imperceptibility to Man, to a modern discourse and disciplinary apparatus, an imperceptibility to normative modalities of existence and desire, that would have been a gift, the gift found in flesh. This is what is rehearsed with each protest for and praise of Black flesh lost to the violence of modernity, to the violence of police and poverty. What is rehearsed and performed is an excess that remains, an excess that is imperceptible though its force moves and vibrates and is generative for thinking and imagining otherwise. Such excess is the abolition from the normative genre of Man. And in such excess is the celebratory possibility of otherwise.

Hallelu, hallelu, hallelujah . . .

Notes

1 Alexander G. Weheliye, *Habeas Viscus: Racializing Assemblages, Biopolitics, and Black Feminist Theories of the Human* (Durham, NC: Duke University Press, 2014).
2 Weheliye, *Habeas Viscus*, 24.
3 Weheliye, *Habeas Viscus*, 43.
4 Weheliye, *Habeas Viscus*, 138.
5 Hortense J. Spillers, "Mama's Baby, Papa's Maybe: An American Grammar Book," in *Black, White, and in Color : Essays on American Literature and Culture* (Chicago: University of Chicago Press, 2003), 206.
6 Nathaniel Mackey, *From a Broken Bottle Traces of Perfume Still Emanate: Bedouin Hornbook, Djbot Baghostus's Run, Atet A.D.*, 1st ed. (New Directions, 2010), 15.
7 Sylvia Wynter, "Unsettling the Coloniality of Being/Power/Truth/Freedom: Towards the Human, after Man, Its Overrepresentation—an Argument," CR: *The New Centennial Review* 3, no. 3 (2003): 257–337, doi:10.1353/ncr.2004.0015.
8 Arthur Jafa, *Dreams Are Colder Than Death*, Documentary (2014).
9 Wynter, "Unsettling the Coloniality of Being/Power/Truth/Freedom."
10 Leanne Betasamosake Simpson, *As We Have Always Done: Indigenous Freedom through Radical Resistance*, 3rd ed. (Minneapolis: University of Minnesota Press, 2017).
11 Simpson, *As We Have Always Done*, 33.
12 Mark Rifkin, *Beyond Settler Time: Temporal Sovereignty and Indigenous Self-Determination* (Durham, NC: Duke University Press, 2017).
13 Rifkin, *Beyond Settler Time*, 179.
14 Delores S. Williams, *Sisters in the Wilderness: The Challenge of Womanist God-Talk* (Maryknoll, NY: Orbis Books,1995), 159.
15 Daniel Patrick Moynihan, "U.S. Department of Labor—History—The Negro Family—The Case for National Action," accessed April 6, 2011, http://www.dol.gov/oasam/programs/history/webid-meynihan.htm.
16 Denise Ferreira da Silva, "To Be Announced: Radical Praxis or Knowing (at) the Limits of Justice," *Social Text* 31, no. 1 (March 20, 2013): 43–62.
17 Sylviane A. Diouf, *Slavery's Exiles: The Story of the American Maroons* (New York: New York University Press, 2014).
18 Timothy James Lockley, *Maroon Communities in South Carolina: A Documentary Record* (Columbia: University of South Carolina Press, 2009), ix.
19 M. [Monique] Allewaert, "Swamp Sublime: Ecologies of Resistance in the American Plantation Zone," *PMLA* 123, no. 2 (March 2008): 341–42.
20 Diouf, *Slavery's Exiles*, 14.
21 Weheliye, *Habeas Viscus*, 135.

CHAPTER TWO

Denise Ferreira da Silva

Reading the Dead

A Black Feminist Poethical Reading of Global Capital

Facing the mountain we speak with our dead so that they will reveal to us in their word the path down which our veiled faces should turn. The drums rang out and in the voice of the earth our pain spoke and our history spoke. "For everyone, everything," say our dead. Until it is so, there will be nothing for us. —Zapatista National Liberation Army, "Second Declaration of the Lacandona Jungle," June 1994

In the conflicts caused by the territorial expansion of "junior" mining companies . . . different ways of seeing and experiencing the world, namely use value and exchange value, are pitted against each other. From the Rio Bravo to Tierra del Fuego, disputes are arising because of the incompatibility between short-term speculative mining activity and the existential long-term approach of local and regional populations; between mining on the one hand and farming, silvo-pasture and fishing on the other; between the limited generation of jobs leading to local social disparities and the social, cultural, economic and environmental backwardness caused when the company withdraws. —Saúl Vicente Vásquez, "Study on the Extractive Industries in Mexico and the Situation of Indigenous Peoples in the Territories in Which Those Industries Are Located"

Item 8 of the 12th Session of UN Permanent Forum on Indigenous Issues, "Future Work of the Permanent Forum, Including Matters of the Economic and Social Council and Emerging Issues," dealt with the impact of mining upon Indigenous peoples. The documents discussed included a commissioned study on Indigenous protests against the mining industry in Mexico.[1] At first, the study seems to support Indigenous people's arguments that, in Mexico (as in many other countries), public interest now means the interests of global capital. It acknowledges that Mexico's recent mining boom is part of a "global trend," as countries, in Latin America in particular, have reformed their "laws and administrative regulations to encourage and attract capital for investment in mining."[2] It also quotes the assertion of Mexico's Ministry of Economic Affairs that "mining in Mexico is currently the third most successful industry in terms of attracting investment—behind the oil industry and automotive and electronic exports."[3] It describes how the notions of public interest and priority undermine "the preferential right that the Constitution gives to Indigenous peoples, who are unlikely to have the financial and technical resources to outbid large multinational or national corporations, should they attempt to do so. It also nullifies their right to consultation and consent as guaranteed in the international legal instruments signed by Mexico."[4] This study could be instrumental to Indigenous and rural people's legal battles. It could. And it might. Unfortunately, however, its analysis of Indigenous insurgencies against the Mexican state and the Canadian mining companies fails to articulate their political significance. For when explaining the core of the conflict, the author chooses to construct it as an effect of cultural difference: "Differences of culture and ways of thinking among the actors (the states, the mining companies, the communities, etc.)," it argues, "represent a great challenge not only to dialogue and ad hoc negotiations in conflict situations but also to the construction of a common interest, which is the basis for the formulation of public policy."[5]

Listening to the presentation I was intrigued by how organized protest against land expropriation can be explained as an actualization of cultural difference. What I do in this chapter is not so much to answer this question but to outline an approach that describes Indigenous peoples' protests as what they are: the articulation of a political subject emerging against the colonial apparatus for land and labor expropriation that has been so crucial for the accumulation of capital.

Returning to my question: it is no surprise that Indigenous people's organized protest in Mexico is described as expressions of different set of values. For since at least the 1980s, cultural difference has been the basis for demands from social (racial and gendered-sexual) subaltern subjects precisely because it allows for the delimitation of the social trajectory of exclusion and the articulation of the particular subjectivity emerging from it. Inclusion strategies, based on recognition, such as diversity and multiculturalist programs, as well as the syntax and lexicon of second- and third-generation human rights, borrow from social scientific knowledge—the anthropological studies that deploy the notion of cultural difference and the sociological analytics of exclusion, which does no more than to recount the many ways in which states fail to fulfill their task of promoting social equality (causing social harm, social exclusion, poverty, environmental damages—which comes with their right to sovereignty over the territory). Put differently, the human rights framework, national constitutions, and social scientific tools available to support demands for the realization of these rights rehearse the same liberal grammar. In them, items of the arsenal of raciality, such as the notion of cultural difference, operate as always, as tools of political-symbolic violence, by occluding of the juridic-economic relevance of Indigenous and other anticolonial and anticapitalist protests by transforming them into actualizations of fixed ("traditional") beliefs of the past, instead of reading them as expressions of an Indigenous "radical resurgent present," to borrow Leanne Simpson's phrase.[6]

In this chapter I deploy a Black feminist poethical reading method designed to capture Indigenous insurgencies as anticolonial and racial critiques of global state-capital. Ignoring the onto-epistemological pillars—namely, separability, determinacy, and sequentiality—actualized in social categories and concepts that compose the available critical arsenal, I foreground the fundamentally juridic-economic character of these confrontations. The inspiration for this exercise comes from Indigenous and rural anticolonial and anticapitalist protests against the return to an economic development program based on mega-agricultural projects and natural resource exploitation. Let me just mention three: the Zapatistas (Mexico), Idle No More movement (Canada),[7] and the Encontro Unitario dos Trabalhadores, Trabalhadoras e Povos do Campo, das Aguas, e das Florestas (United Meeting of the Male and Female Workers and the Peoples from the Countryside, the Waters, and the Forests) (Brazil).[8] My main concern is how, because of the onto-epistemological assumptions guiding our critical work, these Indigenous and rural insurrections against state-capital and their demands for justice are immediately translated into actualizations of their cultural difference/identity without political and transformative force.

Toward a framing of justice consistent with these radical challenges to state-capital, the Black feminist poethical praxis aims to contribute to a vision of justice grounded in the view that the only acceptable response to the radical (not metaphorical) call for decolonialization is the demand for nothing less than the return of the total value expropriated from and yielded by the productive capacity of Native lands and slave bodies.[9] Framed as a Black feminist poethical contribution to the critique of global capital—that is, the present figuring of the state-capital duo—what follows is nothing more than a sketch, with each section merely touching the core of the many moves necessary to begin. Even if only as an outline, it presents a method that not only does not repeat but also dissolves the effects of existing critical tools. Not surprisingly, the itinerary is rather simple: I begin with an example of this translation of Indigenous political expressions into actualizations of cultural difference and close with an outline—actually more like notes—on reading the dead as a method for the critique of global capital.

Notes on a Raw Materialist Method

The effect of an object on the capacity for representation, insofar as we are affected by it, is **sensation**. That intuition which is related to the object through sensation is called **empirical**. The undetermined object of an empirical intuition is called **appearance**. I call that in the appearance which corresponds to sensation its **matter**, but that which allows the manifold of appearance to be intuited as ordered in certain relations I call the **form** of appearance. Since that within which the sensations can alone be ordered and placed in a certain form cannot itself be in turn sensation, the matter of all appearance is only given to us a posteriori, but its form must all lie ready for it in the mind a priori, and can therefore be considered separately from all sensation.
—Immanuel Kant, *Critique of Pure Reason*

For everything is a plenum, which makes all matter interconnected. In a plenum, every motion has some effect on distant bodies, in proportion to their distance. For each body is affected, not only by those in contact with it, and in some way feels the effects of everything that happens to them, but also, through them, it feels the effects of those in contact with the bodies with which it is itself immediately in contact. From this it follows that this communication extends to any distance whatsoever. As a result, every body is affected by everything that happens in the universe, to such an extent that he who sees all can read in each thing what happens everywhere, and even what has happened or what will happen, by observing in the present what is remote in time as well as in space.
—G. W. Leibniz, Philosophical Essays

When setting up his transcendental aesthetics at the beginning of *Critique of Pure Reason*, Immanuel Kant's first move is to displace The Thing and

Matter. Both are disavowed in the statement that knowledge/science does not concern The Thing in-itself, but only phenomena, already an effect of the pure intuitions of time and space. My intention here is not to dispute Kant's claims or advance a critique of his program. The radical move here is refusal: refusal to engage, to maintain thinking within the limits of the very distinction between matter and form, which cannot but request the onto-epistemological pillars of modern thought in order to assemble its grounds. Taking off with the given distinction between the substractum (materia prima), without seeking to capture it with the attributes of the subject (such as life or self-determination), I move to figure Matter as The Thing. Of course, I am writing with a good number of early and contemporary philosophers and theorists, many inspired by Gilles Deleuze, who will go unnamed. My inspiration is not Deleuze but Gottfried Wilhelm Leibniz's description of the plenum.

The method I am after begins and stays with matter and the possibility of imaging the world as *corpus infinitum*. I am borrowing, and as I borrow I am also translating, reading Leibniz's with the contemporary Italian artist Michaelangelo Pistoletto's formulation of canvas infinita, which I find resembles Leibniz's, the world is not one in which the Subject projects (reflects and recognizes) itself onto everything, as the determining force. It is one in which everything is indeed always already also an expression of everything else in the unique way it can express the world—imagine difference without separability. This is not difficult if you notice how every other article in the field of particle physics describes a plenum similar to Aristotle's description of matter and change: "Changes will be from given states into those contrary to them in several respects. The matter, then, which changes must be capable of both states. And since things are said to be in two ways, everything changes from that which is potentially to that which is actually. . . . Therefore not only can a thing come to be, incidentally, out of that which is not, but also all things come to be out of that which is, but is potentially, not actually."[10] For potentiality (I prefer the term "virtuality") seems to be precisely what has been puzzling particle physicists throughout the twentieth century. Very successful experiments—from the technological point of view—that fail to find particles obeying efficient causality, as they violate the limits of space-time (the still theoretical tachyon particles that seem to exceed Albert Einstein's speed of light limit), determinacy (Werner Heisenberg's disturbing finding), separability (John Stewart Bell's nonlocality or spooky effects at distance), and sequentiality (also a violation due to quantum entanglement). What interests me is that these elements, materia prima, that constitute (have constituted and will constitute) everything in the universe, the content of every body, violate the modern grammar; they remain Thing. Whatever can be said is said about the object (particle, wave, vibration, emanation of a field)—that is, after measurement—Kant would obviously agree with that! Yet that they can be talked about at all violates the Kantian and the Hegelian programs. My method moves toward description of existence that takes into account both actuality (reality as space-time), but also takes into account virtuality—the world as Matter, that is, Plenum.

How to apprehend the world anew, without separability, determinacy, and sequentiality presumed in the very categories and concepts—that is, the forms of the subject—which are still our critical tools and raw materials? Abstraction or reflection has to go. This is a job for intuition. I am thinking with Hortense Spillers's articulation of the flesh as the ethical ground from which to critically consider conquest and slavery—namely, the wounded flesh exposes total violence as a means that ensures profit and its accumulation through the appropriation of total value, that is, that global capital consists in nothing more than the expropriated productive capacity of slave bodies and Native lands. For the flesh and soil expose the limits of space-time, that is of the (social) scientific and historical accounts of colonial and racial subjugation, which cannot but reproduce what elsewhere I call the racial dialectic. For flesh is no more and no less than what has been (which nourishes us as animal, vegetable, or mineral) and of what has yet to become, that which returns to the soil to be broken down into the nano elements, the particles that emerged at the beginning and remain in the composition of everything that happens and exists in the universe. The Dead's words have ethical force: everything for everyone. For if the flesh holds, as a mark/sign, colonial violence, the Dead's rotting flesh returns this marking to the soil, and the Dead then remain in the very compositions of anything, yes, as matter, raw material, that nourishes the instruments of production, labor, and capital itself. That is how the dead slave/Native lives in/as capital.

What I am proposing then is an approach to reading, as a materialist practice, one that includes imaging of what happens and has happened as well as what has existed, exists, and will exist otherwise—all and at once. From without the subject and its form, the World, becomes the stage of indeterminacy, that is, of The Thing or matter released from the grips of the forms of the understanding. Beyond Kant's forms and laws (and rules), Hegel's Spirit (whose materiality is also that of phenomena), and the concepts and categories of historical materialism (but as a constituent of Karl

Marx's raw material), all that exists and happens refers to the Thing or prime matter. I'll conclude with a comment on the kind of onto-epistemological departure that reading history from the horizon of death demands.

"By the General Law of Value . . ."

If the value of 40 lbs. of yarn = the value of 40 lbs. of cotton + the value of a whole spindle, i.e., if the same working-time is required to produce the commodities on either side of this equation, then 10 lbs. of yarn are an equivalent for 10 lbs. of cotton, together with one-fourth of a spindle. In the case we are considering the same working-time is materialised in the 10 lbs. of yarn on the one hand, and in the 10 lbs. of cotton and the fraction of a spindle on the other.
—Karl Marx, *Capital, vol. 1*

What is it about modern grammar that renders the Zapatista Dead's words without political (in the strict meaning of addressing the state) significance (both as meaning and value), transforming them into expressions of beliefs that refer to a time before exposure to Europeans, their reason, and the tools and modalities of violence it justifies? When I turn to the original presentation of the historical materialist text, I find how the pillars of modern thought that sustain reason's ruling render the Dead's words incomprehensible.[11] This is not loss because that incomprehensibility also exposes how transcendental reason has not been able to comprehend everything, the Thing, or matter. Post-Enlightenment Reason comprehends what it engulfs, which is only what separability, determinacy, and sequentiality can work with, and which is always already translated as form, more precisely as temporal (historical or social) ones that, in the historical materialist text, for instance, are figured as juridical devices, such as title and contract.

For example, here is how it appears when, deploying a Black feminist reading device, which I call blacklight, I try to find an answer for an obvious question in Marx's presentation of the theory of value in *Capital*, volume 1, chapter 7.[12] The question: How is it that slavery and conquest are only relevant as moments of primitive accumulation (violent preconditions) and not as crucial to the ongoing accumulation of (industrial and financial) capital in the late eighteenth and throughout the nineteenth century and beyond? If there is something upon which Marxists do not disagree it is that labor time materialized in a commodity accounts for its exchange value. What most do not question is what happens to the materialized labor in the commodities that enter as raw material (cotton) and instrument of production (the iron used in the spindle). What happens to these materializations of slave labor in Virginia and Minas Gerais working on conquered (Indigenous) lands (cotton) and extracted (gold) from conquered lands? My point with these questions is that if one accepts determinacy, as it operates in the attribution of productivity to human activity—that is, that social labor time determines value—why is the claim not taken seriously that accumulated (exchange) value that constitutes global capital includes both the surplus value appropriated from the wage (contract) labor and the total value yielded by slave (title) labor on colonized lands. The answer is because exchange value is measured "by the quantity of labour expended on and materialized in [a commodity], by the working-time necessary, under given social conditions, for its production."[13] Unfortunately, my claim is incomprehensible—much like the Zapatistas' Dead—because it refuses determinacy (and sequentiality) in the differentiation (separation) of social conditions.

Let me explain how determinacy operates in both moments. First, it appears in Marx's statements on the production of value in his consideration of the "labour process independent of the particular form it takes under given social conditions."[14] I am not refusing this deployment of determinacy here for the sake of this argument because doing so would break with the basic tenet of historical materialism. This would defeat the purpose of this chapter, which is to challenge the disavowal of slave labor as productive of exchange value. In any event, determinacy operates here in two distinctions: (a) when considering the "labor process" in general, between labor and its objects (means of production or instruments of production): land, raw materials, and so forth; that is, in Marx's statement that living labor is the sole subject, the productive force: "the soil (and this economically speaking, includes water) . . . is the universal subject [meaning object] of labour,"[15] and (b) in Marx's argument, when considering labor as a "value-creating activity," that the labor expended in creating raw materials—such as cotton and iron or gold—is also mere object: "The raw material serves now merely as an absorbent of a definite quantity of labour," it is changed in the process of spinning (by the labor time in it) into the yarn, which as the product is "nothing more than a measure of the labour absorbed by the cotton."[16] Under capitalist social conditions of production, the social labor time expended in the production of cotton disappears in the process of production of the yarn; it is used by the spinner. Though it enters in the price the capitalist paid for the cotton and the spindle, it has no significance (explanatory value) to the exchange value of the commodity, the yarn. In this distinction between the labor process in general and (surplus) value-creating labor, the productive capacity (that is, their capacity to work) of Native lands and enslaved bodies vanishes into/as raw material. They have no part in surplus value, because what counts is living labor time.

Second, the key statement in the explanation of the law of value is the phrase "under certain social conditions." For *Capital* is also a piece of sociological theorizing, and its main concern is to provide a clear and distinct description of capitalist social conditions, according to the formalizing trust of classical knowledge and the temporal trust of Hegel's account of history. More important, what distinguishes capital accumulation is the particular historical stage, in which freedom has an economic and juridical shape. It requires "free laborers, in the double sense that neither they themselves form part and parcel of the means of production, as in the case of slaves, bondsmen, &c., nor do the means of production belong to them, as in the case of peasant-proprietors; they are, therefore, free from, unencumbered by, any means of production of their own." Hence, the enslaved laborer picking cotton on the plantations in Virginia or mining in the mountains of Minas Gerais does so under social (economic and juridic) conditions of unfreedom, as "part and parcel of the means of production."[17]

For Marx, they do not enter in the reproduction (accumulation of) capital because the land where the cotton grows and the bodies of those who tend the land and pick the cotton are instruments of production, not dead labor, but raw material. That is, slave labor does not count as dead/past labor. However, because the raw material (cotton and gold) would not exist without it, it enters the calculation of the value of the yarn as an underdetermined element in the conditions of production. At the same time, as such, as raw material, slave labor also differs from the cotton it creates for the production of the yarn. For, as noted above, the cotton is a raw material whose exchange value disappears once living labor transforms it into an elementary component of the yarn—that is, when it realizes it use value. But the price of the slave's labor is already surplus value and his/her labor is extracted, rather than willfully applied to its subjects. More important, the slave is presented as a raw material given by nature, like the soil (land and water), and not one that is in itself use value (that is the product of past labor).[18]

"In slave-labor," Marx argues, "even that part of the working-day in which the slave is only replacing the value of his own means of existence, in which, therefore, in fact, he works for himself alone, appears as labor for his master. All the slave's labor appears as unpaid labor. In wage-labor, on the contrary, even surplus labor, or unpaid labor, appears as paid. There the property-relation conceals the labor of the slave for himself; here the money-relation conceals the unrequited labor of the wage-laborer."[19] Evidently, if one accepts this second operation of determinacy, in the differentiation of social conditions of production, my claim that the accumulated surplus value that constitutes capital contains the total value yielded by slaves laboring on Native lands is absolute nonsense. But it is nonsense, it seems, precisely because the settler slave owner did expropriate the *total value*.

Though necessity guides the original presentation of historical materialism, its formulation of labor rests on the concept of freedom (as a descriptor of social conditions)—in the two senses Marx highlights above, from land (and other means of production) and to enter into a contract. The juridical forms of title and contract, respectively, account for the determination of two kinds of labor: slave labor, which as raw material, an object, as an instrument of production does not produce exchange value, and *wage labor*, which, even if dispossessed, remains a subject, free and equal. This is what renders my case nonsense, not the statement that slave owners expropriated the total value produced by slave labor in Native lands. What to do? To move to dissolve the categories of historical materialism. If we are to apprehend the words of the Dead (the Native and the slave), our political imagination must learn how to do without separability, sequentiality, and determinacy.

In Lieu of a Conclusion—Reading as Re(De)compositional Practice

Now listen!! What are the Zapatistas' Dead saying? What is in the demand that does distinguish a subject (everyone is us) and an object (everything or nothing), or I and Other: "For everyone, everything," say our dead. "Until it is so, there will be nothing for us." Heed the call from the Zapatistas' Dead, who speak history in the voice of the earth, their flesh and blood nurturing the mountains and rivers of the Mexican southeast, demanding everything to everyone or nothing, the return of the total value yielded by Native lands and slave labor; calling for the end of the rule of state-capital; because global capital is postcolonial capital, that is, it lives off the value yielded by the productive capacity of Native lands and slave bodies, so that the end of the anticolonial struggles, decolonization, will only be accomplished if the line separating the colonial present from the colonial past is erased because this is the only way to seize the colonial future.

What is it that the Dead call for? Listening to the Dead requires seizing the spatiality and temporality that constitute Hegelian and Marxian formulations of the dialectical. Heeding the call of these insurgencies against state-capital, I am convinced, requires a materialist perspective that can answer to the Zapatistas' Dead call for decolonization, or as I prefer, the end of the world as we know it. Emphasis on know! For what the Dead's words and the Zapatistas' reply presumes is an in/distinction between Thing, One, Us—thus violating the basic rules of modern grammar, namely separability, determinacy, and sequentiality.[20] For the Dead (speaking in the mountains and forests) there is no distinction between everything, everyone, and us, no separability (extension and its related attributes, such as solidity), that is. No separation between the Dead and us and everything (what is happened and what is happening), no sequentiality, that is. These functions of our political grammar are presupposed in descriptions of the state and its legal borders and common history and social subjects. A Black feminist po-ethical reading is a kind of radical imaging; it is a compositional method that attends to matter not toward comprehending it in the fixed forms of the understanding or subsuming it to the idea(l)s of Reason. While a tool for critique, Black feminist poethical reading consists in a confrontational method that erases the distinction between the actual and the virtual, as it presupposes that, beyond space-time, all that happens and exists is deeply implicated. As a mode of critical intervention, it is creative in that it images the World as having always already been otherwise than its modern picturing. That is, its deployment of the figural (against the formal) unsettles the onto-epistemological pillars that sustain critical projects derived from the Kantian program. Reading the Dead is imaging, with an intention, a manner of composing and recomposing what is given (global capital) so as to expose fissures through which possibilities can be contemplated and with what is not necessarily followed by what is supposed to come.

As a practice, a praxis, it foregrounds the intuition and the imagination. What do I mean by the intuition? Let's take Kant's description of cognition, in *Anthropology from a Pragmatic Point of View*, in which he identifies three faculties: apprehending (*attentio*), abstracting (*abstratio*), and reflecting (*reflexio*).[21] Apprehension, which is the task of the senses, Kant states, receives "representations in order to produce intuitions" that, because these are already in time and space, become the material for the other two: abstraction takes away "what is common to several of these intuitions in order to produce the concept," and reflection uses the concepts in order to produce cognition of the object" or a judgment.[22] That is, intuitive knowledge (that of impressions/expressions) is always already subjected to discursive knowledge (that of conceptions). Walter Benjamin and Henri Bergson provide counter accounts of intuition as a mode of knowing. However, I do not think, with Bergson, that "what is unique" in an object is inexpressible. I prefer Benjamin's account of the intuition in his Doctrine of the Similar, which is like his image: "The perception of similarity is in every case bound to an instantaneous flash. It slips past, can possibly be regained, but really cannot be held fast, unlike other perceptions. It offers itself to the eye as fleetingly and transitorily as a constellation of stars." Here he also describes language as a the embodiment of previous (a thousand years old) practices of intuitive knowledge: "Language is the highest application of the mimetic faculty: a medium into which the earlier perceptive capabilities for recognizing the similar had entered without residue, so that it is now language which represents the medium in which objects meet and enter into relationship with each other, no longer directly . . . but in their essences, in their most volatile and delicate substances, even in their aromata."[23] Imaging/reading names a method aimed at what is without space-time, but which seeps through as/in language, if it is not conceived as a set of rules but as expression. Language, indeed! I conclude with an invitation to contemplate descriptors of existence that do no reduce it to space-time and the play of its onto-epistemological pillars, namely separability, determinacy, and sequentiality, which translate the Dead's words into the actualization of cultural difference and render the statement that "global capital is post/colonial capital" nonsense.

Notes

1 Vásquez, "Study on Extractive Industries in Mexico."
2 Vásquez, "Study on Extractive Industries in Mexico," 8.
3 Vásquez, "Study on Extractive Industries in Mexico," 7.
4 Vásquez, "Study on Extractive Industries in Mexico," 7.
5 Vásquez, Study on Extractive Industries in Mexico, 10.
6 Simpson, *As We Have Always Done*.
7 For a history of Idle No More, see http://www.idlenomore.ca/story.
8 For more information on the Encontro Unitario dos Trabalhadores movement, see https://encontrounitario.wordpress.com.
9 I would here refer to Jared Sexton's comments on the Zapatista's call. Even though Sexton does not cite this piece (Reading the Dead)—which I presented as a talk (at which he was present) at the University of California, Irvine, in March 2014—or the Zapatistas' declaration, for that matter, I am sure that he is also responding to my call for decolonization: Sexton, "The *Vel* of Slavery: Tracking the Figure of the Unsovereign," 11. In particular, I would like to highlight that the call for decolonization is not one for "radical redistribution"—which would keep it within the liberal grammar. It is a call

for the return of the total value extracted under total violence, which includes the very American (Indigenous) and African (enslaved) lives that were taken as well as the pasts, presents, and futures that were no longer because of their obliteration. More important, because the Dead (these lives) remain outside the scenes of economic and ethical value, there can be no hierarchy—vertically (spatially) or horizontally (temporally) presented—of suffering attached to the demand for decolonization.

10 Aristotle, *Metaphysics*, Kindle version location 3660. Downloaded from https://ebooks.adelaide.edu.au/a/aristotle/metaphysics/index.html. Last accessed September 27, 2018.

11 This should be preceded by the following: Just imagine that I have just finished a review of how the presumption of separability informs the modern grammar, in particular how it sustains determinacy in Kant's account of knowledge, and sequentiality in Hegel's description of the movement of history. Separability—the ontic state presupposed in efficient causality—guides the original presentation of the historical materialist and is at work in all its concepts and categories. It explains both the relation between the subject and its object (Kant's determinacy) and (internal/self-relation that is) the movement of history (Hegel's sequentiality).

12 A version of the argument presented in this section has been published in Silva, "Unpayable Debt."

13 Marx, *Capital. Volume I*, 208.

14 Marx, *Capital. Volume I*, 197.

15 Marx, *Capital. Volume I*, 198–99.

16 Marx, *Capital. Volume I*, 211.

17 Marx, *Capital. Volume I*, 785.

18 Implicated here are, of course, the works of Silvia Federici and Hortense Spillers.

19 Marx, *Capital, Volume I*, 591.

20 For a discussion of these terms, see Denise Ferreira da Silva, "On Difference without Separability."

21 Kant, *Anthropology from a Pragmatic Point of View*, 27.

22 Kant, *Anthropology from a Pragmatic Point of View*, 249.

23 Benjamin, "Doctrine of the Similar," 68.

References

Aristotle. 2018. *Metaphysics*. Translated by W. D. Ross. Adelaide: University of Adelaide. Kindle edition.

Benjamin, Walter. 1979. "Doctrine of the Similar." *New German Critique* 17 (spring).

Ferreira da Silva, Denise. 2016. "On Difference without Separability." In *Catalogo: 32nd Sao Paulo de Art Contemporanea*. Sao Paulo: Fundacao Bienal.

Ferreira da Silva, Denise. 2017. "Unpayable Debt." In *The Documenta 14 Reader,* edited by Quinn Latimer and Adam Szymczyk, 81–112. Munich: Prestel Verlag.

Kant, Immanuel. 1998. *Critique of Pure Reason*. Cambridge: Cambridge University Press.

Kant, Immanuel. 2006. *Anthropology from a Pragmatic Point of View*. Cambridge: Cambridge University Press.

Leibniz, G. W. 1989. *Philosophical Essays*. Indianapolis: Hackett.

Marx, Karl. 1906. *Capital. Volume I*. New York: Modern Library.

Sexton, Jared. 2014. "The *Vel* of Slavery: Tracking the Figure of the Unsovereign." *Critical Sociology* 42, nos. 4–5.

Simpson, Leanne. 2017. *As We Have Always Done*. Minneapolis: University of Minnesota Press.

Vásquez, Saúl Vicente. 2013. "Study on the Extractive Industries in Mexico and the Situation of Indigenous Peoples in the Territories in Which Those Industries Are Located." E/C.19/2013/11, 12th Session Permanent Forum on Indigenous Issues, New York, United Nations. https://undocs.org/E/C.19/2013/11.

CHAPTER THREE

Frank B. Wilderson III & Tiffany Lethabo King

Staying Ready for Black Study

A Conversation

Part 1

I had never met or talked with Frank prior to our telephone conversation in the summer of July 2017.[1] I had, however, encountered his work and contin-ued to labor with his thoughts and prose. I had developed my own relation-ship to his texts and an intimacy that I thought was unique and singular. Coming into the conversation, I had a particular investment in his elaborate cartographies that mapped the ontological positions in the United States in his book *Red, White & Black*.[2] I had worked very hard to understand the schema of the coordinates of whiteness and its world-making project. I had become clearer over the years about the ways that the articulation of a sov-ereign self by "the Native" intersected with the circle of white civil society. And I had come to appreciate and even found the possibility for kinship in the space of the other half of Native people's circle—genocide—that over-lapped with Black people's social death in the Venn diagram of the triadic relationship.

I had studied them, written about them, and set about crafting an under-standing of how to be with, think with, trust or not the possibility of sharing the world and future with Indigenous peoples. I admit I came to the conver-sation with investments. And investments that I wanted to deposit more of my political desires into.

Frank came to our engagement differently. While I can't speak for his intentions, investments, or even anxieties about the conversation, he was poised for a different kind of meeting. Frank seemed to see an opening and a possibility in our exchange. Frank had never met me, but he im-mediately wanted to talk about an article that I had recently written. I was caught off guard. Frank is without the academic pretense that I have often encountered—even when the scholar pretends that it is not there. I was surprised not by the generosity but by Frank's earnest desire to be open. To be changed by the encounter. I had to recalibrate. I was not prepared for this opening, this possibility and moment made for Black study.

As you will notice, during my fourth question and response to Wilderson's articulation of coming into an uncompromising critique and understanding of Native subject formation—through Jared Sexton—I switch topics.[3] I start by conceding that this critique is difficult for some Indigenous scholars and activists "to swallow" but do not admit or talk through my own anxiety and am about the critique. I flee, reluctant to confront the anti-Blackness required in the formation of sovereign Native subjects in the white genocidal and anti-Black nations of the United States and Canada. I cut the conversation short here.

Rather than pursue and talk through this anxiety in the first conversation, I cut the exchange short. After a few days of reflecting on our conversation, I reached out to Frank again. In the spirit of Black study and in order to reciprocate the generosity of Frank's engagement I asked him for another conversation. We picked up at the space of my angst in part two of our conversation weeks later.[4] This time I was prepared for a convening, a meeting, a chance to layer and even unmoor myself. This was the kind of exchange that Frank made himself available for. In the academy, I rarely have to be ready to respond to people changing their minds. It is rare to not have to perform or not be ready to perform. It is rare to have to be open to being affected. Engaging with Frank requires being prepared to talk through—and study—your own stuff with each other. It is to break open and out in order to reconnect at another possibility, another way to think. It is the process of Black study with someone. We talked about a number of things in this conversation (Afro-pessimism, gender, citing Black women scholars, the "Black body," Native studies), but more importantly we talked about what we held out hope for and what we have given up on in the hopes of desiring something else.

TK   Frank, I want to start with some context for our conversation. In 2015, a conference entitled "Otherwise Worlds" was held to provide a less mediated exchange between Native and Black studies scholars to see how we might be able speak to each other. At times, the conversation was difficult. But it was also productive in that we could be honest with each other and admit what we did not know about each other's fields. This conference is the basis for this anthology and the conversation we are having today. While the conference provides some of the context,

I have been looking forward to our meeting for more personal reasons. Your work has been invaluable for my own development as a scholar, as well as for helping me orient myself within the political and ethical discussions that take place in the Americas.

Before, I went into the academy I worked for the Philadelphia Unemployment Project for several years in Philadelphia. I got burnt out after ten years in the white nonprofit world and struggled a lot with the white left. I was also a member of the Black Radical Congress— of which factions were informed by the Marxism of the Communist Party USA—and the Philadelphia chapter of the National Coalition of Blacks for Reparations (NCOBRA). When I went to the academy in 2009 and encountered your book in 2010 it was a relief. It affirmed me and allowed me to feel okay about many of the reservations I was feeling and critiques that I had about my political life and activism. It was such a relief to have my exhaustion with Marxists affirmed, many of whom were founders of the nonprofits in Philadelphia. Your worked affirmed my suspicions with Marxist theory.

FW   What you were butting up against in Philly was similar to what the Communist Party was doing in the ANC [African National Congress]. It was really hard to get around that without becoming a Black renaissance Afrocentric person. We are refugees of other peoples' projects.

TK   Yes, that is very true. In terms of your book, *Red, White & Black*, I have always had questions about your interest in Indigenous thought. Why was that of interest to you and why did it become so central to your work in *Red, White & Black*?

FW   I'm not sure where it started. AIM [the American Indian Movement] was started in my city not too far from where I lived. So the issues of Native American sovereignty and the demands of AIM were part of the University of Minnesota landscape. Looking back on that, I see some of the problems. One of the things was my Dad was running a program on a reservation; it was a joint program with the tribal government. One day, there was a meeting, and people on the reservation did not want to adhere to some of the requirements of the University of Minnesota for which it was a joint program. Politically, I thought his institutional interests were wrong and the Indigenous peoples' interests were right. I thought the University should turn over the resources. At the same time, there was an affective charge that had more

to do with my Dad as a Black person than with him being a representative of the university. The tribal representatives said, "We don't want
you, a nigger man, telling us what to do."

In grad school, I was thinking about how the institutionality of indigeneity is a function of the very concrete resources the university, as
a settler formation, took from them. There was also something important in the libidinal economy that the most highly charged imago is
anti-Blackness. Anti-Blackness is driving the quest for sovereignty as
much as the desire to get rid of the settler.

TK That origin story is so important and enlightening to me. Your experience of growing up where people are constantly negotiating Indigenous sovereignty in the Midwest is very different from my experience on the East Coast. I grew up outside of Philly in Wilmington,
Delaware, and the lack of Native institutions—and the general erasure
of Native presence—did not allow the anti-Blackness of Native people
to surface on a regular basis. It also enables folks on the East Coast to
think that Native people aren't around and negotiating with the state
on a regular basis. I was allowed to set up a romantic relationship with
Indigenous peoples, where I could fill in absences and create these alternative histories where we worked in alliance and didn't bump up
against each other when there was a fight for local resources.

FW I can say that I had some anxiety about making this critique about this
presumptive logic in light of the fact that millions of Native people
have been massacred. But in hindsight, I accept [Jared] Sexton's article [in this volume] as a corrective to my work. You have two things
running. I have deep anger towards the settler state and sorrow for
the millions that were genocided. And at the same time, I have this
critique, which is uncompromising, about Native subject formation.
A critique that says one cannot be "Indian" or anything else without
being anti-Black. It is a necessary element to being alive.

TK *That is hard to swallow for Indigenous folks. It is also hard for me
to swallow, and I find myself stuck, conflicted, and unresolved about
that.

Toward another direction, I have been in conversations with others
and myself about how white and non-Black folks are taking up Afro-
pessimism. Some of my anxiety is emerging when and where I see
non-Black folks working under the guise of, "I'm doing the political

work and exposing anti-Black racism," but they are primarily doing their antiracist political work through theorizing Black death and flesh. I often see these folks thinking of, or theorizing, Black death and flesh at the level of metaphor and aestheticizing it in order to make it more malleable. This then becomes "the work." I find myself recoiling from that kind of work. Do you have any thoughts about what white and non-Black folks are doing with Black death and Afro-pessimistic work?

FW   I hear exactly what you're saying, and I grieve over it. Sometimes, I try not to know to get my own work done. As a general rule, it is difficult for Black people to make anything and to hold onto it for more than thirty seconds before the world takes it for its own purposes. Afro-pessimism is going the way of jazz, where it will be for everyone else. Or hip-hop. Patrice Douglass asked me, how do we keep Afro-pessimism for Blacks? And I said, it's like our bodies, we can't. What it becomes is something to animate someone else's projects, and then we'll be dispossessed of Being. That doesn't mean I'm not writing, but I don't know what to do about it. It's akin to lynching as David Marriott describes. The lynched body becomes something through which community can build because it is the not quite human thing to which Humans can ultimately compare themselves.

TK   I had a Black queer woman graduate student who told me about how her white professor thoughtlessly (or maybe not) displayed photos of lynched Black bodies the very weeks that Philando Castile and Alton Sterling were murdered. She became ill during the class and left. She eventually withdrew from the class. I never cease to be surprised by the way that non-Black people just play with Blackness. I don't know what to do with non-Black students who want to work on Blackness; luckily, I have not had that many make the attempt. Have you had to deal with white and non-Black students who want to engage Black studies through Black bodies? What is your response?

FW   The response is an art and not a science. Each time has its own context. As a general rule, I am more direct, and preliminarily set boundaries more with graduate students than undergraduate students. If I am dealing with an undergraduate student, I think they might be wrong-headed but earnest. At UCI [UC Irvine], our relationship with under-grad students is often mediated through TAS. With grad students, I try to say, "what I would like you to do is take down your own people;

as opposed to fetishizing and wallowing in Blackness." The insurgent gesture in Afro-pessimism is that there is not just a grammar of Black suffering but a finger that points to humanity as being deserving of destruction because of its very being and not just its actions. In other words, it's an unflinching critique of Human *capacity*, rather than a critique of unethical and/or discriminatory acts performed. That aspect, that affective side of Afro-pessimism, is important for giving critical recognition to Black rage for your existence, your capacity to be Human, and not just your actions. This part is rarely taken up. Non-Black people cannot fathom the fact that it's their cultural coherence and not their cultural practices that is the problem.

TK   Thank you. There is so much work that could be done on whiteness and how its coherence requires parasitism in order to survive. I think white folks have so much to do in that respect. There is this ongoing and enduring question of how does whiteness require Black death. Deal with that. What's with this obsession with us?

FW   Your question about the students is really deep. What it reminds us of is that we are in a novel position of having some authority while, at the same time, the student is our master. I supervise their exams, etc. But at the level of paradigm, I am their slave. When they get huffy, they are speaking through that paradigm. In the moment, I can't say I will only work with people with whom I agree with their politics. But I will say, this is how it's going to be: I will push back. You don't have to agree. You have to show me that you understand the material, not that you agree with me, or that you consider yourself to be an Afro-pessimist. That's all you need to do to get your PhD and have me sign off on it. But what I won't do is blurb your book when you publish your dissertation. I don't want your reputation intertwined with mine beyond our professor-student relationship. I have work to do in the world (beyond the academy); work which does not include you.

TK   That makes me think about what I should be investing in as I work with non-Black students. I cannot make my supervision of non-Black students about their transformation into being a non anti-Black person. That will take much longer than the two years I have with them or the seven or so years you might spend with a doctoral student. Why burden myself with that commitment? Your insight about our paradigmatic relationship as slaves having to answer to our masters (as students) makes me think more deeply about where the push back comes from when a student says, "this is what I want." It really is, as you say, a demand that "you need to make it happen." It is not just about the intellectual or political differences that emerge between Black professors and students but the power relations between master and slave. As Afro-pessimism becomes sexy and not "ours" anymore, these are things to think about.

FW   In your recent article, you critique Deleuzian scholars who desire posthumanity because they have a humanity that depends upon Black and Indigenous genocide. How did you come to write that?

TK   I wrote the article, "Humans Involved: Lurking in the Lines of Post Humanist Flight," in response to what I still see as an uncritical and celebratory reception of Deleuzian and Guattarian nonrepresentational theory by white folks.[5] I think its ability to escape white embodiment and, more specifically, white violence while claiming to have invented a "new" way of encountering the human and nonhuman material world as fundamentally interconnected is only possible through the murder of Indigenous and Black people. More specifically, what enrages me is the way that nonrepresentational and posthumanist discourse disavows Indigenous worldviews that don't (and for centuries did not) rely on the western boundaries between human and things in order to discover these white "new materialisms" as if they had not existed before. It is precisely because white conquistadors and colonizers wiped out these Indigenous worldviews that they can be rediscovered as new and novel. White people should pay attention to this genocidal process of disavowal in their own epistemic systems. That's a project.

TK   I had an opportunity to meet Saidiya Hartman recently. However, I was not able to talk about her 2003 conversation with you.[6] This might be my projection, but your exchange with her in "The Position of the Untought" made me think about my recent experiences with abolitionist politics and activism. I remember that in that interview, you had some concerns about it, specifically who the leadership was, who is participating, and how it was becoming visible. Can you say more about your feelings about the prison abolition movement as it currently exists and how people are conceiving of conceptualizing abolition?

FW   I don't know much about it in the present. But in 2002, Jared Sexton, Zakiyyah Jackson, and I were involved in different kinds of abolition spaces in Berkeley at the time. We were involved in trying to get political prisoners released. We were also involved in the first launch of Critical Resistance while we were in graduate school. What I felt was happening was that the Critical Resistance people in general were thinking captivity as a common paradigm for all people and not understanding the rise of the prison industrial complex. They were construing the rising rates of incarceration of Latino and Asian men, and more Latina and Asian women, as of a parallel universe to the captivity of Black people. Incarceration and captivity for Latinos, Asians, and Muslims *is a function of a historic experience*; but captivity *is a constituent element* of Black life. If we read Saidiya Hartman's *Scenes of Subjection* as an allegory of the present, then we can begin to see how consent cannot figure into the adjudication of Black injury, because Black people are not endowed with consent—to be either solicited or violated. Specifically, she is talking about how the rape of Black female slaves cannot be considered a violation (which causes the process of adjudication to cave in on itself) because she has no consent that can be abrogated by way of sexual violation. (Yes, her examples are from the nineteenth century, but they are *paradigmatically* applicable today. The end of chattel slavery does not mark the end of slavery.) But it also means that the word "injury" is a word that gains no coherence when it comes to Black people. I felt that if we were to read Hartman's work, not as a historical document, but as an allegory of the present, that we can see that the legibility of other people's historical experience [of captivity] is dependent upon Black people's ubiquitous and transhistorical paradigm of captivity. Jared makes this point in his article [in this volume] that abolition as a politics is never about resurgence, recovery, or recuperation. It would be okay if Black peoples could be in coalition to provide the scaffolding for recovery, resurgence, and recuperation. But we also know that we have Black people in the room, and so it's about something different. The abolition movement wasn't willing to do that; I don't think any movement is willing to do that. As Hartman says, no one wants to be as free as Black people will make them, because they will be free of their own cultural coordinates, not just free of their oppressive dynamics. Let's work from there. What Sexton is talking about in abolition through Blackness is degeneration, decline, and dissolution. An uprooting of the notion of presenting any order of determination from taking root; a politics without claim or even demand; a politics whose demand is too radical to be formulated in advance of its deeds. That's what makes Black bodies so exciting to people at one level and so terrifying at another register. What I saw is that what Critical Resistance really wanted was the affect, the energy that comes from the demand of Blackness, a politics without a claim, but it wanted to contain that within a very coherent and purposeful vision of resurgence, recovery, and recuperation. That is what I mean about Blackness as the refugee of other peoples' movements.

Hartman was at Berkeley at the time and her book, *Scenes of Subjection*, blew me away.[7] I used to be a post-Gramscian and worked with the Communist Party in South Africa. But when folks like [Michael] Hardt talk about the lack of consent, they mean that now with globalization, the command modality of capitalism imposes its will ubiquitously across the globe; there is no longer the space and time of respite once vouchsafed by hegemony and civil society. But Hartman shows that Black peoples never operated through consent. For us, there's nothing temporal about the loss of consent; one cannot narrate this loss this way. Subalterns can, but Blacks cannot. There's nothing temporal (or historical) about the loss of something one never possessed. So why can't we think abolition through that. The abolition movement is the place for white joy and excitement, but it's not about abolition as it could be.

TK   Even though you're reflecting back on this dynamic in your past experiences, you are speaking about dynamics that exist in the current moment. This year, I went to a training that was organized by a coalition of multiracial social justice activists in the city of Atlanta with the goal of introducing folks to the concept of abolition. I showed up, expecting to see the usual folks from the Black social justice community, and 80 percent of the people were white. It was also being facilitated by a white presenting person—they may have identified as a person of color—to my dismay. I decided this wasn't the place for me, as people were talking about "reforming the prison away" or becoming excited by the idea that as a Marxist a part of the work of abolition was "abolishing the notion that cops were workers" to make themselves feel better. This was not the conversation I wanted to have. The energy of Blackness was animating the room but Black people were not there. Abolition now has this currency in activist movements, and its momentum is certainly animated by Black struggle but not necessarily Black people.

On another note, Frank, I definitely see the influence of Hartman on your work. I'm now thinking about and concerned about how we engage and cite her work within the Afro-pessimistic tradition. I and a few other Black women are noticing and talking about how they see people invoke your work and Jared's work, but they don't even cite or know Hartman's work. How can we address some of the sexism in the academy that avoids taking Hartman seriously? How do we take misogyny seriously within the Black intramural?

FW   I am so in agreement with you. Critical theory has been a masculinist space. I am upset about the lack of citational practice. Are you talking about Afro-pessimism specifically?

TK   Those who use an Afro-pessimistic frame. People will cite you and Jared, but when asked if they have read Saidiya Hartman, they don't know her work. And no one wants to take this on in terms of this particular kind of erasure. How do we interrupt this masculinist tendency to just cite Black men in Black critical theory?

FW   I don't have a programmatic answer to that. The moniker "Say Her Name" is something we can think of with this. Afro-pessimism is an outgrowth of Black feminist theory; particularly the work of Spillers and Hartman have helped us think about structure and relationality. The term comes from the 2002 interview and it's Hartman's word; it's not my word. This is the problem of Afro-pessimism, as you have pointed out, and Black studies in general. Scholars cite Black men more than Black women. We should see how the lessons in Hartman's book provide a spotlight on the intramural as it relates to gender. She writes about how a Black woman was raped by her master, and then kills him and goes on trial. The lawyer adjudicated the case by highlighting the injury to the Black man's pride rather than the Black woman's body. The point is that in the libidinal economy, the value of masculine violation is so high as to erase the actual real bodily trauma of Black females. The only way Black injury could be imagined to have a voice is through the Black male defendant. This dynamic is carried over into political organizing as well as in Afro-pessimism. Intuitively, there is the centering of the Black male voice with the Black female voice being unthought. Hopefully this can be highlighted because this erasure is the very thing that Afro-pessimism is talking about.

TK   How do we take up gender within an Afro-pessimistic frame?

FW   I don't like to be prescriptive. But what I find is necessary is the way in which violence is thought and mediated on through sexuality. Violence happens through Blackness without an endgame. That impinges upon every area of Black life. Violence is constitutive of sexuality in Blackness in a way that it is not constitutive in other subjects. One has to move through the categories even if they don't apply structurally. The violence that produces the slave cannot be consented to by the slave because the slave cannot provide consent. That makes you a very different kind of sexual being than a person who can consent. [Judith] Butler, brilliant as she is, has not been able to theorize a violence that happens prior signification (meaning prior to instantiation as a subject) in the way Hartman has. And it is this regime of violence which actually forecloses the possibility of Black people being positioned as Human subjects (and, again, makes Human subjects legible as subjects in contradistinction to the Slave).

TK   And Spillers. I tell students to pay attention to what Spillers says at the end of "Mama's Baby, Papa's Maybe." If these categories don't cohere at the level of flesh, we are people who don't have anything to prove, right? There's no way you are going to fulfill the mandates of heteronormativity, or even queerness, right? It's not going to work for you.

     Thank you for taking both of them so seriously in your work. Now, I want to spend this last bit of time we have asking about what you are working on? I know that you used to be in a theater department. How is that experience and training informing your current work?

FW   Writing can be very anxiety-producing. Or at least it is for me. What we are dealing with as Black critical thinkers is painful stuff. The cost of an Afro-pessimistic book is higher than a Deleuzian book. Can one actually write Afro-pessimistic books? There's a lot of interest in Afro-pessimism, and that is not always a good thing. It's akin to the deployment of black bodies in theater departments at universities. I used to work in such a department. It wasn't a fun thing to watch.

     There is so much pornotroping of Black men and women in these departments when they stage plays. I had to fight these battles, so I had to transfer my line. One of the members of the department (who did not want to go on the record) told me that a white woman in that department had had the nerve to say, "We're all over here suffering from post-traumatic Frank syndrome." When I was just speaking up for Black people, telling them, "Stop staging your fantasies through our bodies." But somehow they are the victims.

TK   I have no words for that, I don't. You just gave me an awareness when you talked about pornotroping of why I can't talk to white people about how much they appreciate the film *Moonlight* and the work of Tarell McCraney. I'm afraid about where the conversation will go. How am I going to do it?

FW   This is what kills us, because it hurts you in your chest.

TK   I think my own anxiety as it concerns my own writing is that my academic and therefore writing work is something I cannot escape. For my academic colleagues and, to some extent, if I am honest about how I experience my work in the context of the academy, my anxiety can at times stem from whether I feel like I am appreciated enough. And we're always doing a self-assessment in terms of our marketability. I didn't have to do this in the other kind of work I did before I became an academic.

FW   It's like we are never not working. Thanks for that, it spoke to something that was gnawing at me.

Part 2

When Frank and I spoke again later, it was in order to finish a conversation that I felt was unfinished. I felt that very early on, I rerouted our conversation away from the territory of Native subjectivity. My own apprehension surfaced and prevented a full fleshing out of some of the more difficult terrain of Black and Indigenous relations.

TK   Frank, thank you so much for being willing to speak with me again. I really felt like I had to continue this conversation with you to really allow you—and me—the opportunity to finish or rather open up some things. I am also putting my cards on the table, about how I come to this conversation and where we left off last time. I think that in my own work, I have tried to hold hope that Native and Black folks can speak to each other. What I thought I found was an opening in *Red, White & Black*. I was compelled by your idea of Black flesh and Indian flesh—Black flesh created out of slavery and Indian flesh created out of genocide. And that Indigenous people in the genocidal mode could talk to Black peoples as fungible, accumulable things. And when you started to talk about Jared's work, particularly, the "*Vel* of Slavery" [in this collection] early in our first conversation as a corrective to your work, I started to think, maybe I have to change my mind if Frank changed his mind.[8] I also have to be clear that I am currently in the process of writing a book [*The Black Shoals*] that looks for these moments of discursive exchange or where we "hear" each other. I think that trepidation made me stop the conversation prematurely. I prevented you and us from talking about how you have really sat with and thought about Native studies and Native philosophies, Native cosmology and Native thought. So I wanted you to be able to think through that this time.

FW   I want to say I share your anxiety at the level of emotion and the level of intent. I also shared it theoretically when I wrote *Red, White & Black*. Jared's work had already been generative and formative for me. He holds things very unflinchingly. He does not link an analysis of a problem with a prescription for how to solve the problem. That's the heat that Afro-pessimism gets because few people are able or willing to theorize like that. Matthew Arnold said in *Culture and Anarchy* that the workers can and *should* become more enfranchised than the British aristocracy is willing to allow, and they and their children should have free access to education; but they should not be taught a mode of thinking that could lead to a French Revolution in England. Arnold wanted to keep both the working class and the aristocracy in check. He was saying, "If we keep going down this road, the aristocracy, it's going to drive England into the ground. We need a middle ground but it can't be revolutionary." And he thought educating the working class while clipping the wings of the aristocracy would achieve this; but the working class needed a pedagogy that shackled problems to solutions (description must always come with prescription); otherwise, they would find the solutions in the streets—and those solutions would not contribute to the rise of capital and the middle class. "Sweetness and light" must prevail over anarchy (from below and from above). Afro-pessimism does not come with a prescriptive component. No answer to either Arnolds *or Lenin's*, for that matter, question, "What is to be done?" Black folks will figure that out when we're on the move. I was in graduate school with Jared, and we were dealing with various campaigns. One was a campaign to stop a proposition that would send youth to state prisons. People would say, if you are for prison abolition as the long-term goal on the path of the reformist campaign, how are we going to stop crime? And I remember at one of these debates, Jared said, I won't talk to you about crime and punishment. I will only talk to you about crime. At a later time, I will talk about punishment. To have that conversation together is to have a conversation about the solution. Theoretically, we believe Black embodiment is a problem that does not have a coherent solution. (We're not simply being recalcitrant and difficult.) One of the claims Sexton is making in the "*Vel* of Slavery," thanks to Native scholars, is that there is a distinction between colonialism and settler colonialism. It's a powerful intervention. But you're still talking the politics of a claim, the politics of redress, the politics of dispossession. And that very conversation itself crowds out Black suffering. I've come over to that because I think that even though in 2010 I theorized should Indigenous theorization of suffering jettison sovereignty as an essential dynamic and stay in the elements of genocide, I have found there is just not enthusiasm among First Peoples in Canada and Native peoples in the US to follow that path. So just on the level of on-the-ground activism, I just get hammered by people who tell me to focus on the historical concrete thing of Indian people having lost land. So we're not going to have a conversation of the abjection of Blackness with the partial abjection of Nativeness. There is just no desire. The book you're doing could be a new chapter in that. I think this structure of feeling is hegemonic, that no matter how good the argument is, folks refuse to be authorized by a Black ensemble of questions. I don't think it's a calculated thing. I just think that's how Native peoples are like white people in the libidinal economy. I don't have time for these people, that's my attitude. Does that mean I don't champion the release of Leonard Peltier? Does that mean I don't champion the destruction of the United States and the honoring of treaties and more so that land is returned to Indians? No, I want those things. But I also fundamentally don't believe Black peoples have any coalition partners—not even with Native Americans or First Nations Peoples in Canada. And this marks a shift in my thinking since *Red, White & Black*. Even Native Americans, when in coalition with Blacks, are going to crowd out discussion of our grammar of suffering (and often go so far as to lump us in with the settlers). Here's another component of this. Jared makes the point that what you get out of Blackness is a politics without claim. And no one seems to be taking that on. Saidiya

Hartman said to me when I wrote my dissertation that I was going to get all this flak because it (my critique of Indigenous ontology) is not camouflaged. And she was right. Afro-pessimism is not just an analysis of the preconscious suffering that civil society imposes upon Black people—the withholding of rights. It's also about the collective unconscious and how the mind works creating Blackness as a necessary object of abjection, through primary processes of articulation, not just secondary processes—how conscious speech belies primary desires. You can't control your unconsciousness. Jared has come along and shown me that we embody an essential antagonism because you cannot articulate what would make Black people whole. And that makes everyone anxious. Let's say we look up in the perfect world where Native peoples engage Afro-pessimism. Blackness is the absence of subjectivity and that's so powerful. That's why people want Black peoples in their movement. Why don't Native people, instead of articulating sovereignty as the key thing, why don't they see that their grammar of suffering, as horrifying as it is, is not as bad as the Black grammar of suffering. Why do we have to be, in the face of the evidence, the number one subject of suffering? I don't want to be the number one subject of suffering, I would much rather be a disposed colonial subject than a slave for whom there is no story of dispossession.

TK   Are you saying, why is it that in the face of Black suffering, the Native person can't say, wow, that's not what I experience? And I don't necessarily have to experience it. Is that what you are saying? You want Native people to be able to say, my suffering is horrible, but in the face of Black suffering, and its politics without a claim or a demand, that is a whole different order of existence that I am unfamiliar with?

FW   I don't understand the question.

TK   I just wanted to be sure I heard you. You were helping me think of the anecdotes I use when I hold out this hope. I think I shared with you I used to be part of the INCITE chapter in Toronto. There was this moment when we as Black and Indigenous people got each other. There were three Black women that were part of INCITE, and we sat with an Anishinaabe woman for two years trying to work this out. We were having deep conversations about the problems of sovereignty with our Anishinaabe sister. We were saying, even this idea of getting rid of the Canadian state, getting rid of the US, creating a new subjectivity, creating new language systems, how do you account for Native peoples' anti-Blackness. And one sister asked the Anishinaabe sister directly, how can you guarantee that Native people won't incarcerate and kill us like white people do? And the Anishinaabe woman sat back and was completely crestfallen, and said, I never considered that in my understanding of sovereignty. She said that she would have to shift. Her idea about sovereignty would have to be about Black survival. We would have to undo the prison system in order to free the land. So we are back to the land.

So I have to check myself here, because I'm sure I don't have a full understanding about what Native peoples mean by land. I think in Black studies we tend to be reductive about land. But what I hear Jared say is that Native peoples will still ground themselves in a kind of coherence. So even if she says I will rethink or undo sovereignty, she still has land to fall back on, which has a particular kind of coherence with the human and the self, particularly for white folks. As you were talking, it helped me think about those experiences I had with INCITE. Because there we were with Black and Native flesh. We weren't where Jared is, but we were willing to move in light of Black suffering. Again, you said people often come to us with emotional, experiential examples. It makes me consider whether these experiences can lead to long-term transformation? In the end, we decided to put our work together on hold. We were at an impasse. We still want to hold one another and Black and Indigenous people but do not know how to move forward.

FW   I agree with everything you are saying, you said it all.

TK   But let us get back to what you didn't get a chance to talk about. Why did you choose to think with Ward Churchill, Vine Deloria, Leslie Marmon Silko, etc., in your book? Was there something about what they were saying that allowed you a point of entry?

FW   First, let me say I am not someone who cares about whether Churchill is a properly registered Cherokee, and hence would say he is not worth listening to, like this Hawaiian scholar, J. Kēhaulani Kauanui, was saying to me at this talk.

TK   I just saw a chronicling of your and Kauanui's exchange in a recent *American Quarterly* article.[9]

FW   Look, in general, when I travel it's to connect with other Black people and have a space to think about Black suffering. I don't think anyone can be taught to accept the essential dynamic of Black suffering. I simply believe the psyche has processes that are contradictory and hypocritical. I think Blackness necessarily remains in the realm of the imaginary. I believe there is a structural imposition that prevents bringing Blackness into subjectivity. I used to try to work with that. Now I try to have a way of talking that is a metaphorical middle finger. That energy makes Black people feel good about my talk. I feel good about centering peoples who have been genocided at the level of analysis. Can you restate the question again?

TK   No, I like where we were going. I was reading that article a few days ago, and I had a lot of problems with it. First, I found J. Kēhualani Kauanui uncritical of Patrick Wolfe. Secondly, she said that you said "we're not going to agree." Which is true. But I felt like we were not going to get anywhere in the article. But her beef is interesting. In her argument she uses Bacon's Rebellion to argue that people who were in the process of becoming Black, but not in the way we know Blackness today, chose to participate in Native genocide. She dismisses your question of why are you so focused on Black people's role in the assault on Native people? She just says Black peoples have subjectivity and can do violence to Native folks. Now she brought this up, but it makes me think of the unconscious, and how it might be working in terms of her focus. In the article, she says the Occoneechees sold out the Susquehannock as they sought a strategic alliance with the participants of the rebellion. So my question is, why doesn't she have an issue with the Occoneechees who were also complicit in the genocide of the Susquehannock? Why are you only concerned about Black folks' (who were not yet Black in the way we know) complicity and not about how one nation of Indigenous people participated in the genocide of another nation?

FW   Exactly, she was one of those people who said Churchill isn't even Native as a way to dismiss my argument. She didn't know how the libidinal economy is subtended by violence. How the collective unconsciousness works with structural violence. You know what, in 1997, I didn't either. I had to go through psychoanalysis. Then I had to go through how psychoanalysis is as anti-Black as is Marxism. This is the drive of Black liberation, which is different than the drive of Indigenous liberation. What I was arguing in my books is that world-making is an anti-Black project. I don't like that statement. It gives me a lot of pain.

However, my pain is not a counter argument. If anything, it gives the (painful) argument more validity. But she was arguing several layers below the level of abstraction at which I was speaking. She was saying this is how our world was destroyed and this is how Black people participated in the destruction of our world. And my argument is that you first talk to me about how the world is made? How is space transposed into place and how does paradigmatic violence play into that? And Black people are always making place out of space and making event out of duration. But the structure of gratuitous violence *acts as an injunction against anyone else accepting Black place names or Black timed events.* Native peoples are told that their world is incompatible with the European world. But *we're* told we have no right to make or inhabit worlds at all (whether Native or European). I realized that her unconscious anti-Blackness was not giving me any authority at the level of theory; not because she disagreed with me but because she had nothing to say about the actual Afro-pessimist argument; and everything to say about the historical facticity of Black participation in Native subjugation. She was keeping herself from being able to understand that I was not saying that Black people have never committed horrible crimes against Native peoples. But I was saying that I dealt with that in my discussion of Vine Deloria complaining about Black Buffalo Soldiers and Black people becoming Christians. Vine Deloria did not understand that slavery is not about Black people picking cotton and being in chains: that's the historical facticity of *some* experiences of slavery, not a paradigmatic explanation of slavery. Slavery is a dynamic in which subjectivity cannot cohere. She could have said, "Hey buddy your meta-critique of relationality is wrong and here is how relationality is *not* anti-Black; I'll explain how Indigenous world making is *not* anti-Black." That would have been a genuine response to my talk. But she didn't meet me there. She stayed at her level of scholarship, and the historical dynamic. That's a trap. One which I simply refuse to fall into. And that's what happened. Some Black people came up, and said, "That's what I was thinking but didn't know if I could say it." And that's all I care about. Not because I'm a jerk, because I am a jerk, but because she didn't actually engage what my book said or what I said in my lecture.

Now coming to back to the original question, what I realized was that the Native writers were reluctant to have a sustained engagement with violence. But Black writers were not reluctant. But Silko, Churchill, and [Haunani-Kay] Trask had the sustained engagement with violence, even though the tools they were using were from the social sciences. I wanted to see if there were Native peoples talking about violence compared to culture.

TK   I am trying to have conversations with Native studies scholars about my more recent analytical shifts. I'm ready to talk about conquest, but not about settler colonialism. I can't really have this conversation about language, culture, spiritual laws, and land. But I can talk about the brutal ways conquest created the human through Black and Indigenous death. Some folks can hear it and some cannot. Some can't hear my beef with Patrick Wolfe. Like OK, we've traveled with his idea that settlement and invasion are a "structure and not an event," but we can't keep going there because eventually you're going to be talking about the human space, labor, and work. Something—a discourse—within which Black people cannot be heard. Some Indigenous peoples don't want to have a conversation on Black terms.

FW   I have a tendency to be flippant. I'm still willing to have the conversation. I've spent my teens in the '70s when I was an internationalist, and my twenties and thirties in South Africa, and the forties in grad school, really wanting this embrace between Black and Native peoples. I would like that. I still think there is an injunction against it. But I want it.

TK   I don't think you are being flippant. You have put the time into that. You were sharing that you grew up in Minnesota and knew people in AIM. For most of my political life, I have only worked with Black folks, and didn't come into any consciousness about Indigenous genocide until my thirties. So when I was in Toronto in 2006 I was hit with it. A consciousness about Indigenous genocide is much more present there than on the East Coast in the US. I mean it's in the atmosphere. You can feel it. The very presence of Native activists in the streets of Toronto representing for the Six Nations encampment and blockade in Caledonia was right in my face. I was also confronting this issue with my Anishinaabe friend who was working with Native youth whose rates of suicide were astonishingly high at the time. She was constantly trying to prevent the death of Native youth and working with the Murdered and Missing Indigenous women movement. So I was horrified about genocide and that she was working with Native death every day, but also about my ignorance of it. I felt guilty, and so I am still invested in kind of letting the reality of genocide hit me and work through it. So I know I'm in a different place than where you are, where you are—you are, exhausted—you've been arguing with folks for decades that still haven't moved. So I don't think you're being flip.

FW   I don't want to in any way belittle the tactile suffering of Native peoples. I've spoken twice in Toronto and once in London [Ontario]—an hour from there. What I felt in the room, Native people were guilt-tripping Black peoples into not being enough into Native issues. But the biggest example was when I was with Jared and the now deceased Joel Olson, who does whiteness studies. There was this radical whiteness conference in Denver. They brought us to speak and AIM people to speak. I suggested to them that Zakiyyah Jackson speak since they didn't have any Black women speaking. The first year, the organizers were really into the analytic framework that Ward Churchill was offering, which was very powerful at the time. One reason I got fired from UC Santa Cruz was trying to get him to speak there. The second year (in Denver)—and this is the danger of the white gaze—the white organizers would read more work by Black intellectuals than Native intellectuals. The work we were doing was showing how violence was part of the libidinal economy. The Native people were really upset. Zakiyyah was the next to the last speaker and Ward Churchill was the last speaker. I worshipped him as a theorist at the time, but he did not sit through any of the Black talks. And, toward the end of the conference, he and his entourage were very abusive to Zakiyyah Jackson while she was at the podium. He came in with his uniformed bodyguards (AIM paramilitary gear), four of them, and he sends his uniformed bodyguards on the stage *while she was talking*; and they ran behind her, again, while she was speaking, and said it was a security check. (In other words, this pageantry was, putatively, about a Secret Service–like security check—never mind the fact that a Black woman was speaking on the stage that they needed to secure—before Churchill spoke, to prevent assassination attempts). After that, I was just through with him. Why did they do it? They were tired of her talk bleeding through the time he thought he should be speaking. We (Churchill and I) got into a heated repartee on what had happened. On top of that, unlike Jackson, Churchill didn't even come prepared. He spoke extemporaneously. I just left. He told the organizers that he wanted to meet me to talk about what happened. (I guess some kind of rapprochement with *me*, not Jackson; he made no overtures toward her, nor did his people.) His people told me he wanted the two of us to meet up the next day. And I didn't do that. I'm through with him as a politico. I'm not through with him as a theoretician. And the reason I'm done with him as a politico has nothing to do with whether he has the proper papers from the Cherokee Nation. That's just a moment of madness like so many others.

TK   So when you're talking about your travels in Canada, this anxiety that Black people have about not being down with Indigenous peoples is deep to me. Black people in Canada are always thinking about Indigenous genocide, even in a context where there are no Black studies programs. But I don't know how many Indigenous folks have showed up to get Black studies in Canadian universities. That kind of anxiety has always been weird to me given the kind of leverage Indigenous peoples actually do have in Canada. In a 2006 conference, there was discussion on Blackness, Indigeneity, and diaspora. Then in a moment of frustration, a Mi'kmaq scholar called Black peoples settlers. Then the white people in the audience were laughing and saying she was right. I thought, how is this even possible? What have you been reading that Black people could ever share the same ontological position as white settlers?

FW   When it comes down to it, we as Black peoples have the generosity to understand the grammar of suffering of others, but there's no generosity coming back to us. It's always what we have to be taught, and not what we can teach others. That lack of engagement works at every level of abstraction—at the level of the interpersonal, the institutional, etc., and the level of the imaginary of Native society once liberated. In some way, in different modalities, everyone is like Abraham Lincoln who said Blacks should be free but I can't imagine them living with us.

TK   Thank you so much for your time, Frank.

FW   I'm glad you are doing this work. I don't think the work you, Jared, or I are doing will change Native peoples' minds. But I think it will give Black people permission to speak the unspeakable. And that's what is important.

Notes

1 Our conversations took place on July 2 and July 26, 2017.

2 Frank B. Wilderson III, *Red, White & Black: Cinema and the Structure of U.S. Antagonisms* (Durham, NC: Duke University Press, 2010).

3 I marked the question with an asterisk (*).

4 We continued our conversation on July 26, 2017.

5   Tiffany Lethabo King, "Humans Involved: Lurking in the Lines of Posthumanist Flight," *Critical Ethnic Studies* 3, no. 1 (2017): 162–85.

6 Saidiya V. Hartman and Frank B. Wilderson, "The Position of the Unthought," *Qui Parle* 13, no. 2 (2003): 183–201.

7 Saidiya Hartman, *Scenes of Subjection* (New York: Oxford University Press, 1997).

8 Jared Sexton, "The *Vel* of Slavery: Tracking the Figure of the Unsovereign," *Critical Sociology* 42, nos. 4–5 (2014): 583–97.

9 J. Kēhaulani Kauanui, "Tracing Historical Specificity: Race and the Colonial Politics of (In)Capacity," *American Quarterly* 69, no. 2 (2017): 257–65.

BOUNDLESS
ONTOLOGIES

Part II

CHAPTER FOUR

Tiffany Lethabo King

New World Grammars

The "Unthought" Black Discourses of Conquest

At some point during the stretch of dark on the night of June 24, 2015, in the North End of Boston at Christopher Columbus Park, the statue of the itinerant sailor was doused in red paint. Simulating blood, paint covered portions of forehead, face, and a shoulder of Columbus's folded arms. The crimson paint ran down the conquistador's back into a pool of bloody red that surrounded his feet. On the foundation block upon which the bloodied figure stood, a tag spray-painted in black letters with each word stacked upon the other read "BLACK-LIVES-MATTER." The tag was graffitied on the back side of the foundation block upon which the statue stands. For the fifth time since its design and placement in the park the statue had been defaced. This time an aesthetic and political inscription of protest enveloped the statue in a collage of red, white, and black. Beyond its local coverage in the Boston metro area, national news sources provided additional coverage of the incident.[1] Labeled an act of "vandalism," the incident was presumed to be a part of the string of acts of vandalism and defacement of Confederate monuments across the southeastern part of the US immediately following the massacre of nine African Americans in Charleston, South Carolina. This incident of vandalism in the northeastern city of Boston elicited a number of responses.

The overwhelming sentiment conveyed was a sense of incredulity. People could not seem to wrap their heads around why Columbus had become a target of defacement by "allegedly" black actors. A volunteer from the Friends of Christopher Columbus Park was interviewed by the local ABC News affiliate in Boston. Volunteer Jean Brady remarked, "Why here? I mean it just seems so out of place."[2] Local news station reporters from ABC interviewed two individuals who were unaware of the event and happened to be visiting the waterfront on the day the story was covered. The reporter showed them images of the defaced statue. Upon seeing the image, one of the visitors responded confoundedly, "Oh look, there's blood there," as if the association of blood with Christopher Columbus was some kind of non sequitur or at least an out of place association in relation to the historical figure.[3] The edited news clip then returns to the volunteer Jean Brady who still seems unable to make this incident square within the space and time of Boston or Christopher Columbus. Brady expressed that she and residents in the North End and waterfront neighborhoods did not believe that the act of vandalism had anything to do with the Black Lives Matter movement. As a self-described sympathizer of the movement, Brady found it hard to believe that the people who belong to or believe in this cause would participate in an act like this. Brady incredulously states that "this is not what they would do."[4] A few days later, the *Boston Herald* interviewed local founder and lead organizer of Black Lives Matter–Boston, Daunasia Yancey. Yancey said that while members of Black Lives Matter Boston had nothing to do with the political act of public resistance, "we fully support it."[5]

In the comments section that appears on a number of the online sources that reported the story, commentators left a range of responses that evinced a certain kind of disconnect and inability to make the relationship between Black death, Black rage, and Christopher Columbus. Readers' comments ranged from those that insulted the intelligence of the "vandals," to ones that characterized the act as an appropriation of Native American issues, to responses that relegated Black death and white supremacist violence to the space of the Confederate South, much like Jean Brady who was interviewed by ABC. One comment left on Media Equalizers' website where the news article appeared is particularly telling.[6] A commentator with the username Jack Sparrow simply weighed in with, "What a moron. Columbus had nothing to do with Africans in America."[7] For the purposes of this essay, we might call this inability to make this kind of connection a form of "colonial unknowing" that runs rife among the US and North American public.

It can be argued that this kind of historical amnesia, willful ignorance, or North American agnosia about Columbus's role in the slave trade and the way that conquest invented and instantiated Blackness as a form of abjection in the modern world is due to North American quotidian circulations of colonialist common sense. For many, Columbus and the unfortunate yet inevitable genocide of Indigenous peoples are traditionally treated as unrelated to Black life and death within public discourses of the history of the Americas. Even leftist critiques of the everyday acts of commemoration and public forms of pedagogy that naturalize conquest are typically singularly focused on Columbus the murderer, not on Columbus the enslaver. This results in a kind of "colonial unknowing" and denial that is evinced in the way that the various news sources produced and circulated the idea that the supposedly Black vandals were misdirected in their public critique and protest. The tone and framing of most of the coverage presumed that Columbus and conquest had nothing to do with Black people. While North Americans' disavowal of the violence of Christopher Columbus as well as the conquistador's role in the slave trade is certainly a form of colonial unknowing worthy of interrogation, I am interested in the way a similar form of unknowing is reproduced within contemporary leftist critical theories including (white) settler colonial studies in North America. This chapter inquires whether or not the preoccupation of North American white settler colonial studies (as well as other critical theories) with settlement, settler subjectivity, and land make it increasingly difficult to register the far-reaching and ongoing violence of conquest in everyday life.

This chapter poses the following questions: Why have we decided that we are done with the rubric and temporality of conquest? What if we made a conceptual return to the terrain of conquest, the conquistador, and conquistador modes of life? What happens when we pay attention to the ways that Black contemporary politics and Black studies have paid attention to conquest? I argue that an analytical return to and tarrying with conquest enables a different kind of conversation and ethical engagement among scholars in Black studies, Native studies, ethnic studies, settler colonial studies, and other critical discourses. Realizing that the relations of conquest have far from abated encourages a reframing and rethinking of some of the urgent questions and interdisciplinary concerns that critical theories continue to grapple with in the neoliberal university. For example, rather than acting on the compulsion to ride the newest theoretical turn's intellectual current (i.e., white settler colonialism) and apply it as a mandatory analytical tool in order to demonstrate an analytic agility and relevance, perhaps the impulse to do so should be probed. For example, I have struggled rather transparently with whether or not to engage settler colonial studies from the scholarly and political site of Black studies.

At this particular intellectual and political crossroad, at which the defaced Columbus statue tagged with "Black Lives Matter" becomes a placemarker, I am obligated to ask different questions. Rather than pursuing the current question of the moment, "What would it look like for Black studies to take up issues of settler colonialism?," I am compelled to pursue a different problematic. These concerns center a new question: "How has Black studies been talking about genocide, colonization, settlement, and slavery?" And more important, why has the Black discourse of conquest remained a space of "unthought"[8] within contemporary critical theories like white settler colonial studies in North America?

It's Bigger Than Settler Colonialism

According to the origin story that settler colonial studies tells about itself, it is a distinct area of study that emerges in the 1990s primarily out of Australian settler scholarship. As an area of study, it regards settler colonialism as a "distinct social, cultural and historical formation with ongoing political effects."[9] Its genesis is indebted to the intellectual labor of Australian scholars like the late Patrick Wolfe, Lorenzo Veracini, and Ed Cavanaugh. In 2010–11, the open access journal called *settler colonial studies* launched its inaugural issue. With an open access journal, the field had the infrastructure and capacity to travel transnationally and gain appeal. As a transnational theoretical movement it traveled from Australia and New Zealand to Canada, South Africa, the US, and other imperial European sites.

To date, the late Patrick Wolfe remains a seminal figure in the field and his body of work continues to influence the burgeoning North American field of settler colonial studies. In 2006, Wolfe compellingly made the case that settler colonialism was a more apt theoretical frame and structure from which to think through and "beyond" genocide as a way of conceptualizing the elimination of the Native in settler societies. Wolfe theorizes that settler colonialism is a "structure" rather than an "event."[10] As a structure, settler colonialism is an ongoing process that can contain other formations. Wolfe's work acts as an intervention due to the way it extends the field of analysis for tracking settler colonial relations. In the article "Settler Colonialism and the Elimination of the Native," Wolfe theorizes settler colonial relations in a way that gives the structure a kind of elasticity—Michel Foucault's influence is evident—that allows it to intersect or work through formations other than the nation-state. According to Wolfe, as a structure, settler colonialism— and its logic of elimination—looms much larger than genocide. Wolfe proclaims that "to this extent, it is a larger category than genocide."[11] Using a similar logic and refrain, this chapter argues that conquest is a larger conceptual and material terrain than settler colonialism and far more suited for the regional/hemispheric particularities of coloniality in the Americas and the specific ways diasporic Blackness gives conquest, genocide, and settlement its form and feel.

As the unique (and productive) social and theoretical concerns of oceanic settler-Indigenous relations traveled transnationally and landed in North America, some of the particular historical legacies and contemporary machinations of relations of conquest in the Americas and the Atlantic were effaced and disappeared. Writing this critique of settler colonial studies in the wake of Patrick Wolfe's death makes me reflect on the possibilities and limits of his work in a new way, one less motivated by a form of "gotcha criticism" than one urged by ethics. An ethical engagement and critique of the work of Wolfe and other white settlers forces us to grapple with white human(ist) and earnest intentions and attempts to enact decolonization in everyday thought and practice. However, the intended and unintended consequences of white annunciations of decolonial theory and praxis still require rigorous engagement and scrutiny. Wolfe's work provides the substance from which to do this ethical work.

Wolfe's work from Oceania, as well as the work of white male scholars, caused a marked shift in the way North American discourses of genocide, coloniality, and settlement resonated in the academy. There was an excitement, particularly among white male scholars who were not engaged in or connected to the kind of scholarship and activism that women of color, specifically the formation INCITE, introduced in the early 2000s.[12] The overwhelming (and at times) uncritical adoption of settler colonial discourses from an oceanic context enacted a discursive shift that fields such as ethnic studies, American studies, Native studies, and Black studies is still contending with. The discursive shift privileges a theoretical and ethical engagement with settlers, settlement, and settler colonial relations that displaces conversations of genocide, slavery, and the violent project of making the human (humanism). In 2007, Carole Pateman examined the ascendancy of the discursive regime of settlement and the settler contract within British legal discourse. Pateman argued that the discourse of settlement has been a way of concealing the violence of conquest for centuries.[13] I am curious about the redeployment of the discourse of settler colonialism in the emerging field of North American settler colonial studies. I wonder if it is functioning as a ruse and a way of distracting critical theory from grappling with the relations of conquest as well as urgent political and theoretical concerns of Native studies and Black studies and movements concerned with Missing and Murdered Indigenous women and Black Lives Matter.

On one level, as the fervor over white settler colonial studies grows, a form of discursive genocide is performed as Native scholars, texts, and analytics disappear from the conversation. Further, an actual discussion of Native genocide is displaced by a focus on the white settler's relationship to land rather than their parasitic and genocidal relationship to Indigenous peoples. Settler colonialism also suffers from an acute form of unknowing in relation to Blackness and slavery. Land, space, and (white settler) subjectivity become rubrics of analysis that are elaborated upon and theorized through a resuscitation of humanist Continental theory.[14] Humanist modes of legibility reassert themselves through Karl Marx's worker, capitalist, and property, and Foucault's analysis of disciplinary power at the level of the individual and governmentality and biopolitics at the scale of population. Settler colonialism forces its interlocutors into conversations rife with humanist analogies and discussion of resolutions that Native studies and Black studies (specifically Afro-pessimists)[15] with a steadfast commitment to abolishing genocide and humanist forms of sovereignty would resist.

These analytic and political imperatives within strains of Native and Black studies are important to preserve within discussions of coloniality in the Americas. While white settler colonial studies' interventions are important—and should not be dismissed—it is also important to notice the ways that settler colonial studies' primary preoccupation is with the settler's relationship to land (or terra nullius). This focus on terra nullius and land disappears the settler's relationship to violence and the intricate and violent processes of the human's self-making. A focus on settlers and their relationship to land displaces the way the settler also becomes the conquistador/a (human) through Native genocide and Black dehumanization. Further, genocide or Wolfe's "structural genocide" often becomes a secondary and provisional concern of the field. In Wolfe's own synopsis of settler colonial power the relationship to land is the privileged site of analysis: "In sum, then, settler colonialism is an inclusive, *land-centered project* that coordinates a comprehensive range of agencies, from the metropolitan center to the frontier encampment, with a view to eliminating Indigenous societies. Its operations are not dependent on the presence or absence of formal state institutions or functionaries."[16]

Further, drawing on Cole Harris's work, Wolfe deploys a Marxian analysis in order to draw attention to settler colonialism's "principal momentum."[17] "Combine capital's interest in uncluttered access to land and settlers' interest in land as livelihood, and the principal momentum of settler colonialism comes into focus."[18] Wolfe effectively categorizes and names settler colonialism a land-centered project as opposed to a genocide-centered project. In the well-rehearsed passage from the germinal 2006 essay, setter colonialism's land-centered and oriented project is placed in the active, animating, and independent clause of the sentence. Genocide becomes a by-product and subordinate clause, "with a view to eliminating Indigenous societies"[19] that merely functions as a modifier.

If we also think with the figure of the conquistador Columbus tagged with "Black Lives Matter," we can maintain a focus on the ways that Native genocide and Black enslavement as a dehumanizing and property-making venture ensured the historical and current conditions of possibility (on the land-made property) for conquistador subjectivity. The conquistador and conquistador relations and modes of life (which can become subjectless discourses) are the historic and ongoing daily processes of white human self-actualization that require the making of the Indian as nonhuman and the making of the Black slave as forms of property. The making of the conquistador—as the human—can be tracked methodologically as bloody, bodily, discursive, and sensual (and affective) enactments of perverse and gratuitous violence as well as theoretically approached and narrated as a way of deftly and surgically reading the minutiae of its quotidian discursive moves and affectations. Further, a focus on conquest can reroute attention to Black studies' critiques of the human and humanism. I argue that it is in this discourse of conquest that we find Black studies lingua franca for staging a discussion with Native studies as an interlocutor. Further, Black discourses of conquest fill in the conceptual gaps of Blackness that currently vex and confound white settler colonial studies.

Bringing Black Lives into the Frame through Conquest and the Human

Conquest can be traced as a mode of speech and thinking within the work of a number of Black scholars. Understanding the mechanizations of conquest from within Black studies requires placing an emphasis on the making and remaking of the human (Christian, European Man, economic man, and so forth) as an object of study. According to Alexander Weheliye, Black studies has "taken as its task the definition of the human itself."[20]

Weheliye expounds, "Given the histories of slavery, colonialism, segregation, lynching and so on, humanity has always been a principal question within black life and thought in the west; or rather, in the moment in which blackness becomes apposite to humanity, Man's conditions of possibility lose their ontological thrust, because their limitations are rendered abundantly clear. Thus, the functioning of blackness as both inside and outside modernity sets the stage for a general theory of the human, and not its particular exception."[21] Like Weheliye's project in *Habeus Viscus*, I use the works of Hortense Spillers and Sylvia Wynter as models for the ways that Black intellectual traditions stalk the making of the human through the relations of conquest. Spillers's and Wynter's urgent questions about how the human is made require an interrogation of how conquest shapes processes of self-actualization in relation to Black and Indigenous peoples and our Cartesian concept of land as other than human. I also bring Frank Wilderson's discussion of the everyday and banal yet gratuitous violence of the making of Settler/Master/Human subjectivity into conversation with Spillers in order to think about conquest as an ongoing set of relations. Further thinking about conquest as a set of relations, mode of life, and forms of thought/knowing deserves a more robust elaboration and theorization.

Examining Spillers's and Wynter's work, the discourse of conquest functions as a grammar that endows the scholars with multiforked tongues. This tongue's polyvocality enables a simultaneous utterance and consideration of slavery and genocide. More importantly, Spillers and Wynter think about the emergence of the hierarchy of the human species as an epistemological order that is able to appear only in contradistinction to "human Others" or Man's Other. The European-Christian can only rise to the apex of the summit of humanity through the invention and subjugation of the Native and Black as the heathen and then eventually the irrational, sensual abject muck in which the last link of the great chain of being hangs. A part of Weheliye's exploration of Wynter's and Spillers's bodies of work entails an in-depth exploration of the ways they expound upon the bloody and always ongoing process of crafting and recrafting Man. "Wynter's and Spillers' thinking provides alternate genealogies for theorizing the ideological and physiological mechanics of the violently tiered categorization of the human species in western modernity, which stand counter to the universalizing but resolutely Europe-centered visions embodied by bare life and biopolitics. They do so—in sharp contrast to Foucault and Agamben—without demoting race and gender to the rank of the ethnographically particular, instead exposing how these categories carved from the swamps of slavery and colonialism [genocide] become the very flesh and bones of modern Man."[22] In addition to the violent and mutable procedures that reproduce Man, Weheliye also locates these processes in the swampland of slavery and colonialism, specifically genocide.

What is particularly fruitful about a meditation on Wynter and Spillers at the same time is that both scholars reorganize the geo-temporal dimensions of conquest in ways that expand their spatial and temporal frames beyond the conventional time-space coordinates of 1492 and the New World. In Wynter's body of work, the shores of West Africa during the 1440s become inaugural moments of conquest.[23] In a similar adherence to the space and time of Wynter's conquest, Spillers makes a similar move and situates conquest on the shores of Guinea. When Spillers turns to the archive in the essay "Mama's Baby, Papa's Maybe," she finds Gomes Eannes de Azurara's "Chronicle of the Discovery and Conquest of Guinea, 1441–1448" and says that "we learn that the Portuguese probably gain the dubious distinction of having introduced black Africans to the European market of servitude."[24] For both Wynter and Spillers, the beginnings of conquest begin with the landing of the Portuguese on the shores of western Africa. The fifteenth through the eighteenth centuries give birth to a number of epistemological revolutions within Europe (secularism, the Enlightenment, planetary vision) that make conquest imaginable and executable, giving birth to the human as an exclusive category—that of Man. Man demands the invention and negation of the Negro and Native in order to know her/his self. In Wynter's essay "1492: A New Worldview," which marks the quincentenary of the Columbian voyage, in addition to discussing Columbus's version of Christian humanism and the introduction of alternative geographies, Wynter proposes a "triadic model" (White-Native-Black) rather than a dyadic model (White-Native) to understand the antagonisms that would bring forth the notion of the modern human and inform conquest.[25]

This triadic model is echoed in Spillers's text "Mama's Baby, Papa's Maybe: An American Grammar Book." As Spillers plots the unfolding of an economy of signification in which the captive emerges through a series of mutilations, Spillers also focuses on the time-space of the "socio-political order of the New World."[26] This sociopolitical "order with its human sequence written in blood, represents for its African and indigenous peoples a scene of actual mutilation, dismemberment, and exile."[27] The human and its "sequence" or repetition and arrangement for its continuance is a mode of being that requires genocide, mutilation, displacement, and the negation of Black and Indigenous peoples and their ways of living. Conquest is constituted by a violence formidable enough to encompass both slavery and Native genocide as it writes and extends itself as the human-conquistador across Wynter's and Spillers's Atlantic.

While Spillers does not explicitly take on Native genocide in this essay, a reparative read could view this text as a possible point of departure for thinking about Blackness and Indigeneity as nonhuman, ethnic bodies—and "flesh"—in relationship to the human's process of self-actualization. Black and Native flesh is certainly a space of engagement in the work of Frank Wilderson. In *Red, White & Black*, Wilderson reworks and alters Spillers's conceptualization of flesh in order to elaborate upon the way the making of the human requires the unmaking of Black and Native bodies as nonhuman matter. Wilderson's deployment of Spillers's "body" and "flesh" engenders the human with a body. Conversely, the nonhuman (Slave and Savage) is fleshly matter that exists outside of the realm of the body and thus humanity. Under the ontological universe of political economy, the Native is rendered nonhuman "flesh." The Black/Slave is rendered nonhuman flesh under both "political" and "libidinal" economies. Though Wilderson does not identify Black and Native bodies as ontological equivalents, Native (the Savage's) and Black (the Black's) grammars of suffering do share the urgent concerns of the flesh. Wilderson sets forth the conditions of possibility that result in the making of Black and Native flesh.

> The Middle Passage turns, for example, Ashanti spatial and temporal capacity into spatial and temporal incapacity—a body into flesh. This process begins as early as the 1200s for the Slave. By the 1530s, modernity is more self-conscious of its coordinates, and Whiteness begins its ontological consolidation and negative knowledge of itself by turning (part of) the Aztec body, for example, into Indian flesh. In this moment the White body completes itself and proceeds to lay the groundwork for the intra-Settler ensemble of questions foundational to its ethical dilemmas (i.e., Marxism, feminism, psychoanalysis). In the final analysis, Settler ontology is guaranteed by way of negative knowledge of what it is not rather than by way of its positive claims of what it is.[28]

In exploring the diacritics at work in the making of the human, Wilderson momentarily identifies a moment of interlocution in which the discourse of conquest serves as passage for Black and Native grammars. When speaking in terms of the flesh, a space of possible dialogue emerges under rare conditions in which Wilderson argues that the "genocidal modality of the 'Savage' grammar of suffering articulate[s] itself quite well within the two modalities of the 'Slave's' grammar of suffering, accumulation and fungibility."[29] For Wilderson, both of these grammars find it difficult to assume narrative form within the lexicon made available by humanism and the contemporary polemics of the white left. It is virtually impossible for the Native or the Black to speak through these registers of intelligibility, which are predicated on their very death.

While Indigenous theorists like Robert A. Williams have traced the legacy of conquest within Anglo-American legal discourse in the nineteenth and twentieth centuries, there are other ways that conquest appears in the realm of the everyday. Sylvia Wynter and Jodi A. Byrd provide incisive examples of how to mine the philosophical and epistemic traditions of the West (structural and poststructural theories) in order to reveal the reproduction of a pious universalism even in their liberatory and nonidentitarian inflections. Critical theories' universalism fails to interrogate humanist impulses and the ways that it reproduces conquest and empire even when it espouses to advance anti- and posthumanist thought. In Wynter's text "Beyond the Word of Man," Marxism and feminism are categorized as epistemological shifts that are internal to Western culture. In fact, they only reproduce different genres of Man or humanism in the guise the "proletarian/Worker" and "woman/Gender."[30] These new versions that expand the category of Man move us from the first version of Man (found in the sixteenth, seventeenth, and eighteenth centuries) to modern man—or what Wynter refers to as Man2. The second version or "late modern" Man (the nineteenth century to the present) is birthed from the economic revolution and rationalization of empire.

Marx's worker and its female counterpart could both become intensified Foucauldian individuals and subjects due to the enslavement of Blacks that expelled them outside of the limits of the human-worker. The "worker" and the "woman" in fact constitute the normative human bourgeois family that was reproduced through Charles Darwin's evolutionary process of natural selection. Further, the birth of the "heterosexual" and "homosexual" as variations of human sexual identities in the nineteenth century are simply more variations of late modern Man within Wynter's theorization of the modern human. These subjects and the critical theories that birthed them are also the theoretical building blocks of much of white settler colonial scholarship.[31]

Continental theory has a long legacy of cordoning off the gratuitous violence that birthed and continues to structure its intellectual tradition. Continental theory has not typically had the stomach for sustaining an investigation of the kind of unspeakable violence that enabled the Marxist worker, the Foucauldian subject-as-discourse, and queer and affective theories' subjectless discourses (one can only strive for subjectlessness if you possess it) to exist. Even in its postidentitarian, nonrepresentational, and subjectless modes, Continental theories' transgressive moves (affective, sensational, masochistic) and the erasure of the (white) body-as-subject has been more effective in covering the bloody trail of white/human self-actualization than it has been successful at offering a way around and beyond the entrapments of liberal humanism.

Conquest/Colonialism/Settler Colonialism

As this chapter critically examines the way that settler colonial studies and other critical theories become the preferred discourse for examining coloniality in North America, it does not call to move beyond discussions of settlement and settler colonialism. As reminded by the work of Indigenous feminist scholar Maile Arvin, letting go of or turning our backs on settler colonialism is not the answer. For one of the consequences would be to bury or forget settler colonialism's theoretical genealogy and beginnings in the works of Native feminists.[32] Genealogies are important, contrary to Deleuzian and Guattarian rhizomatic and nomadic thinking.[33] Native feminists like Haunani-Kay Trask deployed and homed the way that settler colonialism was invoked in order to maximize its explanatory power without letting it subsume a larger discussion of Native genocide and conquest. Native feminisms in particular have a way of holding in tension discussions of genocide, conquest, colonialism, and settler colonialism. Trask's work is also a model for the ways that genocide and settlement could work in tandem with slavery and anti-Black racism.

In Trask's 1993 work, *From a Native Daughter: Colonialism and Sovereignty in Hawaii*, painful and sustained attention is given to the brutal nature of genocide in a way that does not reduce genocide to an epiphenomenon of settler colonialism. Additionally, when Trask invokes settler colonialism (one of the first to do so) she uses "settler" as a modifier and descriptive term of the kind of colonialism she is examining rather than conducting extensive ruminations and examinations of the analytic import of the terms "settler," "settlement," and "settler colonial relations." These white settler units of analysis and terms do not perform heavy conceptual lifting and analysis in ways that overwrite and crowd out genocide in Trask's text. Cook's, the British Empire's, and the United States' forms of genocide remain the focus and the distinguishing feature of settler colonialism.

For example, the active, animating, and meaningful portions of Trask's prose describe the genocide of Native peoples. Trask writes, "Modern Hawai'i, like its colonial parent the United States, is a settler society; that is, Hawai'i is a society in which the indigenous cultures and people have been murdered, suppressed, or marginalized for the benefit of settlers who now dominate our islands."[34] The sentence above is put into motion and animated by the naming of the kinds of violence committed by settlers for their benefit or self-actualization. Far from a "damage-centered"[35] statement, the use of the verbs "murdered, suppressed, or marginalized" direct our attention to the methods and processes of genocide that settlers/conquistadors use to self-actualize.[36] Genocide is theorized as a relational process in which Indigenous peoples experience multiple kinds of death in order for conquistador/settlers to live. Further, in Trask's essay "The Color of Violence," settler colonialism, colonialism, and genocide are specific yet supple and agile analytics that do not bracket one another off in the ways that Veracini and Cavanaugh's 2010 theorization makes settler colonialism irreducible and incommensurate.[37]

Trask's work creates an opportunity to think about colonialism as a form of conquest fundamentally constituted by slavery as much as it is by genocide. When Trask reflects on the imperialism of the United States a number of forms of violence that white settler colonial studies brackets off are considered. For example, Trask proclaims that "today, the United States is the most powerful country in the world, a violent country created out of the bloody extermination of Native peoples, and the enslavement of the forcibly transported peoples, and the continuing oppression of dark-skinned peoples."[38] Frank Wilderson's version of Afro-pessimism even finds resonances between Trask's work and Black theorists of social death. In *Red, White & Black*, Wilderson discerns a sense or feeling of abandonment within Native studies (specifically in the work of Leslie Marmon Silko, Ward Churchill, Gerald Taiaiake Alfred, Vine Deloria, and Trask) that resonates with the sense/feeling of abandonment in some of the work of Afro-pessimists.[39] Wilderson regards Trask as one of these abandoned Native scholars who is reluctant and perhaps unwilling to invest in or broker an "eventual articulation between overlapping elements of Native sovereignty and elements of settler ontology."[40] Wilderson reads Trask as someone who is likely to recoil at the idea of a negotiation between the constituent parts of sovereignty and white civil society that are antagonistic to the possibility of Black life. In fact, Wilderson says that Trask "will not countenance" this kind of alliance as a form of Native freedom.[41]

The parasitic and genocidal violence required to unmake the Native and the Black in order for the white human to self-actualize is also hard to conceptualize within the discourse of an imported settler colonialism. In order for settler colonialism to function as a transnational theoretical frame it must be subject to some elasticity and give. Transnational circuits generally feature reciprocal exchanges in which the "traveling" object, subject, or discourse is also transformed as it alters the social relations where it lands. A question that this chapter poses is, How might Native and Black studies discourses of conquest disfigure and transform white settler colonial studies traveling from Oceania?

Conquest, its subjects (conquistadors), and its daily instantiations (modes of conquering) must be spoken in a sharper vernacular and hypoglossic speech that can give signification to its forms of violence that remain unnamed in the wake of discourses of settlement. Perhaps the defacement and bloodying of a conquistador whose legacy still moves through and shapes everyday life in North America and the Americas is a way of bringing to language what remains at times unthought or at least unspoken. Extradiscursive and ungrammatical performances, defacements, and modes of living that confound normative modes of organizing and concealing colonial violence must also coexist with this new grammar. Rather than the "BLACK LIVES MATTER" tag eclipsing Native lives, why couldn't this current defacement be absorbed into a longer history of incidents of defacement—many of them initiated by Indigenous communities in protest of Columbus Day celebrations. In 2010, in protest of Columbus Day celebrations in Boston, Indigenous people beheaded the statue of Columbus. Black and Indigenous protest against conquistador ways of life have already been talking to one another in ways that exceed certain forms of humanist narrativity and intelligibility available within discourses of settler colonialism. The recent defacement of Columbus could represent an (ongoing) act of revolt that confronts the murders and disappearances of Native women in the northwestern part of Turtle Island, the ongoing destruction of Native life and the murderous onslaught against Black women, transpeople, and all Black life forms in ways that traverse and inform one another.

Notes

"New World Grammars: The 'Unthought' Black Discourses of Conquest" was originally published in *Theory & Event* 19, no. 4. © 2016, Johns Hopkins University Press. Reprinted by permission.

1 Julia Craven, "Political Activists Throw Blood Back in Christopher Columbus' Face," *Huffington Post*, July 2, 2015, http://www.huffingtonpost.com/2015 /07/02/columbus-monument-vandalized_n_7716138.html. Bob McGovern,

"Vandalism No Way to Make Point," *Boston Herald*, July 1, 2015, http://www
.bostonherald.com/news_opinion/local_politics/2015/06/pol_vandalism_no
_way_to_make_point.

2 Craven, "Political Activists Throw Blood Back in Christopher Columbus' Face."

3 Craven, "Political Activists Throw Blood Back in Christopher Columbus' Face."

4 Craven, "Political Activists Throw Blood Back in Christopher Columbus' Face."

5 McGovern, "Vandalism No Way to Make a Point."

6 Brian Maloney, "Now It's Columbus under Attack: Boston Statue Defaced with 'Black Lives Matter,' Red Paint," mediaequalizer.com, July 1, 2015, http://mediaequalizer.com/brian-maloney/2015/07/now-its-columbus-under-attack.

7 Maloney, "Now It's Columbus under Attack."

8 Saidiya Hartman and Frank Wilderson, "The Position of the Unthought," *Qui Parle* 13, no. 2 (2003): 183–201.

9 Penelope Edmonds and Jane Carey, "A New Beginning for Settler Colonial Studies," *Settler Colonial Studies* 3, no. 1 (2013): 2–5.

10 See Patrick Wolfe, "Settler Colonialism and the Elimination of the Native," *Journal of Genocide Research* 8, no. 4 (2006): 387–409, quote at 390; and *Settler Colonialism and the Transformation of Anthropology: The Politics and Poetics of an Ethnographic Event* (London: Continuum, 1998).

11 Wolfe, "Settler Colonialism and the Elimination of the Native," 402.

12 In 2005, when Andrea Smith's book *Conquest: Sexual Violence and American Indian Genocide* (Cambridge: South End Press, 2005) was released, until about 2010, largely Native feminist and Native American studies discourses about genocide, colonialism, and conquest shaped the way the disciplines of American, ethnic, women's, and gender studies and other critical fields discussed genocide, colonialism, and "settler" colonialism.

13 In Charles Mills and Carole Pateman's *Contract and Domination* (Cambridge: Polity Press, 2007), Pateman's examination of the emergence of the settler contract within the legal discourse of the British Crown reveals an attempt at discursive distancing. Pateman's essay marks as significant the ways that Western legal thought makes a shift from the discourse of conquest (subduing) to a discourse of settlement (which is supposed to index contracts and consent). Pateman reviews literature that illumines the ways that the British Empire attempted to put a discursive or theoretical gulf between themselves and the "atrocities that accompanied Spanish conquest." This discursive shift from one of conquest (violence) to one of planting settlements, establishing contracts, and consent was not an indication of the British rejection or disavowal of gratuitous violence, but a means of concealing the violence of conquest by invoking the discourse of settlement. Settlement becomes a euphemism that invokes a relationship to terra nullius as land or wilderness (including beasts, not people) that need to subsumed under the "law of

nature." The discourse of settlement also confers the power to engage in private war (or private-individual genocide) to the settler from its introduction in the sixteenth century through the early nineteenth century.

14 See Wolfe's *Settler Colonialism and the Transformation of Anthropology* and "Settler Colonialism and the Elimination of the Native"; Scott Lauria Morgensen, *Spaces between Us: Queer Settler Colonialism and Indigenous Decolonization* (Minneapolis: University of Minnesota Press, 2011); Mark Rifkin, "Indigenizing Agamben: Rethinking Sovereignty in Light of the 'Peculiar' Status of Native Peoples," *Cultural Critique* 73, no. 1 (2009): 88–124; and Mark Rifkin, *When Did Indians Become Straight? Kinship, the History of Sexuality, and Native Sovereignty* (Oxford: Oxford University Press, 2010).

15 See Jared Sexton's "The *Vel* of Slavery: Tracking the Figure of the Unsovereign," *Critical Sociology* (2014): 1–15; https://doi.org/10.1177/0896920514552535.

16 Wolfe, "Settler Colonialism and the Elimination of the Native," 393.

17 Wolfe., "Settler Colonialism and the Elimination of the Native," 394.

18 Wolfe., "Settler Colonialism and the Elimination of the Native," 394.

19 Wolfe., "Settler Colonialism and the Elimination of the Native," 394.

20 Alexander G. Weheliye, *Habeas Viscus: Racializing Assemblages, Biopolitics, and Black Feminist Theories of the Human* (Durham, NC: Duke University Press, 2014), 20.

21 Weheliye, *Habeas Viscus*, 19.

22 Weheliye, *Habeas Viscus*, 29–30.

23 See Sylvia Wynter's "Beyond the Word of Man: Glissant and the New Discourse of the Antilles," *World Literature Today* 63, no. 4 (1989): 637–48; "1492: A New World View," in *Race, Discourse, and the Origin of the Americas: A New World View*, ed. Vera Lawrence Hyatt and Rex Nettleford (Washington, DC: Smithsonian Books, 1995), 5–57; and "Unsettling the Coloniality of Being/Power/Truth/Freedom: Towards the Human, after Man, Its Overrepresentation—an Argument," CR: *The New Centennial Review* 3, no. 3 (2004): 257–337.

24 Hortense J. Spillers, "Mama's Baby, Papa's Maybe: An American Grammar Book," *Diacritics* 17, no. 2 (1987): 65–81, 70.

25 Wynter, "1492: A New Worldview," 5.

26 Spillers, "Mama's Baby, Papa's Maybe," 67.

27 Spillers, "Mama's Baby, Papa's Maybe," 67.

28 Frank B. Wilderson III, *Red, White & Black: Cinema and the Structure of U.S. Antagonisms* (Durham, NC: Duke University Press, 2010), 215.

29 Wilderson, *Red, White & Black*, 28.

30 Wynter, "Beyond the Word of Man."

31 See Morgensen, *Spaces between Us*; Rifkin, "Indigenizing Agamben"; Rifkin, *When Did Indians Become Straight?*

32 See Maile Arvin's paper "Polynesia Is a Project, Not a Place," presented at the Otherwise Worlds Conference, Riverside, CA, April 10, 2015.

33 For a discussion of the importance of Native/Indigenous genealogies in the face of nonrepresentational theory like that of Gilles Deleuze and Félix Guattari, see the work of Jodi A. Byrd in *The Transit of Empire: Indigenous Critiques of Colonialism* (Minneapolis: University of Minnesota Press, 2011) and Eve Tuck's essay "Breaking Up with Deleuze: Desire and Valuing the Irreconcilable," *International Journal of Qualitative Studies in Education* 23, no. 5 (2010): 635–50. Genealogies have a way of remembering the "anti-humanist" traditions of Native/Indigenous peoples that the West's form of violent Enlightenment humanism wiped out through genocide. The only reason that we experience European postmodern/poststructuralist antihumanist impulses like those found within Deleuzian thought as novel and as an epistemic revolution is because Indigenous and Native peoples' cosmologies and epistemologies that did not recognize boundaries between nature/culture or the human and the Western sensuous world were wiped out and had to be remade by the West.

34 Haunani-Kay Trask, *From a Native Daughter: Colonialism in Hawaii* (Honolulu: Latitude 20 Books, 1993).

35 See Eve Tuck, "Suspending Damage: A Letter to Communities," *Harvard Educational Review* 79, no. 3 (2009): 409–28.

36 Trask, *From a Native Daughter*, 25.

37 See Edward Cavanaugh and Lorenzo Veracini, "Definition," Settler Colonial Studies blog (2010), https://settlercolonialstudies.blog/about-this-blog/.

38 Haunani-Kay Trask, "The Color of Violence," *Social Justice* 31, no. 4 (2004): 8–16, 9.

39 Wilderson, *Red, White & Black*, 12.

40 Wilderson, *Red, White & Black,* 164.

41 Wilderson, *Red, White & Black*, 164.

CHAPTER FIVE

Jared Sexton

The *Vel* of Slavery

Tracking the Figure of the Unsovereign

The *vel* returns in the form of a *velle*. That is the end of the operation.
Now for the process. —Jacques Lacan, "Position of the Unconscious"

Introduction

In the spring of 2011, the Department of Equity Studies and the Centre for
Feminist Research at York University in Toronto hosted a three-day international conference entitled "Our Legacy: Indigenous-African Relations across
the Americas." Professor Bonita Lawrence initiated the event after publishing a pair of articles on the principal theme (Amadahy and Lawrence 2009;
Lawrence and Dua 2005).[1] This and similar gatherings of late suggest that
the emergent political-intellectual discourse in the North American context
regarding "communities of colour and their relationship to settler colonialism" (Jafri 2012) is driven more precisely by an abiding concern, or anxiety, about the position and function of African-derived people. It has to do
with a formulation of the fundamental relations between racial slavery and
settler colonialism in the development of global modernity (Dirlik 2007).
Insofar as such interests are geared toward an engagement with struggles
for abolition and reconstruction, on the one hand, and decolonization and
resurgence, on the other, they invariably highlight "the paradoxical nature of
freedom in Indian Territory" (Saunt 2004).

I adumbrate below the intervention of Indigenous scholars and their allies
on the theory and practice of antiracism in the contemporary United States
and Canada. I attempt to discern several convoluted elements: (1) a folk concept of racial slavery with a truncated account of its historical formation
(in which slavery is reduced to a species of coerced migration and forced

labor instituted in the seventeenth century); (2) an elision of slaveholding and the dissemination of anti-Blackness among Native peoples throughout the continent (in which Indian slavery is either ignored or marginalized and anti-Blackness is conflated with colonial white supremacy); (3) a liberal political narrative of emancipation and enfranchisement immune to the history of Black radicalism (in which the postbellum achievement of full Black citizenship, or "civil rights," is both taken for granted and mistaken for the substantive demands of "freedom, justice, and equality"); and (4) a misidentification of Black inhabitation with white and other non-Black settlement under the colonial heading (in which "the fact of Blackness" is disavowed and the fundamental racism of colonialism is displaced by the land-based contest of nations). These elements draw from and contribute to the discourse of postracialism by diminishing or denying the significance of race in thinking about the relative structural positions of Black and non-Black populations, not in order to assert the colorblind justice of American or Canadian society or to extol the respective virtues and vices of "model" and "problem" minorities, but rather to establish the contrasting injustice of their settler colonial relations with Indigenous peoples. The convolution has been suggestive—even symptomatic—and the sustained encounter is long overdue or long under way depending on the vantage point. The argument in this chapter could be considered a symptomatic reading of the problematic of sovereignty as an element of (settler) decolonization. It is motivated by a desire for (settler) decolonization without, and against, sovereignty. To that end, we might consider Black studies as the field of interpretation in relation to the discourse of Native studies at the point where the latter loses touch with itself and unconscious knowledge emerges as interference in the logic of theoretical elaboration. "Some critics will take it on themselves to remind us that this proposition has a converse. I say that this is false" (Fanon 2008, 83).[2]

Unsettling Decolonization

Native studies in the North American academy has attained critical mass in the last generation and commands growing attention across the interdisciplinary humanities and social sciences as scholars rethink their research and teaching protocols in response to the emergent scholarship and the collective pressure exerted by Native scholars, students, and communities. There are in Canada and the USA at present more than half a dozen peer-reviewed academic journals published by major university presses and nearly thirty programs of advanced study leading to graduate certificates, master's degrees, or doctorates.³ Over the preceding two decades, a new generation of schol-ars trained within or in relation to the Native studies programs established since the 1960s has come of age, producing a steady stream of book-length studies and edited collections. While the focus here is regional, it bears re-peating that the intellectual enterprise has long been *global*, linking scholars throughout the Americas to those in Africa and Asia, the Antipodes and the Pacific Islands.

The fruition of Native studies represents, among other things, the institu-tional inscription of the Fourth World in academic discourse.⁴ The Fourth World, as concept and movement, indicates a critique of the limitations of the anticolonial politics of Third Worldism and a reassertion of an internally differentiated Indigenous lifeworld that precedes and exceeds the tripartite division of the earth.⁵ As a matter of practical-theoretical activity in the pro-duction of knowledge, Native studies marks an intervention upon the study of colonialism in the most general sense, establishing and refining the pri-mary distinction between its metropolitan and settler forms. Put differently, it is an analytic *differentiation* between colonialism and settler colonialism. One of the clearest formulations of this position is provided in the work of Lorenzo Veracini (2010) and in the scholarship gathered together under his founding editorship at the journal *Settler Colonial Studies*.⁶

Veracini uses the introduction to the inaugural issue to outline what he terms "a proper appraisal of settler colonialism in its specificity," based upon the following premise: "Colonizers and settler colonizers want essentially different things" (Veracini 2011, 1). These essentially different desires pro-duce structurally divergent fundamental directives. Whereas the colonizer demands of the Native "you, work for me," the settler colonizer demands of the Native "you, go away." Surely, colonialism and settler colonialism can and often do coexist within the same social formation, and even the same agent or agency with a particular order can issue colonial and settler colonial demands at once or in turn. But this empirical coincidence does not dissolve the need for analytic differentiation. More to the point, if the divergent spatio-temporal and relational logics of colonialism and settler colonialism cannot be fully comprehended, then the respective political-intellectual projects of decolonization and settler decolonization cannot be broached.

Veracini establishes that settler colonialism has been theoretically sub-sumed beneath the conceptual rubric of colonialism. As a result, the histori-cal and geographical parameters of colonization become truncated and the political dimensions of the former situation—and long-standing, ongoing resistance to it—become illegible. For instance, the racial logic of colonialism tends to insist on permanent and unbridgeable differences between "the colonizer and the colonized," to borrow the title of Albert Memmi's famous 1957 text. Accordingly, the preoccupation of the colonial order falls upon the segregation and exclusion of the Native population from the mainstream institutions of the colony, except for token positions of quasi authority, in order to continue the colonizer's domination—a relation that Jean-Paul Sartre described, in his introduction to Memmi's treatise, as a "relentless reciprocity" (Memmi 2003, 24). This fundamental division between the colonizer and the colonized is pursued in the historic instance through the production and reproduction of racial difference (Fanon 2008).[7]

The colonial paradigm preserves the colonizer and the colonized as categories of racial difference and maintains the populations in that state, even when relations of production for the political and libidinal economies of colonialism request or require the deployment of genocidal violence. The spatiotemporal logic of colonialism is permanent division in the service of hierarchy, and the relational logic of what Frantz Fanon identifies as colonialism's characteristically stalled or frozen dialectic is one of interminable encounter ("something that wants itself ongoing"). Decolonization in this context entails breaking the colonial relation, ending the encounter, and removing the colonizer from the territory in order to destroy the zoning that creates spaces for different species and enables such massive exploitation. In this, decolonization destroys the positions of both the colonizer and the colonized.

Settler colonialism, by contrast, seeks over time to eliminate the categories of colonizer and colonized through a process by which the former replaces the latter completely, usurping the claim to Indigenous residence. "You, go away" can mean the removal of the Native population, its destruction through direct killing or the imposition of unlivable conditions, its assimilation into the settler colonial society, or some combination of each. As under the colonial paradigm, settler colonialism may deploy techniques for the production of racial difference, but it need not assume the strong form of permanent division. Likewise, settler colonialism may exploit the labor of the colonized en route, but the disappearance of the Native is its raison d'être. The spatiotemporal logic of settler colonialism is transience in service of demographic substitution and its relational logic is one of radical nonencounter ("something that wants itself terminated"). Decolonization in this context entails articulating the colonial relation, revealing the encounter, and transforming the elementary terms of cohabitation. In this, *settler* decolonization destroys the positions of both the colonizer and the colonized.

However, we should underline a crucial difference between decolonization and settler decolonization. While it is true that decolonization seeks to undermine the conditions of possibility of colonialism, in expelling the colonizer—rather than eliminating him *as* colonizer—it holds open the possibility of return in the form of neocolonialism. Settler decolonization, in turn, seeks to undermine the conditions of possibility of settler colonialism, but its trajectory involves consequences that are more severe, as it were, because the colonizer, having taken root on conquered land, must stay and live under a new dispensation. Undergoing conversion to Native lifeways and submitting to Native sovereignty and its related modes of governance, the erstwhile colonizer ceases to exist *as* colonizer, having been taken in by the Native community or repositioned, materially and symbolically, as a migrant engaged in an open-ended practice of reconciliation, or both. Indeed, "the struggle against settler colonialism must aim to keep the settler-indigenous relationship ongoing" in order to transform both of the operative terms and not only the relation itself (Veracini 2011, 7).

This may seem like settler decolonization provides a nonviolent alternative to the violence of decolonization, but to frame things in this way would be to miss the point entirely. The settler colonial paradigm that informs Native studies does not only demand specificity in our understanding of colonialism. This is not, in other words, a conceptual distinction among previously conflated varieties or forms of colonialism, but rather the analytic differentiation of heterogeneous political phenomena. Settler colonialism is not a particularly extreme form of colonialism. More to the point, in the space forged by the theoretical object of settler colonialism, in its delineation with respect to colonialism, a *radicalization* of decolonization is enabled and, in my view, that radicalization *is* settler decolonization. As a result of discrepant material conditions, settler decolonization must needs not only, like decolonization, reclaim land and resources, assert the sovereignty of the Indigenous people, protect or renew decolonial forms of collective life, and establish or reestablish decolonial forms of governance, but also, unlike decolonization, it must *pursue* the settler and undercut the very basis of his capacity and even his desire to rule. The project might be phrased as a rearticulation of Captain Richard Pratt's old Indian-hating maxim: kill the settler in him, and save the man. The analysis of settler colonialism developed within Native studies is less a friendly amendment or point of clarification for the analysis of colonialism in general—simply broadening its scope—and more a critique and a challenge to contemplate a more profound liberation altogether.

Settler decolonization pursues liberation in and as Indigenous resurgence, and obstacles to that resurgence, whether structural or ideological, must be confronted. Here, the critique of colonialism rehearsed above redounds upon the Indigenous critique of antiracism.[8] From within the conceptual apparatus attendant to the 2011 "Our Legacy" conference, thinking about "Indigenous-African relations" in the North American context means, above all, challenging "the manner in which anti-racism in Canada [and the USA] excludes Indigenous peoples." This exclusion is far more than oversight; it indicates misrecognition of the nature of the state against which antiracist politics is organized and to which the demands of antiracist politics are addressed. Because Canada and the USA are settler colonial states, any progressive reform of relations with non-Native Black populations at best fails to disrupt that prior settler colonial situation and at worst serves to entrench its power and further conceal its basic facts. Antiracism that is not grounded in the movement for settler decolonization is constrained to a politics whose "horizon of . . . aspiration largely is full inclusion in the nation as citizens" (Rikfin 2009, 102). That is, antiracism without Indigenous leadership is a wager for Black junior partnership in the settler colonial state.

Bonita Lawrence and Enakshi Dua (2005) are clear on several interrelated points to this end. First, any "dialogue between antiracism theorists/activists and Indigenous scholars/communities requires talking on Indigenous terms" (Lawrence and Dua 2005, 137). Second, antiracism must find a way "to place antiracist agendas within the context of sovereignty and restoration of land," a practice that requires learning "how to write, research, and teach in ways that account for Indigenous realities as foundational" (Lawrence and Dua 2005, 137). Third, the "pluralistic method of presenting diverse views" must yield to a "synthesis" that takes on "Indigenous epistemological frameworks and values" (Lawrence and Dua 2005, 137). For these authors, this is the way by which African Americans (in the hemispheric sense of the Americas) can transform themselves from settlers to allies "in the interests of a deeper solidarity" (Amadahy and Lawrence 2009, 105).

Let me add that I find no problem with the synthetic gesture that rejects the "pluralistic method of presenting diverse views." The impetus behind the demand for Black people to adopt Indigenous ontology, epistemology, and ethics, to speak on Indigenous terms, and to situate their politics within the context of sovereignty is consistent with the movement for settler decolonization described above. In other words, settler decolonization sees in antiracism the same pitfalls it sees in decolonization: both leave the colonizer intact and may even rely upon his continued existence for matters of recognition and redistribution. This point goes some way in explaining why there is a strong current *within* Native studies cautioning its audience to avoid emulating Black political struggle insofar as it is restricted to antiracist aims.[9] The advice offered to Native people and the critique and challenge posed to non-Native Black people (or to Black people pursuing decolonization elsewhere) are recto and verso of a single axiom: "emancipatory potential" is to be found in "the possibility of the return of a land-based existence" (Waziyatawin 2012, 82). Democratizing the settler colony as belatedly enfranchised citizens and subjects, or simply creating distance between colonizer and colonized without canceling both terms, is to forfeit the possibility of genuine freedom for all while contributing to the destruction of "the lands, waters, and ecosystems upon which [Native] people [and ultimately all life] must survive" (Waziyatawin 2012, 68). Hence, "To acknowledge that we all share the same land base and yet to question the differential terms on which it is occupied is to become aware of the colonial project that is taking place around us" (Lawrence and Dua 2005, 126). In the broadest sense, the problem is posed as the difference between an Indigenous and exogenous relation to the land, a problem of the terms of occupation. This frames the question of land as a question of sovereignty, wherein Native sovereignty is a precondition for or element of the maintenance or renaissance of Native *ways* of relating to the land. Surely, denial of sovereignty imperils Native ways of relating, but sovereignty does not thereby guarantee this way will be followed. This is why much discussion *within* Native studies is dedicated to thinking critically about what Waziyatawin (2012, 68) terms "the continued cooptation of our people into civilization's fallacies and destructive habits." How to resist such lures and the resultant disconnection from the land?

If the keywords of Native studies are *resistance* (to settler colonial society and the global industrial civilization that comprises it) and *resurgence* (of Native ways of life in and for our time), and if the source of both is a form of *self*-recognition among Indigenous peoples—"with the understanding that our cultures have much to teach the Western world about the establishment of relationships within and between peoples and the natural world that are profoundly non-imperialist" (Coulthard 2007, 456)—then it stands to reason that Black-Native solidarity would pivot upon Black people's willingness "to provide material and moral support to . . . the Indigenous movement on Turtle Island" (Amadahy and Lawrence 2009, 128). Solidarity here does not mean reciprocity. Because it is claimed that the "majority of diasporic Black struggles . . . want equity *within* the laws, economy, and institutions of the colonial settler state" (Amadahy and Lawrence 2009, 128, emphasis added), there is little to be gained from the Indigenous encounter with Blacks.

Are Native calls for Black solidarity simply expedient in a situation of settler colonialism? My sense is that there is something more complicated, and concerning, at work. If one surveys the writing on Black-Native solidarity in the field of Native studies, one finds frequent reference to histories of shared struggle, strategic alliance, and cohabitation in place of or alongside acknowledgment of histories of Indian slavery, ongoing exclusion of Black Native people, and pervasive anti-Black racism. In drawing up the historical balance sheet this way, scholars suggest there is ground for Black-Native solidarity in the present. Even where there is no denial or minimization of the history of Indian slavery, even where Native anti-Black racism is recognized and the struggles of Black Native people are affirmed, an argument is forwarded that solidarity in this moment can be retrieved from the past and refashioned for the future. In this sense, Native peoples are seeking to reunite with lost allies, namely, those enslaved Africans from the early colonial period who demonstrated "a spiritual worldview, land-informed practices, and were held together by kinship structures which created relationships that allocated everyone a role in the community" (Amadahy and Lawrence 2009, 127). This is political solidarity derived from "cultural similarities."

The implications of this claim are considerable. If Black-Native solidarity is founded upon shared Indigenous worldviews, practices, and kinship structures, then the prerequisite for Black people to move, politically and ethically, from settlers to allies "in the interest of a deeper solidarity" with Native people is, in a word, *re-indigenization*. In so doing, Black people on the North American scene not only become politically relevant to settler decolonization but also, en route, redress "the true horror of slavery"— the loss of culture: "Diasporic Black struggles, with some exceptions, do not tend to lament the loss of Indigeneity and the trauma of being ripped away from the land that defines their very identities. From Indigenous perspectives, the true horror of slavery was that it has created generations of 'de-culturalized' Africans, denied knowledge of language, clan, family, and land base, denied even knowledge of who their nations are" (Amadahy and Lawrence 2009, 127).

From Indigenous perspectives, diasporic Black struggles would, first and foremost, need to lament the loss of indigeneity that slavery entails, a process that requires acknowledging that the loss is both historic and ongoing. This would be a more proper posttraumatic response than "internalizing colonial concepts of how peoples relate to land, resources, and wealth" (Amadahy and Lawrence 2009, 127). However, what becomes curious upon even the briefest reflection is the fact that "denied knowledge of language, clan, family, and land base"—and the consequent temptation toward "internalizing colonial concepts"—is precisely what Native resistance and resurgence is struggling against to this day. To wit: "I believe that the systematic disconnection (and dispossession) of Indigenous Peoples from our homelands is the defining characteristic of colonization" (Waziyatawin 2012, 72). So, deculturalization, or loss of indigeneity, is a general condition of Black and Native peoples, not one that Native people can restrict to Black people in order to offer (or withhold) sympathies.

The structuring difference between settler colonization and enslavement is to be found precisely in the latter's denial of "knowledge of who their nations are"—that is, *deracination*. On this count, the loss of indigeneity for Native peoples can be named and its recovery pursued, and that pursuit can (and must) become central to political mobilization. The loss of indigeneity for Black peoples can be acknowledged only abstractly and its recovery is lost to history, and so something else must (and can) become central to political mobilization. Not the dialectics of loss and recovery but rather the loss of the dialectics of loss and recovery as such, a politics with no (final) recourse to foundations of any sort, a politics forged from critical resources immanent to the situation, resources from anywhere and anyone, which is to say from nowhere and no one *in particular*.

From Indigenous perspectives, this baseless politics can only ever be a liability. Without a base, which is to say a land base, a politics of resistance can only succumb to "civilization's fallacies and destructive habits." The quest for equality is perhaps the most pernicious of those fallacies. The conclusion of this line of thinking is that, due to "the trauma of being ripped away from the land that defines their very identities," landless Black people in diaspora cannot mount genuine resistance to the settler colonial state and society; they can only be held apart from it *as slaves*. Which is to say that, without the benefits of a land base and absent the constitutive exclusion of slavery, Blacks are destined to become white, and thus *settlers*, in thought and action; moreover, they have effectively become so postemancipation.[10] But rather than argue that Black people in North America do, in fact, have significant, if attenuated, Indigenous worldviews, practices, and kinship structures or, in any case, can learn such from others in order to begin fighting the *good* fight;

I submit we must consider the possibility that (1) the "Black Diasporic struggles" under examination are irreducible to antiracism, (2) that antiracism is irreducible to demands upon the state, and (3) that demands upon the state are irreducible to statist politics.[11] Blacks need not be Indigenous or enslaved Africans, or a mix of the two, in order to be allies to Native peoples in the Americas, whatever that might mean. And I say all of this without a need to mention the "notable exceptions" otherwise known as the Black radical tradition.[12] What if there are, and will have always been, ways to pursue settler decolonization otherwise than as Indigenous peoples and their immigrant allies, a movement from *within* that slavery whose abolition is yet to come?

Of course, not all Native studies scholars adhere to this cultural criterion of political solidarity. But even among those attempting to coordinate struggles among Black and Native peoples on a political basis, related problems arise. The contributions of Andrea Smith in the last decade are perhaps most generative on this note (Smith 2006, 2010, 2012, 2013). In a series of recent articles, Smith proposes one way to reframe the relational field of "people of color" in North American political culture by thinking through the multiple logics of white supremacy, in relation to the enforcement of normative gender and sexuality, as a sort of permutation. The author thus nominates the three pillars: Slavery/Capitalism, Genocide/Colonialism, and Orientalism/War (Smith 2010). We might recast them here as Racial Slavery, Settler Colonialism, and Orientalism, with the understanding that all are coeval, at least, with the history of capitalism. Each pillar operates according to a respective logic: the proprietary logic of slavery (through which captive Africans are rendered property of slaveholders and regarded as such by the larger society), the genocidal logic of settler colonialism (through which Indigenous peoples are dispossessed of land, water, and resources and made to disappear *as* Indigenous peoples), and the militarist logic of Orientalism (through which the people of Asia, the Middle East, and eventually Latin America are constructed as inferior, yet threatening, "civilizations" subjected to imperial warfare and its domestic ramifications).

The aim of this tripartite scheme is to illustrate for each pillar how those inhabiting its logic might become complicit in the victimization of those inhabiting the other; the object is the fostering of strategic alliances across multiple axes of power, rather than a politics based on notions of shared victimhood along a single axis. For present purposes, we are prompted to develop approaches to political struggle that address *both* the Indigenous/settler binary *and* the slave/master binary, working for settler decolonization while dismantling the hierarchy established by racial slavery. And these movements would be set about in tandem with the movement to end American imperialism abroad. Smith's formulation seeks to ascertain the fundamental dynamics in the relative positioning of various social groupings. The adjudication of those dynamics may involve not only the old canard of compromise (politics reduced to the art of being uncomfortable), but also the creation of new abilities to think in different registers in turn or at once. To this end, "we might focus on actually building the political power to create an alternative system to the heteropatriarchal, white supremacist, settler colonial state" (Smith 2012, 87).

While the three pillars model seeks to typify and diagram interrelated logics, it makes no explicit attempt at analytical synthesis or integrated political strategy. Synthesis and strategy are implied, however, a point that becomes clear when we look more closely at the working definitions of racial slavery and settler colonialism. In "Three Pillars," Smith describes the logic of slavery as one that "renders Black people as inherently slaveable—as nothing more than property." She goes on to situate slavery as the "anchor of capitalism," but in a peculiar way:

> That is, the capitalist system ultimately commodifies all workers—one's own person becomes a commodity that one must sell in the labor market while the profits of one's work are taken by someone else. To keep this capitalist system in place—which ultimately commodifies most people—the logic of slavery applies a racial hierarchy to this system. This racial hierarchy tells people that as long as you are not Black, you have the opportunity to escape the commodification of capitalism. This helps people who are not Black to accept their lot in life, because they can feel that at least they are not at the very bottom of the racial hierarchy—at least they are not property; at least they are not slaveable. (Smith 2006, 67)

We can agree that under the capitalist system one must sell their labor power and that it will be commodified as labor, which is to say it will be converted into a factor of production. We can agree that under the capitalist system the surplus value of social labor—not the bourgeois notion of individual work—is appropriated by the owners of the means of production and converted into profit. That is the basic structure of labor exploitation under capital.[13] We must object, however, that labor exploitation is a commodification of "one's own *person*" or that the capitalist system "ultimately commodifies most *people*." If this were true, then slavery as the conversion of person into property would simply be an extreme form of labor exploitation.[14] Or, vice versa, exploitation would be an attenuated form of slavery.

In either case, there would be only a difference of degree rather than kind between exploitation and slavery. At any rate, disabusing ourselves of anti-Black racism would, for Smith, enable us to see that they inhabit the same logic and that Black struggles against racial slavery are *ultimately* struggles against capitalism.

Something similar happens with respect to Smith's statement of the relation between racial slavery and settler colonialism. When she returns, in a more recent article on "Voting Rights and Native Disappearance," to reprise her concept of racial slavery, she has this to say about the ideological formation of anti-Black racism and its effects on critical intellectual production: "Because Africa is the property of Europe, Africa must then appear as always, already colonized. . . . The colonization of Africa must disappear so that Africa can appear as ontologically colonized. Only through this disavowed colonization can Black peoples be ontologically relegated to the status of property. Native peoples by contrast, are situated as potential citizens. Native peoples are described as 'free' people, albeit 'uncivilized'" (Smith 2013, 355).

Smith rightly argues that the racist designation of Native people as free, albeit uncivilized, precitizens is not a privilege (i.e., proximity to whiteness) in relation to the racist designation of Black people as unfree anticitizens incapable of civilization (i.e., antipode of whiteness) because the civilizing mission through which Native peoples are forcibly assimilated into the settler colonial society is, in fact, a form and aspect of genocide. Yet what is missed in the attempt to demonstrate that Black studies is also, like Native studies, concerned with colonization is the plain fact that colonization is not essential, much less a prerequisite, to enslavement. In other words, to say that it is *only* through "disavowed colonization" that Black people can be "ontologically relegated to the status of property" is a feint, just as it is to suggest that capitalism "ultimately commodifies most *people*." In this case, enslavement would be enabled by a prior colonization that it extends *perforce*. If this were true, then slavery as the conversion of person into property would simply be an extreme form of colonization. Or, vice versa, colonization would be an attenuated form of slavery. In either case, there would be only a difference of degree rather than kind between colonization and slavery. At any rate, disabusing ourselves of anti-Black racism would, for Smith, enable us to see that Black struggles against racial slavery are *ultimately* struggles against colonialism.

Colonization is not a necessary condition of enslavement because (1) slaves need not be colonial subjects, or objects of colonial exploitation, and they do not face the fundamental directive of colonialism, "you, work for me," though slaves often enough labor; and (2) slaves need not be settler colonial subjects, or objects of settler colonial genocide, since they do not face the fundamental directive "you, go away," though slaves often enough are driven from their native land. But the crucial problem with this formulation of the relations between racial slavery, settler colonialism, and capitalism (leaving aside any problems with the pillar of Orientalism) has to do with the *drive* to confound the position of Blacks in order to describe them as exploited and colonized *degree zero*. Regarding the latter, Smith writes, "Africa is the property of Europe"; *Africa* rather than the *African*. As in the reduction of slavery to the exploitation of labor, there is here a dreadful elision of the permanent seizure of the body essential to enslavement.[15]

What can be done to a captive body? Anything whatsoever. The loss of sovereignty is a fait accompli, a by-product rather than a precondition of enslavement. Genocide is endemic to enslavement insofar as slavery bans, legally and politically, the reproduction of enslaved peoples *as* peoples, Indigenous or otherwise, whether they are removed from their native land, subjected to direct killing, unlivable conditions, or forced assimilation; or they are kept in place, allowed to live, provided adequate means, or supported in their cultural practices.[16] Native studies scholars misrecognize "the true horror of slavery" as deculturalization or the loss of sovereignty because they do not ask what slavery is in the most basic sense—its local and global histories, its legal and political structures, its social and economic functions, its psychosexual dynamics, and its philosophical consequences. Perhaps they do not want to know anything about it, as they evaluate it through the lens of their own loss and lament and redress it through the promise of their own political imagination. Slavery is not a loss that the self experiences—of language, lineage, land, or labor—but rather the loss of any self that could experience such loss. Any politics based in resurgence or recovery is bound to regard the slave as "the position of the unthought" (Hartman and Wilderson 2003).[17]

Abolishing Sovereignty

There is by now a literature on the historical relations between Black and Native peoples in the Americas, including, in the US context, the award-winning work of Tiya Miles (2006, 2010) and the signal contribution of Barbara Krauthamer (2013).[18] But Frank B. Wilderson's *Red, White & Black* may be the first sustained attempt to theorize, at the highest level of abstraction, the structural positions of European colonists, Indigenous peoples, and African slaves in the "New World" encounter and to think about how the conflicts and antagonisms that give rise to those positions in the historic instance establish the contemporary parameters of our political ontology. At this writing, Wilderson's text has not been taken up in the field of Native studies, despite dedicating fully a hundred pages to addressing directly the machinations of settler colonialism and the history of genocide and to critically reading a range of Indigenous thinking on politics, cosmology, and sovereignty. This is not a brief in favor of Wilderson's project as resolution or answer. The upshot of *Red, White & Black* is a provocation to new critical discourse and just such an invitation is offered midway, even as it acknowledges the grand impediment: "What, we might ask, inhibits this analytic and political dream of a 'Savage'/Slave encounter? Is it a matter of the Native theorist's need to preserve the constituent elements of sovereignty, or is there such a thing as 'Savage' Negrophobia? Are the two related?" (Wilderson 2010, 182).

We might understand something else about the historical relations between Black and Native peoples if we bear in mind that the dynamics of Negrophobia are animated, in part, by a preoccupation with sovereignty. We have learned already that settler colonialism is governed by a genocidal commandment and that, as a direct result, survival becomes central to Indigenous movements for settler decolonization. We have also learned that sovereignty, even disarticulated from the state form, is the heading for thinking about this survival as a matter of politics.[19] Yet, in its struggle against settler colonialism, the claim of Native sovereignty—emerging in contradiction to the imposition of the imperial sovereignty of Euro-American polities[20]— "fortifies and extends the interlocutory life of America [or Canada or . . .] as a coherent (albeit genocidal) idea, because treaties are forms of articulation, discussions brokered between two groups presumed to possess the same kind of historical currency: sovereignty" (Wilderson 2003, 236).

This point is not mitigated by the fact that Native sovereignty is qualitatively different from, and not simply a rival to, the sovereignty of nation-states. What links these statements discursively is an "ethico-onto-epistemological" (Barad 2007) point of contact: "At every scale—the soul, the body, the group, the land, and the universe—they can both practice cartography, and although at every scale their maps are radically incompatible, their respective 'mapness' is never in question" (Wilderson 2010, 181).[21] Capacity for coherence makes more than likely a commitment "to preserve the constituent elements of sovereignty" (Wilderson 2010, 182) and a pursuit of the concept of "freedom as self-determination."[22] The political de-escalation of antagonism to the level of conflict is mirrored by a conceptual domestication at work in the field of Native studies, namely, that settler colonialism is something already known and understood by its practitioners. The political-intellectual challenge on this count is to refine this knowledge and to impart it. The intervention of Native studies involves bringing into general awareness a critical knowledge of settler colonialism.

We might contrast the unsuspecting theoretical status of the concept of settler colonialism in Native studies with its counterpart in Black studies: racial slavery. I remarked above that any politics of resurgence or recovery is bound to regard the slave as the position of the unthought. This does not suggest, however, that Black studies is the field in which slavery is, finally, thought in an adequate way. The field of Black studies is as susceptible to a politics of resurgence or recovery as any other mode of critical inquiry. Which is to say that the figure of the slave and the history of the emergence of the relational field called racial slavery remain the unthought ground of thought *within* Black studies as well. The difference, provisionally, between these enterprises is that whereas Native studies sets out to be the alternative to a history of settler colonialism and to pronounce the decolonial intervention, Black studies dwells within an uninheritable, inescapable history and muses upon how that history intervenes upon its own field, providing a sort of untranscendable horizon for its discourse and imagination. The latter is an endeavor that teaches less through pedagogical instruction than through exemplary transmission: rather than initiation into a form of *living*, emulation of a process of *learning* through the posing of a question, a procedure for study, for *Black* study, or Black *studies*, wherever they may lead.

Native studies scholars are right to insist upon a synthetic gesture that attempts to shift the terms of engagement. The problem lies at the level of thought at which the gesture is presented. The settler colonial studies critique of colonial studies must be repeated, this time with respect to settler colonialism itself, in a move that returns us to the body in relation to land, labor, language, lineage—and the capture and commodification of each— in order to ask the most pertinent questions about capacity, commitment, and concept. This might help not only to break down false dichotomies, and perhaps pose a truer one, but also to reveal the ways that the study of slavery is already and of necessity the study of capitalism, colonialism, and settler colonialism, among other things; and that the struggle for abolition is already and of necessity the struggle for the promise of communism, decolonization, and settler decolonization, among other things. Slavery is the threshold of the political world, abolition the interminable radicalization of every radical movement. Slavery, as it were, precedes and prepares the way for colonialism, its forebear or fundament or support. Colonialism is, as it were, the issue or heir of slavery, its outgrowth or edifice or monument. This is as true of the historic colonization of the Third World as it is of the prior and ongoing settler colonization of the Fourth.[23]

"The modern world owes its very existence to slavery" (Grandin 2014a).[24] What could this impossible debt possibly entail? Not only the infrastructure of its global economy but also the architecture of its theological and philosophical discourses, its legal and political institutions, its scientific and technological practices, indeed, the whole of its semantic field (Wilderson 2010, 58). A politics of abolition could never finally be a politics of resurgence, recovery, or recuperation. It could only ever begin with degeneration, decline, or dissolution. Abolition is the interminable radicalization of every radical movement, but a radicalization through the perverse affirmation of deracination, an uprooting of the natal, the nation, and the notion, preventing any order of determination from taking root, a politics without claim, without demand even, or a politics whose demand is "too radical to be formulated in advance of its deeds" (Trouillot 2012, 88).[25]

The field of Black studies consists in "tracking the figure of the *unsovereign*" (Chandler 2013, 163) in order to meditate upon the paramount question: *"What if the problem is sovereignty as such"* (Moten 2013)? Abolition, the political dream of Black studies, its unconscious thinking, consists in the affirmation of the unsovereign slave—the affectable, the derelict, the monstrous, the wretched[26]—figures of an order altogether different from (even when they coincide or cohabit with) the colonized Native: the occupied, the undocumented, the unprotected, the oppressed. Abolition is beyond (the restoration of) sovereignty. Beyond the restoration of a lost commons through radical redistribution (everything for everyone), there is the unimaginable loss of that all too imaginable loss itself (nothing for no one).[27] If the Indigenous relation to land precedes and exceeds any regime of property, then the slave's inhabitation of the earth precedes and exceeds any prior relation to land—landlessness. And selflessness is the correlate. No ground for identity, no ground to stand (on). Everyone has a claim to everything until no one has a claim to anything. No claim. This is not a politics of despair brought about by a failure to lament a loss, because it is not rooted in hope of winning. The flesh of the earth demands it: the landless inhabitation of selfless existence.

Notes

"The *Vel* of Slavery: Tracking the Figure of the Unsovereign" was originally published in *Critical Sociology* 42, no. 4–5 (2014). © 2014, SAGE Publications Ltd. Reprinted by permission.

1 See the official conference website: http://www.yorku.ca/laps/des/conference/index.html. The conference, held April 29–May 1, 2011, featured presentations and performances by over fifty participants. For a critical response, see B. Lawrence and E. Dua, "Decolonizing Anti-Racism," *Social Justice* 32, no. 4 (2005): 120–43. The latter argument makes important conceptual distinctions between and among immigrants, settlers, and colonists, but it does not resolve the problem pursued in this chapter.

2 On the symptom, see J. Lacan, *Écrits: The First Complete Edition in English*, trans. B. Fink (New York: W. W. Norton, 2006). "They do not see that the unconscious *only has meaning in the Other's field*; still less do they see the consequences thereof: that it is not the effect of *meaning* that is operative in interpretation, but rather the articulation in the symptom of signifiers (*without any meaning at all*) that have gotten caught up in it" (714, emphasis added). On symptomatic reading and the problematic, see L. Althusser and É. Balibar, *Reading Capital*, trans. B. Brewster (London: Verso, 1997), especially part 1.

3 For overviews of the field, see D. A. Mihesuah and A. C. Wilson, eds., *Indigenizing the Academy: Transforming Scholarship and Empowering Communities* (Lincoln: University of Nebraska Press, 2004); C. S. Kidwell and A. Velie, eds., *Native American Studies* (Lincoln: University of Nebraska Press, 2005); and R. Kuokkanen, *Reshaping the University: Responsibility, Indigenous Epistemes, and the Logic of the Gift* (Vancouver: UBC Press, 2007).

4 See G. Manuel and M. Posluns, *The Fourth World: An Indian Reality* (Toronto: Collier-Macmillan Canada, 1974); P. McFarlane, *Brotherhood to Nationhood: George Manuel and the Making of the Modern Indian Movement* (Toronto: Between the Lines, 1993); and, generally, the work of the Center for World Indigenous Studies, including its publication *The Fourth World Journal*. For discussion of Indigenous women in relation to the Fourth World concept, see A.-E. Lewallen, "Strategic 'Indigeneity' and the Possibility of a Global Indigenous Women's Movement," *Michigan Feminist Studies* 17 (2003): 105–30.

5 For recent treatments of the "Three Worlds" concept and Third Worldism, see M. Berger, ed., *After the Third World?* (New York: Routledge, 2009), and V. Prashad, *The Darker Nations: A People's History of the Third World* (New York: New Press, 2007).

6 *Settler Colonial Studies* (Taylor and Francis) was founded in 2011. On the history of US settler colonialism, see W. Hixson, *American Settler Colonialism: A History* (New York: Palgrave Macmillan, 2013). I should add that this article does not address the emergent scholarship of Tiffany King, "Labor's Aphasia: Toward Antiblackness as Constitutive to Settler Colonialism," *Decolonization*

(June 10, 2014), who rightly argues that anti-Blackness, and more specifically the production of Black fungibility, is constitutive to settler colonialism. I hope to say something about her important intervention in subsequent work. Suffice it to say that it is not only settler colonialism that requires the material and symbolic production of fungible Black bodies, but also, as I suggest herein, the political discourse and imagination of settler decolonization and Native sovereignty.

7 See F. B. Wilderson III, *Red, White & Black: Cinema and the Structure of U.S. Antagonisms* (Durham, NC: Duke University Press, 2010), for an attempt to rethink the racial logic of colonialism, described by Frantz Fanon, as the disavowed racial logic of slavery, which is to say anti-Blackness.

8 It redounds upon the Indigenous critique of feminism as well: M. Arvin, E. Tuck, and A. Morrill, "Decolonizing Feminism: Challenging Connections between Settler Colonialism and Heteropatriarchy," *Feminist Formations* 25, no. 1 (2013): 8–34.

9 See, for instance, G. Coulthard, "Subjects of Empire: Indigenous Peoples and the 'Politics of Recognition' in Canada," *Contemporary Political Theory* 6 (2007): 437–60. For Coulthard, Fanon is right that the politics of recognition is a dead end, yet he is nonetheless "ultimately mistaken regarding violence being the 'perfect mediation' through which the colonized come to liberate themselves from both the structural and psycho-affective features of colonial domination" (455). Black thought can, in this way, inform and inspire, but it cannot *orient* Indigenous politics.

10 As a rule, Native studies reproduces the dominant liberal political narrative of emancipation and enfranchisement. See, for example, E. Cook-Lynn, "Who Stole Native American Studies?," *Wicazo Sa Review* 12, no. 1 (1997): 9–28. For a critique of emancipation that distinguishes it from the abolition of slavery, see G. Binder, "The Slavery of Emancipation," *Cardozo Law Review* 17 (1995): 2063–102. See also, generally, S. Hartman, *Scenes of Subjection: Terror, Slavery, and Self-Making in Nineteenth-Century America* (New York: Oxford University Press, 1997).

11 Andrea Smith acknowledges that "it may be possible to strategically engage the US political system without granting it legitimacy" (366), but on this count it only seems to be true in the case of Native peoples: A. Smith, "Voting and Indigenous Disappearance," *Settler Colonial Studies* 3, nos. 3–4 (2013): 352–68. Whenever Black civil rights are addressed, they are reduced to bids for inclusion in the state and civil society and capable of producing, at best, a form of liberal multiculturalism based upon a bankrupt politics of recognition.

12 The seminal study of the Black radical tradition is, of course, C. Robinson, *Black Marxism: The Making of the Black Radical Tradition* (Chapel Hill: University of North Carolina Press, 2000). For recent additional sources, see C. B. Davies, *Left of Karl Marx: The Political Life of Black Communist Claudia Jones* (Durham, NC: Duke University Press, 2007); R. D. G. Kelley, *Freedom*

Dreams: The Black Radical Imagination (Boston: Beacon, 2002); and B. Ransby, *Ella Baker and the Black Freedom Movement: A Radical Democratic Vision* (Chapel Hill: University of North Carolina Press, 2005).

13 I am gesturing, of course, to ideas outlined in Karl Marx's 1847 lectures to the German Workingmen's Club of Brussels, later serialized as *Wage Labor and Capital*, and subsequently developed in his 1859 *A Contribution to the Critique of Political Economy* and his 1867 magnum opus, *Capital*, vol. 1.

14 "African Americans have been traditionally valued for their labor, hence, it is in the interest of the dominant society to have as many people marked 'Black', as possible, thereby maintaining a cheap labor pool": A. Smith, "Heteropatriarchy and the Three Pillars of White Supremacy," in *The Color of Violence: The INCITE! Anthology*, ed. INCITE! Women of Color Against Violence, 66–73, at 71 (Boston: South End Press, 2006).

15 The elision of the body can be found again in M. Rifkin, "Indigenizing Agamben: Rethinking Sovereignty in Light of the 'Peculiar' Status of Native Peoples," *Cultural Critique* 73 (2009): 88–124, who seeks to shift the reception of the political philosophy of Giorgio Agamben from a focus on the biopolitics of race to the geopolitics of place, with a correlative reworking on Agamben's notion of "bare life" as "bare habitance." Without adjudging Rifkin's reading of Agamben, we note that to displace race with place by juxtaposing body with land and rights with sovereignty—thereby juxtaposing Blacks-as-*embodying* with Natives-as-*inhabiting* (without thinking diacritically about Black inhabitation and Native embodiment)—serves to disembody and deracialize Native peoples, which is to say to gain or maintain *distance* toward racial Blackness, in order to pursue the critical discussion of metapolitical authority.

16 "To some degree the standard-of-living issue is universal: it applies to feudalism as well as to capitalism, to slave as well as free societies. But a slave was a slave, whether he lived a healthy hundred years or a sickly forty, whether she was better fed than a Polish peasant or more miserably housed than an American yeoman. . . . We can only measure the substance of such criticism if we understand why '*slavery*' and '*freedom*' do not refer to material well-being. . . . Freedom and slavery are at bottom political categories; they refer to the distributions of power in society." J. Oakes, *Slavery and Freedom: An Interpretation of the Old South* (New York: W. W. Norton, 1990), xv–xvi.

17 One should hear in this phrase the resonance between a political theory of the universal particular and a psychoanalytic theory of the unconscious. I hope to take this up in subsequent work.

18 These titles demonstrate not only the continuity between white and Native forms of racial slavery in the eighteenth and nineteenth centuries, but also the *centrality* of Native slavery to the history of racial slavery as such. Centrality is indicated here not as a measure of empirical preponderance, but rather of legal and political significance.

19 On the critical differences between conceptions of Native sovereignty and the sovereignty of the nation-state, see L. Simpson, "I Am Not a Nation-State,"

Voices Rising, November 6, 2013, accessed August 1, 2014, http://nationsrising
.org/i-am-not-a-nation-state/.

20 "[An] origin is constituted as such only as an effect of displacement":
N. Chandler, *X: The Problem of the Negro as a Problem for Thought* (New York:
Fordham University Press, 2013), 138.

21 For a powerful meditation on cartographic incoherence and incapacity, see
D. Brand, *A Map to the Door of No Return: Notes to Belonging* (New York:
Random House, 2001).

22 For a fundamental critique of sovereignty and freedom as self-determination,
see D. F. da Silva, *Toward a Global Idea of Race* (Minneapolis: University of
Minnesota Press, 2007).

23 See, for instance, R. Blackburn, *The Making of New World Slavery: From the
Baroque to the Modern, 1492–1800* (London: Verso, 1997); T. Green, "Build-
ing Slavery in the Atlantic World: Atlantic Connections and the Changing
Institution of Slavery in Cabo Verde," *Slavery and Abolition* 32, no. 3 (2011):
227–45; P. Manning, *Slavery and African Life: Occidental, Oriental, and
African Slave Trades* (New York: Cambridge University Press, 1990); B. Solow,
Slavery and the Rise of the Atlantic System (New York: Cambridge University
Press, 1991); S. Wynter, "1492: A New World View," in *Race, Discourse, and the
Origins of the Americas*, ed. V. Lawrence and R. Nettleford (Washington, DC:
Smithsonian Institution Press, 1995).

24 For a more fulsome argument, see G. Grandin, *The Empire of Necessity:
Slavery, Freedom, and Deception in the New World* (New York: Metropolitan
Books, 2014).

25 This reference to the Haitian Revolution does not only take it as a world-
historical emblem of abolition but also views it within the ongoing abolitionism that ties it to "a much larger and perhaps even more successful
slave rebellion in the United States." S. Hahn, "A Rebellious Take on African
American History," *Chronicle of Higher Education*, August 3, 2009, http://
chronicle.com/article/On-History-A-Rebellious-Take/47497.

26 See, respectively, Silva, *Toward a Global Idea of Race*, on the affectable;
Wilderson, *Red, White & Black*, on the derelict; and H. Spillers, *Black, White
and in Color: Essays on American Literature and Culture* (Chicago: University of Chicago Press, 2003), on the monstrous; and D. Marriott, "Whither
Fanon?," *Textual Practice* 25, no. 1 (2011): 33–69, on the wretched.

27 "What would the *politics* of a dead relation, a slave, look like": F. B. Wilderson, "Biko and the Problematic of Presence," in *Biko Lives! Contesting the
Legacies of Steve Biko*, ed. A. Mngxitama, A. Alexander, and N. Gibson (New
York: Palgrave Macmillan, 2008), 106, emphasis added. For recent writing on
the global commons, see P. Linebaugh, *Stop Thief! The Commons, Enclosures,
and Resistance* (Oakland: PM Press, 2014); K. Milum, *The Political Uncommons: The Cross-Cultural Logic of the Global Commons* (London: Ashgate,
2010); and J. Shantz, *Commonist Tendencies: Mutual Aid beyond Communism*
(Brooklyn: Punctum Books, 2013).

References

Althusser, L., and É. Balibar. 1997. *Reading Capital*. Translated by B. Brewster. Verso: London.

Amadahy, Z., and B. Lawrence. 2009. "Indigenous Peoples and Black People: Settlers or Allies." In *Breaching the Colonial Contract: Anti-Colonialism in the US and Canada*, edited by Arlo Kempf, 105–36. New York: Springer.

Arvin, M., E. Tuck, and A. Morrill. 2013. "Decolonizing Feminism: Challenging Connections between Settler Colonialism and Heteropatriarchy." *Feminist Formations* 25, no. 1: 8–34.

Barad, K. 2007. *Meeting the Universe Halfway: Quantum Physics and the Entanglement of Matter and Meaning*. Durham, NC: Duke University Press.

Berger, M., ed. 2009. *After the Third World?* New York: Routledge.

Binder, G. 1995. "The Slavery of Emancipation." *Cardozo Law Review* 17: 2063–102.

Blackburn, R. 1997. *The Making of New World Slavery: From the Baroque to the Modern, 1492–1800*. London: Verso.

Brand, D. 2001. *A Map to the Door of No Return: Notes to Belonging*. New York: Random House.

Chandler, N. 2013. *X: The Problem of the Negro as a Problem for Thought*. New York: Fordham University Press.

Cook-Lynn, E. 1997. "Who Stole Native American Studies?" *Wicazo Sa Review* 12, no. 1: 9–28.

Coulthard, G. 2007. "Subjects of Empire: Indigenous Peoples and the 'Politics of Recognition' in Canada." *Contemporary Political Theory* 6: 437–60.

Davies, C. B. 2007. *Left of Karl Marx: The Political Life of Black Communist Claudia Jones*. Durham, NC: Duke University Press.

Dirlik, A. 2007. *Global Modernity: Modernity in the Age of Global Capitalism*. Boulder, CO: Paradigm.

Fanon, F. 2008. *Black Skin, White Masks*. Translated by Charles Lam Markmann. London: Pluto Books.

Grandin, G. 2014a. "How Slavery Made the Modern World." *Nation*, February 24. http://www.thenation.com/article/178509/how-slavery-made-modern-world.

Grandin, G. 2014b. *The Empire of Necessity: Slavery, Freedom, and Deception in the New World*. New York: Metropolitan Books.

Green, T. 2011. "Building Slavery in the Atlantic World: Atlantic Connections and the Changing Institution of Slavery in Cabo Verde." *Slavery and Abolition* 32, no. 3: 227–45.

Hahn, S. 2009. "A Rebellious Take on African American History." *Chronicle of Higher Education*, August 3. http://chronicle.com/article/On-History-A-Rebellious-Take/47497.

Hartman, S. V. 1997. *Scenes of Subjection: Terror, Slavery, and Self-Making in Nineteenth-Century America*. New York: Oxford University Press.

Hartman, S. V., and F. B. Wilderson III. 2003. "The Position of the Unthought." *Qui Parle* 13, no. 2: 183–201.

Hixson, W. 2013. *American Settler Colonialism: A History*. New York: Palgrave Macmillan.

Jafri, B. 2012. "Privilege vs. Complicity: People of Colour and Settler Colonialism." *Equity Matters*, March 21. http://www.ideas-idees.ca/blog/privilege-vs -complicity-people-colour-and-settler-colonialismx.

Kelley, R. D. G. 2002. *Freedom Dreams: The Black Radical Imagination*. Boston: Beacon.

Kidwell, C. S., and A. Velie, eds. 2005. *Native American Studies*. Lincoln: University of Nebraska Press.

King, T. 2014. "Labor's Aphasia: Toward Antiblackness as Constitutive to Settler Colonialism." *Decolonization*, June 10. http://decolonization.wordpress .com/2014/06/10/labors-aphasia-toward-antiblackness-as-constitutive-to -settler-colonialism/.

Krauthamer, B. 2013. *Black Slaves, Indian Masters: Slavery, Emancipation, and Citizenship in the Native American South*. Chapel Hill: University of North Carolina Press.

Kuokkanen, R. 2007. *Reshaping the University: Responsibility, Indigenous Epistemes, and the Logic of the Gift*. Vancouver: University of British Columbia Press.

Lacan, J. 2006. *Écrits: The First Complete Edition in English*. Translated by B. Fink. New York: W. W. Norton.

Lawrence, B., and E. Dua. 2005. "Decolonizing Anti-Racism." *Social Justice* 32, no. 4: 120–43.

Lewallen, A.-E. 2003. "Strategic 'Indigeneity' and the Possibility of a Global Indigenous Women's Movement." *Michigan Feminist Studies* 17: 105–30.

Linebaugh, P. 2014. *Stop Thief! The Commons, Enclosures, and Resistance*. Oakland: PM Press.

Manning, P. 1990. *Slavery and African Life: Occidental, Oriental, and African Slave Trades*. New York: Cambridge University Press.

Manuel, G., and M. Posluns. 1974. *The Fourth World: An Indian Reality*. Toronto: Collier-Macmillan Canada.

Marriott, D. 2011. "Whither Fanon?" *Textual Practice* 25, no. 1: 33–69.

McFarlane, P. 1993. *Brotherhood to Nationhood: George Manuel and the Making of the Modern Indian Movement*. Toronto: Between the Lines.

Memmi, A. 2003. *The Colonizer and the Colonized*. 4th ed. Translated by H. Greenfield. New York: Routledge.

Mihesuah, D. A., and A. C. Wilson, eds. 2004. *Indigenizing the Academy: Transforming Scholarship and Empowering Communities*. Lincoln: University of Nebraska Press.

Miles, T. 2006. *Ties That Bind: The Story of an Afro-Cherokee Family in Slavery and Freedom*. Berkeley: University of California Press.

Miles, T. 2010. *The House on Diamond Hill: A Cherokee Plantation Story*. Chapel Hill: University of North Carolina Press.

Milum, K. 2010. *The Political Uncommons: The Cross-Cultural Logic of the Global Commons*. London: Ashgate.

Moten, F. 2013. "Notes on Passage: An Epistemology, Paraontology, Insovereignty." Paper presented at the Graduate Center, City University of New York, April 12.

Oakes, J. 1990. *Slavery and Freedom: An Interpretation of the Old South*. New York: W. W. Norton.

Prashad, V. 2007. *The Darker Nations: A People's History of the Third World*. New York: New Press.

Ransby, B. 2005. *Ella Baker and the Black Freedom Movement: A Radical Democratic Vision*. Chapel Hill: University of North Carolina Press.

Rifkin, M. 2009. "Indigenizing Agamben: Rethinking Sovereignty in Light of the 'Peculiar' Status of Native Peoples." *Cultural Critique* 73: 88–124.

Robinson, C. 2000. *Black Marxism: The Making of the Black Radical Tradition*. Chapel Hill: University of North Carolina Press.

Saunt, C. 2004. "The Paradox of Freedom: Tribal Sovereignty and Emancipation during the Reconstruction of Indian Territory." *Journal of Southern History* 70, no. 1: 63–94.

Shantz, J. 2013. *Commonist Tendencies: Mutual Aid beyond Communism*. Brooklyn: Punctum Books.

Sharma, N., and C. Wright. 2008. "Decolonizing Resistance, Challenging Colonial States." *Social Justice* 35, no. 3: 120–38.

Silva, D. F. da. 2007. *Toward a Global Idea of Race*. Minneapolis: University of Minnesota Press.

Simpson, L. 2013. "I Am Not a Nation-State." *Voices Rising*, November 6. Accessed August 1, 2014. http://nationsrising.org/i-am-not-a-nation-state/.

Smith, A. 2006. "Heteropatriarchy and the Three Pillars of White Supremacy." In *The Color of Violence: The INCITE! Anthology*, edited by INCITE! Women of Color Against Violence, 66–73. Boston: South End Press.

Smith, A. 2010. "Indigeneity, Settler Colonialism, White Supremacy." *Global Dialogue* 12, no. 2. Accessed August 1, 2014. http://www.worlddialogue.org /content.php?id=488.

Smith, A. 2012. "The Moral Limits of the Law: Settler Colonialism and the Anti-Violence Movement." *Settler Colonial Studies* 2, no. 2: 69–88.

Smith, A. 2013. "Voting and Indigenous Disappearance." *Settler Colonial Studies* 3, nos. 3–4: 352–68.

Solow, B., ed. 1991. *Slavery and the Rise of the Atlantic System*. New York: Cambridge University Press.

Spillers, H. 2003. *Black, White, and in Color: Essays on American Literature and Culture*. Chicago: University of Chicago Press.

Trouillot, M-R. 2012. *Silencing the Past: Power and the Production of History*. Boston: Beacon.

Veracini, L. 2010. *Settler Colonialism: A Theoretical Overview*. New York: Palgrave Macmillan.

Veracini, L. 2011. "Introducing." *Settler Colonial Studies* 1, no. 1: 1–12.

Waziyatawin. 2012. "The Paradox of Indigenous Resurgence at the End of Empire." *Decolonization* 1, no. 1: 68–85.

Wilderson, F. B., III. 2008. "Biko and the Problematic of Presence." In *Biko Lives! Contesting the Legacies of Steve Biko*, edited by A. Mngxitama, A. Alexander, and N. Gibson, 95–114. New York: Palgrave Macmillan.

Wilderson, F. B., III. 2010. *Red, White & Black: Cinema and the Structure of U.S. Antagonisms*. Durham, NC: Duke University Press.

Wynter, S. 1995. "1492: A New World View." In *Race, Discourse, and the Origins of the Americas*, edited by V. Lawrence and R. Nettleford. Washington, DC: Smithsonian Institution Press.

Andrea Smith

Sovereignty as Deferred Genocide

It was more just the country should be peopled by Europeans than continue the haunt of savage beasts. —*State v. Foreman* (1835)

I have come to kill Indians, and believe it is right and honorable to use any means under God's heaven to kill Indians. . . . Kill and scalp all, big and little; nits make lice. —Col. John Milton Chivington

The relationship between Native and Black peoples in the United States has often been articulated as one in which Black peoples have been exploited for their labor and Native peoples have been exterminated for their land. Black studies scholars have troubled the first part of this relationship. As Frank Wilderson argues, "The slave is not a laborer but an anti-Human, a position against which Humanity establishes, maintains and renews its coherence."[1] Furthermore, "If workers can buy a loaf of bread, they can also buy a slave."[2] However, the second part of this relationship is often not similarly questioned. As Wilderson articulates this relationship: "Give Turtle Island back to the 'Savage.' Give the life itself back to the Slave."[3] The struggle for the Indian can be and has often been simply summarized as a "demand for land." Because Native struggle becomes articulated as a demand for land, then Native peoples presumably do not have an absolute antagonistic relationship with whiteness—because they can claim land, they are essentially partially human. A demand for sovereignty thus becomes equated with a demand for land, which then requires that Native peoples ostensibly must be able to enter the realm of the human to even be able to assert sovereignty. Black peoples, by contrast, argues Jared Sexton, occupy the "unthought" of sovereignty. This is why the struggle against anti-Blackness, according to

Sexton, is distinct from the struggle for decolonization, because the agent of decolonization must necessarily occupy the category of the "human." As Sexton states in this volume: "Slavery is not a loss that the self experiences—of language, lineage, land, or labor—[and by extension the goal is not the recovery of these losses as sovereignty implies] but rather the loss of any self that could experience such loss."

I question the assumption that colonization is ultimately about the theft of land and then by extension decolonization is ultimately about the return of stolen land. Rather, colonization is about the creation of land and hence it is also about the creation of the human itself. That is to say this assumption presumes that land is always already property that can be owned by the "human." As many Native scholars and activists have argued, however, land should not necessarily be seen as a commodity that can be bought and sold and controlled by a group of humans.[4] The presumption of land as property makes invisible alternative conceptions of "land" as a relative that does not exist in sharp distinction from "humanity." That is, for the structural relationship of white/Black and hence human/nonhuman to exist, the distinction between human and nonhuman (or human and land) must be made meaningful. Before there can be the theft of land there must be a creation of something called land that can be stolen. Thus, perhaps the Native does not exist in a midway point between the human and the nonhuman—rather the creation of the Native is the creation of the grid of intelligibility upon which the antagonistic relationship between the human and nonhuman can even exist.

Rather than the position of the Native being one that oscillates between "the living and the dead,"[5] the Indigenous marks the creation of the division between the living and the dead or between the human and the nonhuman. As such, the Native as such can never actually exist. It remains the trace of a different grid of intelligibility altogether. It is thus always disappearing—disappearing into whiteness or disappearing into Blackness, but the Native itself cannot exist. "The lived violence of this biopolitical categorization and partitioning is encapsulated by the fact that, as Native Americans, they are 'under the jurisdiction of a department that otherwise manages "natural resources."'"[6]

The legal origin in the United States of what Joseph Pugliese describes as the classification of Native peoples as "natural resources" can be seen in the "doctrine of discovery." In *Johnson v. McIntosh* (1823), the Supreme Court held that, while Indigenous people had a right to occupancy, they could not hold title to land on the basis of the doctrine of discovery. The European nation that "discovered" land had the right to legal title. Native peoples were disqualified from being "discoverers" because they did not properly work. "[T]he tribes of Indians inhabiting this country were fierce savages, whose occupation was war, and whose subsistence was drawn chiefly from the forest. To leave them in possession of their country, was to leave the country a wilderness."[7] As they did not work, Native peoples had the ontological status of things to be discovered—the status of nature. By "work" I mean the ability to transform nature into property. That is, as Tiffany Lethabo King notes, while Black women certainly labored under slavery, their labor did not qualify as work because it could not produce property for themselves, only for the settler/master.[8] Black peoples, with the ontological status of property, cannot produce property. Native peoples, with the ontological status of nature, can only create more nature. They, as well, cannot transform nature into property, and hence cannot qualify as workers, and by extension, as humans.

Wilderson, Tiffany Lethabo King, and many other scholars have challenged the notion that slavery is exploited labor by arguing that work implies a human laborer that can be exploited. However, the doctrine of discovery suggests that work is not a prior category that belongs to the human. Rather, work is the operation that divides the human from the nonhuman. One does not simply work the land if one has the ontological status of human. Work creates the land in the first place by transforming it from a set of relations to a thing that can be commodified.

Disappearing into Whiteness

The Native then is the trace of a grid of intelligibility by which the boundaries between land, creation, human, and things become meaningful. Some "Native" peoples have the opportunity to disappear into whiteness through work, but this then makes them no longer Native. The Native does not exist in a bounded relationship with nonhumanity such that the category of work is meaningful in the first place. For instance, the Dawes Allotment Act, which divided Indigenous lands into individual allotments, was deemed necessary because only through individual property ownership could Native peoples have a need to work. In the 1887 Indian Commissioner's Report, J. D. C. Atkins explains how allotment will "free" Native peoples into the status of workers. "It must be apparent . . . that the system of gathering the Indians in bands or tribes on reservations . . . thus relieving them of the necessity of labor, never will and never can civilize them. Labor is an essential element in producing civilization. . . . The greatest kindness the government can bestow upon the Indian is to teach him to labor for his own support, thus developing his true manhood, and, as a consequence, making himself-relying and self-supporting."[9]

The report warns that allotment will not work overnight: "Idleness, improvidence, ignorance, and superstition cannot by law be transformed into industry, thrift, intelligence, and Christianity speedily."[10] Nonetheless, the pathway toward civilization requires Native peoples to adapt to a capitalist work model. Of course, as I have argued elsewhere, when Native peoples began to work, they will still never be human (i.e., whiteness)—as the trace of the alternative grid of intelligibility remains. For instance, Native peoples were not actually trained to be successful in the capitalist system. And when they were successful, this created problems for capital (i.e., the controversies around Indian gaming),[11] because as Glen Coulthard notes, capitalism is supposed to be white,[12] and Native peoples can never really escape their status as "nature" just as Black peoples perpetually live in the afterlife of slavery.[13]

Thus, Native peoples seem to be promised a provisional humanity, but it is a promise that can never be fulfilled. First, as Maile Arvin notes, this promised humanity exists not to benefit Native peoples, but to enable whiteness a proximity to indigeneity such that whiteness can then possess it and lay claim to all that is Indigenous.[14] Second, Indigenous peoples can lay claim to humanity and thus lay claim to land only when they are no longer Indigenous because humanity is defined as that which is fully distinguishable from land and nature.

Furthermore, as Robert Nichols notes, settler colonialism sets the very terms of its contestation. And the terms of the contestation set by settler colonialism is antiracism. That is, the way we are supposed to contest settler democracy is to contest the gap between what settler democracy promises and what it performs. But, as Nichols notes, contesting the racial gap of settler democracy is the most effective way of actually ensuring its universality.[15] Thus, borrowing from this analysis, settler colonialism does not just operate by racializing Native peoples as racial minorities rather than as colonized nations, but also through domesticating Black struggle within the framework of antiracist rather than anticolonial struggle. Anti-Blackness is effectuated through the disappearance of colonialism in order to render Black peoples as the internal property of the United States such that Black struggle must be contained within a domesticated antiracist framework that cannot challenge the settler state itself. Through anti-Blackness, not only are Black peoples rendered the property of the settler state, but Black struggle itself remains its property—solely containable within the confines of the settler state. Thus, rather than presume that Black struggle is in fact an antiracist struggle and hence sharply distinct from Indigenous struggle, as often articulated with Native studies,[16] it is important to see that anti-Blackness makes Black struggle legible only through the lens of civil rights and antiracism.

Thus, the colonialism that never happened—anti-Blackness—helps reinforce the colonialism that is settled: the genocide of Indigenous peoples. For the so-called Indian problem to disappear, the United States must itself appear hermetically sealed from both internal and external threats that would threaten its legitimacy and continued existence. Indigenous peoples must disappear as internal threats who are sadly in a constant state of vanishing but nonetheless are in no position to unsettle the settler state. Essentially, the colonization of Indigenous peoples must remain "settled." Meanwhile, the external threat posed by a global Black anticolonial struggle disappears by rendering Africa as the property of the United States and hence no longer external to it, hence this colonization must disappear altogether.

These colonial projects presume that nature has the status of being a "thing." That is, the ability to "work" nature is what bestows humanity to the colonizer. Consequently, any analysis of raciality must concern itself with the construction and thingification of nature itself. For Indigenous peoples to be removed from their land bases, land first has to be thingified. As Dian Million notes, our typical paradigm for articulating Indigenous struggles as a "land"-based struggle may itself be a result of this colonial discourse. That is, under our current legal system, the only way Indigenous peoples can intervene when there is colonial encroachment on Indigenous lands is to argue, it's not *your* land; it's *our* land. One cannot argue that land should not be owned by anyone. But as I have discussed elsewhere, many Native scholars and activists argue that land should not be a commodity that can be owned and controlled by one group of people.[17] Rather, all peoples must exist in relationship with all of creation and care for it. Consequently, the principles of Indigenous nationhood that emerge from these relationships are principles of inclusivity, mutual respect, and interrelationality with all other nations.

However, contends Million, the term "land" itself does not speak to the manner in which Indigenous peoples have relationships with all of creation, the entirety of the biosphere. Thus, the term "land" itself truncates what these relations signify in order to facilitate the commodification of a piece of creation that is separated from the rest of the biosphere. Thus, contrary to Sexton's assertion, it is not that Indigenous liberation can be articulated through a cognizable demand—for land or resources. Rather, extending

Nichols's analysis, Indigenous struggle is only legible in the formulation of a demand—a demand for land and resources befitting a minoritized group seeking recognition. It cannot be understood in terms of challenging reality and relationality as defined by the Settler/Master, or challenging what Native studies scholar Andrea Derbecker describes as the "fungibility of land."[18]

Disappearing into Blackness

Thus, the relationship between indigeneity and whiteness is constituted through a logic of disappearance. However, while Native scholars have explored this relationship, there has been insufficient attention to how this disappearance into whiteness is enabled by a simultaneous disappearance into Blackness. Here, the work of Dian Million and Frank Wilderson provide a helpful foundation for analyzing these simultaneous disappearances.

Wilderson argues that the structural antagonism between Indigenous peoples and whiteness is not around colonization/sovereignty, but genocide.

> Of course, the "Savage" ontological modality of genocide ratchets the Settler/"Savage" struggle up from a conflict to an antagonism and thus overwhelms the constraints of analogy. Suddenly, the struggle between the Settler and the "Savage" is "like" nothing at all, which is to say it becomes "like" the struggle between the Master and the Slave. Suddenly, the network of connections, transfers, and displacements between the "Savage's" semiotics of loss and the Settler's semiotics of gain is overwhelmed—crowded out—by a network of connections, transfers, and displacements between a genocided thing and a fungible and accumulated thing.[19]

He juxtaposes genocide against sovereignty: "Genocide, however, has no speaking subject; as such it has no narrative. It can only be apprehended by way of a narrative about something that it is not—such as sovereignty."[20] However, the endpoint of the "sovereignty" offered by colonization, as Glen Coulthard and Dian Million note, is also genocide. That is, this sovereignty is the state administration over the spectacularity of Indigenous suffering that has no end.[21] Echoing Wilderson's analysis, Million critiques some strands within ethnohistory that reject the use of the word "genocide" to describe the histories of Indigenous peoples. Native peoples had "agency," so the argument goes, and hence they could not have been subject to genocide.[22] Essentially, a focus on sovereignty rather than genocide shifts Indigenous politics from eradicating genocide to engaging in, to use Dylan Rodriguez's term, genocide management.

The infamous *Dred Scott* decision (1857) concretizes this analysis. In this decision, Justice Peter Daniel explains in his concurring opinion that Black peoples have the ontological status of property that derives from their origins in Africa as the property of Europe. Consequently, this ontological status does not change simply because one's owner relinquishes his property rights. Black peoples remain property whether or not an individual owns them.

> Now, the following are truths which a knowledge of the history of the world, and particularly of that of our own country, compels us to know— that *the African negro race never have been acknowledged as belonging to the family of nations*; that as amongst them there never has been known or recognized by the inhabitants of other countries anything partaking of the character of nationality, or civil or political polity; that this race has been by all the nations of Europe regarded as subjects of capture or purchase; as subjects of commerce or traffic; and that the introduction of that race into every section of this country was not as members of civil or political society, but as slaves, as *property* in the strictest sense of the term.[23]

Because Africa is deemed the property of Europe, Africa must then appear as always, already colonized. Thus, there can be no actual peoples in Africa or nations in Africa to colonize. As a result, the categories of "Indigenous" and "Black" become mutually exclusive. Indigenous peoples are subject to settler colonialism, whereas the colonization of Black peoples must be disavowed. As Tiffany Lethabo King notes, the entire project of settler colonialism must then disappear Blackness.[24] The "Natives" in Africa, however, who disappear into Blackness no longer bear the trace of this colonialism and hence are subject to a double disappearance. As a result, many works within Indigenous studies cast Black peoples as simply subject to racism while remaining somehow unimpacted by colonization—enabling their casting as "settlers."[25]

Jared Sexton contends in this volume that colonization is not a necessary condition of enslavement because (utilizing Lorenzo Veracini's articulation of colonialism versus settler colonialism): "(1) slaves need not be colonial subjects, or objects of colonial exploitation, and they do not face the fundamental directive of colonialism, 'you, work for me,' though slaves often enough labor; and (2) slaves need not be settler colonial subjects, or objects of settler colonial genocide, since they do not face the fundamental directive 'you, go away,' though slaves often enough are driven from their native land."[26]

This reasoning tends to presume that colonization is primarily about driving people away from land. However, this presumes that colonialism has not impacted what we consider to be "land." Instead, colonialism creates the divide between land, resources, and "humanity" and hence creates the categories themselves. For Black peoples to become "things" or nonhumans, nonhumans have to be created as a meaningful category. Thus, while Sexton holds that Black peoples occupy the "unthought of sovereignty," colonization itself makes alternative conceptions of reality unthinkable. "Sovereignty" can be equated not simply with control of land or resources but with the ability to articulate reality at all.

Genocide operates then through a synthesis of operations involving a disappearance of some into Blackness and some into whiteness. The disappearance of Native peoples into Blackness operationally disappears their disappearance, and it operates simultaneously with Indigenous disappearance into whiteness by making a disappearance into whiteness seem a desirable goal.

To illustrate, in Virginia, the courts initially ascribed Native slaves with the same status as Black slaves. However, gradually more Native peoples were removed from the category of Blackness until in 1806, the Supreme Court in *Hudgins v. Wright* declared that "all *American Indians* are *prima facie* FREE."[27] This freedom, however, is predicated on the immutable slavery of Black peoples. "For the Africans are absolute slaves in their own country, none but the King being a freeman there."[28]

Contemporaneously with this decision, however, the New Jersey courts held that Native and Black peoples shared the same legal status.

> The *habeas corpus*, in this case seems to have been sued out under the supposition that an Indian could not be a slave under our laws. But this idea . . . cannot be urged with any shew of reason. They have been so long recognized as slaves in our law, that it would be as great a violation of the rights of property to establish a contrary doctrine at the present day, as it would in the case of Africans: and as useless to investigate the manner in which they originally lost their freedom. . . . No discrimination is made between negroes and Indians. The slavery of Indians therefore, by our laws, stands precisely upon the same footing, and is to be governed by the same rules as that of Africans.[29]

Native peoples were thus simultaneously positioned as Black and non-Black. This relationality of simultaneous Black/non-Blackness is typified in the 1800s debate about what do about the so-called "Indian problem." Carl

Schurz, at that time a former commissioner of Indian Affairs, concluded that Native peoples had this "stern alternative: extermination or civilization."[30] Henry Pancoast, a Philadelphia lawyer, advocated a similar policy in 1882: "We must either butcher them or civilize them, and what we do we must do quickly."[31] In other words, Native peoples have only one option, disappearance. However, they may disappear either into whiteness (civilization) or Blackness (extermination) in which Indigenous disappearance itself disappears.

However, the threat of disappearance into Blackness makes disappearance into whiteness appear as both survival and a choice rather than a deferred genocide. Sovereignty as a practice of deferred genocide can be seen in the Cherokee nation cases. Legal scholar Robert Williams has compellingly argued that while Native nations rely on the Cherokee nation cases as the basis for their claims to sovereignty, all of these cases rely on a logic based on white supremacy in which Native peoples are racialized as incompetent to be fully sovereign. Rather than uphold these cases, he calls on us to actually overturn these cases so that they go by the wayside as did the *Dred Scott* decision.

> I therefore take it as axiomatic that a "winning courtroom strategy" for protecting Indian rights in this country cannot be organized around a set of legal precedents and accompanying legal discourse that views Indians as lawless savages and interprets their rights accordingly. Before rejecting out of hand this axiom that the precedents and language the justices use in discussing minority rights are vitally important to the way the Court ultimately identifies and defines those rights, I ask Indian rights lawyers and scholars to consider carefully the following question: Is it really possible to believe that the court would have written *Brown* the way it did if it had not first explicitly decided to reject the "language in *Plessy v. Ferguson*" that gave precedential legal force, validity, and sanction to the negative racial stereotypes and images historically directed at blacks by the dominant white society?[32]

Williams points to the contradictions involved when Native peoples ask courts to uphold these problematic legal precedents rather than overturn them. "This model's acceptance of the European colonial-era doctrine of discovery and its foundational legal principle of Indian racial inferiority licenses Congress to exercise its plenary power unilaterally to terminate Indian tribes, abrogate Indian treaties, and extinguish Indian rights, and there's nothing that Indians can legally do about any of these actions."[33]

In addition, further reading into these cases demonstrates that the "sovereignty" promised in them is not only limited but also designed to be temporary. Eventually, Native peoples should "mature" into whiteness and disappear as Native peoples. Thus, in this case, even the provisional humanity promised to some Native peoples is not humanity at all insofar as it too must disappear. For instance, in a concurring opinion to *Worcester v. Georgia* (1832), which, on one hand, upheld the right of the Cherokee nation to be free of state laws because of their semi-sovereign status, also explained that the sovereign status of Native peoples was not permanent. Rather, Justice John McLean implies that the recognition of Native sovereignty is primarily a strategic one—one designed to facilitate European access to land and resources until such time that it would be in a position to expropriate them.

> The exercise of the power of self-government by the Indians, within a state, is undoubtedly contemplated to be temporary. This is shown by the settled policy of the government, in the extinguishment of their title, and especially by the compact with the state of Georgia. It is a question, not of abstract right, but of public policy. I do not mean to say, that the same moral rule which should regulate the affairs of private life, should not be regarded by communities or nations. But, a sound national policy does require that the Indian tribes within our states should exchange their territories, upon equitable principles, or, eventually, consent to become amalgamated in our political communities.[34]

Temporary sovereignty is essentially a deferred genocide, but it is the legal framework adopted when the alternative option is immediate genocide. The result then, as that when we focus on Indigenous "survivance," is that the memories of the Indigenous peoples who have not survived completely disappear. Kim TallBear illustrates this tendency in her critique of Russell Means's argument that "that *we* will survive, even if there is only one tribe left in the Amazon or one tribe left in the Arctic."[35] Contends TallBear: "Means used the word *we* to signify indigenous people from around the globe as one race of people—as if two surviving tribes in the Amazon and the Arctic could carry forth the cultural practices and histories of thousands of tribes."[36] As her work implies, many Native communities have not only disappeared, but their disappearance has disappeared and their extinction cannot be mourned. Thus, we cannot forget that all Native peoples were given the option of assimilation. And it is perhaps the threat of Blackness that impels Native peoples to escape into whiteness—and hence to desire simply a deferred genocide.

Ashon Crawley and Denise Ferreira da Silva in this volume suggest that we could perhaps think of disappearance as something different—something perhaps in conversation with fugitivity—the call for the end of the world as we know it. That is, an end to colonial intelligibility, an end to relationality based on commodification, an end to Western man.[37] Native studies could be informed by Wilderson's call: "From the coherence of civil society, the Black subject beckons with the incoherence of civil war, a war that reclaims Blackness not as a positive value, but as a politically enabling site."[38] Further, "in allowing the notion of freedom to attain the ethical purity of its ontological status, one would have to lose one's Human coordinates and become Black. Which is to say one would have to die."[39]

Certainly, many Indigenous movements have organized based on the principle that genocide does not have the last word. However, the process of decolonization cannot be reduced to a "return" to land but to an alternative reality altogether that requires radical breaks with Western epistemology.[40] In particular, decolonization requires a deconstruction of the radical separation of "humanity" from the rest of creation—a separation that enables white supremacy and anti-Blackness. Coya White Hat-Artichoker challenges the tendency within Native organizing and Native academia to define indigeneity in exclusivist terms. She asks what it would mean if indigeneity was not defined in terms of scarcity—that it is something only a few can have. What if, instead, indigeneity was understood as powerful and potentially world-transforming? Similarly Dawn Moves Camp asks what would happen if we took the commonly repeated phrase "we are related" seriously. Such expansive notions of indigeneity provide a glimpse of alternative grids of intelligibility that colonization attempts to disappear and suggest a future whose endgame is not genocide. As Hat-Artichoker and Paulina Helm-Hernandez argue:

> We believe it is an outgrowth of colonialism that an individualistic "American" sense of identity, one that seeks to overpower and erase the culture of kindness and kinship our community can offer when at its best, has taken root in our modern culture. At its worst, we've seen assertions made on our behalf that some have a more "legitimate claim" to our shared ancestry than others. The weight of atrocities such as the trans-Atlantic slave trade and the pillaging and plundering of our continental resources and lands for the gain of European monarchies, nations and "New World" capitalists are to this day resting on our ground

and in our bones. Because of those parallel and overlapping oppressions that indigenous, mestizo, black/African, and Caribbean people have endured, our stake in each other's survival is greater than we have been led to believe; our ancestors wept together at the loss of our homelands, at the loss of our mothers and fathers, our loves and our babies, our sacred practices and rituals, at the loss of our autonomy and histories. As people of resistance and resilience, however, we know that not all has been lost, and it has been part of our shared spiritual imperative to continue to reclaim our ancestry, our languages, and our claim to each other as kin. It is through this reclaiming that we see glimmers of what is possible, what promise lies on the other side of our shame and grief, when we unbind ourselves from the lie that there is a singular indigenous experience, a singular claim over who we are and what constitutes our communities. We have the opportunity, now more than ever, to see the full depth and breadth of who we are as shared descendants of the American continent tribal nations, of Antilles Indians, of Africans brought to the Caribbean and this continent as slaves.

We are indigenous.[41]

Notes

Epigraphs: *State v. Foreman*, 16 Tenn. 256, 265 (1835); Dee Brown, *Bury My Heart at Wounded Knee: An Indian History of the American West* (New York: Macmillan, 2007), 86–87.

1 Frank B. Wilderson III, *Red, White & Black: Cinema and the Structure of U.S. Antagonisms* (Durham, NC: Duke University Press, 2010), 11.

2 Wilderson, *Red, White & Black*, 13.

3 Wilderson, *Red, White & Black*, 2

4 Patricia Monture-Angus, *Journeying Forward: Dreaming First Nations' Independence* (Halifax: Fernwood Publishing, 1999); Mishuana Goeman, *Mark My Words: Native Women Mapping Our Nations* (Minneapolis: University of Minnesota Press, 2013); Leeanne Simpson, "Queering Resurgence: Taking on Heteropatriarchy in Indigenous Nation Building," Leanne Betasamosake Simpson, June 1, 2012, http://leannesimpson.ca/2012/06/01/queering-resurgence-taking-on-heteropatriarchy-in-indigenous-nation-building/.

5 Wilderson., *Red, White & Black*, 25.

6 Joseph Pugliese, *State Violence and the Execution of the Law: Biopolitical Caesurae of Torture, Black Sites, Drones* (London: Routledge, 2013), 54.

7 *Johnson v. McIntosh*, 21 U.S. 543, 590, 5 L. Ed. 681 (1823).

8 Tiffany Jeannette King, "In the Clearing: Black Female Bodies, Space, and Settler Colonial Landscapes," PhD diss., University of Maryland, College Park, 2013.

9 Report of the Secretary of the Interior, 50th Congress, 1st Session, House of
   Representatives, Ex. Doc 1, Part 5, p. 7. Washington Government Printing
   Office, 1887.

10 Report of the Secretary of the Interior, 50th Congress, 1st Session, 4.

11 For a fuller discussion, see Jessica Cattelino, *High Stakes: Florida Seminole
   Gaming and Sovereignty* (Durham, NC: Duke University Press, 2008).

12 See Glen Coulthard, *Red Skin, White Masks: Rejecting the Colonial Politics of
   Recognition* (Minneapolis: University of Minnesota Press, 2014).

13 Saidiya Hartman, *Lose Your Mother: A Journey along the Atlantic Slave Route*
   (London: Macmillan, 2008).

14 Maile Arvin, "Pacifically Possessed," Department of Ethnic Studies (La Jolla,
   CA: UC San Diego, 2013).

15 Robert Nichols, "Contract and Usurpation: Enfranchisement and Racial Governance in Settler-Colonial Contexts," in *Theorizing Native Studies*, ed. Audra
   Simpson and Andrea Smith (Durham, NC: Duke University Press, 2014).

16 See, for instance, Mark Rifkin, *Beyond Settler Time: Temporal Sovereignty and
   Indigenous Self-Determination* (Minneapolis: University of Minnesota Press,
   2017); Mark Rifkin, *Settler Common Sense: Queerness and Everyday Colonialism in the American Renaissance* (Minneapolis: University of Minnesota
   Press, 2014).

17 Andrea Smith, "Indigeneity, Settler Colonialism, White Supremacy," in *Racial
   Formations in the Twenty-First Century*, ed. David Martinez HoSang, Oneka
   LaBennett, and Laura Pulido (Berkeley: University of California Press, 2012).

18 Personal conversation, February 15, 2016.

19 Wilderson, *Red, White & Black*, 182.

20 Wilderson, *Red, White & Black*, 213.

21 Coulthard, *Red Skin, White Masks*; Dian Million, *Therapeutic Nations: Healing in an Age of Indigenous Human Rights* (Phoenix: University of Arizona
   Press, 2013).

22 Dian Million, "Felt Theory: An Indigenous Feminist Approach to Affect and
   History," *Wicazo Sa Review* 24 (Fall 2009).

23 *Dred Scott v. Sandford*, 60 U.S. 393, 475–77, 15 L. Ed. 691 (1856). Emphasis
   added.

24 Tiffany Lethabo King, "New World Grammars: The 'Unthought' Black Discourses of Conquest," *Theory & Event* 19, no. 4 (2016).

25 See, for instance, Rifkin, *Beyond Settler Time* and *Settler Common Sense*.

26 Jared Sexton, "The *Vel* of Slavery: Tracking the Figure of the Unsovereign,"
   Critical Sociology 42, nos. 4–5 (2014): 9.

27 *Hudgins v. Wright*, 11 Va. 134, 139 (1806). Emphasis in original.

28 *Robin v. Hardaway*, 1772 WL 11 (Va. Gen. Ct. Apr. 1772).

29 *State v. Van Waggoner*, 6 N.J.L. 374, 374–77 (1797).

30 David Wallace Adams, *Education for Extinction: American Indians and the
   Boarding School Experience, 1875–1928* (Topeka: University Press of Kansas,
   1995), 15.

31 Adams, *Education for Extinction*, 12.
32 Robert A. Williams Jr., *Like a Loaded Weapon: The Rehnquist Court, Indian Rights, and the Legal History of Racism in America* (Minneapolis: University of Minnesota Press, 2005), xxxiii.
33 Williams, *Like a Loaded Weapon*, 151.
34 *Worcester v. State of Ga.*, 31 U.S. 515, 593, 8 L. Ed. 483 (1832).
35 Kimberley TallBear, "Racialising Tribal Identity and the Implications for Political and Cultural Development," in *Indigenous Peoples, Racism and the United Nations*, ed. Martin Nakata (Australia: Common Ground Publishing, 2001), 169–70.
36 TallBear, "Racialising Tribal Identity," 170.
37 Alexander G. Weheliye, *Habeas Viscus: Racializing Assemblages, Biopolitics, and Black Feminist Theories of the Human* (Durham, NC: Duke University Press, 2014).
38 Frank B Wilderson III, "The Prison Slave as Hegemony's (Silent) Scandal," in *Warfare in the American Homeland*, ed. Joy James (Durham, NC: Duke University Press, 2007), 33.
39 Wilderson, "Prison Slave," 23.
40 Smith, "Indigeneity, Settler Colonialism, White Supremacy."
41 Coya White Hat-Artichoker and Paulina Helm-Hernandez, "A Love Letter to All of Our Indigenous/Native/Mestiza LGBTQ Familia," *Huffington Post*, July 25, 2013. https://www.huffpost.com/entry/a-love-letter-to-all-of-our-indigenousnativemestiza-lgbtq-familia_b_3645414.

References

Adams, David Wallace. 1995. *Education for Extinction: American Indians and the Boarding School Experience, 1875–1928*. Topeka: University Press of Kansas.
Arvin, Maile. 2013. "Pacifically Possessed." Department of Ethnic Studies. La Jolla, CA: UC San Diego.
Brown, Dee. 2007. *Bury My Heart at Wounded Knee: An Indian History of the American West*. New York: Macmillan.
Cattelino, Jessica. 2008. *High Stakes: Florida Seminole Gaming and Sovereignty*. Durham, NC: Duke University Press.
Coulthard, Glen. 2014. *Red Skin, White Masks: Rejecting the Colonial Politics of Recognition*. Minneapolis: University of Minnesota Press.
Goeman, Mishuana. 2013. *Mark My Words: Native Women Mapping Our Nations*. Minneapolis: University of Minnesota Press.
Hartman, Saidiya. 2008. *Lose Your Mother: A Journey along the Atlantic Slave Route*. London: Macmillan.
Hat-Artichoker, Coya White, and Paulina Helm-Hernandez. 2013. "A Love Letter to All of Our Indigenous/Native/Mestiza LGBTQ Familia." *Huffington Post*, July 25. https://www.huffpost.com/entry/a-love-letter-to-all-of-our-indigenousnativemestiza-lgbtq-familia_b_3645414.

King, Tiffany Jeannette. 2013. "In the Clearing: Black Female Bodies, Space, and Settler Colonial Landscapes." PhD diss., University of Maryland, College Park.

King, Tiffany Lethabo. 2016. "New World Grammars: The 'Unthought' Black Discourses of Conquest." *Theory & Event* 19, no. 4.

Million, Dian. 2009. "Felt Theory: An Indigenous Feminist Approach to Affect and History." *Wicazo Sa Review* 24 (Fall): 53–76.

Million, Dian. 2013. *Therapeutic Nations: Healing in an Age of Indigenous Human Rights.* Phoenix: University of Arizona Press.

Monture-Angus, Patricia. 1999. *Journeying Forward: Dreaming First Nations' Independence.* Halifax: Fernwood Publishing.

Nichols, Robert. 2014. "Contract and Usurpation: Enfranchisement and Racial Governance in Settler-Colonial Contexts." In *Theorizing Native Studies*, edited by Audra Simpson and Andrea Smith, 99–121. Durham, NC: Duke University Press.

Pugliese, Joseph. 2013. *State Violence and the Execution of the Law: Biopolitical Caesurae of Torture, Black Sites, Drones.* London: Routledge.

Rifkin, Mark. 2014. *Settler Common Sense: Queerness and Everyday Colonialism in the American Renaissance.* Minneapolis: University of Minnesota Press.

Rifkin, Mark. 2017. *Beyond Settler Time: Temporal Sovereignty and Indigenous Self-Determination.* Minneapolis: University of Minnesota Press.

Simpson, Leeanne. 2012. "Queering Resurgence: Taking on Heteropatriarchy in Indigenous Nation Building." Leanne Betasamosake Simpson, June 1. http://leannesimpson.ca/2012/06/01/queering-resurgence-taking-on-heteropatriarchy-in-indigenous-nation-building/.

Smith, Andrea. 2012. "Indigeneity, Settler Colonialism, White Supremacy." In *Racial Formations in the Twenty-First Century*, edited by David Martinez HoSang, Oneka LaBennett, and Laura Pulido, 66–90. Berkeley: University of California Press.

TallBear, Kimberley. 2001. "Racialising Tribal Identity and the Implications for Political and Cultural Development." In *Indigenous Peoples, Racism and the United Nations*, edited by Martin Nakata, 163–74. Australia: Common Ground Publishing.

Weheliye, Alexander G. 2014. *Habeas Viscus: Racializing Assemblages, Biopolitics, and Black Feminist Theories of the Human.* Durham: NC: Duke University Press.

Wilderson, Frank B., III. 2007. "The Prison Slave as Hegemony's (Silent) Scandal." In *Warfare in the American Homeland*, edited by Joy James, 23–34. Durham, NC: Duke University Press.

Wilderson, Frank B., III. 2010. *Red, White & Black: Cinema and the Structure of U.S. Antagonisms.* Durham, NC: Duke University Press.

CHAPTER SEVEN

Chad Benito Infante

Murder and Metaphysics

Leslie Marmon Silko's "Tony's Story" and Audre Lorde's "Power"

It is not necessary for a black man to hate a white man, or to have any particular feelings about him at all, in order to realize that he must kill him. Yes, we have come, or are coming to this, and there is no point in flinching before the prospect of this exceedingly cool species of fratricide—which prospect white people, after all, have brought on themselves. —James Baldwin

Both continents, Africa and America, be it remembered, were "discovered"—what a wealth of arrogance that little word contains!—with devastating results for the indigenous populations, whose only human use thereafter was as the source of capital for white people. On both continents the white and the dark gods met in combat, and it is on the outcome of this combat that the future of both continents depends. —James Baldwin

In the opening epigraphs from James Baldwin's 1972 book-length essay *No Name in The Streets*, Baldwin concludes the text by imagining an intimate yet dispassionate rendition of murder that he calls "this exceedingly cool species of fratricide."[1] Baldwin then goes on to imagine a scenario where he shoots a white man who is holding a gun to the head of his "brother." He says that he would pull the trigger coolly, without hesitation or remorse, without hate or passion, indicating that no such feelings are necessary for Black and Native people to employ retributive murder as an ethical response to white violence.

Baldwin concludes this meditation even more dramatically by imagining retributive murder, what I am calling via Baldwin "cool fratricide," as powerful enough to produce a divine conflict—theomachy—between the joined Black and Indigenous "dark gods" of the Earth colluding against the white gods of Europe. Baldwin fleetingly imagines the continental discovery and connection of Africa and the Americas, Blackness and Indianness—through slavery and conquest—as ethical justifications for a cool and effortless murder of white life and Western metaphysics. *No Name's* apogee indicates that when Black and Indigenous characters kill or imagine killing white characters and representations of whiteness, they sometimes deploy the dual histories of Black slavery and Indigenous genocide as ethical justifications for the use of such violence. However, this double reference in Black and Indigenous literature is hardly ever sustained; it occurs in fits and starts, spurts and sputters, pointing to a powerful accord that cannot be held fully in view because of mediating colonial structures and because of the ethical violence their intimacy might avow.

Using *No Name in the Street* as an opening, this chapter takes the retributive justice and murder implied in "cool fratricide" and the fleeting yet metaphysical connection between Africa and the Americas, Blackness and Indianness, as an invitation to read Black and Native American literature together through their shared dreams of white death and retaliatory violence. I also argue that these representations of violence do not reflect hatred but in fact are an attempt at care both within and between Black and Indigenous communities. As such, I use the murder in "cool fratricide" as a heuristic to do more work than Baldwin might have intended—in ways that might irk him or make him shout, "Oh, pioneers!"[2] I use literary representations of vengeance to connect and read Black and Native American literature together, to read Blackness and Indianness as entangled, through their shared depiction of retributive violence against whiteness—even in moments where they do not (over)represent their connection. I extend Baldwin's work to Native American literature because he indicates that it is the combined efforts of the dark gods of Africa and the Americas that will wage metaphysical war—theomachy—against the white gods of Europe. At such an angle, we can see, as Frank Wilderson says, a "network of connections, transfers, and displacements between a genocided thing and a fungible and accumulated thing."[3] In this, the "dark gods" are not metaphysically coherent, but stress the abject nonbeing of Black and Indian life-in-death that enables the (white) world.

Particularly, I apply this heuristic to read Leslie Marmon Silko's 1974 short story "Tony's Story" and Audre Lorde's 1978 poem "Power" to argue that Silko's and Lorde's rendition of murder suggest that when Black and Native people are killed and targeted with impunity, that this "rendition of fratricide," as a retributive response, first, asks metaphysical and ethical questions about the nature of life itself (what does it mean to live in the afterlives of slavery and conquest) and, second, points to the paradigmatic intimacy between Blackness and Indianness. This intimacy reflects the global and metaphysical structures of Black slavery and Native conquest.

Metaphysics

Two of Baldwin's contemporaries, Audre Lorde and Leslie Marmon Silko, offer similar imaginings of cool and ethical murder tied to metaphysics. After being repeatedly harassed by a white state trooper, the Indian narrator of Leslie Marmon Silko's 1974 short story "Tony's Story" says to his friend, "'We've got to kill it Leon. We must burn the body to be sure. . . . Don't worry, everything is O.K. now, Leon. It's killed. Sometimes they take on strange forms.'"[4] Similarly, the Black mother that narrates Audre Lorde's 1978 poem "Power" concludes the poem by contemplating murder: "and one day I will take my teenaged plug / raping an 85 year old white woman / who is somebody's mother / and as I beat her senseless and set a torch to her bed / a greek chorus will be singing in 3/4 time / 'Poor thing. She never hurt a soul. What beasts they are.'"[5]

In "Power," Lorde poeticizes the all too familiar story of the Black Mother who makes ready the grave of her dead son, taken by the *Police* as a trace of chattel slavery and anti-Blackness. The narrating voice of the Black Mother chronicles the murder of her child, her trauma, and the trial of the acquitted officer who kills him. She then offers a riposte, a musing, on the abject powers and poetics endemic to the Black woman's condition by murdering an elderly white woman. Silko's "Tony's Story" tells of two Laguna Pueblo young men, Tony and Leon, who are endlessly perused by a "Big Cop" as the contemporary faith and practice of settler conquest. Tony dreams the conflict as a metaphysical clash in the destroyed vernacular of Indigenous lifeworlds, and uses murder to question the Indian's abjection. As the old Silko adage goes, Tony has to invent ceremony in its absence; and like many of Silko's other stories, murder and violence enter as central action and concept in Indigenous ceremony and politics against a marauding white world.

Lorde's poem and Silko's short story, as objects, express the centrality of murder in Black and Native living and literature. Both recount real world events: the actual death of a ten-year-old Black boy at the hands of a police officer in Queens, New York City, in 1973,[6] and the murder of a state trooper by two Native men on an Acoma reservation in 1952.[7] While driving, Lorde hears the verdict of the case over the radio—the officer was not indicted by the grand jury. She pulls over and pens "Power" with murder as the inspiration and structure of the poem.[8] "Tony's Story" is Silko's rewriting of Simon Ortiz's rendition of a popular story of a true event of a reservation killing. Murder is magnified as essential to the structure of Indigenous life in its constant refraction and repetition as narrative opening that blurs the distinction between the violence represented in literature and the literary violence of the real. This is why both Silko and Saidiya Hartman indicate that the most pernicious violence against Black and Indigenous life is their transformation into literary metaphor and device.[9]

Murder's constancy in Black and Native living is the impetus for the writing of both texts, the opening of Black and Native narrative (im)possibility. But this merely reflects that the murders inherent in slavery and conquest do not only reflect historical phenomenon generally. Rather, in their global scope, material intensities, and the continued life of their conceptual categories, slavery and conquest can be said to aspire to metaphysics in their repetition in Black and Indian daily life. Black slavery and Indigenous conquest narrativize the emergence of globe, planet, world, our first order of *nomos*.[10] It is through the terms of slavery and conquest that international law becomes constituted as a global phenomenon and defines white life as "*Homo religious*,"[11] producing race as a "meta-cosmic narrative."[12] In stories where Black and Native characters murder white life, we see explicitly the conjunction between colonial movements and cosmological mapping, where the secular sciences and their racial and colonial conceptions begin to articulate metaphysical principle in defining life, planet, and universe on white Euro-American terms. An attempt to map the Black and Indigenous body, then, is also an attempt to map geography, to map globe, to map the cosmos.[13]

In Lorde's poem the white officer who kills a ten-year-old Black boy seems to inhabit a transcendental space unresponsive to the evidence and truth that the law holds as sacrosanct: "The policeman who shot down a 10-year-old in Queens / stood over the boy with his cop shoes in childish blood / and a voice said "Die you little motherfucker"/ and there are tapes to prove that."[14] When the officer shoots, the poem separates his action from the voice that issues the command of the boy's death—it is described as "a voice." The voice follows the action of the shooting as the philosophy attempting to justify the act already committed. The disjoint between the officer's performance of the murder and the issue of its command—"Die you little motherfucker"— cultivates a metaphysical abstraction that separates the world of signs and symbols from the officer's corporal existence. He leaves his body behind toward a pure abstraction of voice that represents the divine command of the law. The command of the boy's death, then, seems to be divinely sanctioned. It comes from nowhere and nothing in particular, sanctioned as a transcendental fact that the officer executes without question and as the immanent performance of white being.

The poem's abstraction of the officer's voice aspires to universality, collectivity, and singularity. And in the poem there are three groups that represent this collective-singularity: the *Police* officer who kills the boy, the jury that acquits him, and the Greek chorus that mourns the old white woman's death. All three are immanent with the murder's arrival, and rather than offering a lament at the boy's death, they offer approval. The poem concludes with the chorus because it represents a matrix of Western religious, social, and aesthetic sentiments that confer the "pleasures of community."[15] The chorus figures as literary tradition and frame, as the development of narrative and literature as mythological locus, and as the (un)consciousness of Western universalism and humanism. The accord between these collectives—and the Greek chorus's mourning in particular—evidences the immutability of Black suffering, and an ironic and satiric sting that mocks the supposition of white ignorance and innocence. The law, rather than thwarting Black and Native death, conspires to actualize its occurrence through murder's narrative power of becoming.

The violence that the Black Mother experiences is compounded by the twelfth juror, a Black woman, whose body is transformed into a tool against Black life itself. The poem says that the law alters "the first real power she ever had / and lined her own womb with cement / to make a graveyard for our children."[16] These lines indicate that the power the law confers to the Black body, under its own institutional auspice and whim, ascribes Black agency as criminality, and performs what Anthony Farley calls "the perfection of slavery."[17] Here, freedom-conferred *is* a manifestation of an enslaving and colonizing will.[18] This produces in constant repetition and transformation the ungendering of the Black body by the law, anti-Blackness, and sexual violence. The trauma of slavery's isolation, its rupture of cosmological location, repeats as generational mark, as "the stamp of the commodity haunts the maternal line and is transferred from one generation to the next."[19] But to line the Black Mother's womb with cement, of course, is not only to foreclose heterosexual reproductive capacity—since life, "reproduction," and heterosexuality, for the slave, is not guaranteed—but any condition of transformation and repetition inherent in life itself. The rape of the old woman indexes this history of sexual violence and attempts to locate the theft of the body, maternity, and life itself. Sexual violence and the 3/4 beats of the chorus is indicative of 3/5 compromises and other practices that in lieu of murdering the Black and Native body seeks to murder/break the spirit—to perform metaphysical excision.

Gendered and sexual violence produce metaphysical death by making the "miracle" of life itself a repeating and mimetic curse. The narrating Mother is forced to inhabit the space of her son's dead body. She is forced to live his death in constant repetition, as the natural conditions of her surroundings. Repetition's gendered and naturalizing function makes violence dreary, and in its tedium retributive violence is her attempt to "make power out of hatred and destruction. / Trying to heal my dying son with kisses / only the sun will bleach his bones quicker."[20] "Destruction" represents the mother's suffering as well as the means of her contemplating her condition in and out of abjection. Nevertheless, the sun that bleaches his bones returns his body to the desert of the Earth. His body and the body of the lamenting Black Mother represents, as Tiffany Jeannette King explains, a "unit of space measurement" that "makes plantation space, populate the plantation space with workers and commodities and order the plantation as a non-Native realm of existence."[21] The poem queries how the Black body is transformed into metaphor, commodity, and geography by locating the disappearance of life as concept, of motherhood as capacity, into the figure and body of an old white woman. I will return to this moment shortly.

In "Tony's Story," metaphysical abstraction comes by way of Tony's use of the destroyed vernacular of Native lifeworlds. Tony inverts the colonial rendering of Indigeneity as malefic other and the Euro-American as benevolent and divine, performing what J. Kameron Carter calls "a decoding of divine discourse."[22] Nevertheless, it is not merely this theological inversion that throws into high relief the metaphysical drama of anti-Black and settler conquest, but rather through the very actions of the Big Cop himself.

In one of Tony and Leon's encounter with the officer, he says, "I don't like smart guys, Indian. It's because of you bastards that I'm here. They transferred me here because of Indians. They thought there wouldn't be as many for me here. But I find them."[23] Indianness is both the question and the answer to a "how" and "why" of the cop's placed existence in a given "here." It is because he targets Indians that the cop is made to move, but it is also because he is made to move that he targets Indians. The cop's transit from an unknown "there" and "then" to a particular "here" and "now" is metonymic of the creation of what Jared Hickman calls "a truly global conception of life—in the double sense of metaphysical coherency and geo-cultural scope . . . world."[24] This tautology moves away from the facticity of the officer's body-in-place toward a cosmic wholeness and imagines Indianness as the "transit" through which a particular relationship to a given geopolitical and metaphysical "here" is made manifest.[25] The Native body becomes a paradigmatic means of apprehending and understanding notions of terrestriality and futurity projected onto/into the infinite recesses of space. This is made even more apparent by the use of the nomenclature produced at the site of the settler encounter with Indian territory to describe modern planetary relationships to outer space. This is also why Jodi Byrd begins her pivotal text, *Transit of Empire,* with the 1769 cosmological mapping of the transit of Venus.[26] The officer's geopolitical tautology aspires to cosmic wholeness and allows him to exist as transcendent principle. And, as such, he projects his essence and presence beyond the facticity of his body to all places and all times; he becomes, in a word, omnipresent. This white omnipresent imagining of futurity and planetary wholeness necessarily demands replaying the trauma of Native dispossession and dismemberment.

When the young men encounter the officer in other parts of the story, they in fact never encounter him at all; what they meet is a feeling. On entering a gas station Tony knows there is something wrong; he says, "I went into the store for some pop. He was inside. I stopped in the doorway and turned around before he saw me, but if he really was what I feared, then he would not need to see me—he already knew we were there. Leon was waiting with the truck engine running almost like he knew what I would say."[27] What is significant about this scene is the tenuousness of the cop's physical presence through which he manifests himself as present even in his absence—the feeling of his presence goes before him. Anti-Black violence and settler conquest, like religion, belongs "to the sphere of psychological emotion, that it essentially has to do with shivers and goose bumps."[28] Even Leon feels the presence of the officer in his readiness upon Tony's exit. What they both feel and fear is the weighty presence of their own murder at the hands of the *Police.*

In the installation of the white Euro-American in all places and all times, as "lords of all the world," and through the material fact of being targeted, Tony and Leon become a cosmological coordinate of Indigenous belonging to be mined and extracted.[29] The officer's abstraction through law and violence is framed in the opening of the story by the San Lorenzo Day festivities. The patron saint of librarians, cooks, and comedians, San Lorenzo functions satirically as a joke that mocks the Christian power of archival and universal singularity and its cannibalistic tendencies in its consumption of Indigenous skins and Black flesh.[30] The Spanish Requerimiento of 1513, the true and unilateral treaty, draws the American Indian into a geopolitical corpus of the globe. Here, in the first instance, violence and conquest is used to facilitate the Native's fictitious end through an imagined production of pure absence and negativity—that is, genocide.[31] The Requerimiento makes possible the English and American treaty as a positive principle that confers sovereignty and makes the Native reappear as a constant metaphor for a false and civil inheritance of land. This fiction assumes metaphysical murder but nevertheless necessitates the Native's constant reappearance as a symbol that transfers Indigenous land and Indigeneity, facilitating the genocidal grafting and supplanting of white Euro-American belonging onto Indigenous space. Although this "paradigmatic Indian," to use Jodi Byrd's term, seems to be ever "disappearing" and "passing away," it imbues the Indian with a countervailing principle of everywhereness that is a kind of nothingness. In the nothing of everywhere anyone and everyone can be made "Indian" or "Native," and, subsequently, no one is.[32] As a result, the Indian is always waiting to be encountered, while it is simultaneously already gone.

In both texts, transcendence and abstraction separates the officers from their bodies to cultivate a metaphysical and universal conception of life as white life. The officers come to represent life itself in the assumed universality of the law and in the assumption of the innocence and ignorance of white people. But the officers' performance of violence indicates that universal abstraction comes by way of the brute and material power of murder, chattel slavery, sexual violence, and settler conquest-occupation. These institutions become metaphysical because they labor to develop a sense of planetary wholeness and a cosmic imagination—as scientific truth and theological essence, as the divine power to create and destroy at will. Law and philosophy, in order to universalize the white body, must deny the tenuous and affective fleshiness of the white body, a tenuousness and hypercorporeality reserved for Blackness and Indianness.

"Power" and "Tony's Story" use murder as a form of retributive justice to wrest the white body from its coveted position of disembodied universalism and point to the fact of its fragility, its materiality, its particularity with literary and punctuated acts of imaginary violence. Testing the boundaries of the equality and balance in white law and civility, these representations of retributive murder attempt to produce what Courtney Baker calls a "justice discursive system" or to "even the keel" by responding to Black and Native death in kind. Murder in these texts cuts the body of the Euro-American, but it cuts his/her metaphysics doubly in tethering it to the body against its universal abstraction by Western philosophy and law.[33] "It is an economy motived not by profit," Baker explains, "but by fair distribution of its reward and gains. Ethical inquiry is the project of identifying these inequalities as systemic injustices and of interrogating more just alternatives."[34] Murder's emphasis on white corporality in "Power" and "Tony's Story" is nothing if not the dissolution of the deification of the Euro-American. We can say that representations of retribution in literature are also a performative attempt at valuing Black and Native life in an anti-Black and settler colonial world.

Murder

Lorde's narrator endeavors to unmake the law by murdering an old white woman who is the manifest performance of the law's fictive innocence and false contrition. But the Black Mother's performance of murder is already assumed by Blackness. Blackness is the condition of the slave "as either will-less object or a [criminal,] chastened agent."[35] The criminality ascribed to the Black woman's body demonstrates the impossibility of calling this encounter between a Black woman's "flesh" and a white woman's body sororicide. This is because the mother's ungendered capacity negates and performs both masculine and feminine inflections of gender. She performs fratricide as a double reference to the impossibility of her intimacy with white women through the language of womanhood and life itself. The attribution of being-as-criminality assumes the murderous eruptions of the Black body as the justification for its subjection. But this ascription is a refusal of "reasonable resistance" as possibility and sanctions Black death in the cultivation of a presumption of "the ignorance and innocence of the white world."[36] The Black Mother's lamentation and the murder of her son assumes criminality and villainy as the immanent character of Black being and politics. The *Police*'s targeting and killing of Black and Indigenous children, in both literature and the real, becomes an anticipatory defense, a preemptory violence, against a possible counterviolence inherent to those bodies themselves—the demon that lurks in perpetuity beneath the dusky surface of Black and Indigenous skin, waiting to kill, murder, massacre, and revolt.

The "nearest socket" that transforms the Mother's energy from potentiality to a murderous kinetics is simultaneously the "desert of raw gunshot wounds" that riddles her son's body. She says, "I am trapped on a desert of raw gunshot wounds / and a dead child dragging his shattered black / face off the edge of my sleep / blood from his punctured cheeks and shoulders / is the only liquid for miles."[37] In the face of the powers of the *Police*, the Black body becomes a "territory of cultural and political maneuver," a cultural and political "unit of space measurement," as Hortense Spillers and King, respectively, explain. Particularly, the Black female body performs this work both materially and metaphorically by peopling the United States as plantation space and non-Native space.[38] The "territoriality" of the Black body endows it with a topological quality; it becomes a porous terrain of violence, registering as desert and deserted. And, yet, despite the inhospitable fact of Black life and the Black body, this desert is nonetheless inhabited. The speaker of the poem is "trapped" here as both the figure of the lamenting mother and as the source of a murdering kinetics of her Black politics. She resides in the broken places of her son's body, inhabiting the openness of his wounds as her location of targeting and her dreaming otherwise.

The poem's transition from the "desert of raw gunshot wounds" to the "whiteness of the desert" facilitates the whitening of space as non-Black, non-Native space—it facilitates a settler colonial function in slavery's spatial logics.[39] Here, anti-Blackness entices as sustenance, the cannibalistic consumption of the Black child's blood as "the only liquid for miles." Anti-Blackness promises redemption by inviting her to consume her son's body, where the world of songs and magic would be readily at hand. But to consume her son's body would "allow her power to run corrupt as poisonous mold." And this the narrator cannot do if she wishes to love her son in death, if she wishes to learn "to make power out of hatred and destruction / trying to heal my dying son with kisses." She must reject the false quenching of her thirst offered by his liquid blood.

Attempting to heal her "dying son with kisses" and to touch the destruction within herself, the narrating Mother murders. This violence mediates between the particular experience of her dirges and her son's death with a concern for life itself under white institutions of power. Her violence draws the white body close to the law and performs the law's self-evident truths of equality by approximating the value of an old white woman to that of a dead Black child. The destruction that the narrator learns is reflected in the tension between her kisses that attempt to rescue her son and the sun that bleaches his bones quicker. From the swiftness of the sun and the deep feeling of her kisses that attempt to heal bullet holes, the Black Mother harnesses the energies of the sun and the wounds of her son's body as the source of an ethical and retributive murder, performing both vengeance and care. Learning to use the abject power within herself, the narrator uses this to effect a transformation of her son's "gunshot wounds" into the "nearest socket" that in turn changes her. She says,

I have not been able to touch the destruction
within me.
But unless I learn to use
the difference between poetry and rhetoric
my power too will run corrupt as poisonous mold
or lie limp and useless as an unconnected wire
and one day I will take my teenaged plug
and connect it to the nearest socket
raping an 85 year old white woman
who is somebody's mother
and as I beat her senseless and set a torch to her bed
a greek chorus will be singing in 3/4 time
"Poor thing. She never hurt a soul. What beasts they are."[40]

Using the power of poetry, she cuts the power of the *Police* in being made to inhabit the space of her dead son's body, the narrator locates her own suffering and her son's materiality as the site of an ethics and aesthetics of care and intimacy that manifests as the murder of white characters. Despite the tensed and frustrated tone of the poem that leads to this moment, the opening line of the murder, "and one day," is indeterminate and nonchalant. This lack of concern with the precise place and time of the deed converts the malice and forethought necessary for murder into a cool connection of energies and possibilities. Rather than reading this scene as a masculinist performance of insertion, I interpret the metaphor of wire, socket, and plug as a performance of connectivity and shared energies, of energies moving and being made to move from potentiality to kinetics, and connecting the narrator with the person whose life she takes and with her dead son. It combines the broken and abject wounds of her dead son, with her own anguish and frustration, the denatured power and violation of the twelfth juror, and transforms these abjected parts into an intimate act of care that manifests as murder.

The nearness of the narrator and the old women points out the absence of such closeness with her own son. The desert sun dries his bones more quickly than her kisses can heal him. The killing intimacy of the sanctified body of the old white woman and the Black Mother's flesh is the inspiration for the Greek chorus and their solicitation of grief, shock, and horror. Line eight of the last stanza of the poem uses maternity to emphasize the violence in the lines that precede and follow it—"raping an 85 year old white woman / who is somebody's mother / and as I beat her senseless and set a torch to her bed."[41] The emphasis on the old woman's maternity promises the fictive universality of motherhood and birth—we all, at least in theory, have mothers. By saying that the elderly woman is someone's mother and by emphasizing her age, the poem appeals to the sentiment, purity, and innocence of white maternity to demonstrate that it is nothing if not the theft of the Black woman's being and capacity to mother. Her son's childhood innocence and her capacity for life and mimetic repetition are stolen by the law and planted here, in the heart and body of the old woman, who, along with the chorus, comes to represent the abstraction of law and its power.

In the Black Mother's act of violence, one can see, as King sees in her study of Black and Native women's literature, "a saturated and leaky image . . . a hybrid flesh-land thing, but I also saw the land being violently and radically altered."[42] In this leaky image, the ebb and flow of energies, in the metaphors of plug, socket, and wire, mimic the ebb and flow of an oceanic feeling. Here, the desert of the poem is also the desert of the sea. The sea becomes desert and deserted because terrestrial life, human life, cannot inhabit its spaces, cannot find grounded sustenance.[43] To paraphrase Spillers, the slave in Middle Passage across the Atlantic exists in the noplace and nonbeing of an oceanic feeling and becomes unmade, an undifferentiated object for the master.[44] The poem's metaphor of kinetic energies reflects the push and pull effect/affect of the "oceanic feeling": immersion and delay, sinking and stillness, lapping movement and stasis. Spillers draws us to the geopolitical space of the Americas and the violent "order, with its human sequence written in blood, [that] represents for its African and Indigenous peoples a scene of actual mutilation, dismemberment, and exile." Spillers's imagining of "flesh" is imagined as the constitutive relation between stolen Africans and America's mutilated Indigenous peoples. "This profound intimacy of interlocking detail" names Indian "skins" as an intimate of Black "flesh," drawing attention to the relation between the genocidal violence that clears away the Native and chattel slavery that steals and plants the Black body in the New World and on the plantation: a genocided object and an enslaved thing.[45]

In this process, the ungendering violence of slavery and conquest present the Black and Indigenous body as elastic metaphors of increase and decrease, imagined as opposing, refracted, and sometimes interchangeable extremes on the horizontal axis of power.[46] As such, the raw desert of gunshot wounds of Lorde's "Power" expresses a paradigmatic and abject intimacy with the drought ravaged Laguna Pueblo desert that opens Silko's short story. Both spaces are desert and deserted; the story begins, "it happened one summer when the sky was wide and hot and the summer rains did not come; the sheep were thin, and the tumbleweeds turned brown and died."[47] The oppressive heat that opens the short story, foreign even to the desert itself, represents the appropriation of the Native land and body—as the philosophical appropriation of context. Tony encounters this heat most powerfully upon his return home after another encounter with the Big Cop. He says, "I didn't feel safe until we turned off the highway and I could see the pueblo and my own house."[48] He describes the heat and emptiness of the village and adds, "The door was open, but there was only silence, and I was afraid that something had happened to them. Then as soon as I opened the screen door the little kids started crying for more Kool-Aid, and my mother said 'no,' and it was noisy again like always."[49] The relief and safety at escaping the reach of the officer, upon sight of home, is short lived. Home's cavernous silence, its unbearable heat, and Tony's fear that "something had happened to them" summarizes Native life against the elimination and genocidal practices of settler conquest.

After this pivotal domestic moment, Tony is reminded of the ability of settler colonialism to transform and inhabit multiple spaces. The brief presence of Tony's mother in the story reframes settler colonial violence "out there" on the highway where the officer lurks to indicate how the officer projects himself into the space of home. As Audra Simpson might explain, Tony's mother's refusal of "no" becomes overburdened with meaning and politics. All at once, it represents the loving and motherly chastising against the synthetic brightness of "more Kool-Aid," the Native woman's resistance against a history of sexual violence implied in progeny, a response to Tony's unasked question about the safety of home, and an anticolonial refusal "in everyday encounters [that] enunciate repeatedly to themselves and to outsiders" a principled resistance to the assumption of the Native's finality.[50] Her refusal produces Tony's realization of the ability of settler colonialism to transform and inhabit multiple spaces and the importance of murder to questioning this ability.

The intimacy between refusal and home imagine home as a nexus of gendered and sexed meaning and performance. Settler colonialism and chattel slavery colonize and map land and body where to map one is to map the other. Such mapping determines the location of one's body in place but also cosmologically in a world of signs and meaning. Leon, Tony, and Tony's mother's gendered meaning reflect the transformation of the Native ungendered body into the object of land through conquest that also metaphysically murders the ground zero of the Native's lifeworld in the transformation of the Native relative of land into material object—a double gesture in the metaphysical murder of body and soul in place.[51] By stealing and conquering land and body, "particularly women's bodies through sexual violence" and by "recreating gendered relationships," settler colonialism secures its hold on Native land and body as a generational phenomenon.[52] The precariousness of home in the story, coupled with his mother's refusal, evidence the gendered matrix of settler colonialism that transforms the Native body into an indigenizing function. The Native body is made a cache of Indigenous belonging that transfers Tony's and Leon's "indigeneity" to the occupying force of the Big Cop.[53]

Eventually Leon seeks protection from the governor of the state, hoping that his service in the military will count as agentive power or phallic currency deserving of protection. However, when it is made clear that the law can provide no succor, Leon offers instead the protection of an "arrowhead on the piece of string." Tony says, "here, wear it around your neck—like mine. See? Just in case . . . for protection." Leon refuses the gift, mocks Tony, and says that all he needs for protection is the ".30–30 leaning against the wall." Tony, however, responds, "you can't be sure that it will kill one of them."[54] Tony registers skepticism not about the bullet's ability to kill the white body but whether or not the bullet can kill the metaphysics of whiteness. He also registers skepticism about Leon's constant dream of masculine power, "I wondered why men who came back from the army were troublemakers on the reservation."[55] And "I couldn't understand why Leon kept talking about 'rights,' because it wasn't rights he was after, but Leon didn't understand that."[56] Tony's relationship to his mother's refusal, his seeming youth and shyness, his inability to speak "much English," his familial memory, his fondness for his friend Leon, improvises an antimasculinist performance of murder that indicates intimacy and feeling as the source of its political maneuver rather than an assertion of phallic agency. Tony indicates that it is not "rights" that the Big Cop wants but Indigenous land and life itself, to possess life and land as objects. In light of this, Tony takes Leon's suggestion that a gun can kill a white man and improvises it by shooting without aiming and intention. He attempts to displace the centrality of masculine power inherent in Leon's imagining of murder by combining it with the broken and abject parts of Native living. Tony shoots because the officer raises his club as if to beat and kill Leon. Here, murder expresses itself as an act of community defense and care.

Leon refuses Tony's gift because he does not think that the broken bits of Indian being and nonbeing can orient his politics. Instead, he appeals to the power of white law and war. His appeal to the state indicates how racial up-lift, sovereignty, and recovery become the most coherent Native American political narratives. However, these narratives necessarily foreclose a politics of abjection, which, in turn, occludes abjection's ontological and material corollary, murder. By a politics of abjection, I mean a wading through and strategic engagement with the conditions and the processes that dehuman-ize and create the social death of the Native—the possibility of inhumanity that pressures and exceeds capacities of being. In literature, a politics of ab-jection murders the potency of the category of the white "human" and when possible the human himself/herself. This politics finds value in colonially dismembered bodies and revels in destruction and the negation of transcen-dence and uplift. Employing such a politics, these characters are careful not to construe this engagement as a desire for subjugation. Tony's attempt to value those around him indicates that Native abjection is not only a site of pathology but also an occasion to lament the violence against the Native and to revel in the destructive forces of violence out of Indianness.[57] Tony finds value in the broken bits and pieces that make up his world. The story's emphasis on heat and Native dissolution offer an aesthetic of negativity that exceeds normative notions of politics and that ultimately concludes in cool and retributive murder.

As settler conquest and chattel slavery sanctifies the white body they si-multaneously cast Indianness and Blackness as its malefic other. Accord-ingly, violence is expected of Tony, assumed as endemic to Indianness. How-ever, he performs this expectation of violence against itself by performing murder effortlessly and without the "malice aforethought" expected in mur-der's legal meaning. Tony shoots without noticing when the officer prepares to beat Leon with a club. He says, "The shot sounded far away and I couldn't remember aiming. But he was motionless on the ground and the bone wand lay near his feet. . . . The head wobbled and swung back and forth and the left hand and the legs left individual trails in the sand. The face was the same. . . . The gas tank exploded and the flames spread along the underbelly of the car. . . . 'Don't worry, everything is O.K. now, Leon. It's killed. They sometimes take on strange forms.'"[58] The raised club of the officer places Tony and Leon's Native (male) bodies in a state of anticipatory anxiety con-cerning the possible violence to be enacted against them but also an anxiety about a smooth and unnamable response of retributive murder. This state of anxiety and tension is what Darieck Scott identifies as "arrested activity, as a trembling, held back by a restraint, on the edge of a new conscious-ness (an inchoate theoretics) that readies itself to direct the body in activity (i.e. revolutionary action)."[59] Despite Tony's recognition of the necessity of murder beforehand, the manner of the murder, Tony's aiming and shooting without knowing and feeling, is performed coolly, calmly.

In a story where the Native body is punctuated by the Big Cop's constant targeting, Tony questions this fact through a kind of anatomization. The moment of the murder is an autopsy that observes the officer's body and its relationship to the surrounding environment and the absolute materiality of death. Tony notices the body's movement in the sand and separates out the parts of his body: feet there, a wobbling head, left hands and legs, an unmoved face. The Euro-American denies this fragile fleshiness of the body by assuming the universality of life as white life, relegating the Black and Indigenous body and land to a hypercorporeality. "This exceedingly cool species of fratricide"—to return to Baldwin's name for such representations of literary, retributive murder—represents a repressed state of political anguish that endeavors to balance the violence experienced by Tony and Native peoples by imagining the body of the officer as equal in value to that of land and the lives of Tony's family and friends.

"Cool fratricide" breaks with the supposition of the Native's extinction because while it does not guarantee "renewed autonomy," it is, as Philip Deloria might explain, "a pocket of stubbornness in the midst of the sweep of the American empire."[60] Tony's aiming and shooting without notice or memory evidences the precarity of Native life as the very articulation of Native politics—it is a stubborn "outbreak" of rebellious questioning.[61] Murder is not triumph but reflects the Indian's perpetual dishonor of defeat in one's own country. In the difference between war and murder, murder assumes the elimination and assimilation of the Native by the power and rule of civil law. Without ground and language, Tony exists in a state of abjection where he must invent and improvise new ceremonies and practices.

Tony shoots the officer without knowing or feeling. By improvising murder, he performs fratricide as a cooling enactment that counteracts the heat that opens the story. The narrative ends when the officer's blood acts as the longed-for quenching of the desert's drought, and when the officer's body is emphasized and punctuated in space. The emphasis on the materiality of the white body and its relationship to dust and dirt refuses its fictive flight into divinity; this moment excises the white body's propriety claim to life itself and returns it to the natural environment. Nature responds to this act in the affirmative by consuming the spilt blood, taking it as offering and salve for Black and Native life in and against death. The natural world of the story responds to the officer's murder by punctuating the ethics of Tony's actions with the sublime formation of "thunder clouds in the west," portending the return of revitalizing waters.

Fire and Metaphysical Transformation

By way of conclusion, the Black Mother burns the bed and body of the old white woman. Tony burns the car and body of the officer. Tony says, "We've got to kill it Leon. We must burn the body to be sure. . . . they sometimes take on strange forms."[62] Using fire's primal energies, both speakers attempt to combat the abstract yet real quality of the *Police* and white violence. Even in murder, Tony cannot be sure that the officer is dead because his metaphysics seems to function independently from his body. The fire that concludes both pieces attempt to perform Baldwin's theomachy. Baldwin's apogee forcefully portends divine war because the text recognizes, as Hartman explains, the impossibility of "fully [redressing] this pained condition without the occurrence of an event of epic and revolutionary proportions . . . the incompleteness of redress is therefore related to the magnitude of the breach . . . and to the inadequacy of the remedy."[63] Fire, continental catastrophe, and divine war conclude these texts as an ethical question pertaining to the unfathomable nature of the crime of chattel slavery and settler conquest and the impossible task of their remedy. The primal energies of fire hedge a bet against the transformative capacity of these institutions and their metaphysics by reducing, and so connecting, white life to its smallest and most abstract material components of dust, dirt, particle, atom, energy, and carbon.

Nevertheless, the magnitude of the crime and its remedy belie the condition by which this unworldly violence is made the stuff of the everyday. Additionally, murder is somewhat a counterintuitive Black and Native tool. Unlike "killing" that assumes no immediate order of politics or "revolt" that abandons the order of the law altogether, murder assumes the law wholeheartedly; it is a crime that belongs within the bounds of the legal codes of civil society. Murder asks questions about slavery and conquest because it cannot unmake the structure of the law in its small and isolated scope.[64] This is why murder asks questions rather than offers a political route because it can only point to the largeness and longevity of settler conquest and chattel slavery rather than attend to it.[65] "Tony's Story" and "Power" ask about the salience of life as material and metaphysical concept in Black and Native living; it asks whether the life of a ten-year-old Black boy is worth less than that of an aged white mother; or whether the life and structure of a belligerent cop is worth more than that of a Native veteran. Both renditions of murder attempt to comprehend the death of self and kin, of life and cosmo-logical placedness in the face of chattel slavery and settler conquest. Such a desire for positive relation is also the same reason Baldwin believes he would pull the trigger in defense of his brother. Black and Native shared dreams of white murder represented in literature symbolize an impossible demand for life itself.

Such coupled invocations bind these two peoples together in a syncretic and metaphysical abjection, a condition of absence and nonbeing that cul-tivates a politics of collusion rather than one of coalition. Coalitional poli-tics are grounded in identitarian recognition and empathic feeling that redounds on the individual without recourse to an analysis of structural or metaphysical violence. A focus on identity dismisses the metaphysical economy of violence between structure and individual feeling that deter-mines intra-minoritarian conflict and the way that groups of people are con-scripted and positioned with and against each other. The consort of chattel slavery and settler conquest as institutions produce Black and Indigenous life as syncretic intimates. I use syncretism not to mean the facile "union of communities" or its linguistic emphasis on merging different inflections. I use the word in relation to an older sense that refers to two communities that "combine against a common [third] enemy."[66] Such a connection points to the way that Blackness and Indianness are often imagined as opposing extremes in a US political and national schema; but, also, how this schema situates them in collusion and combination against a singular and common enemy—the white Euro-American Settler-Master. Syncretism, or a "politics of collusion," emphasizes a shared ethical and nefarious political praxis from positions imagined as frictional in their abjection. Here, the benchmark for political and poetic engagement between Blackness and Indianness need not be the elusive fiction of identity but a political praxis oriented toward the in-evitable and eventual death of Western metaphysics and white domination. This anticipated outcome is the expiration, expropriation, death, uprooting, "by any means necessary," of the Western and white Euro-American's uni-versal definition of life on planet Earth. In dreaming of the end of the white world, these literary representations of retributive murder are in fact repre-sentations of a longing and desire for community safe from violence. Both renditions of murder attempt to comprehend the death of self and kin, of life and cosmological placedness in the face of chattel slavery and settler con-quest. However, the retributive murder in "cool fratricide" also indicates that community and care cannot be a panacea or succor for all wounds; care and community cannot rouse the dead from their dying, cannot always heal the wounds of those who have been lost and broken, but they can, as Wilderson explains, conjure "feelings powerful enough to bring the living to death."[67]

Notes

1 Baldwin, James, *No Name in the Street*, (New York: Vintage Books, 1972), 182–83.

2 Baldwin, *No Name in the Street*, 182–83. As a phrase, Baldwin's "cool species of fratricide" reflects his sardonic self-critique of his own former belief in the necessity of Black and white amelioration. Fratricide satirically mocks the fraternity and brotherhood promised under the law, and is modified by a Black masculine abject performance of "cool." This alchemy of feeling and violence conjures a rendition of murder that performs as an act of intramural Black care without any particular feeling toward white life. The "brother" Baldwin rescues is his brother in Blackness and abjection. Rather than being merely disinterested murder, Baldwin's fratricide cuts the difference between cold and hot blood, between crimes of logic and crimes of passion, refuting Albert Camus's facile split between the two. "Cool fratricide" is interested in feeling because it recognizes that the law and revenge are merely metonyms of one another; and so is interested in feelings only insofar as they point to a feeling of ethics. Feelings of retribution and vengeance is the essence of the law distilled to its most basic parts. "Cool fratricide" seeks to demystify the law by indicating that feeling is the source and structure of international law.

3 Frank B. Wilderson III, *Red, White & Black: Cinema and the Structure of U.S. Antagonisms* (Durham, NC: Duke University Press, 2010), 182.

4 Leslie Marmon Silko, "Tony's Story," in *Storyteller* (New York: Arcade, 1981), 128–29.

5 Audre Lorde, "Power," in *The Black Unicorn: Poems* (New York: W. W. Norton, 1978), 108–9.

6 Jim Dwyer, "A Police Shot to a Boy's Back in Queens, Echoing since 1973," *New York Times*, April 16, 2015. https://www.nytimes.com/2015/04/17/nyregion/fired-at-queens-boy-fatal-1973-police-shot-still-reverberates.html.

7 Lawrence J. Evers, "The Killing of a New Mexican State Trooper: Ways of Telling an Historical Event," in *The Study of Native American Literature: An Introduction*, ed. Andrew Wiget (Boston: Hall, 1985), 18.

8 Lexi Rudnitsky, "The 'Power' and 'Sequelae' of Audre Lorde's Syntactical Strategies," *Callaloo* 26, no. 2 (Spring 2003): 473–85.

9 Leslie Marmon Silko, "An Old Time Indian Attack in Two Parts," 212–13, in *Nothing but the Truth: An Anthology of Native American Literature*, ed. John Lloyd Purdy and James Ruppert (Upper Saddle River, NJ: Prentice-Hall, 2001); Hartman, *Scenes of Subjection*, 7.

10 Jodi Byrd, "Mind the Gap: Indigenous Sovereignty and the Antinomies of Empire," in *Anomie of the Earth*: *Philosophy Politics and Autonomy in Europe and the Americas* (Durham: Duke University Press, 2015), 120–22; Carl

Schmitt, *Nomos of the Earth in International Law of the Jus Publicum Europaeum*, trans. G. L. Ulmen (New York: Telos Pres, 2003), 4.

11 J. K. Carter, "Paratheological Blackness," *South Atlantic Quarterly* 112, no. 4
(2013): 597.

12 Jared Hickman, "Globalization and the Gods," *Early American Literature* 45,
no. 1 (2010): 154.

13 Byrd, Jodi, *Transit of Empire: Indigenous Critiques of Colonialism* (Minneapolis: Minnesota Press. 2011), xx–xxi.

14 Lorde, "Power," 108–9.

15 Joshua Billings, Felix Budelmann, and Fiona Macintosh, *Choruses, Ancient
and Modern* (Oxford: Oxford University Press, 2013), 1–2. In their study, they
explain that for the Greeks, "To be without choral experience was not only
to be uneducated, but to be cut off from a major form of social interaction of
religious worship and of aesthetic pleasure. . . . To take part in a chorus was to
be embedded in a social texture and to have a share in the pleasures of community" (1–2).

16 Lorde, "Power," 108–9.

17 Saidiya V. Hartman, *Scenes of Subjection: Terror, Slavery, and Self-Making
in Nineteenth-Century America* (New York: Oxford University Press, 1997),
80–81; Anthony Patrick Farley, "Perfecting Slavery," *Loyola University Chicago
Law Journal* 36 (2005): 221–51.

18 Farley, "Perfecting Slavery," 102.

19 Saidiya V. Hartman, *Lose Your Mother: A Journey along the Atlantic Slave
Route* (New York: Farrar, Straus and Giroux. 2007), 80.

20 Lorde, "Power," 108–9.

21 Tiffany Jeannette King, "In the Clearing: Black Female Bodies, Space, and Settler Colonial Landscapes," PhD diss., University of Maryland, College Park,
44.

22 Carter, "Paratheological Blackness," 599.

23 Silko, "Tony's Story," 125.

24 Hickman, "Globalization and the Gods," 151.

25 Byrd, *Transit of Empire*, xx–xxi.

26 Byrd, *Transit of Empire*, xx–xxi.

27 Silko, "Tony's Story," 125.

28 Giorgio Agamben, *Homo Sacer: Sovereign Power and Bare Life*, trans. Daniel
Heller-Roazen (Stanford: Stanford University Press, 1998), 78–80.

29 Anthony Pagden, *Lords of All the World: Ideologies of Empire in Spain, Britain,
and France c. 1500–c. 1800* (New Haven, CT: Yale University Press), 5.

30 Maria Herrera-Sobek, *Celebrating Latino Folklore: An Encyclopedia of Cultural Traditions* (Santa Barbara, CA: ABC-CLIO, 2012), 1017.

31 Daniel Castro, *Another Face of Empire: Bartolome De Las Casas, Indigenous
Rights, and Ecclesiastical Imperialism* (Durham, NC: Duke University Press,
2007), 61.

32 Byrd, *Transit of Empire*, xxxv.

33 Fred Moten, *In the Break: The Aesthetics of the Black Radical Tradition* (Minneapolis: University of Minnesota Press, 2003), 1–2.

34 Courtney Baker, "The Grift of Death? The Ethics of Murder Narratives," *Parallax* 22, no. 1 (2016): 52.

35 Hartman, *Scenes of Subjection*, 80.

36 Hartman, *Lose Your Mother*, 169.

37 Lorde, "Power," 108–9.

38 King, "In the Clearing," 44; Hortense J. Spillers, "Mama's Baby, Papa's Maybe: An American Grammar Book," *Diacritics* 17, no. 2 (1987): 67.

39 King, "In the Clearing," 44. King is important here because she argues that the Black female body is a site of Native and Black interaction because the power that the settler exerts over geographic space—through Indian geno-cide—is intimately tied to the power exerted over Black women's bodies. For King, Black women's bodies make "plantation space, populate the plantation space with workers and commodities and order the plantation as non-Native realm of existence."

40 Lorde, "Power," 108–9.

41 Lorde, "Power," 108–9.

42 King, "In the Clearing," 48.

43 Gilles Deleuze, *Desert Islands and Other Texts: 1953–1974*, trans. David Lapou-jade and Michael Taormina (Los Angeles: Semiotext(e), 2004), 11.

44 Spillers, "Mama's Baby," 67. It is interesting to note, then, that Sigmund Freud's notion of the "oceanic feeling," though brief, excludes the caesura that is so vital to oceanic space and time. In this respect, Freud's definition of the "oceanic feeling" is incomplete. To say that the oceanic and Blackness have as their ontological referent a cutting or a mutilation is to identify the inher-ent contradictions central to these spaces, positions, and beings. To identify Blackness is to identify the contradiction of the human-as-object. Likewise, to come to know the ocean, on its own terms, is to know death in the scien-tific birthplace of life. Freud describes the "oceanic feeling" as "a sensation of 'eternity,' a feeling as of something limitless, unbounded—as it were, 'oce-anic'" (Sigmund Freud, *Civilization and Its Discontent,* trans. James Strachey [New York: Norton, 1930], 7–8). However, what Freud fails to point out is that the unbound nature of the oceanic forestalls any possible referent. The oceanic feeling, then, and by extension Blackness, is not simply a sensation of something limitless or unbound, it is also the sensation of foreclosure, delay, and stasis.

45 Spillers, "Mama's Baby," 67; Wilderson, *Red, White & Black*, 182.

46 Byrd, *Transit of Empire*, 12; Alexander G. Weheliye, *Habeas Viscus: Racial-izing Assemblages, Biopolitics, and Black Feminist Theories of the Human* (Durham, NC: Duke University Press, 2015), 1. Taken together, "blood quantum" and "the one drop rule" form a matrix of blood in the hypo-descent slave law of *partus sequitur ventrem* in 1662 and the Indian "hy-perdescent" slave law in 1705 Virginia that introduces the explicit practice

of blood quantum (Saidiya Hartman, "The Belly of the World: A Note on Black Women's Labors," *Souls* 18, no. 1 [2016]: 166). In his 2000 article "Blood Quantum: A Relic of Racism and Termination," Jack D. Forbes explains, "Many Native People have gotten so used to the idea of 'blood quantum' (degree of 'blood') that sometimes the origin of this racist concept is forgotten. Its use started in 1705 when the colony of Virginia adopted a series of laws which denied civil rights to any 'negro, mulatto, or Indian' and which defined the above terms by stating that 'the child of an Indian, and the child, grandchild, or great grandchild of a negro shall be deemed accounted, held, and taken to be a mulatto'" (http://boitano.net/history/native-american/genocide/Jack%20D_%20Forbes%20-%20Blood%20Quantum%20A%20Relic%20Of%20Racism%20And%20Termination.htm). Arica L. Coleman, in her study *That the Blood Stay Pure: African Americans, Native Americans, and the Predicament of Race and Identity in Virginia* (Bloomington: Indiana University Press, 2013), explains further: "Applied within the context of Virginia, people of mixed-race ancestry came to be defined by degree of 'blood' with the advent of the definition of mulatto in 1705. Within this context, ancestry based on the concept of degree of admixture was used as a means to exclude mixed-race people from the privileges of White-ness, of which the most salient pertained to land rights. White settlers, determined to wrestle every square inch of land away from American Indians, made numerous attempts to rob Indigenous populations of their reservations by using the language of blood and admixture to reclassify American Indians from aborigines to free Negroes" (82).

47 Silko, "Tony's Story," 123.

48 Silko, "Tony's Story," 127.

49 Silko, "Tony's Story," 126–27.

50 Audra Simpson, *Mohawk Interruptus: Political Life across the Borders of Settler States* (Durham, NC: Duke University Press, 2014), 105.

51 Sarah Deer, *The Beginning and End of Rape: Confronting Sexual Violence in Native America* (Minneapolis: University of Minnesota Press, 2015), xv; Mishuana Goemen, *Mark My Words: Native Women Mapping Our Nations* (Minneapolis: University of Minnesota Press, 2013), 33.

52 Goeman, *Mark My Words*, 33.

53 Philip Joseph Deloria, *Indians in Unexpected Places* (Lawrence: University Press of Kansas, 2004), 21.

54 Silko, "Tony's Story," 127.

55 Silko, "Tony's Story," 125.

56 Silko, "Tony's Story," 127.

57 Julia Kristeva, *Powers of Horror: An Essay on Abjection* (New York City: Columbia University Press 1984), 1. Kristeva explains that "there looms, within abjection, one of those violent, dark revolts of being, directed against a threat that seems to emanate from an exorbitant outside or inside, ejected beyond the scope of the possible, the tolerable, the thinkable. It lies there, quite close, but it cannot be assimilated" (1).

58 Silko, "Tony's Story," 108–9.

59 Darieck Scott, *Extravagant Abjection: Blackness, Power, and Sexuality in the African American Literary Imagination* (New York: New York University Press, 2010), 64.

60 Deloria, *Indians in Unexpected Places* 20–21.

61 Deloria, *Indians in Unexpected Places*, 20–21, 36.

62 Silko, "Tony's Story," 128.

63 Hartman, *Scenes of Subjection*, 77.

64 For me, my argument here, the revolutionary activity of murder is insular and short lived because it orients itself toward singularity and the concept of the individual inherent in the concept of murder itself. When retributive murder is made to disassociate from its emphasis on the individual through improvised and simultaneous occurrence—and particularly through the simultaneous imagining and occurrence of Black and Native dreams of white death—it unbecomes murder altogether and becomes an ethic and revolutionary stirring inherent to the creative force of nature and life. Put more simply, anticolonial murder becomes truly revolutionary only when it occurs in aggregate and as defense.

65 Patrice Douglass and Frank B. Wilderson, "The Violence of Presence," *Black Scholar* 43, no. 4 (2013): 121; Frantz Fanon, *The Wretched of the Earth*, trans. Richard Philcox, commentary by Jean-Paul Sartre and Homi K. Bhabha (New York: Grove [1963] 2004), 12.

66 OED, Syncretism: Etymology: < modern Latin *syncrētismus* (D. Pareus, 1615), < Greek συγκρητισμός , < συγκρητίζειν to syncretize *v.* Compare French *syncrétisme*, "the joining, or agreement, of two enemies against a third person." http://www.oed.com.turing.library.northwestern.edu/view/Entry/196428 ?redirectedFrom=syncretism#eid. "reconciliation of different beliefs," 1610s, from French syncrétisme (17c.) and directly from Modern Latin syncretismus (used by German Protestant theologian David Pareus, 1615), from Greek synkretismos "union of communities," from synkretizein "to combine against a common enemy," from syn- "together" (see syn-) + second element of uncertain origin. One theory connects it with kretismos "lying," from kretizein "to lie like a Cretan;" another connects it with the stem of kerannynai "to mix, blend;" krasis "mixture." Related: Syncretist; syncretistic. http://www.etymonline.com/index.php?term=syncretism.

67 Wilderson, *Red, White & Black*, 142.

References

Agamben, Giorgio. 1998. *Homo Sacer: Sovereign Power and Bare Life*. Translated by Daniel Heller-Roazen. Stanford: Stanford University Press.

Baker, Courtney. 2016. "The Grift of Death? The Ethics of Murder Narratives." *Parallax* 22, no. 1: 51–65.

Baldwin, James. 1972. *No Name in the Street*. New York: Vintage.

Billings, Joshua, Felix Budelmann, and Fiona Macintosh. 2013. *Choruses, Ancient and Modern*. Oxford: Oxford University Press.

Byrd, Jodi. 2011. *Transit of Empire: Indigenous Critiques of Colonialism*. Minneapolis: University of Minnesota Press.

Byrd, Jodi. 2015. "Mind the Gap: Indigenous Sovereignty and the Antinomies of Empire." In *Anomie of the Earth: Philosophy Politics and Autonomy in Europe and the Americas*, edited by Federico Luisetti, John Pickles, and Wilson Kaiser. Durham, NC: Duke University Press.

Carter, J. K. 2013. "Paratheological Blackness." *South Atlantic Quarterly* 112, no. 4: 589–611.

Castro, Daniel. 2007. *Another Face of Empire: Bartolome De Las Casas, Indigenous Rights, and Ecclesiastical Imperialism*. Durham, NC: Duke University Press.

Coleman, Arica L. 2013. *That the Blood Stay Pure: African Americans, Native Americans, and the Predicament of Race and Identity in Virginia*. Bloomington: Indiana University Press.

Deer, Sarah. 2015. *The Beginning and End of Rape: Confronting Sexual Violence in Native America*. Minneapolis: University of Minnesota Press.

Deleuze, Gilles. 2004. *Desert Islands and Other Texts: 1953–1974*. Translated by David Lapoujade and Michael Taormina. Los Angeles: Semiotext(e).

Deloria, Philip Joseph. 2004. *Indians in Unexpected Places*. Lawrence: University Press of Kansas.

Douglass, Patrice, and Frank Wilderson. 2013. "The Violence of Presence." *Black Scholar* 43, no. 4: 117–23.

Dwyer, Jim. 2015. "A Police Shot to a Boy's Back in Queens, Echoing since 1973." *New York Times*, April 16. https://www.nytimes.com/2015/04/17/nyregion /fired-at-queens-boy-fatal-1973-police-shot-still-reverberates.html.

Evers, Lawrence J. 1985. "The Killing of a New Mexican State Trooper: Ways of Telling an Historical Event." In *The Study of Native American Literature: An Introduction*, edited by Andrew Wiget. Boston: Hall.

Fanon, Frantz. [1963] 2004. *The Wretched of the Earth*. Translated by Richard Philcox, with commentary by Jean-Paul Sartre and Homi K. Bhabha. New York: Grove Press.

Farley, Anthony Patrick. 2005. "Perfecting Slavery." *Loyola University Chicago Law Journal* 36: 221–51.

Fitz, Brewster E. 2003. "Undermining Narrative Stereotypes in Simon Ortiz's 'The Killing of a State Cop.'" *MELUS* 28, no. 2: 105–20.

Freud, Sigmund. 1930. *Civilization and Its Discontent*. Translated by James Strachey. New York: W. W. Norton & Company.

Goeman, Mishuana. 2013. *Mark My Words: Native Women Mapping Our Nations*. Minneapolis: University of Minnesota Press.

Hartman, Saidiya V. 1997. *Scenes of Subjection: Terror, Slavery, and Self-Making in Nineteenth-Century America*. New York: Oxford University Press.

Hartman, Saidiya V. 2007. *Lose Your Mother: A Journey along the Atlantic Slave Route*. New York: Farrar, Straus and Giroux.

Hartman, Saidiya. 2016. "The Belly of the World: A Note on Black Women's Labors." *Souls* 18, no. 1: 166–73.

Herrera-Sobek, Maria. 2012. *Celebrating Latino Folklore: An Encyclopedia of Cultural Traditions*. Santa Barbara, CA: ABC-CLIO.

Hickman, Jared. 2010. "Globalization and the Gods, or the Political Theology of 'Race.'" *Early American Literature* 45, no. 1: 145–82.

Jaskoski, Helen. 1999. "To Tell a Good Story." In *Leslie Marmon Silko: A Collection of Critical Essays*, edited by Louise K. Barnett and James L. Thorson. Albuquerque: University of New Mexico Press.

King, Tiffany Jeannette. 2013. "In the Clearing: Black Female Bodies, Space, and Settler Colonial Landscapes." PhD diss., University of Maryland, College Park.

Kristeva, Julia. 1984. *Powers of Horror: An Essay on Abjection*. New York City: Columbia University Press.

Lorde, Audre. 1978. *The Black Unicorn: Poems*. New York: W. W. Norton.

Moten, Fred. 2003. *In the Break: The Aesthetics of the Black Radical Tradition*. Minneapolis: University of Minnesota Press.

Pagden, Anthony. 1995. *Lords of All the World: Ideologies of Empire in Spain, Britain, and France c. 1500–c. 1800*. New Haven, CT: Yale University Press.

Rudnitsky, Lexi. 2003. "The 'Power' and 'Sequelae' of Audre Lorde's Syntactical Strategies." *Callaloo* 26, no. 2 (Spring): 473–85.

Schmitt, Carl. 2003. *Nomos of the Earth in International Law of the Jus Publicum Europaeum*. Translated by G. L. Ulmen. New York: Telos Press.

Scott, Darieck. 2010. *Extravagant Abjection: Blackness, Power, and Sexuality in the African American Literary Imagination*. New York: New York University Press.

Silko, Leslie Marmon. [1974] 1981. "Tony's Story." In *Storyteller*. New York: Arcade.

Silko, Leslie Marmon. 2001. "An Old Time Indian Attack in Two Parts." In *Nothing but the Truth: An Anthology of Native American Literature*, edited by John Lloyd Purdy and James Ruppert. Upper Saddle River, NJ: Prentice-Hall.

Simpson, Audra. 2014. *Mohawk Interruptus: Political Life across the Borders of Settler States*. Durham, NC: Duke University Press.

Spillers, Hortense J. 1987. "Mama's Baby, Papa's Maybe: An American Grammar Book." *Diacritics* 17, no. 2: 64–81.

Weheliye, Alexander G. 2015. *Habeas Viscus: Racializing Assemblages, Biopolitics, and Black Feminist Theories of the Human*. Durham, NC: Duke University Press.

Wilderson, Frank B., III 2010. *Red, White & Black: Cinema and the Structure of U.S. Antagonisms*. Durham, NC: Duke University Press.

Wynter, Sylvia. 2003. "Unsettling the Coloniality of Being/Power/Truth/Freedom: Towards the Human, after Man, Its Overrepresentation—an Argument." *CR: The New Centennial Review* 3, no. 3: 257–337.

CHAPTER EIGHT

J. Kameron Carter

Other Worlds, Nowhere
(or, The Sacred Otherwise)

in memory of Charles H. Long,
friend, late mentor, and theorist of black religion

Listen, you, I was creating a life study of a
monumental first person, a Brahmin first
person.
If you need to feel that way—still you are in here
and here is nowhere.
Join me down here in nowhere.
—Claudia Rankine, *Citizen: An American Lyric*

so perhaps ritual provides a way through the thicket of impossi-
bles . . . / I am committed to retaining an ambivalence of the sacred
object
—M. NourbeSe Philip, "Wor(l)ds Interrupted"

Otherwise Worlds

This chapter engages the notion of "otherwise worlds," a phrase gifted to us by
Ashon Crawley. It is a phrase that as I think about it, and much like the notion
of "the undercommons" as I think about that phrase too,[1] functions less as a
place and more as a practice—indeed, as I argue here and elsewhere—as
a kind of "malpractice."[2] It functions less as a zone of address, and thus less
as a somewhere and more, if we stay in the shade that poet Claudia Rankine
provides, as a *nowhere* where resides what Fred Moten, commenting on
this very Rankine passage, speaks of as "the trace of a *we* that comes before
[the address]," and even before "the common and vulnerable collectivity the
address calls into existence."[3] Anterior to interpellation and announced at

the moment of its failed annunciation, *nowhere* bespeaks "a strange dream, a strange reverie," Rankine goes on to say, "a strange beach" that "if you let in the excess emotion you will recall the Atlantic Ocean breaking on our heads"[4] down here . . . in the hold . . . *nowhere* . . . before and beyond and at the end of this world. Astrophysically, quantum physically, perhaps meta-physically but in the end simply and ultimately physically or materially no-where potentiates as an alternative imagination of matter everywhere.

In racial capitalism's creases and folds, nowhere is the alternative, an open set of practices carried out agonistically by those *no-bodies* who augment and thereby are a turbulence within the terms of order.[5] Let's be clear: the alternative is already happening. Always has been. For nowhere points to blackness's queerness, to its liminal, monstrous, occultic, poetic strangeness. That strange nowhereness has to do with nowhere's spacetime coordinates as "not-in-between" (more on this in a moment) the oppositional heirarchies that anchor racial capitalism's consumptive violence. One such opposition, the one I target in what follows, is that between the profane and the sacred. This statically conceived opposition has powered the very production, in the factories that were Elmina Castle, and slave ships that were auction blocks and plantations, of racial blackness as fetish object, as propertied, suppos-edly deanimated matter or thing. I hold to matter's persistent animation, to the interinanimation, that makes endurance through capitalism's processes of deanimation for the sake of commodification possible.

What is required to think (black) matter's enduring liveliness, its ani-mated endurance through capitalism as a process of extractive deanimation? This question, along with my ongoing effort to rethink and improvise my way through the semiotics of religious and theological studies at the ensem-blic scene of black study, takes me to some things Moten says in *In the Break* and then more recently in *Black and Blur*.

It is Moten's elaboration in *In the Break* of what he means by "a generative break [within the logically structured, anti-Black World] . . . wherein action becomes possible," that first interests me.[6] Here one hears the insurgency of what in this volume is being thought about not under the rubric of "the World" but in light of what shadows the very idea of the World, namely, "otherwise worlds." Generative break as otherwise action, we are given to understand, is an improvisation through the very idea of World as a logical structure of oppositions and antagonisms. But again, how is this possible? Even more, how might we *think* (which is very different from the question of how might we *know* [as in comprehend]) otherwise worlds? Thinking with Amiri Baraka's improvisation through Martin Heidegger's analytic of

Being and time or Being-unto-death, Moten gives us a clue. He tells us that improvisational action moves past but only because it moves through "normal ontology or time."[7] It does this by virtue of how such action gestures to "the spirit of a totality that is no longer, that has perhaps never been, one." Such action is of "totality's ghost."[8] To think this requires something on the far side of the orientations of pessimism or, for that matter, optimism. It requires "a powerful faith in resurrection, ghosts, spirits, specters, a powerful faith in the possibility of some mystical and therefore totalizing force rising from the abyss . . . You must have faith, in short, in some animus that allows the continual projection of discontinuity, the persistence of a certain structure of life. . . ."[9]

Such faith Moten, more recently in *Black and Blur* and in thinking with C. L. R. James, speaks of as "not-in-between" oppositions, such as the onto-theological opposition between the profane and the sacred, that have powered the anti-Black world.[10] To think appositionally or not-in-between such oppositions is to zero in on what moves dynamically through such oppositions as already exceeding them. This is the concern, as it were, of black faith as black study, which concerns itself with other worlds, nowhere. That is to say, Moten's Jamesian formulation of the not-in-between suggests a pathway by which we might think blackness in its other(wise)worldliness. Black faith here operates gesturally in the religious sense. That is, it operates as a nod to or as "feeling of the numinous" ("das numinous Gefühl . . ."), to borrow from and resituate the important work of historian of religions Rudolf Otto.[11] That gestural nod, or "numen," bespeaks blackness as movement, blackness as dis/orientation, blackness as spirit-possessed dispossession beyond capitalist logics of propertied self-possession. It points to blackness beyond property and thus as non-identical with itself in its non-identity with the notion of an individuated or propertied subject. Here blackness as gesture gestures *das Andere* or Infinity. It signals a mysterious surplus along the lines of a *mysterium tremendum et fascinans*—the mystery that incites both fear and trembling, attraction and repulsion. "Mu" surpasses both modern and postmodern understanding precisely in its promiscuous refusal of scale or to being scaled down to the rational mismeasure of Man.[12] In short, nodding toward the Infinite as signaled in the possibilities of the flesh, blackness gestures toward (and here I one more time annotate Otto through black study) "the Holy Other-wise." Nullifying this world, blackness as numinous nod takes us to *Other Worlds*. Or perhaps even more rigorously put, it takes us *Nowhere*, to the sacred otherwise.

This is what I want to think about in what follows. Indeed, in explicating this, I engage a number of thinkers—from Georges Bataille and Cedric Robinson to Denise Ferreira da Silva, from poets Dawn Lundy Martin to Nathaniel Mackey—though I want to quickly say that most everything I am trying to think about here builds toward a thinking with M. NourbeSe Philip's poem *Zong!*, a text that itself works through what Philip in the above epigraph has called the "ambivalence of the sacred object" as it comes into view in relationship to Black social life and the Middle Passage or the world of racial capital. That ambivalence opens onto the sacred otherwise, a certain malpractice of the sacred, we might say, that itself is what historian of religion Charles H. Long, to whom I have dedicated this chapter, calls the reimagination of matter.[13] It opens onto *Other Worlds. Nowhere.*

Charlottesville, USA

Before getting to *Zong!* allow me to begin to address what I mean by malpractice, and indeed, what I mean by the sacred otherwise. My entry point is a provocatively titled *Washington Post* article sent my way via social media in the immediate aftermath of the white nationalist rally in Charlottesville, Virginia, in August 2017: "U.S. Political Climate Results from 'Theological Malpractice,' D.C. Pastor Says."[14] That phrase—"theological malpractice" adjacent the political—immediately caught my attention.

In the *Post* article the news reporter interviews the pastor of the Metropolitan AME Church of Washington, DC, the Reverend Bill Lamar, who comments that much of the blame for what has happened recently in this country—from the election of a protofascist to the US presidency to the Charlottesville events themselves to the president's response to those events in which he stated an equivalence of blame "on both sides" between white supremacists and the counterprotesters—lays at the feet of many Christians, including many Black Christians. Too many Christians, he says, have abdicated the work of being prophetic and instead have opted for "vague notions of personal salvation" in which Jesus is little more than a heavenly "doorman who opens the portals of eternity." This produces Christians who do "not [give] a damn about the sociopolitical and economic hell which assails many around the world." Rev. Lamar then drops the line from which the *Post* piece gets its title: "What has happened [of late in this country] and what will happen is as much the result of [this] theological malpractice as it is the result of political malpractice."

I want to think with and through this statement, for while I suspect that I share a number of Rev. Lamar's sociopolitical leanings, I nevertheless want to rewrite the terms of his critique and thereby complexify what he seems to be calling for.

Rev. Lamar's comments suggest that the country's fortunes, or, as the case may be, its misfortunes, move in direct relationship to "proper practice" (rather than what he calls "malpractice") in the dual spheres of political rationality and theological rationality. The former we often think as a secular sphere where electoral politics, governance through a system of checks and balances, equality before the law, policies for the "common good," and so forth, take place or are guaranteed. The latter is often thought of as a private domain that considers religion, salvation, and related personal matters of conscience and of the heart. As Rev. Lamar's *Washington Post* comments suggest, these two spheres of the political and the theological offer parallel tracks that contribute to the health and moral well-being of the nation. While Rev. Lamar indicts both spheres of politics and religion, nevertheless the force of his criticism falls decidedly on the so-called private sphere of religion. On asking why this might be the case, it seems the answer lies in the social imaginary Rev. Lamar works with or the picture of society he paints. It is as if, in the picture he paints, the last line of defense to keep the state on the moral straight and narrow, even when or perhaps most especially when political institutions are failing us, is proper theological practice. Religion is our (political) salvation. But what to do when religion does not uphold its societal duty? It is for this reason that Rev. Lamar is keen to call out this particular sphere. "Theological malpractice," or a religious imagination that has abdicated its duty to keep the state on the moral straight and narrow by surrendering to "the sweet bye-and-bye," is as responsible, if not more responsible, for a country gone off the rails than "political malpractice" or the failure of our political institutions.

While I celebrate Rev. Lamar for forcing attention on the dual political and theological operations of our current moment, I want to up the ante: to break from what I see as a limiting presumption within the picture he paints of the Charlottesville incident as expressive of today's general crisis of politicality. This is the presumption of the givenness of the state as the telos of society or the social order. I want to further separate from the way Rev. Lamar perceives the duties of religion insofar as even that perception is a bit captured by the presumption of the givenness of the state as telos of the social. Here, religion does a kind of upholding work, that is, religion's task is to uphold the state, perhaps pushing it toward reform or to make good on its claims to secure freedom for all. But in any case, right or proper theological practice—"orthopraxis" rather than malpractice—moves in close relationship to state order. This presumption of the state as teleological principle of the social, I contend, prevents Rev. Lamar's important critique from going far enough, from perhaps getting to the question of other worlds, nowhere.

It is in the space between the insight Rev. Lamar offers about the twin theo-political operations of the present and the limiting presumption of the state within his yet important account of "what's goin' on" that I want to take initial steps into the concerns of this chapter. More specifically, while in his analysis Rev. Lamar talks about the country's political and theological failings as if they are independent or parallel, and as if all that is needed is better practice in these two spheres working toward a "more perfect union," what he in fact invites is a consideration of how Charlottesville laid bare not a two-track but a singular failure, indeed, a singular terror and violence. This singular terror I name *political theology*. This is the animating problem not just of Charlottesville, Virginia, but of Charlottesville as placeholder for the United States of America. It is the animating problem, shall we say, of "Charlottesville, USA," and so, I will argue shortly, the animating problem of the phenomenon, the closed totality, the enclosure that has come to be called *World*, which I distinguish from the uncloseable, the unsettleable earth.

After an initial consideration in the next section of this chapter ("The Right- and Left-Hand Sacred") to unfold what I mean by the sacred precisely by juxtaposing it with Blackness, I then in the following section ("Political Theology") reframe the Charlottesville incident and the general problem of the political today as nothing less than indexing a general crisis or horror of the sacred that as such points to a general crisis of the violent concept and practice of World. I'm interested in how the notion of the sacred as it comes to be attached to the settler concept of World bespeaks a violent and general horror that, rather than disavowing malpractice, in fact calls for it, a relationship to the earth that exceeds and that is at the end of the (settler's) World and that refuses the very notion of World as an organizing and ordering concept. To dwell in the World's nullification gets close to what I am trying to get at with the idea of malpractice—the malpractice of the sacred or sacred malpractice. What if the malpractice of the sacred, the sacred as released or in flight from the World's enclosure, opens us to the question of otherwise worlds, otherworldly im/possibilities beyond the myth of the World, the mythos of politicality and of racial capitalism? What if malpractice takes us (to) nowhere? I begin to think about this in the "The Right- and Left-Hand Sacred" and "Political Theology" sections even as they serve as a springboard from which I rethink in the remainder the chapter the inherent ambivalence of the notion of the sacred, mobilizing it as a tool for Black thought—that is, as a tool for thinking Blackness precisely as opening up an alternate imaginary of the sacred from which also opens up other worlds, nowhere. Here Blackness indexes sacrality-without-property and without-sovereignty, thus activating other modes of dwelling on and with the earth, other modes of knowing that we might call "abyssal nonknowledge," other socialities or congregationalities that exceed settler politicality. I call this a poetics of the sacred. Stated differently, if in the immediate sections that follow (on "The Right- and Left-Hand Sacred" and "Political Theology") I consider the myth of politicality or political knowledge in which certain energies of the sacred are harnessed to state projects (this is what the Charlottesville white nationalists rallied to defend) to produce a kind of "pure" or neofascist or "right-hand sacred" meant to secure the settler statist homogeneity of (proper) citizenship, then in the rest of this chapter I consider the sacred in its base, heterogeneous, or immanent modalities—that is, the sacred not as grounding figural coherence but as impure or in fugitive, "left-hand" flight, or further still, as a movement or passage or diaspora of spirit that enlivens or animates Blackness precisely in its would-be corpsing. It is with M. NourbeSe Philip's *Zong!* that I aim to put a finer point on this Black radical, which is to say Black maternal or Sycoraxian and monstrous, mode of the sacred—that mode of the sacred that is bound up with the ungivenness of the earth, as bound up with what literary critic Hortense Spillers, adapting Sigmund Freud, sees as earth's "oceanic" condition anterior to sovereign individuation or what in this piece of writing I think about as anterior to sovereignty's genesis of the World; that violent imposition of the World on top of the earth, the imposition of boundaried, ownable place on top of open space.[15] But, first, to the general question of the sacred.

The Right- and Left-Hand Sacred

Building from Émile Durkheim and especially Durkheim's student Robert Hertz, Georges Bataille with Roger Caillois gives us an important initial handle on the sacred in its double-sidedness and as a tool for social theory.[16] In "The Psychological Structure of Fascism," published in 1933, Bataille mobilized a discourse of the sacred to examine what was happening at the time and, crucially, to begin to think toward modes of sociality exceeding onto-politics or politics as we know it.[17] For this, he expands the basic profane/sacred duality that Durkheim bequeathed to French social theory into a distinction between the homogeneous and the heterogeneous. This became for him an analytic framework through which to make sense of fascism. Identified with production, the sphere of the profane or what Bataille called the homogeneous is an exclusively utilitarian realm or a restricted economy of exchange. Conversely, the elements of the sphere of the heterogeneous or what Bataille called the sacred indicate a general economy of an unrestricted expenditure of energy that, though to a point employable and thus "valuable" within a social system to help render the system coherent, even if fragilely so, remains fundamentally excessive, ecstatic, or rapturous.

To borrow a formulation from Caillois, a colleague of Bataille's in a dissident study group that met in the back of a Paris bookstore called the "College of Sociology," we might think of left-hand experiences of the sacred as those in which the sacred is nothing less than the experience of sociality through and as infraction given in "interaffective" excess, given in and as a "collective ecstasy."[18] The sacred here manifests as the experience of innovation and improvisation, what Caillois, in his essay "Brotherhoods, Orders, Secret Societies, Churches," calls an "improvisation of the sacred," that connects with a "mysterious world."[19] For Caillois, such improvisational ecstasy bespeaks a fundamental "metamorphosis of . . . being," an anguished yet joyous dwelling in a kind of blurred communion apart from and in critique of the presumptions of individuation.[20] Akin to Caillois's description of the sacred as that ecstasy that figures as perhaps an anoriginal metamorphosis is what Bataille, with Angela of Foligno, an Italian medieval mystic, figures as a sort of fecund, negative space, but that with Denise Ferreira da Silva I prefer to think of not in terms of negation but of nullification and thus as a zone of "[abyssal] possibilities . . . where the possible is the impossible itself" and in which "ecstatic, breathless *experience* . . . destroys the depths . . . of being by unveiling" a nonpossessable, a nonsubjective zone irreducible to property and thus irreducible to propertied subjectivity.[21] If Bataille would eventually devote an entire book-length study to such "inner experience," where "inner" here is not the interiority of an enclosed, supposedly coherent, individuated self or subject, Caillois would take it up in an essay called "Festivals" that he first presented as a talk to the dissident College of Sociology study group. There he considers the collective effervescence and eruption that characterized ancient festivals and feasts and whose vestiges one finds, he argues, in contemporary carnivals and such. Such festival events of "yesteryear and today," he says, are "always defined by dancing, singing, excitement, excessive eating and drinking. It is necessary to go all out to the point of exhaustion, to the point of sickness. That is the very law of the festival."[22] Here profane or chronological temporality or the time of Man and his Others is disrupted in the name of dwelling in some other experience of temporality beyond the logic of separability. To dwell in the space-time of "difference without separability" is to dwell in the experience of being out of time, of dwelling in time-out, in out-time. It is to be unhistorical, somehow somewhere else. Off beat, nowhere.[23] Such is Caillois's description of "experience," where experience here indicates a condition of *ek-stasis*, a standing in a kind of out-ness. This is a condition of being dispossessed of a self, which is a condition of possession anterior to property, anterior to propertied self-possession, indeed, anterior to a self. A condition perhaps of spirit possession, this socio-ecstasy is given in the ferment of the festival, where the sacred manifests as a sociality of infraction against "taboos" and "rules" meant to ensure propriety and comportment[24]—a tabooed sociality that in the rapture of the festival is nonboundaried and thus nontabooed in the first place. In raptured ecstasy, the element of the heterogeneous fractures onto-politicality. Indeed, it fractures the human, in the face of what the onto-political and/as the onto-theological (i.e., the right-hand sacred, or the sacred reduced to regulation or doctrinal, semiotic, juris-prudential, and political ordering) cannot hold.

The unholdable, the unhaveable—notwithstanding that the juridical-economic order seeks to seize and thus reduce the unhaveable to what's ownable or to property—is in fact uncapturable; it will not fully, if I might invoke Beyoncé, "get in formation." Indexing another horizon of existence (where again, *ex*-istence is necessarily *ek*-static, and thus, we might say, "is-not"), the energies of heterogeneity are for this reason ultimately, Bataille says, an unemployable, "invaluable," or "useless" surplus[25] that indicates a kind of energy-in-flux, a charged or "base matter"[26] that allows the elements of heterogeneity, as Michèle Richman puts it in elaborating Bataille on this point, "to break the conventional barriers upon which homogeneity relies."[27] Bataille associates this break, and importantly, the noncommodifiable knowledge or the nonknowledge from the break and that surges through the break, with what is irreducible to production or monetary and identitarian exchange. This is what makes the heterogeneous powerful and dangerous to systems of politicality or order, why, in other words, it is dangerously because dissidently sacred. Decentralized and acephalous, the heterogeneous, which bespeaks the sacred of "the left-hand" in Bataille's and Caillois's lexicon, indexes "a force that disrupts the regular course of things,"[28] though those very disruptive energies can be recruited for "right-hand" purposes, aggregated to an anointed leader, a political "pastor," as it were, who uses a kind of "pastoral power" to seal the breach of heterogeneity and violently return a polity to homogeneity.[29] To return to "The Psychological Structure of Fascism," Bataille interprets the rise of Adolf Hitler in 1933 and the resulting effects on French politics within this framework and as a manifestation of the right-hand sacred—a recruitment of the wild energies of the sacred to seal the breach of heterogeneity as that breach at the time came to be figured in the Jews and in other undesirables. I read the nationalist protest in the summer of 2017 in Charlottesville in related, right-hand terms.

But to stay with Bataille, in that same essay he keeps his eye trained on the left side of things, which is to say on otherwise worldly movement(s) and moments, where there is always heterogeneity or base energies exceeding the terms of order. He finds examples in this regard in the "untouchables" of India, on the one hand, and among "the destitute" in the economically and socially "less ritualistic" or "advanced civilizations" of the West, as he puts it, on the other. In the latter, "being destitute is all it takes . . . to create between the self and others—who consider themselves the expression of normal man—a nearly insurmountable gap."[30] Whether it be those deemed hereditarily untouchable or whether it be the destitute in "advanced" countries, it is the "lowest strata of society," Bataille contends, "[that] can . . . be described as heterogeneous . . . those who generally provoke repulsion and can in no case be assimilated to the whole of mankind."[31] In their untouchability or destitution, such groups are a heterogeneous element associated with useless expenditure, with "violence, excess, delirium, madness . . . [that] to varying degrees" has that capacity because they are occluded within but are not fully subsumed by the juridical-economic order to unsettle the terms of order.[32] Interpreted as "mobs," they are outlaws or "[breakers] of the laws of social homogeneity." As such, "these impoverished classes," Bataille says, "are characterized by the prohibition of contact analogous to that applied to sacred things,"[33] particularly those tabooed things, those things, as Michèle Richman explains in again elaborating Bataille, that are placed under "restricted contact" and whose collective effervescence indicates a "transgression" or a "negation [that] surpasses itself" in exceeding every closed order "without returning to the original condition or state it had negated."[34] Here we find the sacred in its excessive, left-hand mode of ceaseless volatility, in restless rupture and rapture, as harbinger of a sociality or congregationality or an undercommon dark churchicality without limit or completion.

This brings us to an absolutely vital point around which much of what I want to say in this chapter, and indeed much of my effort to mobilize a discourse of the sacred for Black studies, turns: I mean the ambiguity within the very notion of the sacred itself as both pure and impure. Alexander Riley succinctly clarifies the issues here: "The sacred is not only the *holy or consecrated* but can also be the *accursed*."[35] That is to say, "in addition to being opposed in a binary relationship to the profane [this is Bataille's sphere of the homogeneous], [the sacred] is itself comprised of two opposing binary poles: the forces that maintain physical and moral purity and order, life, and health [the holy that upholds the holy], and those that contribute to impurity, evil, sacrilege, disease, and death [the un/holy or the accursed]."[36] The former sphere of pure divinity depends on an accursed share, an excremental element, to constitute and secure itself, within the terms of a restricted economy of sacrificial exchange, as pure. This doubled or ambivalent sense of the sacred registers in the Latin word from which it derives: *sacer*. Riley goes on to explain how the idea of the sacred can trip us up: hewing close to the Latin sense of *sacer*, "the French *sacré* . . . can mean both, and is frequently used in both senses (*la musique sacrée*, holy or sacred music, and *un sacré menteur*, a damned or accursed liar), whereas the English 'sacred' has in practice lost the second meaning."[37] But it is the recent scholarship of Robert Yelle that, I believe, significantly clarifies in what the ambivalence of the sacred, its constant slippage into potential, left-hand monstrosity and volatility, consists; namely, an interest in territorial logics of property, appropriation and expropriation, and propriety. This is the "ontology of sovereignty that we have inherited" where ontology here signals violent practices that aim to arrest the antinomian "chaos of foundations," that aim to arrest or "sacrifice" the "existence of something wild . . . something untamed and spontaneous."[38] The settler state or secular polity results precisely from efforts to arrest that antinomian something, that anoriginal chaos of foundations, by converting it into property. "This [nonpropertizable] something is what we call the sacred," which must be understood as a practice of in/sovereign or nonroutinized Relation (in the Glissantian sense of the "chaotic fabric of Relation" [*trame chaotique*]) or Love without rule.[39]

This is the sacred in that monstrously wild, anoriginal, and atheological left-hand sense. Indeed, if Bataille associates this forgotten fugitive sense of the sacred, whose relationship to the first or settler sense is not dialectical but excessive or abyssal, with the untouchables and the destitute, then here my Black studies intervention is to stretch the generally Durkheimian formulation of the right- and left-hand sacred, bending along with it even Bataille's more renegade formulation of sacred excess, to that blackened or Black sacral (non)position that aroused the Charlottesville white nationalist rally in the first place as a violent secondary, "right-hand" reaction. This opens up a consideration of the sacred's proximity to Blackness wherein, following Hortense Spillers, we might think of Blackness as a "symptom of the sacred," as terrifying monstrance of that beautiful monstrosity, an inner scar voluntarily claimed in having been called.[40] The monstrosity to be claimed here, this "unbounded sociality," concerns "blackness as matter [that] signals [infinity], another world . . . that which exists without time and out of space, in the plenum"[41]—the sacred otherwise. Here the sacred is obscure and formless, even "oceanic," to stay with Spillers. More akin to that "raw prime matter" of which Denise Ferreira da Silva has recently spoken of as part and parcel of the virtuality of a "black feminist poethics," the sacred here is of the wild, of the wilderness, "a counter-creative significa- tion," Charles H. Long might say.[42] To continue to think under the force of Spillers's, Silva's, and Long's thought, the sacred, in its adjacency to Blackness or as itself symptomatically Black, points to those hermetic energies or those forces of enchantment, to metamorphosis bound to devotional practices of un/knowing. Black sacrality indexes a certain liveliness and aliveness oc- casioned by, moving in relationship to, and yet irreducible to the "spiritual ordeal" of death that is settler modernity.[43] For this reason, Black radical sacrality, which we might just as well think of as the sorcery of (Black social) life itself, unsettles, is ever poised to incite volatility within regimes of po- liticality. That is to say, the sacred, as I am given to thinking about it here as figuring a poetics of malpracticed Black (religious) study, is neither tran- scendental, pure, nor beneficent, but rather base, stank, low to the ground, underground, of and with the earth. All this is to say, I approach the sacred as a kind of "pathological" and *ek-static* threshold before which other, dif- ferential, and unrepresentable "genres" or forms of life, unplottable gather- ings in representation's colonializing ruins, alternative ways of being with the earth, come into view.[44]

From the vantage point of regimes of politicality, Black *ek-static* life, which is to say Black social life, cannot help but be understood as index- ing deviance, deviation, and aberration. Moving "in the break" of the terror of politicality, Black radical deviance is a practice of the social not reduc- ible to politicality—a studied "consent," it has been said, "not to be a single being."[45] This is a malpracticed spirituality, a paratheology, or better still an atheological and thus a *godlessmysticism*[46] that points to frenzied *ex-istence* that is so much more than resistance because such existence is on the far side of the concept, on the far side of the God-concept, on the far side of a God that stalls out as a static concept—on the far side, I mean, of "God as a Failed Figuration," to echo poet Phillip B. Williams, that which grounds "the

American aesthetic."⁴⁷ That malpracticed godlessness bespeaks an interior, collective aliveness constantly ready, expectantly poised for the unexpectant, the experience of the *ek-static*—to be moved, to be terrified, to love, to hate, to live magically, drunkenly, wanderously, wonderously, erotically, joyously, childishly, prayerfully, in the radicality of a certain moving stillness, a certain quarreling, in/sovereign quiet.⁴⁸ This Black (w)hole-iness that (in) sovereignly exceeds the concept we might call "Black rapture." It is along this path that I want to begin to unfold or explicate Black malpractice as the "nonperformance" of modernity's god-terms, as nonperformative breach of the religious contract that subtends the racial contract insofar as the social contract (of race-ism) is necessarily a religious contract.⁴⁹ Stated differently, it is along this path that I want to engage in sacred *poiesis*, a poethics of the fugitive sacred. But first, the problem of political theology as a species, we might say, of anti-Blackness.

Political Theology

From what has just been said, it should already be clear that by political theology I mean more than what Carl Schmitt, whose name is most aligned with this term, meant by it when he said that "all significant concepts of the modern theory of the state are secularized theological concepts."⁵⁰ I mean more than to suggest, again as Schmitt did, a structural similarity between the domains of law and politics, on the one hand, and theology or the religious, on the other, such that the exceptionalism of the latter (as, for example, in the force of the "miracle") is merely transferred to the former (as, for example, with the "state of exception" and the "force of law"). Rather, by political theology I mean the ways that the categories of the political and the theological are mutually affirming. Differing in magnitude, the political and the theological are scalar, internally braided together in the logic of the state, for which reason they cannot be extracted one from the other. As I am using it, political theology is that philosophical, indeed that metaphysical, claim to the rightness, the purity, the would-be gravity of the state as the telos of society, as the horizon of order, as what securitizes the world if not life itself. If this order, which is to say state order, is the ontological horizon of what holds us, if it is a figure of the Being that holds beings (most especially the human mode of being, which within the terms of state order is nothing less than the citizen mode of being, the being that is *homo politicus*), then political theology is the discourse of Being in its projection of the state as the ground of legitimate, political (as opposed to "nonpolitical" or ante-political or anarchic) assembly, on the one hand, and as the ground of juridical sub-jecthood, on the other.

I would like to put a finer point on the problem of political theology by approaching it in terms of the problem of the evisceration of the sacred, or that which hovers "beyond" state-sanctioned horizons of life or what is truly real, what moves as invisibly felt or as a surging, surreal presence that state operations work hard to overshadow in monumentalizing itself, often through monuments. Like a kind of astrophysical dark matter with the un-knowable force of a dark energy that exceeds racial capitalism's gravitational pull by exerting a force from within and that exceeds this (racial) world's epistemological and material circumscriptions, this surging, surreal pres-ence moves at the limit of the state even if on some level within its con-straints. Let us call this limit *Blackness*. America is structured through the horrific regularity, both in spectacular displays but even more so in everyday or mundane displays, of experiencing unincorporable limits to itself. That experience is the experience of the sacred, an experience in which state sov-ereignty or lordly sovereignty is crossed (out), transgressed. Political theol-ogy is a discourse that seeks to eviscerate such an imagination of the sacred. As such, it is a statist discourse predicated precisely on the evisceration of the dark arts of the sacred, those excessive modes of life and knowing. I am interested in that dark knowing that exceeds theo-political constraint—what Georges Bataille spoke of as "nonknowledge" and what he also talked about as "poetry," and what I want to think about here by way of Black radical thought as the astropoetic release of the sacred from categorical capture. This is the Black radical sacred.

As an entry point into this approach to the problem of political theology and to begin to think about the sacred precisely as malpractice, consider Rei Terada's recent essay, "Robinson's Terms," in which she provides a pa-tient and brilliant reading of Cedric Robinson's underexplored first book (his published dissertation, in fact), *Terms of Order: Political Science and the Myth of Leadership*.[51] Her reading of *Terms of Order* offers us a way to understand the trajectory that led Robinson to the thesis he develops in *Black Marxism* that Black radicalism is a complexly differentiated tradition rooted in a revolutionary consciousness that exceeds the terms of political order, which are also the terms of (racial) capitalist order. "Order" emerges or is constituted as the counterrevolutionary evisceration of that which ex-ceeds order. Terada tarries with Robinson as he tarries with the dynamics of this evisceration. What we learn from her reading of Robinson is that if, in positioning "the state [as] the telos of society," the political "depends on and . . . is reflected in [a series of] politico-legalistic settlements" whose narrative languages and philosophical concepts establish "the terms [of] a [settler] tenancy," then what makes the political always already *theological*, even when it prides itself on being secular (which really must be understood as a mode of the theological), is this: in establishing the state as the telos of society and thus as a world that houses (human) being, the political follows, indeed it repeats, the religious logic of "Genesis," or the primordial, cosmo-gonic activity of the gods. As the gods found the world or establish the real by "[projecting] a fixed point into the formless fluidity of profane space, a center into chaos," thus allowing an "ontological passage" that in effect establishes the real,[52] so too the political is predicated on a "cosmocizing"[53] or a worlding of territory, a conversion of earth into territorialized World, by gods/men who imprint "terms of order" onto what is deemed nonpo-litical or formless (*informe*). This cosmocizing or would-be worlding of the earth into ownable, bordered territory entails the production and thus the imposition of spatial order on top of and the vanquishing of nonpolitical space or space charged with dark energy or promiscuous intensities figured as aberrantly racial, sexual, economic, and neurological. These are energies or intensities that are out of this world and that figure an otherwise totality, perhaps that "ontological totality" that propels the Black radical tradition.[54] This, says Terada, is the persistent "existence of what cannot be conceived from the standpoint of the political."[55] Constantly thwarting politicality's claim to being all there is, the nonpolitical represents that open "set of infi-nite alternatives," alternatives that index the impossible as nothing less than the ongoing possibility of what exceeds the terms of political order. Further still, if with Terada (with Robinson) we understand that myth "[functions] to process 'insurmountable contradiction' in the societies from which they arise," then the political, which establishes the terms of settler tenancy as terms of order, is but myth's rationalization, with language serving the utilitarian function of securing the order of signification, the grammar of (political) meaning. Put differently, the political seeks to maintain itself by instituting a form of knowing in which reason is but the declaration of hav-ing won the mythic struggle against an opposing force. This is the struggle of creation itself, a struggle in which Genesis is an effect of struggle. Politi-cal rationality entails the would-be vanquishing or containing or sacrificial "corpsing" of the nonpolitical surround in order to bring into being what in the Western ontotheological tradition has been called "World." And yet, in this instance, formless nonpoliticality bespeaks an abyssal prime matter that as limitless potential for patterning, as "absolute nothingness," is both base resource for the violent production of value *and* at the same time in-dexes a volatile danger to existing patterns of politicality.[56]

We can now address even more directly what is *theological* about the mythic rationality of the terms of political order for the ordering of World. What must be understood is that the previously described dynamic of the political is articulated to what historian of religions Mircea Eliade explains as the production of "sacred space" or the making of "strong, significant space" out of "spaces . . . without structure or consistency," spaces that he describes as "amorphous,"[57] or that we might just as well understand with both Georges Bataille and Hortense Spillers as "monstrous."[58] The bring-ing forth of strong space out of disordered void, or the imposition of form upon a nothingness that in its absolute formlessness, actually cannot be imposed upon; the would-be overcoming of "the fluid and larval modality of chaos" so as to establish, as an "act of the gods who . . . organized chaos by giving it a structure, forms, and norms," the ontological or the "pre-eminently . . . real";[59] and finally, the ritual reactualization of this paradig-matic work of the gods in order to secure a proper place in the world rather than hang suspended in the void of the not-real, the absolute nothingness of nonbeing—these mythic operations ground "religion" in the broadest sense. More still, Eliade describes these operations, to use Terada's Rob-insonian language, as establishing the terms of a settler tenancy. Through that tenancy *homo religiosus* (like and indeed as *homo politicus*) quenches his thirst for real existence in the face of a terrifying nothingness, in the face of that "absolute nonbeing" "that surrounds his inhabited world."[60] In communication with the gods who have, as it were, settled the chaos, *homo religiosus* by feat of ritual repetition repels the abyss and indeed in an ongoing way believes himself to have settled the abyss, lest "by some evil chance, he strays into [that abyss], [and comes to feel] emptied of his ontic substance, as if he were dissolving into [the surrounding] Chaos, and he finally dies."[61]

As a discourse, then, political theology as I mean it proceeds under the logic of a cosmology of settlement, the supposed containment of the sur-round by a settler-God or settler-gods and as reactualized by settler-Man. Here, the sacred has been epistemically annexed to settling, its adhesion underwriting political theology as a discourse that rests on the mytho-theological as the mytho-political founding of the world. Thus, within the terms of political theology, God, State, and Man are all god-terms that name a vanquishing or a supposed conquering of the abyssal, the infinite, the al-ternative, the possibility of the impossible.

But what if we do not assume the political (as seems to be the assumption in Rev. Lamar's comments about the Charlottesville white nationalist rally, his understanding of the general crisis of politicality today, and his understanding of theology's relationship to the political)? What if we do not presume the World? What if, to the contrary, we take seriously the political precisely *as myth* trying to reckon with what monstrously appears as its internal limit, of which the counterprotesters were a monstrous sign? (And here I want to keep in mind that in one etymological derivation monster derives from the Latin word *monere*, which means a divine omen or portent of what cannot be foreseen.) Which is also to ask, what if rather than assuming political theology we think with the likes of Colin Kaepernick whose taking a knee has incited a crisis of politicality, if not a monstrance of what is irreducibly ante-political? What if our study, our writing, takes place within political theology's astrophysical contraction, "in the break" of politicality?[62] These questions propel this chapter's writing practice, which aims to throw language back on itself, to be suspended in, even exiled within, language itself. I am suspended beyond the ontology of the sentence (of politicality), held in an ellipsis, a cloud of ante-political unknowing. What might it mean to write the experience of semiotic exile, to not be sentenced to the sentence while suspended within it, to write the experience of decomposition as the experience of the sacred in its monstrous mode? What "I," what "not-I," can write of parenthetical escape, un/sentenced, un/held within the sentence, "in the break" like sisters in the wilderness of the sentence, in the void of having been theo-politically sentenced?[63] Can (the) I escape the gravitational forces of civilization? What might it mean to occupy escape itself, live the void, be-voided? What is the feeling of the void, the feeling of fugitive suspension, outlawed within the law of the sentence? What of this wandering, this unholding? These are questions inspired by Renee Gladman and Sarah Jane Cervenak, as well as by Layli Long Soldier and M. NourbeSe Philip. My claim in this chapter is that the poetics of what is beyond the (theo-political) sentence is language's taut sentences, the tense of an alternative declension, the domain of the "fourth person singular," where some other experience of language is felt.[64] Here the myth of politicality and thus of being as a being-individuated, of being "I," is always already subject to being sacrificed along with the mode of divinity or the god-terms meant to secure the state. This poetics of the beyond is a poetics of the sacred "'other'-wise," Denise Ferreira da Silva and Ashon Crawley might say.[65] Given this, the Black malpractice of which I here speak is a practice of the sacred overboard, an experience of the sacred detached from or in the absence of its reduction to the stabilizer that has come to bear the name "God" or the gods and as duplicated or mirrored in the divination of the state where the state exists in the image of a stabilizing God.

What I aim for here, then, is a (mal)practice beyond the myth of theo-politicality, an anatheological malpractice. I am after a "practice of outside"— an out not caught in or that already ruptures the dialectic of inside-outside or the notion of a border or a property line, notions of inside-outside that are at the heart of myths of order, state or otherwise. Black out is no ordinary outness. Out even from itself in critique of the notion of a self, Blackness's practiced outness or Black out is "Black rapture." It is akin to what Nathaniel Mackey has called "Mu" in the serial or unending poem of his that bears this name. Approaching the sound of the first two letters of the Greek-derived word myth (*muthos*), Mackey's serial mu-poem encodes a poetics not so much of myth but of what he calls *ythm*.[66] The decomposition of *myth* into *ythm* (or is it the imposition, in keeping with our earlier discussion, of *myth* or propertied world onto larval earth, as a hieroglyphics onto flesh, that we are dealing with?) is fascinating to think through as an expression of Black malpractice.

Descending into language itself as some kind of founding or mythic violence, Mackey malpractices myth by anagrammatically reshuffling it. Yth-mic shuffle "advances a sense of alternative, 'a special view of history,'" that moves in relationship to an alternative sense of language, a dwelling in the flesh of words.[67] What results is the *(rh)ythm* of Black malpractice, an yth-mic overdubbing of myth. With *ythm* the first two letters of *myth* are first inverted (possessive *my*- becomes dispossessed *ym*-) and then splayed open so as to reveal a quantum, cosmic, but also womb space that holds an infinite set of phonemic, phonetic, "parasemiotic" possibilities.[68] That infinite set is signified in the repositioning of the other two letters of *myth*, namely the dental phoneme *th*-, between the inverted and now spaced apart other two letters. The inverted and spaced apart other two letters now hold or, perhaps better put, now care for and become a space of caress for, the dental phoneme *th*-. *Ym*- is the womb for a crippled sound (Mackey says that "ythm is crippled rhythm") created by air vibrating through flesh, air pushed between tongue and teeth and released through the mouth. In this way, the *ym*- of *ythm* is a conduit, a frictional (middle?) passage, a fleshly resonance chamber through which even if under duress life's breath might pass, a quantum gap of pneu-matic respiration, life's harbor, "held but not had / . . . churchical girth."[69]

Such is Mackey's ythmic Mu-poetics wherein due to the "creaking of the word" language becomes a (rh)ythmic paintbrush with which to paint otherworldly, undercommon edifices. Trees paint the sky green and incarnation or larval life sings the flesh, some "other" experience of the sacred. This is an experience of the sacred in the absence of (state) divinity, the experience of an uncontainable outside. Black malpractice is an open field poetics of the Black out. The rest of this chapter explicates, by recursive or serial wandering, that beyond, and that opening of the field that (rh)ythmically cuts the myth of the political. Black malpractice is a ministerial poetics, an ythmic *poiesis* of the beyond.

With this said, we can come back to Rev. Lamar's *Washington Post* interview. I want to locate the deeper impulse of what I take Rev. Lamar to be calling for in relationship to what I have just summarized, that summary pointing to a tradition of the sacred that shadows Rev. Lamar's reading of the Charlottesville incident. Not presuming the state as the teleological principle of the social, this is a tradition that moves from the "groundedness of an uncontainable outside."[70] I want to fold Rev. Lamar's comments into this tradition insofar as it questions modernity as a structure of onto-political theology and thus incites a rethinking of the sacred as what is abyssal to the myth of politicality. Indeed, I would like to (re)turn Black studies to the question of the sacred, a question taken up by the likes of Audre Lorde, Toni Cade Bambara, and M. Jacqui Alexander, among others, and frame it vis-à-vis the im/possibility of Black life within the politico-theological structures of modernity.

I advance here Black radicalism as a movement of *sacred deviancy, deviation, and aberration. Black radical deviance is a (par)atheological practice of the social.* We must study the sacrality of this deviance, the (w)holiness of a Blackness that moves fugitively and ecstatically, like the ancient vagabonds or revolutionary "gyrovagues"—from a compound of the Latin root *gyrus* (meaning "a revolution or a turning round," from which we get our word *gyrate*) plus *vagus* (meaning "wandering")—those monks who, never staying in one place, were mystic wanderers rather than possessive settlers.[71] If the events of Charlottesville, Virginia were a doubling down on or a restatement of a certain counterrevolutionary American settlerism that is not new with Trump but that also must be thought about in relationship to the "post-racialism" of the Obama presidency, then they were only following in the steps of St. Benedict whose counterrevolutionary monastic rule(s) sought to subject the gyrovagues to his rule(s) of obedience and thus settle (down) the sacred by arresting the itinerant, revolutionary energies in the movement of sentient, gyrating flesh. Blackness is gyrovague-ish, given to the insovereign itinerantcy of enspirited flesh, America's phantom limb. Indeed, Blackness is enfleshed spirit and so is (a) spiritual, its wandering an itinerant spirituality. In other words, Black wandering upon the earth, like faith itself, moves as a rapturous, otherworldly excess. Blackness is a lapsarian condition, a "fallen-ness" within the racially gendered world of property, an abiding on and with the unpropertizable, ungiven, and ungiveable earth.[72] Though paradoxical, Black fallenness thus bespeaks Black rapture. We need a protocol for this fall, for the fallenness of Black rapture as a kind of "base faith," the spiritual-ity of a "base materialism."[73] We need a protocol for Black malpractice as a practice of the monstrous, the fugitive sacred, this errantry.

Now I confess that I have no pretensions that in the remainder of this chapter I fully deliver the needed protocol. This is because I am not sure it can be fully delivered. Or, rather, I wonder if its deliverance can only be aspirational—not aspirational in the sense of uplift or as an upward striv-ing to become a proper American, but aspirational in the sense of a certain movement of spirit that manifests in the very form and style or mode of writing in what follows. Such writing I call spirit-writing or *pneumatogra-phy*. That is to say, in aspiring toward a protocol of Black fallenness, I walk a line of blurred distinction between explication and performance. I aim, on the one hand, to further explicate or offer an analysis of what I mean by Black malpractice. In this sense I want to unpack the idea. On the other hand, I want to enact and be enacted by the idea, to create or, perhaps bet-ter, to be poetically, poethically raptured, caught out, felled by, and in this way be all up in the experience of the very malpractice I aim to explicate—held in its suspension, practiced and channeled by malpractice, its possible ritual conjurer, malpractice's would-be instrument, its vibrating reed. This is a matter of method, which is also a matter of the argument itself. What is the methodology of Black radical sacrality, that poetics of malpractice that is a poetics of the sacred?

Poetics of the Sacred

In my effort to explicate this, I would like to linger for a moment on the word *explication* itself, for the blurred distinction of which I spoke above between explication and performance is in fact internal to the very word *explication* itself. The *pli-* in ex-*pli*-cation (from the Latin *plico*, meaning "to fold together") coupled with the prefix *ex-* (from the Greek *ek-*, meaning "out from") suggests an internal communion, a sociality or a being-with, a folding together. Explication draws out or surfaces, splays and displays, that form of life that is not one, that is no-body, that is not a singularity but rather is a folding-together. In this respect, explication is akin perhaps to the activity of weaving or looming. Or just as much, if poet-critic Dawn Lundy Martin be our guide for a moment, explication, given what she says in her meditation on "black poetics," is "as much breaking as it is making. The inverse of hermeneutics as it resists interpretation in favor of something less sure, something more unstable."[74] Immediately following this declaration, Martin pens a curious series of sentences that may be read as practicing the very breaking and making of which she'd just spoken. Set off in italics and moreover as the expression and practice of some sort of poetic knowledge, the sentences have the feel of a poem or of what might be called a micro- or even a minor-poem: *I'm jumping on top of a police car on fire. I'm ecstatic. My heart burns with ecstasy in my sadness.*[75]

The syntax of the first sentence raises questions for how this micro-poem practices or explicates the breaking-making injunction of Black poetic (non) knowledge as Black malpractice. Is the jumping "I" what's on fire here (which may be why it is jumping)? That is, is the I-ness of the "I"—where in the wake of René Descartes and a broader Western philosophical tradition the "I" is often thought of as a self-determined, coherent locus of identitarian stability—what is on fire, what is being burned up, set ablaze in the confrontation with prior embers of multiplicity and instability? Or, might it be that what is burning here is not so much the "I" as it is the police car that that "I" is jumping on? Is that what is on fire? Or perhaps it is both the subjected "I" and the objective policing car, the "subject" and the "object," that are burning. And what of the relationship between the kinetics of the jumping "I," the pyrotechnics of the blazing fire that consumes maybe the subjected "I," maybe the policing car, maybe both, and that third vector in the poem, the ecstatic heart or spirit set ablaze with joy even while singed with sadness?

I pose no "answers" to these questions, but instead want to dwell with their poetic interplay, stay with the splayed ecstatics of a Blackness under fire, on fire, in the fire, as fire, the perhaps Pentecostal, perhaps mystical, perhaps Du Boisian "black flame" fire. Here, blackness might be thought of as that which burns without being burnt up, blackness as that smoky exhaust, blue vespers released in burning heat. This blue(s) exhaust(-ion) puts in mind what the nonconformist fourteenth-century beguine mystic Marguerite Porete, interestingly judged by her inquisitors as a kind of queered "pseudowoman" (*quaedam pseudomulier*), called as she made her way into the fires of the Inquisition, fire's "relinquishment."[76] For Porete, whose vision approximates Sufi mysticism, fire and air coincide in a kind of "co-incidence of opposites." Alchemically combusting, they interact such that their exhaust(ion) releases a freedom that is illegible within the terms of politicality. Such freedom pointed for Porete to otherworldly possibilities, vitalities that exceed and that in fact as she saw it could not be contained by the managerial, priestly class or by inquisitorial governance. The release of which Porete speaks is ecstatic, which is also to say, erotic. Indeed, hers is a social erotics of desire that she saw as the sum and nonsubstance (insofar as she identified this as the abyssal "nothingness") of the sacred. This is a mode of nonindividuated entanglement, a kind of quantum sacrality, that moves on the plane of the "pseudo . . ." and the "para . . ."—again, her grand inquisitors called her a "*pseudomulier . . . ,*" pseudowoman . . . —on the plane of the ellipses attached to these prefixes that will not allow them to be fixed or come to a final resting place. This is the plane of the impossibility, the ungraspability and unknowability of what in Porete's wake Nicolas of Cusa called *posse* or possibility itself.

I read Martin's malpracticing poetics, her micropoetics, as proximate to Porete's mysticism. A Black flame mysticism of the riot is how I want to read what's at stake in Martin's poetics. *I'm jumping on top of a police car on fire. I'm ecstatic. My heart burns with ecstasy in my sadness.* With its imagery of jumping into fiery, aerial suspension, that is to say with its imagery of mystically rapturous (social) movement, Martin's minor-poetics bespeaks spirit possession beyond propertied self-possession. We need a protocol of the spirit, a protocol of this interior zone, which is also a protocol of the earth in its irreducibility to the world of politicality and property. This would be as well a protocol of language's anteriority to itself, a protocol of spirit-language: pneumatology's anagrammatical pneumatography. Such a protocol gives itself in rites of passage, in rituals of apophatic unsaying, in the poetics of an/nihilating fire, in Black mystical nothingness, in the mysticism of a heart jumping and burning in burnt ecstasy without immolation.

Might there be a poetics of celebration here, of riotous ritual of praise, wherein Black joy fleetingly shows up as inconsumably ablaze precisely in the scene of and yet exceeding pain? Immolation without full consumption. Would not such ex/tinguishment and an/nihilation entail the need for a protocol of joy precisely as part of a protocol of spirit, both of which are irreducible to protocol, to rule/s? I raise these questions inasmuch as Martin's minor-poem seems to understand Black joy and Black sadness as bound to each other precisely in the suspension of the spirit, in the suspended ecstatics of the leap itself, in rapture's jump ("*I'm jumping . . . I'm ecstatic . . .*"). I'm interested in the airy, fiery, atmospheric suspension, in the unlocatable not-ness or the knot, the nothingness of "the between" that is the non- or no-place, the Black space of a churchical darkness, the "para-congregationality" between the upbeat and the downbeat of the jump itself. That "blackspace," Alexis Pauline Gumbs and Pierce Freelon help us understand, is sacred.[77] I'm interested in the question of celebration that suspension itself poses.[78] "Our music hurts so much that we have to celebrate. . . . That we have to celebrate is what hurts so much. Exhaustive celebration in and through our suffering, which is neither distant nor sutured," is what Fred Moten calls "black study"[79] and what I am here thinking about under the rubric of malpractice. Black malpractice musics the riot as celebration singed with sadness's potentiating of the alternative. I'm interested in how the three sentences making up what I have been calling Martin's minor, micro-poem ex-*pli*-cate or draw out a social movement of folding, unfolding, infolding, and refolding celebration.

I own that there is something manic, even deranged—by which I mean something like what Nathaniel Mackey, drawing on Spanish poet Federico García Lorca, identifies as a *duende*-like quality—about what I am suggesting here about the method and sociopoetics of Black malpractice, the mysticism of the riot.[80] "The word *duende* means spirit, a kind of gremlin, a gremlin-like, troubling spirit."[81] The troubling comes through as a particular kind of sound in the voice, Mackey commenting on Lorca tells us. A "hurt fractured inside," is how Martin puts it. Announced in "an almost religious enthusiasm . . . [that] shakes the body," that quakes the dancer's voice, that disorients the senses to effect "communication with God by means of the five senses," *duende*'s arrival as "the spirit of the earth" bespeaks, as Lorca himself puts it, "a real and poetic evasion of this world," some "lyric" and "constant baptism [yielding] newly created things."[82] By way of Mackey and Lorca, we can speak of the duende or the rapture of the riot, wherein one hears the "black sounds" of some "deep song," the sonic overflow of spiritual colors, as the undulating eloquence of a perhaps squealed, screeching, scorched but no matter how you put it, troubled voice.[83] "Its eloquence becomes eloquence of another order, a broken, problematic, self-problematizing eloquence."[84] As eloquent disorder, *duende*, we might say, is the explication as the troubled voicing of a fractured inside. Drawing out the fracture, caressing it and being caressed by it perhaps, *duende* is the practice of fractured escape. Jack Spicer, another important influence on Mackey who comes up in Mackey's reflections on *duende*, has called this "the practice of outside." This outside practice, which can show up riotously in writing, in song, in the visual arts, in the streets, which is to say in and as performance, might be understood as (black) spirit's or life's "conversation with the dead, intimacy with death and with the dead," an animacy at the rim of the wound, a "breathing behind the door."[85] That breathing behind the door is a malpracticed breathing, a "longing without object" or toward another world.[86] What Mackey is addressing is wounded breathing or breathing as experiment, as the experimentalism of possibility itself, the practice of what moves uncannily and unsettlingly out of place, what kinetically misbehaves by virtue of an "apparent lack of purpose, efficiency, and function,"[87] though what registers as lack (and Black) here may in fact be thought of as the surplus of the subreal, what yet lives at the end of the world, at the rim of the wound.

The stakes of Black malpractice preliminarily come into view: my discourse considers Black malpractice as a kind of explication of a practiced outness where explication as analysis gives way because it is animated by explication as performance, as atonal, anatheological movement. I want to follow Black malpractice as itself an insovereign, in-explicable movement of what refuses full emplotment and that thus will not stay in place, an "uncanny . . . movement [that] happens for the sake of movement" itself that is always already internally fractal and multiple.[88] This is the movement of a differential (w)hole, of what I noted earlier that Cedric Robinson called "the collective being, the ontological totality," incompletion's totality. As an out-movement that displays a condition of internal folding-in-togetherness, of internal braidings and serial coilings that bespeak some other kind of gathering, Black malpractice is, I guess we could say, *com*plicated.

The trick here then is for my explication to be carried out in such a way that the very malpractice I am concerned with comes into view as itself an alternative imaginary that releases the sacred (and our imaginations of what such a term might mean) from settler logics of sovereignty and the sovereign. This must be an explication that holds malpractice open to its own outside and in this way opens out onto a poetics of the sacred, a movement in which a sociality of deviancy, of deregulated getting together, is itself a transcendently immanent and an immanently transcendent practice of outside. Internal to the sacredness of such deviant out(side)ness is a fundamental claim: Black radical malpractice imagines and is the practice, indeed the ritual conjuring of other modes of being-with, a kind of monastic- or Bedouin-like habit of otherworldly assembling, of convening what the musician N. in *Late Arcade*, the latest installment of Nathaniel Mackey's serial novel *From a Broken Bottle Perfume Still Emanates*, calls "Some Other Sunday."[89] Such malpractice is not *anti*-American, which is not serious enough; irreducible to the political as we know it, the radicalism of Black malpractice is an *ante*-American poetics, the critique of political theology and thus of "God" as governor or world-manager.

Zong! Nowhere

It is at this point that I offer M. NourbeSe Philip's arresting poem *Zong!* as ritual performance of what I have been trying to think through in this chapter. In *Zong!*, Philip poetically engages with the events that took place on the slave ship *Zong* in 1781, when the ship's captain oversaw the throwing overboard of upwards of 150 Africans in order to preserve the ship's dwindling provisions as the ship made its way to Jamaica to deliver its "cargo."[90] Philip tells us that her poetic engagement with this incident is authorized by those thrown overboard from the ship. (More about this below.) The poem's presumption is that those thrown overboard, though left dead or interred in the ocean, as well as left dead or interred in the words of the summary judgment of the court case that unfolded in the wake of the *Zong* events, yet *live* (inside of) death. (The legal case is officially the *Gregson v. Gilbert* case. Gregson was the ship's owner; Gilbert was the insurance company insuring the ship's cargo.[91]) Limiting herself to the words, including the syllables and sounds making up the words, of the summary judgment, which she understands as a "colonial script," Philip commits malpractice (*Zong!*, 196). That is, with a view to recuperating what's been submerged or silenced within the law, what the law censors or proscribes in order to secure the world it prescribes, Philip "breaks and enters" the legal text and thus the law's fundamental *ratio* or logic (or *logos*), its guiding concept; to wit, the "human" (*Zong!*, 200).

It is vital to note that *recuperate* here does not mean "[to recover] the individual identities of the Zong slaves [or] their stories," nor does it mean "to transpose the elisions, silences, and disavowals of the Zong case into a coherent narrative,"[92] into a story subjected to the "ordering mechanism" of "grammar . . . the mechanism of force" (*Zong!*, 192). To do that would be "to do a second violence. To the experience, the memory—the re-membering."[93] Instead, Philip not-tells or rather un-tells the tale by "mutilating" the *Gregson v. Gilbert* court document. In her own words:

> As the fabric of African life and the lives of these men, women and children were mutilated . . . I murder the text, literally cut it into pieces, castrating verbs, suffocating adjectives, murdering nouns, throwing arti-

cles, prepositions, conjunctions overboard, jettisoning adverbs: I separate subject from verb, verb from object—create semantic mayhem, until my hands bloodied, from so much killing and cutting, reach into the stinking, eviscerated innards, and like some seer, sangoma, or prophet who, having sacrificed an animal for signs and portents of a new life, or simply life, reads the untold story that tells itself by not telling. (*Zong!*, 193–94)

In this profound passage, Philip gives us to understand that her procedure of textual production enacts a "potentially generative . . . mystically inflected" textual violence against the mythic violence of the law.[94] "This is the axis on which the text of *Zong!* turns: censor and magician" (*Zong!*, 199). The former, mystically inflected textual violence enacts a kind of shamanic, Sycoraxian, and indeed daemonic release that is a fugitive release of life and breath from that juris-mythic embrace that would contain it.[95] This violence against violence, or this doubling of violence in which the poet's hands are blood-drenched from so much textual dismemberment for the sake of textual de- as re-composition, stages a sacrifice that through the remains releases what remains. The remains that ambivalently offer themselves and withhold something else, are an excess, the undercurrent of a disturbance. Unheld by state projects—in this case, by the slave ship of state—what remains is some primary or anterior, prereflective structure that historian of religions Charles Long identifies with "the archaic symbol." Irreducible to categorization, the archaic harbors inexhaustible possibilities of signification. Like an ideogram lying somewhere between experience and category, the archaic symbol is the reservoir of a spiritual universe. For this reason, it invites different and various types of thought. To "crawl back through history" so as to confront the archaic is to confront a fundamental, prereflective opacity that is anterior to ontology. Anticipating Philip, Long states that it is to confront "Silence" or the sheer potentials of signification or worldmaking as *poiesis*, poetics, poethics. It is to confront the sacred otherwise and thereby to confront the possibilities of "radical critical thought" carried within Silence.

This is what goes unheld by state projects. What remains nonpossessable is nothing less than the opacity of the sacred (the moment of "black religion"), where at this archaic level the sacred must not be understood in terms of ontotheological substance but rather in terms of an exorbitance or in terms of a useless expenditure that plunges the collective poet into a "semantic mayhem" that, as it were, compresses and expands space-time so it "opens up," says Mandy Bloomfield in her provocative reading of *Zong!*, "channels of communication with ancestors."[96] So understood, *Zong!* is a sacred text, or a text that malpractices the sacred, a text whose protocol is sacrifice. However, this is not sacrifice in the sense often observed in institutional religion in its alliance with state power where sacrifice is done with the expectation of something, such as salvation, being returned so as to secure the present toward a certain future. Rather, it is not containable even by institutional religion, which can quell the dangerous energies of the sacred; sacrifice here bespeaks a radical negation of utilitarian production in the name of an insurgency of the nonproductive, in the name of an insurgency of the "sacred instant," in the name, finally, of what holding can't have and what having can't hold but that can get hold of you. This is sacrifice akin to what Bataille might have been trying to get at: "[While] there is a specific motive behind every sacrifice: an abundant harvest, expiation, or any other logical objective; nonetheless, in one way or another, every sacrifice has its cause in the quest for a sacred instant that, for an instant, puts to rout the profane time in which prohibitions guarantee the possibility of life."[97]

Philip's renegade-cum-sacrificial poetics moves in this way. Convening insurgent intimacies or gatherings of spirit and, indeed, of soul, sacrifice here conjures a mode of existence that exceeds and agitates against modern modalities of the individuated self. This is sacrifice given to insovereign headlessness, a practice of what Fred Moten has recently and extensively elaborated as a "consent not to be a single being." Animating Blackness is sacrificial malpractice, an erotics of the sacred given in "differential inseperability."[98] Pointing to and performing this is *Zong!*'s spiritual accomplishment. Philip's poetic "ex-aqua-ing," rather than ex-huming, the remains of those interred in "their 'liquid graves'" (*Zong!*, 202) was a feat of sonic memory as much as it was a kind of shamanic ritual. More specifically, in breaking open the legal text *Zong!*'s collective poet finds therein a religious text of theo-political purity that the collective poet then further breaks open. In breaking open the law (of the subject) she breaks open how we imagine the sacred, and in so doing exposes the juris-theological terms of order that structure the Middle Passage and colonial modernity. Intuitively understanding colonial modernity and its racial logics as ritually enacted (law and religion as, effectively, a shared or transubstantiated ritual), the collective poet breaks open the juris-theological text so as to be swept into the eddies of an insurgent "Silence" (Philip's term), the Silence of another ceremony that somehow, some way is always already there. Nowhere.

Against this backdrop what starts to come into view is this: *Zong!* subtly engages the political theology, and specifically the ritual, ceremonial, and sacramental logics, that harnessed the sacred to the European project so as to underwrite the oceanic and legal internment of those thrown overboard from the slave ship *Zong* and that more broadly ground (racial) capitalism as a project of Western salvation. The European project entailed the would-be deanimation of matter so as to then commodify it or impose on it an equation of value. In fragmenting the words of the court-issued summary judgment surrounding the events that took place on that slave ship and utilizing those words to generate the poem that is *Zong!*, Philip malpractices or, adapting Denise Ferreira da Silva, "hacks the sacred" precisely insofar as the sacred comes to be transubstantiated into the "patriarch form" as an onto-theological form or grammar.[99] More specifically, in breaking open the legal text *Zong!*'s collective poet finds within it a religious text. Further still, the collective poet discovers the religious logics that inform the juris-religious text, making it a juris-sacramental text the fundamental presumption of which is the individual, self-possessed body (politic). Intuitively understanding colonial modernity and its racial logics as ritually enacted (law and religion as, effectively, a shared or transubstantiated ritual), the collective poet theorizes the juris-theological text, breaking it open in a bid to hear the noisy Silence of another ceremony that moves in an insurgent anteriority to the juris-theological terms of order that structure the Middle Passage and colonial modernity, doing so by way of the practice of another ceremony, an otherwise worldly ritual. This is the ritual of other worlds, other words, nowhere.

To elaborate with a bit more textual specificity what I mean, I would like to zero in on one part of *Zong!* In the section of the poem called "Ferrum" (from the Latin meaning "iron" or "chains"), we find a subtle and sophisticated engagement with the ceremonial and, more precisely, sacramental logics of Christian theology that anchored the violence of the *Zong* events and by extension the violence of the Middle Passage and modernity itself. In ex-aqua-ing the dead from the juris-theological text of the *Gregson v. Gilbert* summary judgment, the *Zong!* collective poet-narrator splays the words of the legal text to generate a scene on board the slave ship *Zong* in which those buried in the hold seem to overhear the captain and the sailors on deck partaking in what seems to be the prayers and accompanying hymns of the Christian Eucharist. For convenience of reference, I have reproduced as figure 8.1 the page of the poem that records the scene to which I refer. In traditional Christian theology and church practice, this is the ceremony of eating bread and drinking wine as the body and blood of Jesus Christ. I want to suggest that the scene splayed across the page presents dense "evi / dence of a pa / st drow / ned in no / w . . ." (141, lines 1–2). The collective poet witnesses that this history violently "p / lay[s] on my bo / nes the son / g of bo / ne in b / one" (141, lines 2–3). Bone grating against bone, bone becomes a kind of tuning fork, a resonator. As bone rubs against bone as a bow rubs up against violin strings, a sound is heard, a song is played. What, we might ask, is the song that the collective poet hears playing on "my [collective] bo / nes"? The broken or splayed words that themselves approximate broken or splayed bones and that follow lines 2–3 suggest an answer. What plays on the poet's collective bones are fragments or pieces of words that are broken off and in this way echo the Requiem Mass or the Eucharistic Mass for the dead. This is a Mass replete with a long history of hymns and music offered in the context of funeral prayers, vespers offered for the repose of the soul or souls of one or more deceased persons.[100]

It is worth offering a few words on the Requiem Mass itself in order more fully to appreciate the political theology of the Middle Passage that *Zong!* poetically spots. The Requiem Mass draws on the *Roman Missal*, the liturgical book that contains the texts and rubrics for the celebration of the Mass in the Roman Catholic tradition. More specifically, the Requiem Mass and its settings draw their name from the opening section of the Roman Catholic liturgical celebration of the Eucharist, which begins with the words "*Requiem aesternam dona eis, Domine*" ("Grant them (the dead) eternal rest, O Lord").

Interestingly, fragments of language drawn from the Requiem Mass for the dead are discerned within the language of the court-issued summary judgment of the *Gregson v. Gilbert* legal case and thus make an appearance in the "Ferrum" section of *Zong!* That is to say, in the anticolonial splaying of the legal case a ceremonial or sacramental song of terror is revealed. Thus, *Zong!'s* citation of the sacrament of the Mass breaks open the law in order to reveal the summary judgment of the sovereign judges to be part of a semiotic or signifying system or apparatus. Structuring this semiotic system is a relay between the ritual eating of bread and wine on seas (let's call this the violent liturgy of Middle Passage) and another consumptive ritual, namely, the fundamental transformation or, more to the point the transubstantiation into "Slaves" or "Negroes" of those whose bones are being broken as they are being held below deck as "cargo." This semiotic convergence between the ritual transubstantiation of bread into the body-proper of Christ as (the God-) Man and the concomitant ritual-cum-colonial capitalist transubstantiation of bone into sentient labor power or Slave is an instance of what theologian

t bone stone   of then evi   dence of a pa
st crow   ned in no   w p
        lay on my bo   nes the son
g of bo   ne in b   one sh h ca
        n you he   ar the be   at in bone *pie*
                    je
su pi   e *jes*   u sanctus santuc   sanctus ag
    nu s dei in   san   *ctus* there i
        s *san* say   a *sa*   *nctus* for m
              e a *san*
ctus to the s   ea a s
        anctus to the s   an san   s san s
              san s s   *anctus* i
        am we a   re their e
              yes stare   see thin   gs we ne
ver wil   l let my s   tory my tal
                    e my g   est gift ri
        se up in ti   me to sn
    ap the sp   ine of tim   e *pat*
              er *pa*   *ter* say a *pie je*
    su for me   add a s   *anctus* th
        row in an *ag*   *nu s dei p*
                        ater for me a *mi*
              sa una m   *isa* how man
    y gu   ineas for a *mis*
              a *pate*
        r prat   e the a
              ve ma   *ri a* pra
y *pa*   *ter* pray f   or me
    for th   em sa   y a *san*
        ctus f   or the s   ea but dr
own the can   t *pater* i   t is do   ne lots
        of *pi*   *etas* to   o *pa*
ter

                              & *fi*
        des & sp   es dum d
um de du   m dum th   e no
    ise the   noi   se th
        e drum it do   es not sto
p the *o*   *ba* so   bs a

8.1 An excerpt from M. NourbeSe Philip's poem *Zong!*

Lauren Winner has recently called "the dangers of Christian practice" and of what we might also think of as the horrors of the sacred.[101] As an otherwise ritual of other worlds, *Zong!* witnesses to and is negotiating the horror of the right-hand, racial-capitalist sacred—capitalism's would-be reduction of the sacred to the god-terms of "property," "contract," and "law" through the eucharistic ceremony of the slave ship, the sacrament of the Middle Passage— even as what generates the poem or un/grounds its poetics is precisely the groundless or archaic Silence that gives rise to (black) thought from the improvisational abyss of the im/possible. As a symbol of Silence, blackness from the hold releases the imagination of the sacred. This is what makes Philip's poetics so provocative. In the anticolonial break of *Zong!*'s citation of the eucharistic Requiem Mass, in its broken "S/Zong," the poem itself is summoned or conjured as a witness to the dead and to an ongoing "aliveness."[102] That is to say, in citationality's break (down) into enchanted re-citation, into insurgent chant, otherwise worlds re-sound or surge forth.

First consider *Zong!*'s broken re-citation of the Requiem Mass itself in "Ferrum." What resounds in *Zong!*'s recitation of the Requiem Mass is a song of the remains of the dead, "the son / g of bo / ne in b / one" and that beats "my bo / nes" (141, lines 3–4). That song of terror, sung in ecclesiastical Latin no less, draws from three sections of the Requiem Mass: the "*Sanctus, sanctus, sanctus*" section ("holy, holy, holy," referencing the triune God of the Christian faith), the "*Pie Jesu*" section ("Pious Jesus," referencing a vibrant Christology), and the "*Agnus Dei*" section ("Lamb of God," referencing a theology of salvation by atoning sacrifice). This is what *Zong!* re-cites, what its chant and dissident mode of enchantment "hacks" open.

The broader language of the last two sections, particularly in Andrew Lloyd Webber's version of the Requiem Mass, which seems to be the version *Zong!* inflects, is striking when heard in the context of the historical *Zong* events. In locating the terror of the slave ship *Zong* in relationship to the language in Webber's version of the Requiem Mass, the poem suggests an alignment between the murderous consumption of Black life and the sacrificial and ceremonially salvific consumption of Christ's flesh and blood in the form of the eucharistic Mass. I will say more about this in a moment. But, first, let us consider the specific language of the "*Pie Jesu*" and "*Agnus Dei*" sections of the Requiem song that *Zong!*'s collective poet discerns within the mix of words making up the *Gregson v. Gilbert* legal text and in a broken way recites in broken chant by fracturing them across the poem. Here's the language from the Webber version of the second and third sections, respectively, of the song of the Requiem Mass:

Pie Jesu,
Qui tollis peccata mundi,
Dona eis requiem.

Agnus Dei,
Qui tollis peccata mundi,
Dona eis requiem,
Sempiternam
Requiem.

[Pious Jesus,
Who takes away the sins of the world,
Give them rest.

Lamb of God,
Who takes away the sins of the world,
Give them rest,
Everlasting
Rest.]

The theology embedded in the lyric of the Requiem Mass for the dead suggests that notwithstanding the crisis at sea, with dwindling food and the imminent prospect of losing their lives, the mariners nevertheless hope for salvation in Christ. Eating the bread and drinking the wine of the Eucharist as Christ's flesh and blood gives the mariners assurance of bodily salvation, for in eating the host they become a corporation; they are drawn into Christ's never dying body (politic). That is to say, they are given the gift of bodily integrity and stability amid instability. They become, in other words, saved bodies. But what the poem also invites us to understand is how the ceremony of the Eucharist on the *Zong* ship discloses a ritual structure to the Black Atlantic itself, and thus a ritual structure to the forging of a racial-colonial modernity. The poem breaks open the legal text to disclose its liturgical horizon. This is the horizon that activates the body, or more precisely, that activates the Christ's body politic as the European, enslaving body through exploitative consumption of the enslaved body. Christ's "real presence" through the event of the eucharistic ceremony on the slave ship enfolds or stands forth through and as the mariners. The ceremony of eating Christ's flesh so as to become a body (politic) grants the mariners assurance of bodily security, assurance of salvation. What I am trying to do here is take very seriously the imposition of liturgical, soteriological, and onto-colonial governance through Middle Passage as threshold of modern political economy as itself threshold of "whiteness."

To this end, let's stay with this just a bit longer. For, the (re)production of Christ's body that the collective poet spots as part of the ritual of Middle Passage and that aligns the enslaving-colonizing mariners with Christ as symbolic guarantor or of (white) life in the face of apocalyptic destruction is happening in tandem with another type of consumptive destruction; to wit, the ritualized consumption of what remains alive in the hold. These two consumptions are really one consumption, the second of which we also glimpse in *Zong!*'s "Ferrum" section. Indeed, we hear of this other Eucharist-like, ritual consumption from "one of the strongest 'voices,'" Philip tells us, "in the *Zong!* text [and] who appears to be white, male, and European" (*Zong!*, 204). Figured in the poem as both perpetrator and witness to the *Zong* events, this other voice often addresses, as if in a diary entry or in a letter, a love interest named "ruth" (clipped "t / ruth"?), who herself emerges as a presence in the *Zong!* text. She is figured as one who consoles the European male as he confesses the "sins" he has committed aboard the ship and over his participation in what has happened. In one of these moments of melancholic confession, the European subject confesses to being restless over what's happened on the ship. He uses language that strikingly echoes the eucharistic consumption discourse described above. However, the difference between the two languages of Eucharist-like consumption is that what's being eaten in this scene is not the bread and wine that is Christ's flesh but "negro meat":

> in th / at insta / nce of s / in . . . can s / it no mo / re cl / ams feed on
> we / eds weeds fe / ed on fle / sh we din / e on neg / ro me / at grow
> fa / t (164)

What finally comes into view now is this: the eucharistic consumption of Christ's flesh and blood moves in tandem with the consuming of Black flesh and life, "negro meat." This Janus-faced operation is the moment of the materially transubstantive production of whiteness as religion in and through "the willful expenditure of the Other in an imposing production of the self" in a gesture of consumption.[103] That is to say, by eucharistically ingesting Black flesh as a kind of negative resource, Man is animated, his body vampirically brought to life.

And yet what *Zong!* ultimately points to is how quite unstable this all is. Indeed, that instability registers as a kind of reverb or as the aftereffect of "an excessive and residual Otherness,"[104] of an insurgent "beyond,"[105] of an agitating Silence, that allows for the production of *Zong!* through "sacrificing" the legal text along with the individuated and propertied self it seeks to uphold. *Zong!*'s un-telling of a story that cannot be told but must be told moves in the break of this doubled ritual of fleshly consumption. Indeed, in fracturing not only the legal text but the liturgy internal to the law to enact another ceremony, *Zong!* sacrifices sacrifice without recourse to and in refusal of salvation or a return to "real presence." In Moten's words, "Theory of blackness is theory of the surreal presence."[106] This is the dissident surrealism of "otherwise worlds."

I come back to the "Ferrum" section of the poem to display further what I am getting at here. The collective poet shushes her readers ("sh h / ca / n you he / ar the be / at "? [141, lines 4–5]), urging a quiet upon them so that the poem's auditors can hear what surges through the enchanted re-citation of the Requiem Mass. Such re-citation aims not so much to tell or know anything but to un/tell, and to un/know. This is a feat of engaging that non-knowledge that conditions the violence of theo-legal, which is theo-secular, knowledge. We are invited to overhear (and eventually overdub) a song of "ontotheological terror," the song that is the eucharistic sound of violence on the slave ship:[107] "*pie // je // su pi // e // jes / u sanctus sanctus // sanctus ag // nu // s dei . . .*" (141, lines 5–8). As with the legal text, so too with the theological text buried within it—the collective poet splays the Mass to move through and move around its innards. That is to say, in paralleling her poetics between the *Roman Missal* as religious liturgy and *Gregson v. Gilbert* as legal liturgy, the poet-narrator discloses the transubstantiation of religion and law into one another as that which grounds the (slave ship of) state. This is all ground I have already covered. But what is new is this: in fracturing the already fractured Requiem Mass, the poet-narrator in fact hears some other broken (rh)ythmic song singing or resounding through it. This is the song of another world, the surreality of a "surreal presence." Not the trinitarian "sanctus sanctus sanctus" of the Christian eucharistic liturgy but what the collective poet calls a "sa / nctus to the s / ea," a sea liturgy:

> in / san / ctus there i / s san say / a sa / nctus for m / e a san / ctus to
> the s / ea . . . i / am we a / re their e / yes stare / see thin / gs we ne /
> ver wil / l let my s / tory my tal / e my g / est gift ri / se up in ti / me to
> sn / ap the sp / ine of tim / e . . . (141, lines 8–19)

Notice that in these lines, in the chant that is *Zong!*, being—the conjugated "is" of "to be"—is split open such that the "i" now dangles at the end of the line (see figure 8.1, line 8), incoherently stranded from the "s" that starts on the next line (see figure 8.1, line 9). Further along, and again, the "i" and the "am" of the Cartesian "i am" are set astray from each other (see figure 8.1, lines 13 and 14). And, finally, from the end of what I have quoted above we hear that the un-telling that is going on here moves, in the break and in the wake, we might say, of time understood as progress, the temporality of the subject. *Zong!*'s insurgency "sn / ap[s] the sp / ine of tim /e . . . ," thereby witnessing the space-time of nowhere.

This takes us back to my earlier elaboration of the problem of ontology and genesis or onto-genesis in the "Political Theology" section of this chapter as I was thinking through the problem of "Worlding." We find in the "Ferrum" section of *Zong!* an understanding of the slave ship—which can be extended to the plantation and the racial state—as the ontotheological space-time of the present. More than that, we witness that the ontotheological space-time of the present is predicated on the consumption of the sacred—the conversion of wild potentialities into labor power. And yet, by way of its fractured poetics of the exclamation point, *Zong!* releases the sacred through an ecstatics not of real presence but of the *surreal, subreal* presence, that affirmative space of capacious negation where Lauryn Hill said that everything's everything, everything's all mixed up. In this way, the poem moves with, and finally *through*, the slave ship *Zong*. It dwells with what hovers as "Silence" (Philip's term), an invisible universe, on the far side of the teleological principle of ontotheological "real" presence. *Zong!* is broke(n), (rh)ythmically impoverished. In the break it congregates a dissonant Mass. By this I mean that *Zong!* is a Requiem of an-Other sort, a hemmed in hymn whose notes gather a fugued, fractured, and fractal commune-ion, an undercommune-ion of the undercommons. The resonance of its dissonance indexes some other kind of congregational practice given in the dark churchicality of the sea.

All of this, Philip states or rather punctuates in the poem's titular exclamation point. Through a riotous poetics of Silence, *Zong!*'s exclamation point *ex*-claims or stands "out from" every property claim. It moves dispossessively or spirit-possessively through dispossession. *Zong!* breathes even if by gasping "towards some air."[108] It is the socio-poetic or pneumatic force of a writing that gasps for breath. This is a fractured spirit-writing, a pneumatography, as I call it, that propels *Zong!* Indeed, such writing convenes an alternative sociality, a nowhere church that moves with and through disorder, with and through disordered breathing and poetic palpitations, in its extraceremonial splaying of words, letters, and sounds spread out or floating across the ocean of the page. The gaps in the poem are breathing pockets, pockets of poetic air for ongoing animacies of the earth, air pockets that mimic the gasps for breath of those thrown overboard. Temples of lung and air, those pockets are sanctuaries or un/held spaces of communion, gaps on the page repurposed as a kind of infinite canvas, an open field. We are in the midst of what Philip calls a "poetics of the fragment . . . driven pneumatically by the energy of the breath, the open spaces that then enfold the fragments," spaces that now constitute a surround, a universe that is not of this world, that is fugitive from the very notion of "World," but that is felt through the *precarity* of this world.[109] That feeling is a kind of nonknowledge of a universe given in the noise uprising, that revolution of the sacred in the revolt of Silence that surges through both the legal text and the liturgical text of the Requiem Mass—witnessing to what cannot be told . . . but *must* be told as an un-telling. This is where Philip is pointing when she says that the spaces between words and within words on the pages of *Zong!* may be understood as "ga(s)ps, in-breathings, breathings-out, or a simple holding of the breath," and that these gaps and gasps or fractured, quantum spaces carry "the potential of a universe . . . given that each breath we take is a fragment of the larger breathing and breath [and respiration] of the universe" (39).

Even Philip herself, as "author" of *Zong!*, is no ordinary author, no ordinary authorial "I." Rather, I think of her as spirit possessed beyond propertied self-possession. That is, she is possessed by the collective subject named "Setaey Adamu Boateng," whom Philip understands both as a figure of those deliberately thrown overboard from the *Zong* and as a figure of Sycorax, the healer-witch, obeah woman, and sorcerer from Shakespeare's *The Tempest* who contested the theo-political magic through which Prospero sought to harness the sacred to his project of gentrifying the Caribbean island of Shakespeare's text, to turn the Americas, indeed, the earth itself into his piece of real estate—into a (propertied) World. Philip's authorial "I" emerges as a cumulative, accumulating "we." Re-en-gendered by a Silence that precedes her and that breaks down the space-time of this world, the very notion of a sovereign, possessive author is fractured, exposed to what surges and hovers beyond. The authorial I fractures into a (Black feminist) malpracticed we, a Boateng-Sycoraxian we-ness that is an "I 'n I"-ness. In moving from the single I to a Rastafarian "I 'n I," this "I 'n I"-ness encodes a socio-sacrality that the ga(s)ping "language of Sycorax, whatever that may be," releases.[110] That release manifests as rapturous excess within the disordered linguistic breaks and conceptual brokenness of *Zong!* This rapturous excess points to a ceremony exceeding the ceremony of theo-politicality, a new "Ceremony of Souls" in which both the dead and the earth breathe through an otherwise we-ness, an alternate imaginary of the universe. This is a hydropoetics-become-cosmopoetics of the sacred, the Black radical sacred.[111] Which is but to say that *Zong!* sounds an under-ness—the underlife, the underworld. It re-sounds the subaquatic and the extraterrestrial, what's under the sea and of the heavens, the broken clusters of words and letters that index the sounds that remain at sea are also like stars dotting the cosmic heavens of an open page. As we "read" this strange text or are "read" *by* it and *into* it— experienced most powerfully when Philip *performs* the poem—we become party to an unspeakable underness, an unspeakable language of un-telling.[112] This "mystical language of unsaying" is the language of a strange us-ness, a quantum us-ness of Black malpractice. Or, as Philip herself says,

> When I perform *Zong!*, I allow the words and word clusters to breathe for
> I 'n I—for the we in us that we epigenetically carry within the memory
> of our cells. When I invite the audience to read with me, we collectively
> engage in breathing for the Other—for those who couldn't breathe—then
>> can't now
>> and, perhaps, won't be able to.
>> In doing so we give them a second life
>> I can't breathe;[113]
>>> I will breathe for you. (39)

The Sacred, without World

At the conclusion of this chapter and having come through this all too brief engagement with Philip's *Zong!*, we in fact have returned to where we began: the question and the quest of other worlds, nowhere. I have made a pre-liminary case that *Zong!* is concerned with that nowhere and in its concern re-ritualizes, which is to say theorizes, the sacred otherwise or in its hydro- and cosmopoetic release from property, from politicality. I have argued that to address Charlottesville is to address what symptomatically, fugitively moves at the limit of the otherworldly limit of the world. At that limit the surreal—the subreal, the submerged—flutters as invisibly felt and is apoca-lyptically unveiled as monstrous, as a sacral Blackness that incites volatility. The white nationalists sought to arrest or otherwise repress the vitality of the alternative. The theo-political project of trying to repress the limit so as to divinize and maintain the state in the image of a stabilizing God is precisely what animates American politicality, where American politicality is American religion, a structure of belief bound up with property or settler enclosure, the centerpiece of which is racially gendered governance as a ra-cially gendered capitalism. This project structures being-American, for to be

American is to be under theo-secular apprenticeship to this project, which as such is apprenticeship into racial *belief*—the discipleship of politicization as racialization. In this way, whiteness is that theo-political practice that has for one of its names "America." It was this that underwrote the events of Charlottesville, Virginia (and at the Emanuel AME Church in Charleston, South Carolina with Dylann Roof, and the violence against Sandra Bland and Philando Castile, and . . .). And it is also this that the abolitionism of Black malpractice in its underworldly, materially otherwise worldly sacrality refuses.

All of this is to say that if, as W. E. B. Du Bois told us a century ago,[114] the religion of whiteness is the propertization of the earth, and if that propertizing rests on a mythic substantialization and imperialization of the sacred converted into a brutalizing property-concept that now theo-politically organizes the space-time of modernity, then with Tracy K. Smith, Black malpractice asks, "Is God being or pure force? The wind / Or what commands it?"[115] In raising such a question and as a poetics of the sacred that cannot help but be a poethics of the sacred, Black malpractice contests, refuses, and objects to the god-terms. It contests them because in its thingliness Blackness moves excrementally as extraceremonial excess, as the re-ritualization of life at the scene of political death. In being both beyond property and being its fundamental critique, Blackness ruptures the god-terms in the interest of some other practice of the sacred . . . in the interest of an material otherworldliness without world. Nowhere.

Notes

Parts of this essay are from a book in progress, "Black Rapture: A Poetics of the Sacred."

1 Stefano Harney and Fred Moten, *The Undercommons: Fugitive Planning and Black Study* (New York: Minor Compositions, 2013).

2 J. Kameron Carter, "Black Malpractice (A Poetics of the Sacred)," *Social Text* 37, no. 2 (2019): 67–107.

3 Fred Moten, *Black and Blur* (Durham, NC: Duke University Press, 2017), 243.

4 Claudia Rankine, *Citizen: An American Lyric* (Minneapolis: Graywolf Press, 2014), 73.

5 Denise Ferreira da Silva, "No-Bodies: Law, Raciality and Violence," *Griffith Law Review* 18, no. 2 (2009): 212–36.

6 Fred Moten, *In the Break: The Aesthetics of the Black Radical Tradition* (Minneapolis: University of Minnesota Press, 2003), 99.

7 Moten, *In the Break*, 99.

8 Moten, *In the Break*, 99.

9 Moten, *In the Break*, 99.

10 Moten, *Black and Blur*, 2.

11 Rudolf Otto, *The Idea of the Holy: An Inquiry in the Non-Rational Factor in the Idea of the Divine and Its Relation to the Rational*, trans. John W. Harvey (New York: Oxford University Press, 1958), chapter 3.

12 On "mu," see Nathaniel Mackey's preface in *Splay Anthem* (New York: New Directions, 2006). Besides the meditation on Mackey's work on "mu" and/as "myth" in this essay, see the meditations on "mu" in Fred Moten, "Blackness and Nothingness (Mysticism in the Flesh)," *South Atlantic Quarterly* 112, no. 4 (2013): 737–80; and in Sora Han, "Poetics of Mu," *Textual Practice*, September 17, 2018, 1–28.

13 The reimagination of matter as central to black (religious) studies, runs through the essays collected in *Ellipsis . . . : The Collected Writings of Charles H. Long* (New York: Bloomsbury Academic, 2018). I signal the centrality of Long not just for "black theology" but more broadly for Black studies in "Charles H. Long and Black Studies; or, Black Theology Hesitant."

14 Hamil R Harris, "U.S. Political Climate Results from 'Theological Malpractice,' D.C. Pastor Says," *Washington Post,* August 25, 2017. https://www .washingtonpost.com/local/social-issues/us-political-climate-results-from -theological-malpractice-dc-pastor-says/2017/08/25/2b96d668-8991-11e7-a50f -eod4e6ec070a_story.html?utm_term=.389072179712.

15 On the relationship between logics of property and logics of gift-giving, and within this context on the status of the earth as ungiven and ungiveable, see Sarah Jane Cervenak, "Black Gathering: Arts of Ungiven Life," unpublished manuscript.

16 At the origins of this distinction in French sociology generally and the sociology of religion specifically on the ambiguity of the sacred in its right- and left-hand modalities is Émile Durkheim's *The Elementary Forms of Religious Life*. For Robert Hertz's clarification and development of this, see "The Pre-Eminence of the Right Hand: A Study in Religious Polarity," in *Death and the Right Hand* (Glencoe, IL: Free Press [1909] 1960), 89–113. As for Georges Bataille, engagement with his oeuvre has been greatly aided by Jeremy Biles, Vivienne Brough-Evans, Amy Hollywood, and Michèle Richman, among others. See Jeremy Biles, *Ecce Monstrum: Georges Bataille and the Sacrifice of Form* (New York: Fordham University Press, 2007); Vivienne Brough-Evans, *Sacred Surrealism, Dissidence and International Avant-Garde Prose* (New York: Routledge, 2016); and Michèle H. Richman, *Sacred Revolutions: Durkheim and the Collège de Sociologie* (Minneapolis: University of Minnesota Press, 2002).

17 Georges Bataille, "The Psychological Structure of Fascism," in *Visions of Excess: Selected Writings, 1927–1939*, ed. Allan Stoekl (Minneapolis: University of Minnesota Press, 1985), 137–60.

18 Roger Caillois, "Brotherhoods, Orders, Secret Societies, Churches," in *The College of Sociology*, ed. Denis Hollier (Minneapolis: University of Minnesota Press, 1988), 152. "Interaffective excess" is an idea that represents my effort to think with David Un-Hsien Liu's "Affective Metaphysics." And, finally, much

of the thinking in this paragraph is reflective of my recent discovery of and engagement with Vivienne Brough-Evans's fine work, *Sacred Surrealism*. The first chapter of this work, "The Collège of Sociologie and Dissident Surrealism," has been particularly helpful.

19 Caillois, "Brotherhoods, Orders, Secret Societies, Churches," 152.

20 Caillois, "Brotherhoods, Orders, Secret Societies, Churches," 282.

21 Bataille, *Inner Experience*, trans. Stuart Kendall (Albany: State University of New York Press, 2014), 105. On the vital difference between negation (-1) and nullification (0) towards the infinite or sheer potentiality (∞), see Denise Ferreira da Silva, "1 (Life) / 0 (Blackness) = ∞ - ∞ or ∞ / ∞: On Matter Beyond the Equation of Value," *e-flux* 79 (February 2017).

22 Caillois, "Brotherhoods, Orders, Secret Societies, Churches," 281.

23 Denise Ferreira da Silva, "On Difference without Separability," in *Incerteza Viva: 32nd Bienal de São Paulo: 7 Sept–11 Dec 2016*, ed. Jochen Volz, Rjeille Isabella, and Júlia Rebouças (São Paulo: Fundaçao Bienal de São Paulo, 2016), 57–65. I should also say that the point I'm trying to make here is in keeping with Michael Germana's superb reading of Ralph Ellison's oeuvre: *Ralph Ellison, Temporal Technologist* (New York: Oxford University Press, 2018).

24 Caillois, "Brotherhoods, Orders, Secret Societies, Churches," 282.

25 Bataille, "Psychological Structure of Fascism," 142.

26 Bataille, "Base Materialism and Gnosticism," in *Visions of Excess: Selected Writings, 1927–1939*, ed. Allan Stoekl, 45–52 (Minneapolis: University of Minnesota Press, 1985), 45–52.

27 Richman, *Sacred Revolutions*, 124.

28 Bataille, "Psychological Structure of Fascism," 143.

29 On "pastoral power," see Michel Foucault, *Power*, ed. James D. Faubion, vol. 3 of *The Essential Works of Foucault, 1954–1984* (New York: New Press), 2000.

30 Bataille, "Psychological Structure of Fascism," 144.

31 Bataille, "Psychological Structure of Fascism," 144.

32 Bataille, "Psychological Structure of Fascism," 142.

33 Bataille, "Psychological Structure of Fascism," 144.

34 Richman, *Sacred Revolutions*, 180.

35 Alexander Riley, *Godless Intellectuals? The Intellectual Pursuit of the Sacred Reinvented* (New York: Berghahn Books, 2013), 154.

36 Riley, *Godless Intellectuals?*, 154.

37 Riley, *Godless Intellectuals?*, 154.

38 Robert A. Yelle, *Sovereignty and the Sacred: Secularism and the Political Economy of Religion* (Chicago: University of Chicago Press, 2019), 75, 184.

39 Yelle, *Sovereignty and the Sacred*, 184. Édouard Glissant, *Poetics of Relation*, trans. Betsy Wing (Ann Arbor: University of Michigan Press, 1997), 144.

40 On "symptoms of the sacred" in the context of the Middle Passage, see Hortense J. Spillers, "Mama's Baby, Papa's Maybe: An American Grammar Book," in *Black, White, and in Color: Essays on American Literature and Culture* (Chicago: University of Chicago Press, 2003). 213. Additionally, one

would not be mistaken to hear echoes of Moten's poem "There is blackness" in this sentence.

41 See Silva, "1 (Life) / 0 (Blackness) = ∞ - ∞ or ∞ / ∞."

42 Denise Ferreira da Silva, "Toward a Black Feminist Poethics: The Quest(ion) of Blackness toward the End of the World," *Black Scholar* 44, no. 2 (2014): 81–97; and Charles H. Long, *Significations: Signs, Symbols, and Images in the Interpretation of Religion* (Aurora, CO: The Davies Group Publishers, 1995), 9.

43 Denise Ferreira da Silva, "In the Raw," *e-flux* 93 (September 2018). On the wild and the wilderness, I have in mind Jack Halberstam and Tavia Nyong'o, "Theory in the Wild," *South Atlantic Quarterly* 117, no. 3 (July 2018): 453–64; Saidiya Hartman, "The Anarchy of Colored Girls Assembled in a Riotous Manner," *South Atlantic Quarterly* 117, no. 3 (2018): 465–90; and Delores Williams, *Sisters in the Wilderness: The Challenge of Womanist God-Talk* (Maryknoll, NY: Orbis Books, 1993). On "spiritual ordeal" and hermeticism and modern philosophy, see Joshua Ramey, *The Hermetic Deleuze: Philosophy and Spiritual Ordeal* (Durham, NC: Duke University Press, 2012).

44 My use of the "pathological" here borrows from David Lloyd's recent elaboration of the Subaltern and the Savage in relation to modern aesthetics. See David Lloyd, *Under Representation: The Racial Regime of Aesthetics* (New York: Fordham University Press, 2019).

45 Not just in this sentence but throughout this chapter, I'm involved in an ongoing thinking with poet-theorist Fred Moten. See Fred Moten, *In the Break*, and the recent trilogy, *consent not to be a single being—Black and Blur; Stolen Life* (Durham, NC: Duke University Press, 2018); and *The Universal Machine* (Durham, NC: Duke University Press, 2018).

46 On "godlessmysticism," a notion drawn from Edgar Morin, see Alexander Riley, "Ethnography of the Ek-Static Experience: Poésie Auto-Socioanalytique in the Work of Michel Leiris," *Journal of Contemporary Ethnography* 44, no. 3 (2015): 366.

47 Phillip Williams, "God as Failed Figuration," in *Thief in the Interior* (Farmington, ME: Alice James Books, 2016), 13. The notion of "the American aesthetic" is from Phillip Williams, "Inheritance: The Force of Aperture," in *Thief in the Interior*, 11–12, 12.

48 Kevin Quashie, *The Sovereignty of Quiet: Beyond Resistance in Black Culture* (New Brunswick, NJ: Rutgers University Press, 2012).

49 I have in mind here Sora Han's ground-shifting meditation on the 1857 legal case known in the legal archive as *Betty's Case* (see Sora Han, "Slavery as Contract: *Betty's Case* and the Question of Freedom," *Law and Literature* 27, no. 3 [2015]: 395). At issue in the case is the relationship between freedom and slavery for a slave woman, Betty, whom Chief Justice Lemuel Shaw of the Massachusetts Supreme Court declared free by virtue of her arrival from Tennessee with her owners into the northern free state of Massachusetts. In free territory, Betty's relationship to her owners as a matter of law or a matter

of a kind of legal alchemy from one of property of an owner to one of a free agent contracting out her labor. The question in the case was, Can free will be exercised in any and every way, including the freedom to become a slave again? The reason this legal question arose is because though standing in the transcendent freedom proscribed by law, Betty nevertheless exercised freedom against the very transcendent that law aims to protect; she opts to return to Tennessee with her owners, thus exercising freedom toward unfreedom, toward becoming (again) a slave. Han astutely walks us through the legal issues, arguing that while slavery can be thought about under the rubric of property (which is typically and most often how it is thought about), what *Betty's Case* reveals is that "contract" is the more central category and problematic. It is, Han says, "the condition of possibility for the slave's property status" (403). Han further argues that the kind of freedom Betty enacted was, in fact, an obscenity, an obscene form of freedom, in that this is a practice of freedom that arrives as the negation of legal freedom, "a giving away or a giving up on freedom." Let us call such "malpractice" freedom-prime that moves "in a subterranean realm" even as it shows up in relationship to legal thought. From freedom-prime, which shows up precisely as freedom's malpractice, (legal) freedom's nonperformance, freedom's protocols as imagined within liberal (contract) law are breached, disclosing that in Betty's case, which is to say "the case of Blackness," there is a fundamental indistinction between slavery and (liberal) freedom.

But I must quickly sharpen this statement: the obscenity of Betty's freedom act, her freedom drive, is not merely that it breached the protocols of liberal freedom. Rather, her freedom act discloses liberal freedom as never not already breached by "a form of pure performativity" that, referring to Moten, Han calls "improvisation." Improvisation here indexes a mode of freedom that "cannot be specifically contracted, nor performed against a contract, but is nonetheless a legal form contract law might refer to as nonperformance. We might say that improvisation is the kernel around which contract law's recognition of nonperformance circles, and that which it attempts to defend the promise (of the contracting parties) against" (408).

In "Black Malpractice (A Poetics of the Sacred)" I develop the idea of Blackness as a poetics of the breach, a performative in and against the notions of the sacred that have been recruited to subtend or otherwise sanction the modernist ideas of religion and the secular even as such performative breach against what I have taken to calling "the contract of religion" discloses some other, excessive horizon of the sacred altogether, what I call the Black radical sacred. This connects to what earlier in this chapter I called an "improvisation of the sacred." For another engagement with Han's notion of "nonperformance," see Fred Moten, "Erotics of Fugitivity," in *Stolen Life* (Durham, NC: Duke University Press, 2018). And on my invocation earlier of "the case of Blackness," see Fred Moten, "The Case of Blackness," *Criticism* 50, no. 2 (2009): 177–218.

50 Carl Schmitt, *Political Theology: Four Chapters on the Concept of Sovereignty* (Chicago: University of Chicago Press, [1934] 2005), 36.

51 Rei Terada, "Robinson's Terms," paper presented at the Poetics of Law/Poetics of Decolonization conference, University of California, Riverside, CA, May 21, 2018. I am grateful to Professor Terada for providing me a copy of her paper and allowing me to quote from it.

52 Mircea Eliade, *The Sacred and the Profane: The Nature of Religion* (New York: Harcourt Brace, [1957] 1987), 63.

53 Terada, "Robinson's Terms," 64.

54 Cedric J. Robinson, *Black Marxism: The Making of the Black Radical Tradition* (Chapel Hill: University of North Carolina Press, [1993] 2000), 168, 171.

55 Terada, "Robinson's Terms," 6.

56 The last few sentences reflect a thinking with Mary Douglas, *Purity and Danger: An Analysis of the Concepts of Pollution and Taboo* (London: Routledge, [1966] 2002); Lindon Barrett, *Blackness and Value: Seeing Double* (Cambridge: Cambridge University Press, 1999); David Marriott, *Whither Fanon? Studies in the Blackness of Being* (Stanford, CA: Stanford University Press, 2018); and Silva, "1 (Life) / 0 (Blackness) = ∞ - ∞ or ∞ / ∞."

57 Eliade, *Sacred and the Profane*, 20.

58 See Georges Bataille, "The Sacred Conspiracy," in *Visions of Excess: Selected Writings, 1927–1939*, ed. Allan Stoekl (Minneapolis: University of Minnesota Press, 1985), 178–81; and Spillers, "Mama's Baby, Papa's Maybe."

59 Eliade, *Sacred and the Profane*, 31, 28.

60 Eliade, *Sacred and the Profane*, 64.

61 Eliade, *Sacred and the Profane*, 64.

62 Moten, *In the Break*.

63 Here I echo Nathaniel Mackey's meditations on the sufferings of the non-singular, nonindividuated "I" who dwells in dividuation while suffering individuation. See "Solomon's Outer Wall," in *Eroding Witness* (Pittsboro, NC: Selva Oscura Press, [1985] 2018).

64 Ringing in my head as I write this sentence is something poet Nuar Alsadir says: "The lyric, as a form of ego splitting, becoming multiple, monument to a state of knowing and not-knowing." Nuar Alsadir, *Fourth Person Singular* (Liverpool: Liverpool University Press, 2017), 16.

65 Denise Ferreira da Silva, *Toward the Global Idea of Race* (Minneapolis: University of Minnesota Press, 2007); and Ashon T. Crawley, *Blackpentecostal Breath: The Aesthetics of Possibility* (New York: Fordham University Press, 2016).

66 I am grateful for conversations at the Blackburn Festival: The Mackey Sessions conference at Duke University, September 20–22, 2018, with fellow panelists Norman Finkelstein, Jeanne Heuving, and Peter O'Leary on the theme of "Ythm" in Nathaniel Mackey's poetics. I am particularly grateful for O'Leary's fine paper, "Myth's Ythmic Whatsay," which moves in relationship to what follows here.

67 See Mackey, preface to *Splay Anthem*, xiii.

68 See R. A. Judy, "Sentient Flesh (Thinking in Disorder/Poiēsis in Black)," unpublished manuscript, 2018.

69 Nathaniel Mackey, "A Night in Jaipur," in *Blue Fasa* (New York: New Directions, 2015), 4.

70 Moten, *In the Break*, 26. This is a theme also developed in Harney and Moten, *The Undercommons*.

71 The first serious attempt to curb the gyrovagues of old is to be found in St. Benedict's "Monastic Rule." Indeed, St. Benedict's Rule is counterrevolutionary, it counters the revolution, the turning. It comes into effect against the gyrovague, the wanderer. See Caroline White, ed., *The Rule of St. Benedict* (New York: Penguin Classics, 2008). As for wandering as a problem for (post-)Enlightenment modernity and as it relates to racial and sexual regulation, see Sarah Jane Cervenak, *Wandering: Philosophical Performances of Racial and Sexual Freedom* (Durham: Duke University Press, 2014). I read *Wandering* as contending with the racial-sexual legacy of St. Benedict's monastic Rule and the injunctions of obedience.

72 The ungivenness and the ungiveableness of the earth, see Cervenak, "Black Gathering."

73 Here I am thinking simultaneously with Stefano Harney and Fred Moten, "Base Faith," *e-flux* 86 (November 2017), on the one hand, and with Georges Bataille, "Base Materialism and Gnosticism" and "The Deviations of Nature," in *Visions of Excess: Selected Writings, 1927–1939*, ed. Allan Stoekl (Minneapolis: University of Minnesota Press, 1985), 53–56, on the other.

74 Dawn Lundy Martin, "A Black Poetics: Against Mastery," *boundary 2* 44, no. 3 (2017): 161.

75 Martin, "Black Poetics."

76 On Porete's "pseudowomanhood" and her notion of "relinquishment," see Michael A. Sells, *Mystical Languages of Unsaying* (Chicago: University of Chicago Press, 1994), 117. Throughout this paragraph, I'm thinking alongside Marguerite Porete, *The Mirror of Simple Souls* (Mahwah, NJ: Paulist Press, 1993).

77 In the preface to her poetry collection *Spill*, Gumbs says, "This space, which is a temporary space, which we must leave, for the sake of future travelers and for our own necks, is a sacred dedicated space. Libation for the named and the nameless . . . for black women who made and broke narrative. The quiet, the quarrelling, the queer." Alexis Pauline Gumbs, *Spill: Scenes of Black Feminist Fugitivity* (Durham, NC: Duke University Press, 2016), xii. In Durham, NC, where I currently live, artist-activist and musician Pierce Freelon, who also made a recent run for mayor of the city, has developed a space for the free expression and "afro-futurist" cultivation of young, primarily Black and Brown people of color. It is a sacred space called "blackspace." See Eric Tullis, "Space Is the Place: Durham Gets a Hub for Afrofuturist Thought with Blackspace," *Indy Week*, June, 16, 2016, https://indyweek.com/music/archives/space-place-durham-gets-hub-afrofuturist-thought-blackspace/.

78 Cervenak and I think about "suspension" in J. Kameron Carter and Sarah Jane Cervenak, "Black Ether," CR: *The New Centennial Review* 16, no. 2 (2016): 203–24.

79 Moten, from his talk given at the conference Scenes at 20: Inspirations, Riffs, Reverberations, October 6, 2017. But also his fuller elaboration on celebration in *Black and Blur*, xiii. This paragraph bears the traces of insights from a fine talk by Rizvana Bradley at the same conference on October 6, 2017, which also engaged the question of suspension.

80 Nathaniel Mackey engages the notion of *duende* in "Cante Moro," in *Paracritical Hinge: Essays, Talks, Notes, Interviews* (Madison: University of Wisconsin Press, 2005). Further references will be internal. For more on *duende*, see Frederico García Lorca, "Play and Theory of the Duende," 56–72, and "Deep Song," 1–27, in *In Search of Duende* (New York: New Directions, 2010).

81 Mackey, "Cante Moro," 182.

82 García Lorca, "Play and Theory of the Duende," 62, 57, 72.

83 García Lorca quotes Manuel Torre as saying, "'All that has black sounds has duende.'" He goes on to comment: "And there is no greater truth. These 'black sounds' are the mystery, the roots fastened in the mire that we all know and all ignore, the fertile silt that gives us the very substance of art. . . . 'A mysterious power which everyone senses and no philosopher explains.' The duende, then, is a power not a work. It is a struggle not a thought. . . . This 'mysterious power . . .' is, in sum, the spirit of the earth." See, García Lorca, "Play and Theory of Duende," 57. On the Andalusian music known as "deep song," which also informs Mackey, see García Lorca's profound essay, "Deep Song," 1–27.

84 Mackey, "Cante Moro," 182.

85 Mackey, "Cante Moro," 184, 185.

86 Mackey, "Cante Moro," 185.

87 André Lepecki, *Exhausting Dance: Performance and the Politics of Movement* (New York: Routledge, 2006), 109.

88 Lepecki, *Exhausting Dance*, 109.

89 Nathaniel Mackey, *Late Arcade* (New York: New Directions, 2017).

90 On the history of this incident, see James Walvin, *The Zong: A Massacre, the Law, and the End of Slavery* (New Haven: Yale University Press, 2011), as well as M. NorubeSe Philip's essay, "Notanda," at the end of *Zong!* (Middletown, CT: Wesleyan University Press, 2011). References to *Zong!* and to this essay will occur parenthetically.

91 Philip reproduces the summary judgment of the court case as part of the back matter of *Zong!*.

92 Mandy Bloomfield, *Archaeopoetics: Word, Image, History* (Tuscaloosa: University Alabama Press, 2016), 192.

93 M. NourbeSe Philip, *Genealogy of Resistance, and Other Essays* (Toronto: Mercury Press, 1998), 116, as quoted in Bloomfield, *Archaeopoetics*, 192.

94 Bloomfield, *Archaeopoetics*, 201.

95　In the background of this interpretation of Philip's statement is Walter Benjamin's "Critique of Violence," in *Walter Benjamin: Selected Writings, Volume 1: 1913–1926*, ed. Marcus Bullock and Michael W. Jennings (Cambridge: Belknap Press of Harvard University Press), 236–52; and "Goethe's Elective Affinities," in *Walter Benjamin: Selected Writings, Volume 1: 1913–1926*, 297–360. Between these two crucial texts of the Benjaminian corpus is Benjamin's theorization of divine violence in contrast to mythic violence as well as, in relationship to this distinction, his crucial formulation of the notion of the "daemonic," which I'm aligning with Philip's notion of the shaman and by extension her notion of ritual, glossolalia, and magic, all of which comes to a head with the ghostly, witchly figure of Sycorax, figure of the Black radical, lack feminist sacred. I develop this idea further in my book-in-progress, "Black Rapture." I am grateful to the work of Nijah Cunningham for first sending me down this Benjaminian course of investigation. See Nijah Cunningham, "The Resistance of the Lost Body," *small axe* 20, no. 1 (49) (March 1, 2016): 113–28.

96　Bloomfield, *Archaeopoetics*, 201.

97　Georges Bataille, *Lascaux; or, The Birth of Art* (Lausanne: Skira, 1955), 39.

98　Moten, *Stolen Life*, 244, thinking with Denise Ferreira da Silva. See Silva, "On Difference without Separability."

99　Denise Ferreira da Silva, "Hacking the Subject: Black Feminism and Refusal beyond the Limits of Critique," *PhiloSOPHIA* 8, no. 1 (2018): 19–41.

100　For more information about the Roman Catholic Requiem Mass, see Pietro Piacenza, "Masses of Requiem," *The Catholic Encyclopedia*, vol. 12 (New York: Robert Appleton Company, 1911), http://www.newadvent.org/cathen/12776d.htm. I am grateful for email exchanges with Yale Divinity School professor Teresa Berger that have helped me think through the Requiem Mass.

101　Lauren F. Winner, *The Dangers of Christian Practice: On Wayward Gifts, Characteristic Damage, and Sin* (New Haven, CT: Yale University Press, 2018).

102　On aliveness, I am thinking with Kevin Quashie, "Black Aliveness; or, a Poetics of Being," unpublished manuscript.

103　Barrett, *Blackness and Value*, 28. See also Kyla Wazana Tompkins, *Racial Indigestion: Eating Bodies in the 19th Century* (New York: New York University Press, 2012).

104　Barrett, *Blackness and Value*, 27.

105　On Wynter's "Beyond," see Sylvia Wynter, "Black Metamorphosis," n.d., unpublished manuscript; Greg Thomas, "Sex/Sexuality & Sylvia Wynter's 'Beyond . . .': Anti-Colonial Ideas in 'Black Radical Tradition,'" *Journal of West Indian Literature* 10, nos. 1–2 (2001): 92–118; and J. Cameron Carter, "Black Malpractice (A Poetics of the Sacred)," *Social Text* 37, no. 2 (2019): 67–107.

106　Moten, *Stolen Life*, ix.

107　Here I am extending Calvin Warren's account of anti-Blackness as "ontological terror" to surface the onto-*theological* architecture of that terror and yet think what hovers beyond, within, "(not)(in) between," as Moten with Wynter might say. See Calvin Warren, *Ontological Terror: Blackness, Nihilism, and Emancipation* (Durham, NC: Duke University Press, 2018).

108 Amy De'Ath and Fred Wah, eds., *Toward. Some. Air.: Remarks on Poetics* (Banff, Alberta: Banff Centre Press, 2015).

109 M. NorubeSe Philip, "The Ga(s)P," in *Poetics and Precarity*, ed. Myung Mi Kim and Cristanne Miller (Albany: State University of New York Press, 2018), 31–40. 39. Further references are within the chapter.

110 M. NorubeSe Philip, "A Piece of Land Surrounded," in *A Genealogy of Resistance: And Other Essays* (Toronto: Mercury Press, 1998), 161–73, at 167.

111 I am thinking here with Joshua Bennett and Sarah Jane Cervenak. See Angela Hume, Gillian Osborne, and Joshua Bennett, eds., "Vomiting in the Dark: Towards a Black Hydropoetics," in *Ecopoetics: Essays in the Field* (Iowa City: University of Iowa Press, 2018), 102–17; and Cervenak, "Black Gathering."

112 See Philips's April 24, 2017 talk and performance of *Zong!* as part of the events of "The Black Outdoors."

113 "I can't breathe" were the words of Eric Garner, said eleven times as he was in a chokehold before he died at the hands of the New York City police on July 17, 2014.

114 See W. E. B. Du Bois, "Souls of White Folk," in *Dark Water: Voices from within the Veil* (Amherst, NY: Humanity Books, [1919] 2002).

115 Tracy K. Smith, *Life on Mars: Poems* (Minneapolis: Graywolf Press, 2011), 3.

References

Alsadir, Nuar. 2017. *Fourth Person Singular*. Liverpool: Liverpool University Press.

Barrett, Lindon. 1999. *Blackness and Value: Seeing Double*. Cambridge: Cambridge University Press.

Bataille, Georges. 1955. *Lascaux; or, The Birth of Art*. Lausanne: Skira.

Bataille, Georges. 1985. "Base Materialism and Gnosticism." In *Visions of Excess: Selected Writings, 1927–1939*, edited by Allan Stoekl, 45–52. Minneapolis: University of Minnesota Press.

Bataille, Georges. 1985. "The Deviations of Nature." In *Visions of Excess: Selected Writings, 1927–1939*, edited by Allan Stoekl, 53–56. Minneapolis: University of Minnesota Press.

Bataille, Georges. 1985. "The Psychological Structure of Fascism." In *Visions of Excess: Selected Writings, 1927–1939*, edited by Allan Stoekl, 137–60. Minneapolis: University of Minnesota Press.

Bataille, Georges. 1985. "The Sacred Conspiracy." In *Visions of Excess: Selected Writings, 1927–1939*, edited by Allan Stoekl, 178–81. Minneapolis: University of Minnesota Press.

Bataille, Georges. 2014. *Inner Experience*. Translated by Stuart Kendall. Albany: State University of New York Press.

Benjamin, Walter. 2004. "Critique of Violence." In *Walter Benjamin: Selected Writings, Volume 1: 1913–1926*, edited by Marcus Bullock and Michael W.

Jennings, 236–252. Cambridge: Belknap Press of Harvard University Press.

Benjamin, Walter. 2004. "Goethe's Elective Affinities." In *Walter Benjamin: Selected Writings, Volume 1: 1913–1926*, edited by Marcus Bullock and Michael W. Jennings, 297–360. Cambridge: Belknap Press of Harvard University Press.

Biles, Jeremy. 2007. *Ecce Monstrum: Georges Bataille and the Sacrifice of Form*. New York: Fordham University Press.

Bloomfield, Mandy. 2016. *Archaeopoetics: Word, Image, History*. Tuscaloosa: University of Alabama Press.

Brough-Evans, Vivienne. 2016. *Sacred Surrealism, Dissidence and International Avant-Garde Prose*. New York: Routledge.

Caillois, Roger. 1988. "Brotherhoods, Orders, Secret Societies, Churches." In *The College of Sociology*, edited by Denis Hollier, 145–56. Minneapolis: University of Minnesota Press.

Caillois, Roger. 1988. "Festivals." In *The College of Sociology*, edited by Denis Hollier, 279–303. Minneapolis: University of Minnesota Press.

Carter, J. Kameron. 2019. "Black Malpractice (A Poetics of the Sacred)." *Social Text* 37, no. 2: 67–107.

Carter, J. Kameron, and Sarah Jane Cervenak. 2016. "Black Ether." CR: *The New Centennial Review* 16, no. 2: 203–24.

Cervenak, Sarah Jane. 2014. *Wandering: Philosophical Performances of Racial and Sexual Freedom*. Durham, NC: Duke University Press, 2014.

Cervenak, Sarah Jane. "Black Gathering: Arts of Ungiven Life." Unpublished manuscript.

Crawley, Ashon T. 2016. *Blackpentecostal Breath: The Aesthetics of Possibility*. New York: Fordham University Press.

Cunningham, Nijah. 2016. "The Resistance of the Lost Body." *small axe* 20, no. 1 (49) (March 1): 113–28.

De'Ath, Amy, and Fred Wah, eds. 2015. *Toward. Some. Air.: Remarks on Poetics*. Banff, Alberta: Banff Centre Press.

Douglas, Mary. [1966] 2002. *Purity and Danger: An Analysis of the Concepts of Pollution and Taboo*. London: Routledge.

Du Bois, W. E. B. [1919] 2002. "Souls of White Folk." In *Dark Water: Voices from within the Veil*. Amherst, NY: Humanity Books.

Durkheim, Émile. [1912] 1995. *The Elementary Forms of Religious Life*. Translated by Karen E. Fields. New York: Free Press.

Eliade, Mircea. [1957] 1987. *The Sacred and the Profane: The Nature of Religion*. New York: Harcourt Brace.

Foucault, Michel. 2000. *Power*. Edited by James D. Faubion. Vol. 3 of *The Essential Works of Foucault, 1954–1984*. New York: New Press.

García Lorca, Federico. 2010. "Deep Song." In *In Search of Duende*, 1–27. New York: New Directions.

García Lorca, Federico. 2010. "Play and Theory of the Duende." In *In Search of Duende*, 56–72. New York: New Directions.

Germana, Michael. 2018. *Ralph Ellison, Temporal Technologist*. New York: Oxford University Press.

Glissant, Édouard. 1997. *Poetics of Relation*. Translated by Betsy Wing. Ann Arbor: University of Michigan Press.

Gumbs, Alexis Pauline. 2016. *Spill: Scenes of Black Feminist Fugitivity*. Durham, NC: Duke University Press.

Halberstam, Jack. 2011. *The Queer Art of Failure*. Durham, NC: Duke University Press.

Halberstam, Jack, and Tavia Nyong'o. 2018. "Theory in the Wild." *South Atlantic Quarterly* 117, no. 3 (July): 453–64.

Han, Sora. 2015. "Slavery as Contract: *Betty's Case* and the Question of Freedom." *Law and Literature* 27, no. 3: 395–416.

Han, Sora. "Poetics of Mu." *Textual Practice*, September 17, 2018, 1–28.

Harney, Stefano, and Fred Moten. 2013. *The Undercommons: Fugitive Planning and Black Study*. New York: Minor Compositions.

Harney, Stefano, and Fred Moten. 2017. "Base Faith." *e-flux* 86 (November).

Harris, Hamil R. 2017. "U.S. Political Climate Results from 'Theological Malpractice,' D.C. Pastor Says." *Washington Post,* August 25. https://www .washingtonpost.com/local/social-issues/us-political-climate-results-from -theological-malpractice-dc-pastor-says/2017/08/25/2b96d668-8991-11e7 -a50f-e0d4e6ec070a_story.html?utm_term=.389072179712.

Hartman, Saidiya. 2018. "The Anarchy of Colored Girls Assembled in a Riotous Manner." *South Atlantic Quarterly* 117, no. 3: 465–90.

Hertz, Robert. [1909] 1960. "The Pre-Eminence of the Right Hand: A Study in Religious Polarity." In *Death and The Right Hand*, 89–113. Glencoe, IL: Free Press.

Hollywood, Amy. 2002. *Sensible Ecstasy: Mysticism, Sexual Difference, and the Demands of History*. Chicago: University of Chicago Press.

Hume, Angela, Gillian Osborne, and Joshua Bennett, eds. 2018. "Vomiting in the Dark: Towards a Black Hydropoetics." In *Ecopoetics: Essays in the Field*, 102–17. Iowa City: University of Iowa Press.

Judy, R. A. 2018. "Sentient Flesh (Thinking in Disorder/Poiēsis in Black)." Unpublished manuscript, University of Pittsburgh.

Lepecki, André. 2006. *Exhausting Dance: Performance and the Politics of Movement*. New York: Routledge.

Liu, David Un-Hsien. 2008. "Affective Metaphysics." PhD diss., Duke University.

Lloyd, David. 2019. *Under Representation: The Racial Regime of Aesthetics*. New York: Fordham University Press.

Long, Charles H. 1995. *Significations: Signs, Symbols, and Images in the Interpretation of Religion*. Aurora, CO: The Davies Group Publishers.

Long, Charles H. 2018. *Ellipsis . . . : The Collected Writings of Charles H. Long*. New York: Bloomsbury Academic.

Mackey, Nathaniel. 2005. "Cante Moro." In *Paracritical Hinge: Essays, Talks, Notes, Interviews*. Madison: University of Wisconsin Press.

Mackey, Nathaniel. 2006. Preface to *Splay Anthem*. New York: New Directions.

Mackey, Nathaniel. 2015. "A Night in Jaipur." In *Blue Fasa*, 3–5. New York: New Directions.

Mackey, Nathaniel. 2017. *Late Arcade*. New York: New Directions.

Mackey, Nathaniel. [1985] 2018. "Solomon's Outer Wall." In *Eroding Witness*. Pittsboro, NC: Selva Oscura Press.

Marriott, David. 2018. *Whither Fanon? Studies in the Blackness of Being*. Stanford, CA: Stanford University Press.

Martin, Dawn Lundy. 2017. "A Black Poetics: Against Mastery." *boundary 2* 44, no. 3: 159–63.

Moten, Fred. 2003. *In the Break: The Aesthetics of the Black Radical Tradition*. Minneapolis: University of Minnesota Press.

Moten, Fred. 2008. "There Is Blackness." In *Hughson's Tavern*. Providence, RI: Leon Works.

Moten, Fred. 2009. "The Case of Blackness." *Criticism* 50, no. 2: 177–218.

Moten, Fred. 2013. "Blackness and Nothingness (Mysticism in the Flesh)." *South Atlantic Quarterly* 112, no. 4: 737–80.

Moten, Fred. 2017. *Black and Blur*. Durham, NC: Duke University Press.

Moten, Fred. 2018. "Erotics of Fugitivity." In *Stolen Life*. Durham, NC: Duke University Press.

Moten, Fred. 2018. *Stolen Life*. Durham, NC: Duke University Press.

Moten, Fred. 2018. *The Universal Machine*. Durham, NC: Duke University Press.

O'Leary, Peter. 2018. "Myth's Ythmic Whatsay: Choric Escort, Chronic Dispatch, and Nathaniel Mackey." Paper presented at the Blackburn Festival: The Mackey Sessions conference at Duke University, Durham, NC, September 21.

Otto, Rudolf. 1958. *The Idea of the Holy: An Inquiry in the Non-Rational Factor in the Idea of the Divine and Its Relation to the Rational*. Translated by John W. Harvey. New York: Oxford University Press.

Philip, M. NourbeSe. 1998. *A Genealogy of Resistance: And Other Essays*. Toronto: Mercury Press.

Philip, M. NourbeSe. 1998. "A Piece of Land Surrounded." In *A Genealogy of Resistance: And Other Essays*, 161–73. Toronto: Mercury Press.

Philip, M. NourbeSe. 2013. "Wor(l)ds Interrupted." *Jacket2*. September 17. http://jacket2.org/article/worlds-interrupted.

Philip, M. NourbeSe. 2017. "*Zong!* and the Black Outdoors." *YouTube*, uploaded by Duke Franklin Humanities Institute, August 8. https://www.youtube.com/watch?v=TLQIlExEYmw.

Philip, M. NourbeSe. 2018. "The Ga(s)P." In *Poetics and Precarity*, edited by Myung Mi Kim and Cristanne Miller, 31–40. Albany: State University of New York Press.

Philip, M. NourbeSe (and Setaey Adamu Boateng). 2011. *Zong!* Middletown, CT: Wesleyan University Press.

Piacenza, Pietro. 1911. "Masses of Requiem." *The Catholic Encyclopedia*, vol. 12. New York: Robert Appleton Company. http://www.newadvent.org/cathen/12776d.htm.

Porete, Marguerite. 1993. *The Mirror of Simple Souls*. Mahwah, NJ: Paulist Press.

Quashie, Kevin. 2012. *The Sovereignty of Quiet: Beyond Resistance in Black Culture*. New Brunswick, NJ; Rutgers University Press.

Quashie, Kevin. "Black Aliveness; or, a Poetics of Being." Unpublished manuscript.

Ramey, Joshua. 2012. *The Hermetic Deleuze: Philosophy and Spiritual Ordeal*. Durham, NC: Duke University Press.

Rankine, Claudia. 2014. *Citizen: An American Lyric*. Minneapolis: Graywolf Press.

Richman, Michèle H. 2002. *Sacred Revolutions: Durkheim and the Collège de Sociologie*. Minneapolis: University of Minnesota Press.

Riley, Alexander. 2013. *Godless Intellectuals? The Intellectual Pursuit of the Sacred Reinvented*. New York: Berghahn Books.

Riley, Alexander. 2015. "Ethnography of the Ek-Static Experience: Poésie Auto-Socioanalytique in the Work of Michel Leiris." *Journal of Contemporary Ethnography* 44, no. 3: 362–86.

Robinson, Cedric J. [1993] 2000. *Black Marxism: The Making of the Black Radical Tradition*. Chapel Hill: University of North Carolina Press.

Schmitt, Carl. [1934] 2005. *Political Theology: Four Chapters on the Concept of Sovereignty*. Chicago: University of Chicago Press.

Sells, Michael A. 1994. *Mystical Languages of Unsaying*. Chicago: University of Chicago Press.

Silva, Denise Ferreira da. 2007. *Toward a Global Idea of Race*. Minneapolis: University of Minnesota Press.

Silva, Denise Ferreira da. 2009. "No-Bodies: Law, Raciality and Violence." *Griffith Law Review* 18, no. 2: 212–36.

Silva, Denise Ferreira da. 2014. "Toward a Black Feminist Poethics: The Quest(ion) of Blackness toward the End of the World." *Black Scholar* 44, no. 2: 81–97.

Silva, Denise Ferreira da. 2016. "On Difference without Separability." In *Incerteza Viva: 32nd Bienal de São Paulo: 7 Sept–11 Dec 2016*, edited by Jochen Volz, Rjeille Isabella, and Júlia Rebouças, 57–65. São Paulo: Fundaçao Bienal de São Paulo.

Silva, Denise Ferreira da. 2017. "1 (Life) / 0 (Blackness) = ∞ - ∞ or ∞ / ∞: On Matter Beyond the Equation of Value." *e-flux* 79 (February).

Silva, Denise Ferreira da. 2018. "Hacking the Subject: Black Feminism and Refusal beyond the Limits of Critique." *PhiloSOPHIA* 8, no. 1: 19–41.

Silva, Denise Ferreira da. 2018. "In the Raw." *e-flux* 93 (September).

Smith, Tracy K. 2011. *Life on Mars: Poems*. Minneapolis: Graywolf Press.

Spillers, Hortense J. 2003. "Mama's Baby, Papa's Maybe: An American Grammar Book." In *Black, White, and in Color: Essays on American Literature and Culture*, 203–29. Chicago: University of Chicago Press.

Terada, Rei. 2018. "Robinson's Terms." Paper presented at the Poetics of Law/Poetics of Decolonization conference, University of California, Riverside, CA, May 21.

Thomas, Greg. 2001. "Sex/Sexuality & Sylvia Wynter's 'Beyond . . .': Anti-Colonial Ideas in 'Black Radical Tradition.'" *Journal of West Indian Literature* 10, nos. 1–2: 92–118.

Tompkins, Kyla Wazana. 2012. *Racial Indigestion: Eating Bodies in the 19th Century*. New York: New York University Press.

Tullis, Eric. 2016. "Space Is the Place: Durham Gets a Hub for Afrofuturist Thought with Blackspace." *Indy Week*, June 16. https://indyweek.com/music/archives/space-place-durham-gets-hub-afrofuturist-thought-blackspace/.

Walvin, James. 2011. *The Zong: A Massacre, the Law, and the End of Slavery*. New Haven, CT: Yale University Press.

Warren, Calvin L. 2018. *Ontological Terror: Blackness, Nihilism, and Emancipation*. Durham, NC: Duke University Press.

White, Caroline, ed. 2008. *The Rule of St. Benedict*. New York: Penguin Classics.

Williams, Delores. 1993. *Sisters in the Wilderness: The Challenge of Womanist God-Talk*. Maryknoll, NY: Orbis Books.

Williams, Phillip B. 2016. "God as Failed Figuration." In *Thief in the Interior*, 13. Farmington, ME: Alice James Books.

Williams, Phillip B. 2016. "Inheritance: The Force of Aperture." In *Thief in the Interior*, 11–12. Farmington, ME: Alice James Books.

Winner, Lauren F. 2018. *The Dangers of Christian Practice: On Wayward Gifts, Characteristic Damage, and Sin*. New Haven, CT: Yale University Press.

Wynter, Sylvia. N.d. "Black Metamorphosis." Unpublished manuscript.

Yelle, Robert A. 2019. *Sovereignty and the Sacred: Secularism and the Political Economy of Religion*. Chicago: University of Chicago Press.

BOUNDLESS
SOCIALITIES

Part III

CHAPTER NINE

Maile Arvin

Possessions of Whiteness

Settler Colonialism and Anti-Blackness in the Pacific

I confess: I avoided watching the 2011 Academy Award–winning movie *The Descendants* (directed by the acclaimed Alexander Payne of *Sideways* and *Nebraska*, and starring George Clooney) for a long time. I had read the book of the same name, by Kaui Hart Hemmings, on which the movie is based.[1] I have complicated feelings about the book—a witty and often wrenching portrayal of a rich Native Hawaiian family that doesn't seem to feel, look, or know much about being Native Hawaiian. Though I recognize such struggles, about feeling or being disconnected from your own culture and nation, as a very Native story (or perhaps, more precisely, as the story of settler colonialism), I don't recognize the ending of Hemmings's story. After much turmoil, the protagonist of her novel decides not to sell the land he has inherited from his family. It is hard to connect with the rich protagonists of Hemmings's novel because I don't know any Native Hawaiians who have land to be inherited. I don't know any Native Hawaiians who frequent yacht clubs. And I don't know any Native Hawaiians who seem so completely unaware of the truly amazing achievements of recent cultural revitalization efforts in the Native Hawaiian community—from language revitalization to traditional seafaring (our beloved *Hōkūleʻa* set sail on a three-year, round-the-world voyage in May 2014). But, to each her own, I thought.

When I did finally watch the movie, despite the fact that I knew the story, despite the fact that I spend most of my time writing, researching, and thinking about whiteness and settler colonialism in the Pacific, and despite the fact that I attended (for a time) the very same, very white-dominated private high school in Honolulu that Hemmings (and, incidentally, Barack Obama) attended, I was stunned. In the film, the residents of Hawaiʻi are shown to be, almost entirely, white people. The Hawai'i of the novel I have glimpsed from a distance, the Hawai'i of the film is utterly unrecognizable to me. Asian Americans, who make up at least 40 percent of Hawai'i's population, are barely represented, much less Native Hawaiians. Hemmings herself has a cameo as the lead's assistant and there are a few Hawaiian musicians in another scene. George Clooney is one of the film's most "ethnic" looking characters and, as the lead role, he plays the scion of a poorly fictionalized royal Hawaiian lineage. It must be said: Native Hawaiians look a lot of different ways, but in no way does George Clooney adequately represent us. My concern here is less about authenticity, as I think many of us must suspend disbelief during Hollywood movies if we are to endure them at all. A more representative cast would not fix the problems of the movie. No matter who was cast in the lead role, a viewer could still easily come away from the film with the sense that the main problems facing Native Hawaiians today are (a) being cuckolded and (b) negotiating real estate deals. I am more concerned about questioning the genealogy and the effects produced by the representation of Hawai'i as chiefly a place of white people, some of whom have Native heritage that they find alternately puzzling, romantic, and lucrative. What allows a movie (with the apparent consent of a Native Hawaiian author) to portray Hawai'i as so blindingly white, in both cast and storyline?

There is a long history—in scientific and popular representations—of understanding the Polynesian race (of which Native Hawaiians are understood to be a part) as ancestrally and biologically white. With Western "exploration" and colonization of the Pacific, Oceania was divided into three ethnologically derived areas: Polynesia, Melanesia, and Micronesia. As constructed by European and American imperialists, Polynesia signified the islands where the natives often appeared to be "almost white." Ethnologists, physical anthropologists, and sociologists from the mid-nineteenth through the mid-twentieth century deployed various methodologies to prove that Polynesians had branched off close to the "Aryan stem," and were thus closely akin to Caucasians. White settlers saw Polynesians as "friendly people" with whom they could live safely and securely. In contrast, Melanesians were written about as decidedly more savage and hostile; as "black." The word Melanesia is derived from "melas," meaning "black" in Greek (whereas "Poly" and "Micro" are geographic distinctions: Polynesia, the area of many islands; Micronesia, the area of small islands). Micronesia was somewhere in the middle and could swing either way, racially—sometimes it was seen as related to Polynesia, and at other times it was more akin to Melanesia.

These imposed Western divisions are certainly porous in the lives of Pacific Islander communities. Peoples from across the areas deemed Polynesia, Melanesia, and Micronesia have long made meaningful connections through their shared identities and genealogies (long before settler colonialism, in fact). Maori scholar Alice Te Punga Somerville's groundbreaking book *Once Were Pacific* reminds us, however, that within the Indigenous communities of Polynesia, and Oceania more widely, we must engage the "disjunctures" and "rather embarrassing genealogies of suspicion, derision, and competition between our communities" that are often structured by racism and colonialism.[2] For example, in Hawai'i, many diasporic Micronesian communities have recently begun speaking out against the racism they face daily from other residents of Hawai'i, including, at times, Native Hawaiians. Micronesians, many of whom have been forcibly dispossessed of their homelands and their health from the reverberating legacies of US nuclear testing there, arrive in Hawai'i to find that they are seen as undeserving, welfare-seeking immigrants.

Micronesians in Hawai'i today therefore find themselves caught on the wrong side of the Polynesian/Melanesian divide. This demonstrates that though the Western categories of Polynesian, Melanesian, and Micronesian originate in the 1830s or even earlier, settler colonialism today still effectively operates with these divisions. Under settler colonialism, Indigenous Pacific Islanders are constructed as property—the feminized, exotic possessions of whiteness. Polynesians are ideal in this respect (think of the pervasive image of the light-skinned "hula girl"), but even Polynesians have little control over their own position within settler colonialism. As possessions of whiteness, Polynesians never gain secure power to possess whiteness or identify as white themselves. Neither do they maintain any secure power to identify as nonwhite or Indigenous separate from their supposed whiteness. Polynesian indigeneity—their specific histories and claims to land and water—is thus erased, differently but just as surely as Micronesian indigeneity is erased when they are viewed as immigrants within the very Oceania that has been their home long before the US claimed any part of it.

In this respect, settler colonialism in the Pacific noticeably overlaps with white supremacy, valorizing whiteness in its supposedly most natural state—Polynesians—as a method of naturalizing and normalizing white settler presence in the Pacific. However, in this overlap, settler colonialism seems to offer a way around the rigid boundaries of white supremacy by promising that any non–Pacific Islander can attain the seeming privileges of whiteness or "whiteness in Polynesian-ness," by being a settler. As a conventional Asian American origin story in Hawai'i goes, for example, Japanese and Chinese settlers came to Hawai'i, worked the plantations, saved money, and achieved the "American dream." As theorists of Asian settler colonialism, like Dean Saranillio, have pointed out, this story is told in such a way that settlement and the inclusion of Hawai'i as "America" is naturalized, even though many of those original Japanese and Chinese settlers arrived to and worked in the Hawaiian Kingdom, not Hawai'i as the US territory or state.

Another way that settler colonialism and white supremacy buttress each other, but are not exactly the same, is that "racial mixture" is encouraged under settler colonialism, in order to make Indigenous peoples, and their particular claims to land, less distinct from settlers. Any kind of "mixture" allows Indigenous peoples to be seen as less "authentic," as "dying out." However, the goal of settler colonialism is to mix the population in such a way that it is closer in proximity to whiteness. These ideologies filter down into Indigenous communities in subtle and sometimes surprising ways. For example, many Native Hawaiians are multiracial, and are widely accepted within Native Hawaiian communities if their "racial mix" includes white or Asian. Being Native Hawaiian and Black, however, is often less embraced, less recognizable, and less valorized.

One powerful example of this comes from transgender rights activist and writer Janet Mock's recent, brilliant memoir, *Redefining Realness*, where she shares her experience of growing up as Black and Native Hawaiian in Hawai'i. Where Hemmings's novel, *The Descendants*, depicts the rarified world of O'ahu's moneyed elite, Mock's memoir is set along the streets of working-class Honolulu, and therefore presents, to me, a much more recognizable Hawai'i, in all its complexity. Though acknowledging that Hawai'i was "the home I needed" and "there is no me without Hawaii," Mock's portrait of Hawai'i is not an easy or romantic one.[3] Along with speaking of the abuse she sustained as a transgender person, Mock also notes that the racial order of Hawai'i made her and her brother Chad stand out as mixed Black kids. She writes: "Skin color wasn't necessarily the target as much as our blackness was the target for teasing. I say this because the kids who teased us were as brown as us, but we were black. . . . They teased that Chad and I were popolo, Hawaiian slang for black people. Popolo are shiny berries that grow in clusters in the islands and are so black that they shine purple on branches. Hearing popolo on that playground didn't sound as regal as its namesake berries. It sounded dirty, like something that stuck on our bodies, like the red dirt of the playground."[4]

Mock's account here complicates conventional US understandings of how Blackness is perceived as chiefly a matter of skin color, as it was not her skin color that visibly separated her from the other local kids. Anti-Blackness does not necessarily lodge itself within our communities in well-known or expected ways, which means we have to work that much harder to innovate against it. Mock writes that she has learned that her Blackness does not negate her Native Hawaiian-ness; she does not have to choose between them. Yet, undeniably, Native Hawaiians and Pacific Islanders more generally have work yet to do to truly internalize this lesson within all of our communities. Pursuing this work is key to achieving true decolonization for all of us. When we act to promote our own self-determination and refuse the settler colonial attribution of whiteness to Polynesian-ness, we must also be sure that we do not let anti-Blackness remain intact. Otherwise, our lāhui—our Kanaka Maoli nation—and our Oceania more broadly will continue to be structured by white supremacy and settler colonialism.

Mock's story is structured around her journey to redefine realness—chiefly her realness as a woman, a realness that, for her, was never truly in doubt. What if we also imagined Indigenous self-determination as a process of redefining realness (race, indigeneity, gender, sexuality all included)? As Native Hawaiians, we have never truly doubted our realness as a lāhui, despite centuries of others telling us we no longer exist. As Pacific Islanders, we have never truly believed in the boundaries imposed through the labels of Polynesia, Melanesia, and Micronesia, despite the very material ways these boundaries have differentially structured our various communities' lives. Citing Zora Neale Hurston, Mock tells us: "The dream is the truth." With the movie *The Descendants*, Hollywood has made one dream the truth: the white settler dream of an exclusively white Hawai'i. That dream is deeply structured by both settler colonialism and anti-Blackness. The good news is Native Hawaiians and Pacific Islanders have millions of other dreams and therefore millions of other truths. Let's keep dreaming.

Notes

1 Kaui Hart Hemmings, *The Descendants* (New York: Random House, 2008).
2 Alice Te Punga Somerville, *Once Were Pacific: Māori Connections to Oceania* (Minneapolis: University of Minnesota Press, 2012).
3 Janet Mock, *Redefining Realness: My Path to Womanhood, Identity, Love, and So Much More* (New York: Simon and Schuster, 2014).
4 Mock, *Redefining Realness*, 96.

CHAPTER TEN

Sandra Harvey

"What's Past Is Prologue"

Black Native Refusal and the Colonial Archive

In Meridian, Mississippi, on April 10, 1901, Donnie Simons appeared before the United States Commission to the Five Civilized Tribes, an entity tasked with adjudicating Choctaw citizenship. Testifying before the federal officials was part of the application process for enrollment to the Choctaw Nation. According to the transcripts, the commissioners, who suspected Simons was Black, asked her, "How much Choctaw blood do you claim?" Her response, or rather the stenographer's recording of her response, reflects a moment of epistemological crisis with significant political consequences at the turn of the twentieth century and into the present. Curiously, the stenographer first recorded Simons's answer as "1830." The interrogation continued:

Q Is that how much blood you claim?
A Yes sir.
Q That is a good deal isn't it?
A Yes sir but you see it is from both sides of the family.
Q Your father was a Choctaw Indian?
A Yes sir.
Q How much?
A One half.
Q Was your mother a Choctaw?
A Yes sir.
Q How much?
A I don't know exactly how much she was.
Q How much Choctaw blood do you claim?[1]

Recording Simons's reply, the stenographer typed:

A 1830. 18/30

The line leaves a trace, a moment of authorial hesitation signaling the need for translation. Without the stenographer's intervention it would be unclear how to understand the response. Was Simons referring to a full number, a fraction, or a year? Perhaps it was the year the federal government imposed the Treaty of Dancing Rabbit Creek, which led to Choctaw removal? The stenographer interpreted Simons's response first as a full number and then as a fraction. That simple change—adding the dividing line between eighteen and thirty—made Simons's response legible to the Commission's own coalescing understanding of Choctaw citizenship rooted in Western ideas of blood quantum.

A year later, the commissioners issued a decision stating, "The only evidence offered in this application is the unsupported oral statement of the principal applicant, wherein she attempts to show that she was born in the state of Mississippi in the year 1881 . . . and is possessed of some Choctaw blood but it cannot be ascertained from her statement what degree she claims." Ultimately, the officials concluded, "It is the opinion of the Commission that the evidence in this case is insufficient to determine the identity of Donnie Simons and Booker T. Simons as Choctaw Indians entitled to rights in the Choctaw lands . . . and that the application for their identification as such should be refused, and it is so ordered." Subsequently, Simons's application, the Commission's decision letter, and a Refusal Card were filed together with other unsuccessful petitions in boxes labeled "Refused." They remain there at the US National Archives in Washington, DC. With that, a whole line of descendants of Donnie Simons, starting with her son Booker T. Simons, would not find their ancestor's name on the final rolls of Choctaw citizens and would, therefore, be excluded from the Nation.

The relationship between the colonial archive and colonized peoples is a complex one; this is particularly true of the entangled relationships among and between Blacks and Natives of the Five Civilized Tribes and the US National Archives. On the one hand, their relationships to state archives are overdetermined. For example, citizenship in federally recognized Indigenous nations often relies, at least in part, on one's ability to locate ancestors on late nineteenth-century and early twentieth-century enrollment lists. On the other hand, both Afro-descendants and Natives who have looked for details about their ancestors have long decried the void in the archives where the voice of the colonized "should" be. This foreclosure, of course, is no accidental matter. As Melissa Adams-Campbell, Ashley Falzetti, and Courtney Rivard describe, US archival practices have most often been based on the idea of a "non encounter"—the settler disavowal of Native existence prior to the onset of European colonialism.[2] Further, antebellum slave ledgers documented the economic exchanges of chattel yet did not and could not represent the enslaved as complex political and social subjects.[3] This failure presents Black and Native peoples engaged in decolonial and abolitionist work with a paradox that is part and parcel to the logic of the United States as a settler colonial state: the archive exists as a historically created set of colonial power relations that forecloses our status as sovereign and complex political subjects even as we often turn to it for proof of our existence.

This chapter examines this ambivalent relationship as it emerges through the proceedings of the federal Commission as it adjudicated Black enrollment into the Choctaw Nation at the turn of the twentieth century. I draw on the testimony of two suspected Black applicants for enrollment in the Choctaw Nation, Polly Brookings and Mary Boughman, to demonstrate how enrollment procedures shaped definitions of the nation (both Choctaw and settler) and who might become its citizens. The proceedings did so by building upon (modern, scientific, and cultural) knowledge about the body, blood, race, and even language as indicators of sovereignty. Further, because these colonial archives continue to serve as a referent for present-day enrollment procedures they extend the biopolitical and colonial project of the Western sovereign nation into the twenty-first century.[4]

The Applications for Enrollment submitted to the Commission to the Five Civilized Tribes between 1898 and 1914 catalog the Allotment era as a moment in which the United States reasserted itself as a settler colonial nation with roots in chattel slavery. As the US Civil War ended, the Choctaws, who had fought alongside the South, were forced to concede to a joint treaty that increased the federal government's reach far into Indian Territory. It did so by linking the issue of Black emancipation and citizenship in the Choctaw Nation to the federal appropriation of Choctaw land and the "authorization" of Choctaw sovereignty. The 1866 treaty called for the abolition of slavery, the inclusion of Black Choctaws in the Choctaw Nation, and the parceling off of collective Native land in exchange for federal recognition. As historian Barbara Krauthamer argues, this arrangement produced an economy of Black freedom and Native land as fungibles.[5] For example, under the treaty, the US would pay the Choctaw and Chickasaw Nations $300,000 for 4.6 million acres of land.[6] However, the federal government vowed to maintain control of the payment until the Choctaw and Chickasaw peoples could legally guarantee Blacks the right to vote and the right to citizenship in their nations.[7]

The 1887 Dawes Act and the 1898 Curtis Act authorized the US Office of Indian Affairs to allot Choctaws individual plots of land in Indian Territory while simultaneously usurping collective land in order to sell it to white settlers. Later statutes allowed Choctaws who remained in Mississippi to be recognized as citizens and receive plots of land to the extent that they agreed to leave the state and move to Indian Territory within six months of recognition.[8] The federal land allotment policies called for the federal government to identify members of the Choctaw Nation and establish a commission to carry out the enrollment process in both Indian Territory and Mississippi.

Like Donnie Simons, Polly Brookings and Mary Boughman applied for citizenship in Mississippi in 1901, during the last years of the enrollment effort. They were born and raised in mideastern Mississippi, where Choctaws lived prior to their forced displacement to Indian Territory. Nevertheless, Brookings's and Boughman's families, like numerous others, remained in Mississippi. While they each claimed to be Choctaw "by blood," the Commission refused their petitions. Much more so than in earlier enrollment periods, this Commission's efforts to identify Choctaw peoples depended upon ideas of race that were prominent in late nineteenth and early twentieth-century eugenicist thought. Consequently, the Commission tied the concepts of race and sovereignty together even as the federal legislation on Choctaw enrollment did not include language about race as a criterion for citizenship. Nevertheless, as the testimony analyzed in this chapter illustrates, the enrollment process itself became a race-making mechanism that began to coalesce ideas about indigeneity, whiteness, and Blackness, how these racial categories may or may not interact, and the sort of sovereignty accessible to variously racialized people. Moreover, the practices of the Commission codified the notion of blood as a key criterion for belonging and thus influenced subsequent statutes for federal recognition. Brookings's and Boughman's testimonies offer insight into how ideas of Blackness and Nativeness served to define the limits of sovereign citizenship. What follows is a description of the archives, which store the Commission's proceedings, and a close reading of the testimony provided.

The headquarters of the US National Archives and Records Administration in Washington, DC, is immense, imposing, and stately. Seventy-two Corinthian columns, each about fifty feet high, bolster the building, and the two bronze doors at the main entrance on Constitution Avenue are each almost forty feet tall. Before you reach the doors on Pennsylvania Avenue, you are met with two sizable sculptures, which the administration's website explains are an allegory of the "Future" and the "Past"; the other two sculptures depicting "Heritage" and "Guardianship" are at the opposite side of the building facing the National Mall. On the northeast corner of the archives, inscribed on the "Future" statue is the refrain "What is Past is Prologue." The line points to the teleological nature of the National Archives in modern colonial and imperial contexts, but particularly in the context of US settler colonialism. Deriving from Shakespeare's *The Tempest*, it refers to the structure of Renaissance plays, which often included prologues to set the stage for the main acts. The placement of this refrain on the National Archives provides an uncanny metaphor for the "future" that the building and its corresponding archival practices and performances offer. This is one that supposedly emerges by relegating the violence of displacement, enslavement, and genocide to prologue—that which must be taken as (for)given in order to make possible US national sovereignty.

Among other things, the archives contain the official documents of the United States Commission to the Five Civilized Tribes.[9] They include lists of recognized members as well as applications for enrollment organized into three formations of belonging: "by intermarriage," "by blood," and "Freedmen." The sort of "evidence" presented (or not) in each file greatly depends on the applicants' formation of belonging, which in turn depended upon their suspected race. For example, applications for recognition via "intermarriage" often included tribal and federal government marriage certificates and testimony from wedding officiants. These applicants were mostly recognized as white or "mixed blood": white and Native. They often had access to the materials that matter most as both "documentation" and "evidence," and thus constructed full archives.

In contrast, Black applicants are often contained in the categories of "Freedmen" and, in other cases, "by blood." The Freedmen category is one of the most complicated in terms of the 1890–1914 hearings, in part because of how the various treaties defined the category.[10] The files for these applicants rarely included official or legal documentation. Instead, the pages were filled with in-person testimony or letters from fellow former slaves, Native peoples, and others who attested to the applicant's status.

The files of Black applicants applying for citizenship via blood were equally sparse of official documentation. They generally contained an application card filled out by a stenographer, a notarized transcript of questioning before the Commission, and a decision letter by Commission officials. No marriage certificates or testimony from religious figures were included. There was no record of them having ever received land based on the Treaty of 1830, and their names often had not appeared on earlier Choctaw censuses.

Moreover, the format of the transcripts varied widely and reflected the Commission's understandings of how the witnesses fit or did not fit into the category of "Choctaw." Certainly, the transcripts do not provide the reader with transparent or objective proof of what occurred during the interviews. That is, the reader cannot assume that they are accessing the "authentic" voice of the applicants through the transcripts as primary texts. Rather, the transcripts offer insight into the Commission's developing ideas about race, nation, and citizenship. For example, the layout of the transcripts on the page often resembles a script in which the Commission's question is represented through the "Q" prompt and the applicants' response through the "A" prompt on the line below. This may have the misleading effect of offering a transparent representation of what occurred, word for word, during the testimony. However, oftentimes the Commission's questions and the applicants' responses share the same line, bleeding into each other such that the reader finds it difficult to locate where a question ends and an answer begins; the boundary between the interrogator and the applicant become blurred. Moreover, the transcript contains stenographer notes and commentary including their impressions about the personal appearance of the applicants, what the applicants' hair or skin tone might look like, what languages the applicants spoke well or did not speak, and whether the applicants appeared to be telling the truth. Thus, what is most evident through the transcripts are not the unmediated voices of the applicants but instead the various ways the federal government had come to read, accuse, accept, and refuse Black Choctaw citizenship. When cited in this chapter, I present the testimony spatially in the same format that it appears on the pages of the transcripts.

Brookings's and Boughman's refused applications present almost no official "evidence" to prove their belonging to the Choctaw Nation. There are no state documents to prove their legal position. They did not appear on any previous tribal rolls. They were not fluent in Choctaw. They certainly did not make a credible claim to cultural sovereignty as Choctaw. The question that

I pose is not whether the applicants are telling the truth, whether they are authentically and "by blood" Choctaw, but rather how belonging comes to be concretized in these commissions through the idea of blood, how surveillance and management of Blackness in the nations is maintained after the official end of slavery, and what sort of possibilities arise for Blacks to make a claim—however unbelievable it may be—to a form of Nativeness.

Testify and Signify

In adjudicating Choctaw citizenship claims, the Commission engaged in several discursive moves that characterized Blackness and Nativeness as mutually exclusive categories through which Western sovereignty and citizenship might be understood. First, one of the most significant moves made in both the Commission's proceedings and in archiving its findings for posterity is the increased fixing of Blacks and Blackness to the position of the slave. For example, in developing the enrollment rolls, federal agents often placed Black Choctaws on the Freedmen lists, even when they were known by others in the community to have been Choctaw "by blood."[11]

The tie to slavery was apparent in how the Commission treated the applications for Choctaw nationality via blood. The interrogators often asked suspected Black applicants whether they or their mother or father had ever been a slave. This would likely render an applicant ineligible because having been enslaved signified that one was indeed Black and therefore not Native. For example, according to the archival testimony in the application for enrollment of Mary Boughman, the commissioner asked her,

Q What other nationality was your mother? A Not as I know of.
Q Was your mother a slave? A No sir, we never was slaves. We was free born Choctaws. Never were slaves none of us.
Q You ever been a slave? A No sir, free born.
Q Your father and mother always live in Mississippi? A Free born. Free born Choctaws.

No congressional act stipulated that one could not be recognized as Choctaw by blood if one was or had been a slave. Yet the assumption was that if an applicant had been a slave or a descendant of a slave, they were not Choctaw by blood. Boughman's assertion that she had Choctaw blood, then, was necessarily linked to her assertion that she and her family were never slaves. They had not been emancipated but instead were "Free born Choctaws." Through this line of questioning, the Commission perpetuated the binds of slavery even postemancipation. It did so, paradoxically, by legally codifying the Freedmen status (with few exceptions) as the more plausible way in which Blacks might access sovereignty and political recognition as part of the Choctaw Nation.

Fixing Blackness to the position of the slave put Boughman and other applicants in an impossible situation. That is, the Commission asked those it considered to be former slaves to offer evidence of their genealogical past, of their kinship ties that would offer them a position as a sovereign citizen. Yet it is just the position of the slave, as Orlando Patterson argued, that white supremacy characterized by an indefinite rupture of kinship. Patterson described the status of the slave as emerging through "natal alienation," which "goes directly to the heart of what is critical in the slave's *forced alienation, the loss of ties of birth in both ascending and descending generations.* It also has the important nuance of a loss of native status, of deracination. It was this alienation of the slave from all formal, legally enforceable ties of 'blood,' and from any attachment to groups or localities other than those chosen for him [*sic*] by the master, that gave the relation of slave its peculiar value to the master."[12] Boughman's testimony suggests that what Saidiya Hartman calls the "after life of slavery" was actively enforced during enrollment and allotment.[13] It is this presence—the fixing of Blackness to the position of the slave—that renders Blackness as an impossibility within Western conceptions of both the nation and sovereignty. Within the settler colonial regime, slavery becomes the only inheritable trait assigned to Blackness. The integrity of sovereign nations, thus, required its interrogation, surveillance, and containment. The citizen emerged as that individual who is not a slave, who has free will, autonomy, and self-determination. If a slave could pass for free, the distinction between the two threatened to collapse.

The Commission's proceedings reified and built upon slavery's reduction of Black difference to a notion of race traceable on the body. One might turn to Patterson's description of the slave's "loss of native status" within the white settler imaginary as that which makes this dynamic possible.[14] The nonencounter narrative not only disavows the existence of Native peoples in the West before European settlement but also ignores the fact that enslaved Black peoples were also part of Indigenous communities and nations in Africa before their capture and displacement to the so-called New World. This discursive move forecloses the possibilities to consider Afro-descendants as colonized peoples vying for sovereignty. Instead, it portrays them as emergent citizens to the extent that their difference could be reduced to a biopolitical concept of race, the mark of which was to be traceable within the body. Following this logic, to create the sovereign Choctaw Nation, the Commission needed to locate, quantify, and record sovereign and nonsovereign blood. This was the case even as recognition "by-blood," at the federal level, was not legally or officially dependent on a notion of "quantum" at that time. Nevertheless, "blood" began to take on genea-biological meaning conflated with race, and both race and blood with nation. It was through performances, such as those of the Commission, that this intersection of race, blood, and nation emerged and was policed.

Nevertheless, Black applicants continued to assert their own understandings of how they fit into the political cleavages of both the United States and the Choctaw Nation postemancipation. For example, the commissioner asked Polly Brookings,

Q What proportion of Choctaw blood do you claim to have? A Mississippi Choctaw.

Q What proportion? A Three fourths. My father had three fourths.

Q You have just as much Choctaw blood as your father had? A Yes . . .

Q He claimed to be a Choctaw? A Yes sir.

Q What proportion of Choctaw blood did he claim to have? A About the same I reckon; A little more that I did.

Q You think he had more than you? A Yes sir, he was older than me. I would never have known anything about the Choctaws if it had not been for him.

Q Did he speak the Choctaw language? A Yes, he talked Choctaw and African too. It looked like he did . . .

Q Is your mother living? A No sir . . .

Q Was she a Choctaw? A She was a Choctaw woman.

Q What proportion did she have? A The same that her husband.

Q Three fourths? A My father and her were near about the same.

Q They were both about three fourths Choctaw? A Yes sir.

Q The other fourth was what—negro? A No, white folks.

Q You have some negro in you, have you not? A I couldn't tell you.

Q Do you not associate with the negroes all the time? A Yes.

Q Then you know you have negro blood. A Well, I associates with them.

Q Were you not a slave? A No.

Q Was not your mother a slave? A No sir.

Q Was not your father a slave? A No sir . . .

Q You do not know they were Choctaw Indians? A Yes, but they never went with the Indians.

Q They were negroes were they not? A That is what they were called by the white folks and Indians.

This interview echoes many others in that the commissioner attempted to link Brookings to an inheritance of slavery, and thus reject her application. However, in addition to slavery was the issue of the relationship between blood quantum and language. What might be read as a fair question about cultural-linguistic sovereignty and an unacceptable and even culturally ignorant response, however, must be further interrogated. I argue this is because in the case of the recognition of southeastern Native and Afro-descendant peoples, language is also often reduced to racial difference. In this way, one might read the way language emerges through testimonies like that of Brookings as part of what Hortense Spillers calls a "symbolic paradigm" in which "the human *body* [is] a metonymic figure for an entire repertoire of human and social arrangements," including the arrangement of language as a component of "ethnicity."[15] Within this particular context of racialized belonging, even the proof of language is located on the body.

One might compare Brookings's testimony to certain antebellum runaway advertisements, which suggest that even slaves that spoke the Choctaw language fluently were not assumed to *be* Choctaw. Instead, there was an assumption that Blacks often *passed for* or *resembled* Natives but were not themselves actually Native. An advertisement from the 1834 *Vicksburg Register* in Mississippi demonstrates this point. It offered a $20 reward for "a negro man named JOE, about 25 years old, 5 feet 8 or 9 inches high, yellow complexion, speaks pert, very smart, and intelligent; has a natural black mark on one of his eyes resembling Indian paint; speaks the Choctaw language."[16] The fugitive slave, "Joe," had a mark that "resembles Indian paint" and "speaks the Choctaw language," but his assumed Blackness meant that the Choctaw language must be read as an artificial "trait," one whose authenticity was dependent on ideas of race.[17] In contrast, Brookings's assertion that her father spoke "Choctaw and African too" might be read as a rejection of language tied to ideas of biological race and a turn, instead, toward understanding language within the context of colonialism. Her response brings the specter of Africa and its colonized subjects into the realm of the Choctaw negotiations for sovereignty. It rejects historical narratives of natal alienation and puts forth the possibility of "African" political and social determination, including particular relationships to land.

Brookings's testimony rendered insufficient the expectation that race should be distinguishable on the body. Faced with this dilemma, the commissioner slipped into a different logic by attempting to identify her Blackness through his assumptions about Black sociality. However, when the commissioner insisted that Brookings must be "black" because she "associates" with Black people, Brookings refused. Her response might be considered as reading the commissioner for his ideological slippage. She insisted, "[black] is what they were called by white folks and Indians."

Lastly, the Commission situated Black women as the site of nonsovereignty as its decisions disavowed their capacity to birth Native children even postemancipation. It did this by regularly refusing Black petitions for enrollment by blood, citing the lack of evidence that the applicant's mother and father were legally married. Even if the applicant could claim belonging to the Choctaw Nation through their father's lineage, if their parents were not married, the child's status via the father would not be legally sanctioned. The claim would be illegitimate. An example of this is the commissioner's exchange with Boughman, who claimed her Choctaw inheritance via her father, John Filiyah. The testimony reads:

Q Were your mother and father married?

A Yes sir.

Q When were they married?

A I don't know sir? I wasn't born when they was married. I couldn't tell you anything about that.

Q Have you any evidence of the fact that your father and mother were ever married?

A Well, I believe it.

Q You do?

A Yes, sir.

Q Suppose we didn't believe it?

A I couldn't help that.

Q Could you prove it?

A No sir I couldn't prove it by only myself.

Q Weren't there lots of other people living there at the time your father and mother were married?

A Oh laws I don't know where those people is now. Lord only knows. They may be all dead for all I know but John Filiyah was my father.

Q Before that could do you any good you would have to prove that your father and mother were married?

A That would be hard to prove because I don't know any of the relation but them.

In this exchange, Black Choctaw recognition was scrutinized via blood and "blood" was mediated through the settler state and its heteronormative legal and moral foundation—marriage. Blood itself emerges through the law; it is interpolated rather than innate.

Further, most Black people could not legally marry in antebellum Mississippi when Boughman was born. In fact, one of the major acts taken up in the early years of Reconstruction by the Freedmen's Bureau was to legally wed those Black couples whose relationships had not been recognized by the state prior to emancipation.[18] Within the context of the US federal government, one of the ways in which Blacks emerged as legal subjects was through the institution of marriage, and thus becoming a US citizen was highly dependent on former slaves heeding the heteronormative, civilizing mission of the settler state.

The unwed Black mother, then, became the antithesis to citizenship, and her children continued this legacy of noninclusion and nonfreedom. This paradigm has roots in US slave law, which stated that children born to enslaved women were also slaves. *Partus sequitur ventrem*, the Roman phrase that preceded the US law, signified "that which brought forth follows the womb." Within this framework of white supremacy that undergirded both settler colonialism and chattel slavery, the body of the Black woman produced the "un-free."

Moreover, if the Black woman was understood as the site of nonsovereignty, white settler colonialism considered the Native woman as the physical representation of too much sovereignty—the sovereign outside of the settler body politic. Native feminists have returned to this dynamic in order to trace the proliferation of the heteronormative state. Audra Simpson, for example, writes, "An Indian woman's body in settler regimes such as the U.S. and Canada is loaded with meaning—signifying land itself, the dangerous possibility of reproducing Indian life, and most dangerously, other political orders. . . . Indian women . . . transmit the clan, and with that: family, responsibility, and relatedness to territory."[19] For a white settler, to marry a Native woman was to accumulate land and sovereignty and to produce new citizens mediated through white patriarchy. Within this context, to restrict Native women's reproduction independent of white men was to contain a potential threat to counterimperial, otherwise worlds.

These transits of empire, as Jodi Byrd might call them, moved through white imaginaries of Black and Native wombs.[20] The procedures and practices of the Commission—in particular the authoring and management of difference—delineated Blackness, indigeneity, and their gender formations as the biopolitical limits of Western sovereignty. The work of the National Archives, then, is to render this process a prologue to the US as a nation-state.

Archival Entanglements and Decolonial Futures

By way of conclusion, it is imperative for decolonial movements to discuss and hold each other accountable to the ways in which Black/Native histories emerge together, although situated differently within the white settler imaginary. Thus, we must hold in suspicion the discursive and material confines of the settler state even to the extent that our resistance movements and historical scholarship may unwittingly reify them. This is not a call to flatten differences, particularly with regard to ways of being in the world. Instead it is a call to question how our understandings of these differences have emerged and been shaped through nationalist archival practices and the production of "evidence-based" accounts of the past as prologue. The discourse naturalizing the historical positions of Blackness and Nativeness as mutually exclusive categories produce the limits upon which Black and Native resistance has often been formed. Thus, for example, Black political resistance and scholarship has often been conceived of as aiming toward and imagining various renditions of "freedom"—often in relation to the body and defined through gendered genealogies of liberal thought and otherwise. In contrast, within Anglo settler colonial states, Native people's decolonial resistance has often been described through narratives of relationships to land and sovereignty, both in comparison to and in rejection of its Western renditions. We might begin to question the differences in understanding our efforts in this way and in opening up a movement that puts forth a decolonial politics that is accountable to our historical interconnectedness. What if, as Black critical theorists argue, sovereignty itself is the problem?[21] Or, as they warn, what if our notions of freedom based on emancipation mislead us? Willfully reading the contents of the colonial archive with these vexations in mind opens up the possibility of understanding Black applicants like Brookings or Boughman as threatening a move not simply to attain sovereignty, but to stake a claim—from the position of the nonsovereign, or the "too-sovereign"—to a decolonial future. This sort of reading requires us to embrace what appears to be illogical within the parameters of the colonial archive as a productive provocation. The work, then, becomes one of reading the acts of our ancestors not through the settler state's episteme but instead through the tensions and responsibilities of the unbelievability or impossibility of Black and Native memory and imagination.

Notes

1 All testimony cited in this chapter is from "The Applications for Enrollment of the Commission to The Five Civilized Tribes 1898–1914," National Archives Microfilm Publications M1301, Roll 106. This chapter purposefully replicates the layout the stenographer used to record the testimony, including its inconsistencies, in order to more precisely represent the nuances of the stenographer's thinking.

2 Melissa Adams-Campbell, Ashley Glassburn Falzetti, and Courtney Rivard, "Introduction: Indigeneity and the Work of Settler Archives," *Settler Colonial Studies* 5, no. 2 (2015): 109–16.

3 See Saidiya Hartman, "Venus in Two Acts," *small axe* 12, no. 2 (2008): 1–14; Laura Helton, Justin Leroy, Max A. Mishler, Samantha Seeley, and Shauna Sweeney, "The Question of Recovery: Slavery, Freedom, and the Archive," *Social Text* 33, no. 4 (2015): 1–18; Toni Morrison, "The Site of Memory," in *Inventing the Truth: The Art and Craft of Memoir,* 2d ed., ed. William Zinsser (Boston: Houghton Mifflin, 1995), 83–102.

4 For example, according to the Constitution of the Choctaw Nation of Oklahoma, in order to be recognized one must be a descendent of a "Choctaw Indian by blood whose name appears on the final rolls of the Choctaw Nation" approved in 1906 (Choctaw Nation of Oklahoma 1973, art. II, sec. 1). One might also need a Certificate of Degree of Indian Blood, which is issued by the Bureau of Indian Affairs and shows the member's name, blood degree by tribe, date of birth, and date of issuance. To access this card one must "show direct lineage to a final Choctaw Dawes enrollee register with a blood quantum" (Oklahoma).

5 In line with the federal goal of promoting free labor and private property, the treaty called for Native peoples to enter labor contracts that offered Afro-descendants fair remuneration. Black Choctaws must also be able to serve as witnesses in civil and criminal proceedings in the nation's courts, and they were to have "unrestricted access" to collective tribal lands in order to cultivate crops and build their homes. In exchange, the US "offered" to allot each Choctaw and Chickasaw family 160 acres of previously collective land for private family use. In contrast, future Black citizens of the Choctaw nation would receive forty acres.

6 Barbara Krauthamer, *Black Slaves, Indian Masters: Slavery, Emancipation, and Citizenship in the Native American South* (Chapel Hill: University of North Carolina Press, 2013), 114.

7 Krauthamer, *Black Slaves, Indian Masters*, 114.

8 At the turn of the twentieth century this was a matter of intense debate between Choctaws whose families had remained in Mississippi after removal, the federal government, and Choctaws in Indian Territory. Choctaws in Mississippi argued that they should not have to move to Indian Territory to be recognized. On the contrary, because they were "full-blood" Choctaws,

they deserved to be recognized as both a sovereign band and also as citizens of the United States. However, as Katherine Osburn writes, Congress drafted the 1902 Choctaw-Chickasaw Supplemental Agreement, which stated that Choctaws recognized by the Dawes Commission must move west within six months of recognition in order to obtain their allotments: Osburn, "The 'Identified Full-Bloods' in Mississippi: Race and Choctaw Identity, 1898–1918," *Ethnohistory* 56, no. 3 (2009): 423–47.

9 According to the US National Archives and Records Administration website, the most searched topics include census records, military service records, immigration records, naturalization records, passport applications, and land records. https://www.archives.gov/research/topics.

10 For example, according to the 1866 Choctaw-Chickasaw Treaty with the federal government to be enrolled as a Freedman one needed to have been owned by an officially recognized Choctaw prior to emancipation or to be a descendent of a former slave. Additionally, the applicant or their ancestor needed to have been present in Indian Territory during the signing of the treaty and have remained in the territory as their permanent residence. This of course meant that there was no flexibility for those who had been displaced or had escaped to freedom or to fight with the Union during the Civil War. By 1866, formerly enslaved Blacks needed to have returned to the place of their enslavement, to their masters' land, in order to be recognized as part of the Choctaw Nation. See Article 4, Choctaw-Chickasaw Treaty with Washington, 1866.

11 See Circe Sturm for a description of this phenomenon in applications for enrollment within the Cherokee Nation. She reports that the Dawes Rolls included 4,208 adult Cherokee Freedmen of whom at least 300 "had some degree of Indian heritage." Circe Sturm, *Blood Politics: Race, Culture, and Identity in the Cherokee Nation of Oklahoma* (Berkeley: University of California Press, 2002), 186.

12 Orlando Patterson, *Slavery and Social Death: A Comparative Study* (Cambridge, MA: Harvard University Press, 1982), 7–8. Emphasis added.

13 Saidiya Hartman, *Scenes of Subjection: Terror, Slavery, and Self-Making in Nineteenth-Century America* (New York: Oxford University Press. 1997).

14 Patterson, *Slavery and Social Death*, 8.

15 Hortense J. Spillers, "Mama's Baby, Papa's Maybe: An American Grammar Book," *Diacritics* 17, no. 2 (1987): 65–81, 66, my emphasis; Roland Barthes, "Myth Today," in *Mythologies*, trans. Annette Lavers (New York: Hill and Wang, 1972), 109–159.

16 Douglas B. Chambers and Max Grivno, "Mississippi Runaway Slaves: 1800–1860," Aquila Digital Community (Hattiesburg: University of Southern Mississippi, 2013).

17 Here Hortense Spillers's discussion of the idea of ethnicity as it emerges in the 1966 Moynihan Report is relevant as an example of the results of the construction of "ethnicity" as always reduced to an idea of race when thought to-

gether with Blackness. She wrote, "'Ethnicity' in this case freezes in meaning, takes on constancy, assumes the look and the effects of the Eternal. We could say, then, that in its powerful stillness, 'ethnicity,' from the point of view of the 'Report,' embodies nothing more than a mode of memorial time, as Roland Barthes outlines the dynamics of myth [see Barthes, "Myth Today," 109–59, esp. 122–23]. As a signifier that has no movement in the field of signification, the use of 'ethnicity' for the living becomes purely appreciative, although one would be unwise not to concede its dangerous and fatal effects" (Hortense J. Spillers, "Mama's Baby, Papa's Maybe: An American Grammar Book," *Diacritics* 17, no. 2 [1987]: 66). The effect of timelessness that Spillers identifies in the Moynihan Report echoes the way the components of contemporary ideas of ethnicity emerge in the testimonies this chapter reviews. Within this settler colonial state, while Nativeness becomes an atemporal ethnicity, always referring to an authentic precontact purity, Blackness is reduced to "race," and mapped on the Black body as biological difference. There is no room for language differences when it comes to Afro-descendants and no room for creolization when it comes to the Indigenous.

18 Katherine M. Franke, "Becoming a Citizen: Reconstruction Era Regulation of African American Marriages," *Yale Journal of Law and the Humanities* 11, no. 2 (1999): 251–309.

19 Audra Simpson, "The State Is a Man: Theresa Spence, Loretta Saunders, and the Gender of Settler Sovereignty," *Theory and Event* 19, no. 4 (2016): 1–30, 15. https://muse.jhu.edu/article/633280.

20 Jodi Byrd, *The Transit of Empire: Indigenous Critiques of Colonialism* (Minneapolis: University of Minnesota Press, 2011).

21 See, for example, Fred Moten's "Notes on Passage (The New International of Sovereign Feelings)," *Palimpsest: A Journal on Women, Gender, and the Black International* 3, no. 1 (2014): 51–74; and "Blackness and Nothingness (Mysticism in the Flesh)," *South Atlantic Quarterly* 112, no. 4 (2013): 737–80, and Jared Sexton's "The *Vel* of Slavery: Tracking the Figure of the Unsovereign," *Critical Sociology* 42, nos. 4–5 (2014): 583–97.

References

Adams-Campbell, Melissa, Ashley Glassburn Falzetti, and Courtney Rivard. 2015. "Introduction: Indigeneity and the Work of Settler Archives." *Settler Colonial Studies* 5, no. 2: 109–16.

Barthes, Roland. 1972. "Myth Today." In *Mythologies*, trans. Annette Lavers, 109–59. New York: Hill and Wang.

Byrd, Jodi. 2011. *The Transit of Empire: Indigenous Critiques of Colonialism*. Minneapolis: University of Minnesota Press.

Chambers, Douglas B., and Max Grivno. 2013. "Mississippi Runaway Slaves: 1800–1860." Aquila Digital Community. Hattiesburg: University of Southern Mississippi.

Choctaw Nation of Oklahoma. 1973. *Constitution and Laws of the Choctaw Nation: Together with the Treaties of 1855, 1865, and 1866*. Wilmington, DE: Scholarly Resources.

Choctaw Nation of Oklahoma. 2019. "CDIB and Tribal Membership: Frequently Requested Information." https://www.choctawnation.com/contacts -applications/cdibmembership-information.

Franke, Katherine M. 1999. "Becoming a Citizen: Reconstruction Era Regulation of African American Marriages." *Yale Journal of Law and the Humanities* 11, no. 2: 251–309.

General Records of the United States Government. 1862. "DC Emancipation Act." National Archives. April 16, 1862. Record Group 11.

Hartman, Saidiya. 1997. *Scenes of Subjection: Terror, Slavery, and Self-Making in Nineteenth-Century America*. New York: Oxford University Press.

Hartman, Saidiya. 2008. "Venus in Two Acts." *small axe* 12, no. 2: 1–14.

Helton, Laura, Justin Leroy, Max A. Mishler, Samantha Seeley, and Shauna Sweeney. 2015. "The Question of Recovery: Slavery, Freedom, and the Archive." *Social Text* 33, no. 4: 1–18.

Krauthamer, Barbara. 2013. *Black Slaves, Indian Masters: Slavery, Emancipation, and Citizenship in the Native American South*. Chapel Hill: University of North Carolina Press.

Morrison, Toni. 1995. "The Site of Memory." In *Inventing the Truth: The Art and Craft of Memoir*, 2d ed., ed. William Zinsser, 83–102. Boston: Houghton Mifflin.

Moten, Fred. 2014. "Notes on Passage (The New International of Sovereign Feelings)." *Palimpsest: A Journal on Women, Gender, and the Black International*. 3, no. 1: 51–74.

Moten, Fred 2013. "Blackness and Nothingness (Mysticism in the Flesh)." *South Atlantic Quarterly* 112, no. 4: 737–80.

National Archives. "The Applications for Enrollment of the Commision to The Five Civilized Tribes, 1898–1914." National Archives Microfilm Publications M1301, Roll 106.

Office of Indian Affairs: National Archives. 1831. "Choctaw Armstrong Rolls." Microfilm Roll A–39. Fort Worth, TX: National Archives.

Osburn, Katherine M. B. 2009. "The 'Identified Full-Bloods' in Mississippi: Race and Choctaw Identity, 1898–1918." *Ethnohistory* 56, no. 3: 423–47.

Osburn, Katherine M. B. 2014. *Choctaw Resurgence in Mississippi: Race, Class, and Nation Building in the Jim Crow South, 1830–1977*. Lincoln: University of Nebraska Press.

Patterson, Orlando. 1982. *Slavery and Social Death: A Comparative Study*. Cambridge, MA: Harvard University Press.

Sexton, Jared. 2014. "The *Vel* of Slavery: Tracking the Figure of the Unsovereign." *Critical Sociology* 42, nos. 4–5: 583–97.

Simpson, Audra. 2007. "On the Logic of Discernment." *American Quarterly* 59, no. 2: 479–91.

Simpson, Audra. 2016. "The State Is a Man: Theresa Spence, Loretta Saunders and the Gender of Settler Sovereignty." *Theory and Event* 19, no. 4: 1–30. https://muse.jhu.edu/ article/633280.

Smith, Andrea. 2014. "The Colonialism That Is Settled and the Colonialism That Never Happened." *Decolonization: Indigeneity, Education & Society*, June 20. https://decolonization.wordpress.com/2014/06/20/the-colonialism-that-is -settled-and-the-colonialism-that-never-happened/.

Spillers, Hortense J. 1987. "Mama's Baby, Papa's Maybe: An American Grammar Book." *Diacritics* 17, no. 2: 65–81.

Sturm, Circe. 2002. *Blood Politics: Race, Culture, and Identity in the Cherokee Nation of Oklahoma*. Berkeley: University of California Press.

U.S. National Archives and Records Administration. "A Short History of the National Archives Building, Washington, DC." https://www.archives.gov/about /history/building.html.

U.S. National Archives and Records Administration. 2016. "Resources for Genealogists and Family Historians." https://www.archives.gov/research /genealogy/.

CHAPTER ELEVEN

Cedric Sunray

Indian Country's Apartheid

The things people use against you in life are the things they most fear themselves.

N ever has this been truer than with those who police identity in Indian Country. This chapter addresses the identity policing of those in Indian Country who have or are perceived to have some Black ancestry. More specifically, it is about white privilege among primarily racially white tribal citizens and how they implement this privilege in highly suspect ways. There are two concepts that everyone must know prior to engaging such discussions. Number one is that much of what the individuals and scenarios discussed in this chapter start from is a place of insecurity and complexity that manifests itself in absolute dishonesty. Number two is that this continual battle over identity in Indian Country, which is infused by racism, is not and will never be solved, reconciled, justified, mutually agreed upon, or answered in any way by any opposing parties. If one can understand these key points from the onset, then one is much more likely to view such readings as this not as oppositional or "angry," but rather as simply a discussion infused with realities that has no intention of changing a significant number of minds or correcting a blatant wrong in any manner. In fact, being as open as this chapter is may only serve to cause genuine anger among a segment of its readership with its nonadherence to academic politesse and respectability politics, which serve as walls at times to genuine discussion. Even so, it nonetheless must go forward.

All of this revolves around complex questions with contestable answers and variant origins. Understanding these answers and origins began for me in the 1990s and intensified on a fall day in 2001, while attending one of my morning classes on the campus of Haskell Indian Nations University. The topic of the day was the disenrollment of members of the Seminole Nation of Oklahoma. Our professor had us all sitting in a circle and one by one each student was giving their take on the situation of the Seminole Freedmen's proposed expulsion. An identifiable Seminole student remarked that they should be removed since they were Black and not Indian in her estimation. A student who could only be identified as racially white by sight and who turned out to be a member of the Cherokee Nation of Oklahoma concurred with her statements. Shortly thereafter, one of the Black-phenotype students in the circle began speaking in the Muscogee/Seminole language. When he finished, he looked at the two who had supported the removal of the Seminole Freedmen during the discussion and stated, "Since I know you can't speak our language, I will translate for you in English." You could feel a collective gasp in the room, the type of gasp where someone feeling high and mighty has just been put in their place. It turns out he was an enrolled Seminole Nation tribal member whose family was slated for removal. The Seminole Nation of Oklahoma consists of fourteen bands represented by fourteen chiefs. Two of the bands are considered Seminole Freedmen bands. He and his family were members of one of these. He was raised culturally in the Seminole Nation and, like many Indian Freedmen, he could not only attest to a cultural upbringing but also to being of Seminole Indian blood. That's a still contested notion for some stemming from the way many individuals and families were tribally enrolled in Oklahoma by white government officials who placed many individuals of mixed Indian-Black ancestry on Freedmen rolls while those who were phenotypically white were listed as by-blood.

The argument, though located on the campus in Lawrence, Kansas, did not have its origins there. Nor did the more contemporary prohibition of partially Black or perceived to be partially Black tribes originate there. All the participants in that classroom discussion originated from eastern Oklahoma. In eastern Oklahoma, years later, is where I would truly begin to find the answers to this vexing question, one that could never be adequately answered via research or lived in East and Southeast experience alone.

Haskell, one of the nation's oldest off-reservation Indian boarding schools, which had morphed throughout the generations into a trade school, junior college, and now university, was also at fault for the views held by the two young women. The school, once accessible to those who could prove a one-fourth or more Indian blood degree for attendance, had changed to admitting only those who were connected to federally recognized tribes, no matter their blood quantum. Prior to this, Indian people from historic "non-federal" tribes in the United States, as well as First Nations persons from Canada, had graced her halls. This new prohibition had begun to exclude those tribes from the eastern and southern regions of the US who were perceived to have Black ancestry and simultaneously had been denied official federal recognition. One of those tribes, the MOWA Band of Choctaw Indians, was the Alabama community of my grandfather, and thus a piece of me was discarded in such exclusionary rhetoric. During my time at Haskell, and as the peculiarly placed last member of a historic "non-federal" tribe in the US or Canadian First Nation to attend the school, I mined the archives for evidence of the generational attendance of our historic "non-federal" tribal people in yearbooks, school newspapers, and government documents. There of course was an abundance of material concerning the attendance of these people there. One glaring example was Don Ahshapanek, a Nanticoke elder from Delaware, who was sent over one thousand miles to Haskell as a young teenager, graduated from Haskell Institute, and eventually returned to be a professor there for twenty years.

After the semester concluded at Haskell, I transferred to the University of Kansas, a campus situated only two miles away, and these types of conversations continued. Upon graduation I returned to the community of my upbringing in the Bahama Village section of Key West, Florida, where, as always, I awoke to streets almost exclusively composed of local Conchs, Black people, Black Bahamian and Cuban culture, and worldviews created by people of color and a range of artists, hustlers, and eclectic thinkers.

How a kid of MOWA Choctaw and Scottish-Canadian ancestry with parents hailing from Alabama and Canada ended up growing up in this environment during the 1970s and 1980s is more easily explained than one may assume. My hometown of Key West was not the dream of tourist brochures and beach strewn resorts during the days of my upbringing. An old friend of my parents provides his take on the island during this era in *Florida Travel & Life* magazine's March/April 2012 issue, "It was like the wild, wild West back then . . . smugglers and hush-hush barroom deals of the late '70s and early '80s."[1] More well-known and reputable magazines such as *National Geographic* showed Key West as a primary part of what they dubbed "The Cocaine Empire" (January 1989) and the December 1999 issue stated, "It is not disputed that back in the 1970s . . . the lower Keys were kept alive by drug traffic. It was cash-and-carry. Everybody winked."[2] This is the town where one of my high school coaches was relieved from his duties not for a losing season, but because of a crack cocaine conviction.

My six-foot-five, 245-pound, long-braid-wearing, and charismatic father could not have found a place better suited for his ambitions. After being caught as a young man in his late teens dealing drugs in his native Alabama, my mother and father headed toward South Florida where he eventually became a major player in the drug game, dealing primarily in cocaine and marijuana. My mom became pregnant at this time and their relationship fell apart by the time I was two. My dad became the literal poster child for such contemporary documentaries as *Cocaine Cowboys* and the like. By the time he was twenty-six, he was found dead, leaving behind a "business" employing over twenty men and a mass of material properties and possessions that would be condemned and disappeared by the powers that be.

Newspapers and even *People* magazine dedicated tons of print to my father's disappearance. They found his lifeless body, those of some of his associates, money, and drugs months later beneath the wreckage of his plane. The complexity and at times wreckage of life, along with the dishonesty and hustling traits of others, is something I can see and feel from miles away. Even so, this island and its culture and people will always be my primary identity.

And here I was again heading back down to my island home with my soon to be Kiowa/Ponca wife and daughter. Diving into my teaching and coaching at our local school, I recalled the many diverse, wonderful, and at times traumatic moments I had experienced in our community. How I felt so disappointed in Indian Country's attempted rejection of its Blackness was clearly understood in the context of my own upbringing; one which I now viewed through the laughter of my daughter as she skipped along the same streets where I once played and ate in the houses of those who had cared for me during the first eighteen years of my life; houses where the smell of *ropa vieja, picadilla, frijoles negros* and yellow rice, yellowtail snapper, buttery Cuban bread, and Conch fritters levitated through windows and doorways.

As one of the very few whose roots were not ancestrally tied to this place and whose long, dirty blond hair stood out from most of the island's multigenerational habitants, I first noticed my own white coding and corresponding privilege at the age of ten, though I didn't have the academic words for such. Kids would run "items" down the street for local "pharmacists," like my father, to make some extra money. The Black and racially mixed Cuban-Conch kids would frequently get picked up by the police, while I would whistle on by. Having grown up in the community where I was basically an anomaly, it would not have been possible to not notice my difference, though my full acceptance was never questioned. I viewed myself (and still do to this day) as a Conch, and they viewed me and still view me today as a Conch. Historically, the Conch term originally applied to poor white settlers in the Bahamas and through immigration to parts of Miami and the Florida Keys, in particular Key West; it evolved to encompass the mixed white Bahamian, Black Bahamian, and Cuban generational locals of the island. I am living proof that the race or races assigned to one at birth are not indicative of the culture and community that represents the totality of one's life. Any discussion to the contrary falls flat with me as I lived and live the reality of it.

The nickname given to me by Conch elder Mario Pete Viera Jr. in Mastic Trailer Park where I was raised was "dirty little Cuban." When I went home in July 2018 to assist in a memorial for my closest friend's niece, Mario's granddaughter came through the door proclaiming "There is that dirty little Cuban" before embracing me. The years had passed, the love and acknowledgment had never ceased. Unknowingly, I was for eighteen years unaware of the importance of my parent's racial ancestry, but I was in some ways still crippled by its absence. My father, not I, was referred to as an Indian, though erroneously as Seminole (aside from the Miccosukee, they were the only other tribe in the region). His phenotype and hair color, unlike mine, were the telltale sign to those whose images of Indians were more based on race than nouveau ideas of sovereignty. Others spoke of the literal suitcases of money that he and others like him in the community during those days would haul up and down the Florida Keys from the island to Miami and back again. It seems most had a story or two to share about his life, and the many women who brought up his name had more than I needed to know. These "tellings" were a direct contrast to my mother's very minimal discussion of him—I am sure more so predicated on the feelings of a broken heart than any purposeful omission.

My fiancé, daughter, and I would stay in Bahama Village only a short year and a half, as I accepted a head coaching position in the summer of 2004 at Oklahoma's oldest institution of higher education, Bacone College, in Muskogee, Oklahoma. Members of my tribe had been making the six-hundred-mile journey to the then Indian boarding school, founded four years prior to Haskell, in 1880, for many generations due to our prohibition from the white and Black schools in our area of Alabama. Walking on campus, like so many of my own people had done before, felt like returning to a piece of my reservation home. Identical to my experience at Haskell, I began to search the archives of the school and consistently uncovered the documentary realities of our people's generational lives there.

Thereafter I began coaching and my wife began her position working in the Cherokee Nation of Oklahoma Health Department. We purchased a home in Tahlequah, a short drive from Muskogee, and enrolled our eldest child in the Cherokee Nation Language Immersion School. The reality of eastern Oklahoma's Indian identity wars would soon surface.

That fall of 2004, a student with a white racial phenotype walked into my office on campus and asked me, "Coach, can you help me get an Indian scholarship?" My answer half-jokingly was, "Are you Indian?" His response: "No, but I have a card." He then pulled his Certificate of Degree of Indian Blood (CDIB) out of his wallet and showed me a fraction and connection to the Cherokee Nation of Oklahoma that takes his Indian descent way, way back in time.

Ten years prior to all of this I was sitting at the Bluewater Youth Correctional Facility near my mother's hometowns of Port Albert and Goderich, Ontario, Canada. The circle of inmates were all a part of the Indian Brotherhood group that I was facilitating on a voluntary basis. The only fullblood, who was the oldest and clearly the most dominant member of the group, stood up and scanned the room. After a few moments of silence he remarked, "The difference between me and you all is that you get to choose. You all look white. You will never know the prejudice I go through." The reality that all these young men, including myself, were either enrolled with tribes or could be enrolled with tribes was of little consequence to him. Unlike these young men who were not raised, like myself, in a community of color outside of Indian Country, it was clear they had little understanding of the white privilege he was speaking directly to them about. But, clearly, by the sheer look in their eyes and demeanor by the end of his chastising, they now understood. His words were no less critical toward those darker than himself, which he referred to as simply "niggers," no matter if they possessed Indian ancestry or not.

> Although federal officials claimed that their objectivity gave them the right to interfere in tribal citizenship debates, they were not unbiased mediators. Indeed, many of the decisions rendered by the Interior Department were highly skewed, especially when it came to questions of race. For individuals of mixed Indian-white ancestry, the department concluded that "the appearances are deceptive and inconclusive." They asserted that it was "common knowledge" that some members of an Indian family resembled their white ancestors, while others inherited the physical characteristics of their Indian forebears. . . . Individuals of black-Indian ancestry,

on the other hand, fell more neatly into the era's black-white binary and government officials comfortably ignored their Indian ancestry in favor of a black racial identity. . . . [Agent Fred] Baker [of the Eastern Cherokee Enrolling Commission] could have made the same statement for a number of enrolled families—exchanging the word "negro" for "white"—yet he accepted white Indians on the roll while rejecting black Indians. . . . Baker also more readily enrolled the illegitimate "mixed-blood" Cherokee children of white mothers than the children of black mothers.[3]

While this quote references enrollment factors related to the Eastern Band of Cherokee Indians in North Carolina by Interior Department officials in the 1920s, there are countless examples of this occurring among tribes across the eastern and southern regions of the United States by governmental agents and tribal leaders themselves. Professor Mikaela M. Adams explores this phenomenon among a handful of these tribes in her book, *Who Belongs? Race, Resources, and Tribal Citizenship in the Native South*. These occurrences, as she and others have more recently attested to, are not isolated to prior generations, but have magnified themselves with even greater intensity in the current day.

This racial binary continuation is best illustrated by the actions of Cherokee Nation of Oklahoma tribal citizen R. Lee Fleming, who has become Indian Country's most powerful boundary creator. In his position as the director of the Office of Federal Acknowledgment, he is tasked with determining who is and who is not Indian, though he would argue that he is determining rights to a federal government-to-government relationship in the same way that someone who argues against "illegal immigration" from Mexico attempts to say it is about law, not race. His denial of federal recognition to various petitioning tribes, however, sends the message of inauthenticity of those rejected to many in the mainstream and Indian Country as well. His purposeful inconsistencies in evaluating petitions, as catalogued by hosts of academics, are legendary in the Indian world.

Keneisha M. Green explores this institutionally created degree of inauthenticity in the University of Oklahoma College of Law's *American Indian Law Review*. Her article, "Who's Who: Exploring the Discrepancy between the Methods of Defining African Americans and Native Americans," quotes the words of Lumbee Indian Cynthia Hunt as recorded in the book *Killing the White Man's Indian: Reinventing Native Americans at the End of the Twentieth Century*. "I feels as if I'm not a real Indian until I've got that BIA [Bureau of Indian Affairs] stamp of approval. . . . You're told all your life that you're Indian, but sometimes you want to be that kind of Indian that everybody else accepts as Indian."[4]

Raised in affluence in Maryland, the blond, light-skinned, and blue-eyed bureaucrat Lee Fleming never had to endure the scrutiny of his heritage due to his lived white privilege. His father, a noted businessman on the East Coast, was white and his mother was of mixed white and Cherokee ancestry, with her family originally being from Oklahoma. He eventually attended Northeastern Oklahoma State University in Tahlequah, Oklahoma (capital of the Cherokee Nation of Oklahoma), and then went on to work for his tribe under the Wilma Mankiller administration. During this time he was known for his research on "non-federal" tribes and Indian claimants and his disdain for such persons. During this transitional period into the Indian world in his twenties, he was immediately protected by his status as an enrolled member of a federally recognized tribe. Despite all of this, he has held a two-plus decade stranglehold on the Bureau of Indian Affairs federal list of Indian Country's haves and have-nots, with the accompanying large-scale protections and salary afforded such individuals.

That previously mentioned disdain has been particularly leveraged against eastern and southern tribes that he perceives to have some Black ancestry. One such case is illustrated by his denial of my own tribe's federal recognition petition initially in 1999. Hearing of this denial, Professor Don Rankin recounted a disturbing incident by letter to the leadership of the MOWA Band of Choctaw Indians concerning statements made at a June 1995 Genealogy Seminar conducted by Sharon Scholars Brown at Samford University in Alabama. R. Lee Fleming was also a presenter at the conference, and one year later he would join the Bureau of Acknowledgement and Research/Office of Federal Acknowledgement within the Bureau of Indian Affairs (BIA). Dr. Rankin's letter states, "Someone brought up the MOWA Choctaw and their attempt at federal recognition. At this stage, several people had gathered around and we were talking. Ms. Brown responded in an even professional tone of voice that she felt that they would not be successful. When asked why, she responded that the MOWA Choctaw had black ancestors and in her opinion were not Indian. Mr. Lee Fleming, who was at that time the Tribal Registrar for the Western Band of Cherokee (Cherokee Nation of Oklahoma) and one of the lecturers, agreed with her. I was shocked at their statements."[5]

The denial of the MOWA Choctaw petition was an architectural masterpiece for the now seasoned Washingtonian who, in the midst of the transference of power of the assistant secretary of Indian affairs, his direct supervisor, had come across a "moon and the stars aligning" situation to legitimize his prejudices. Fleming persuaded the newly appointed Assistant Secretary Kevin Gover (Pawnee Nation of Oklahoma), who was only two days into the job, to deny the petition. Having not reviewed the MOWA Choctaw submission, Gover, a racially identifiable American Indian, took Fleming at his word. After leaving the position a few years later, Gover had many misgivings. On April 21, 2004, he provided testimony before the Senate Committee on Indian Affairs on proposed Senate Bill 297. In his testimony addressing the "Structural Issues with the Federal Acknowledgment Program," Gover provided the following statement: "First, I strongly believe that certain petitioners, which already have been denied recognition, should be permitted another opportunity under the revised process established by this bill. . . . Into this category I would place Mowa Choctaw."[6]

By the time of former assistant secretary Gover's comments, it was too late for the tribe. Numerous appeals had gone unanswered and responses to Fleming's comments and clear racist beliefs that tribes could not possess some degree of Black ancestry, or even just a perception of Black ancestry, and be validated under his watch were upheld. The tribe's federal lawsuit contesting his actions was thrown out of court on a statute of limitations argument, and the facts of the case were never heard. A decade later, in a response letter to MOWA Choctaw questions regarding Fleming's racial bias, the acting principal deputy for the Assistant Secretary of Indian Affairs George Skibine (Osage), who is racially white identifiable, the son of a famous Osage ballerina, and raised in France, stated, "The Secretary of the Interior declined to order further reconsideration of this matter by letter dated November 26, 1999. We are sorry that we could not be of help to the MOWA Band of Choctaw Indians in this matter."[7]

The power of anti-Black racism, oddly directed at an identifiable Indian tribe, showed that avoidance and bureaucracy had once again triumphed. For individuals such as Fleming and Skibine, historic documents are "cherry picked" in terms of racial designation. Where historic tribes, such as the MOWA Choctaw, are listed as Indian on census and military records, they are avoided. Mulatto, white, and Black listings in other years and documents are quickly accepted as fact and used as evidence against petitioners. My wife, the daughter of a full-blood Kiowa mother and enrolled Ponca father, is listed in her military service documents as Hispanic. My daughter has been listed as Asian/Pacific Islander in legal documents. Both are identifiable American Indian women. Myself, by far the whitest in the group, has been listed on federal immigration documents since birth as Indian. (My mother and father were living in Florida during her pregnancy, but wanting me to be born in her country of origin, they traveled to Canada when she was eight and a half months pregnant and returned with me shortly after my birth.) If the irony and misnomer of legal identification between the three of us does not draw attention to the clear troubles inherent in legal documentation when it comes to race, then I would find it hard to find something that does.

Fleming's journey to the top of Indian Country's racial identity policing paralleled that of historic figure and twentieth-century State of Virginia registrar Walter Plecker, who made it his life mission to eradicate Virginia tribes whom he deemed as "Negroes passing as Indians." While Fleming has stood against Virginia's tribes himself, he made one more recent exception in the 2016 federal recognition of the Pamunkey. In an effort to show that the process he leads is legitimate, a point of view heavily criticized by tribal leaders, historians, and academics throughout the United States, he supported the petition of the Pamunkey in his positive findings report by stressing, as support for their authenticity as Indians, their codified prohibition on Black intermarriage.

The phenomenon of federal recognition based on proximity to whiteness and distance from Blackness was also expressed thirty-eight years earlier, in 1978. At that time, Terry Anderson and Kirke Kickingbird (Kiowa), an attorney, were hired by the National Congress of American Indians to research this issue and present a paper on their findings to the National Conference on Federal Recognition, which was being held in Nashville, Tennessee. Their paper, "An Historical Perspective on the Issue of Federal Recognition and Non-recognition," closed with the following statement: "The reasons that are usually presented to withhold recognition from tribes are 1) that they are racially tainted with the blood of African tribes-men or 2) greed, for newly recognized tribes will share in the appropriations for services given to the Bureau of Indian Affairs. The names of justice, mercy, sanity, common sense, fiscal responsibility, and rationality can be presented just as easily on the side of those advocating recognition."[8]

It is clear that one's proximity to Indian racial classification is not what drives the federal recognition process and therefore "official" identification of racial Indianness. The system, which is controlled by whites, as well as primarily racially white tribal members from various federally recognized tribes across the nation and also to a much smaller extent by individuals of primarily Indian ancestry, is one imbued with a white cultural lens and therefore with white privilege. The percentage of mixed-Black or Black employees present within the Bureau of Indian Affairs may literally exemplify the lowest percentage of any federal agency in the United States, for instance.

Indian Country's power broker's approvals are one's distance from "Blackness." The closer to perceived Black racial identity an Indian tribe is, the more likely they are to not be recognized by the federal government. The closer to white racial identity a tribe is, the more likely they are to be recognized by the federal government and to hold influence and decision making power in Washington, DC.

But how is it possible that tribes residing on recognized Indian reservations or who attended Indian boarding schools operated by the federal government and closely related missions or who were prevented from attending white or Black schools during the segregation period, or a combination of these, could not be recognized by the federal government?

How is it possible that tribes for whom the federal government listed blood quantums when they sent their members to Indian boarding schools (when the requirement for enrollment was a minimum of one-fourth Indian blood) could not be recognized today? How is it that those people who attended those same schools as Office of Federal Acknowledgement director Lee Fleming's own mother, a 1939 Chilocco Indian School graduate, could not be Indian today? Why is it that Fleming can draw from the Indian boarding school experience of his own family member while conveniently forgetting the similar experiences of others?

In pondering these questions, for which I have my own clear set of explanations, I flash to Oklahoma in 2016 and to the chambers of the state legislature's Native American Caucus. They had just passed HB2261, which makes it a jail-time offense to produce art, write, or provide visual performances as Indian if one is not an enrolled member of a federally recognized tribe in the United States. The primary authors and drivers of the legislation are members of the Cherokee Nation of Oklahoma, with the father of the current chief of the Cherokee Nation of Oklahoma and former Oklahoma House of Representatives member Chuck Hoskin being one of the primary architects, along with white-phenotype and former state senator and Cherokee Nation of Oklahoma citizen John Sparks being the other. Senator Sparks would never respond to repeated inquiries I had with him concerning this issue. Their tribe, the Cherokee Nation of Oklahoma, is the same tribe that is noted for the attempted expulsion of its Cherokee Freedmen descendants (i.e., Black Cherokees) in the 2000s. During Chuck Hoskin Jr.'s tenure as a tribal council member and secretary of state for the Cherokee Nation of

Oklahoma prior to his taking the reins as chief, he did nothing to change this injustice, which began during the former administration of Chief Chad "Corntassel" Smith, a noted anti-Freedmen and anti-"nonfederal" tribe activist.

Chief Chad Smith also accepted a campaign pledge from convicted lobbyist Jack Abramoff and then hired him the following year.[9] Jack Abramoff was a primary player behind the ill-fated MOWA Band of Choctaw Indians' federal recognition effort, receiving millions to upend the MOWA Choctaw and other tribes.

When I publicly questioned Chief Smith about his ability to lead despite living a life such as this, one of his anonymous supporters at the time responded via the internet that "Chief Smith has never betrayed the PUBLIC trust!!" This is the type of bar we have set for ourselves in Indian Country. Thankfully, a federal court judge in August 2017 reversed the decision prohibiting Cherokee Freedmen enrollment, and the Black Cherokees are once again entitled to full tribal citizenship, though deep wounds remain from the decade-long battle.

Back to the state legislature's Native American Caucus, we find that aside from one or two individuals, everyone in it is Caucasian identifiable and some were supportive of Cherokee Freedmen removal as well. Like the young man who strolled through my office in 2004 and the hundreds like him who have strolled through my offices and classrooms at various educational and tribal institutions since, everyone in the Caucus was also enrolled with a federal tribe. In 2017, HB2261 was halted by a federal judge due to an ongoing federal lawsuit and the reality that the legislation does not adhere to the Federal Indian Arts and Crafts Act, which defines Indian artists in broader terms. At the end of March 2019, another federal judge discontinued the legislation altogether and the State of Oklahoma was once again tied to the original federal legislation, thus allowing members of historic state-recognized "non-federal" tribes to continue to define their artwork as Indian produced.

My first published piece was as an eighteen year old, and it spoke directly to the issue of white privilege in Indian Country. Not the privilege of white people negatively impacting Indian Country, but the privilege of white people, who also happen to have CDIB cards, leading Indian Country. And this is where things get even more complex for the casual or even at times more seasoned observer. As I was leaving an educational event at the Choctaw Nation headquarters near Durant, Oklahoma, in November 2019, I was speaking with another attendee who told me she was a citizen of the

Cherokee Nation and also remarked in the same breath, "but only a little bit Cherokee. I am just one-sixteenth." My response to her was that she was practically a full-blood in terms of her blood positionality in relation to the majority of members within her tribe. She was perplexed. She told me that she thought she was the minimum that one could be to be enrolled with the Cherokee Nation. When I told her that there were those of as minimal as 1/8,192 Cherokee ancestry in her tribe, she was shocked. And this is why the Cherokee Nation of Oklahoma is so powerful. These arguments of identity are so far in the proverbial weeds that the average onlooker has no idea of what is going on. Surely, if an enrolled citizen of their own tribe doesn't even know the criteria for legalistic belonging, how would the average American? The façade falls apart quickly when people understand that much of the federal funding going to the tribe isn't actually assisting the minority of identifiable Cherokee people, but is actually being syphoned off to those who many would consider their white neighbors. In Indian Country, however, we are not supposed to talk about this and if we do, we are to be marginalized, have our identity attacked, and then be provided a lecture on tribal sovereignty. Noted Indigenous academic Brian Klopotek addresses this when he argues, "We too rarely account for the multiplicity of social and political positions within a community, preferring the simplicity of well-intentioned declarative statements about supporting tribal sovereignty that carry a secret, homogenizing, nationalist 'conceptual prison' for Indians within them."[10]

When my first piece was published, I was a teenager and knew hardly anything of Indian Country, but my university's location in the Washington, DC, metro area consistently put me in to contact with white-phenotype members of the Cherokee Nation of Oklahoma. Little did I realize that the families in the Virginia tribes who I frequently visited with during this time period were the real victims of those white-phenotype individuals nearby who controlled the actions of the Department of the Interior and Bureau of Indian Affairs. Twenty-five years later I have left a wake of articles regarding this subject in magazines, newspapers, online publications, academic journals, and books. Despite my own and a number of other writers' discussions of this subject, it continues to be one of the largest elephants in the room.

For those who have grown up in predominantly white environments and whose own, now enrolled, family members had previously looked down on identifiable Indians, it is virtually impossible for them to understand white privilege. To acknowledge it is to discredit their own newly found place in Indian Country or to admit that they come from a tribe where the majority, through multigenerational intermarriage, have long since abandoned the racial phenotype and in most cases corresponding cultural realities, including racism directed at them, of racially identifiable Indian people. This is why I remark that this is an unsolvable situation where the trenches of thought have been long established and reinforced.

Today, many academics and critics inside and outside of Indian Country argue that blood quantum is an illegitimate form of tribal identification. I would agree with this sentiment fully if it were not for the overshadowing and convenience that this "blood quantum as colonial oppressor narrative" creates for the federally recognized white Indian bearer of the message who wants others' eyes off of their "lack" of any significant racial heritage. To dismiss it in this context as the acceptance of a blood system created by whites for the purpose of Indian extermination is too simplistic a dismissal. And it is far too convenient for the "Indian" academic or artist who simply wants to put their federal tribal affiliation in brackets next to their name when submitting their works without having to explain the totality of their ancestry and typically non-Indian cultural upbringing. In contrast, a brown, identifiable member of a historic "non-federal" tribe immediately has their authenticity questioned once their affiliation such as Nanticoke, Lumbee, MOWA Choctaw, Haliwa-Saponi, and so forth, is placed in brackets next to their scholarship. No matter how valued the scholarship, no matter how lived the prejudice and Indian life, there always seems to exist an invisible asterisk. Even the few who have found some semblance of academic respect have to constantly deal with the paternalism thrown their way, whether intentional or not. An example of this occurred in October 2019 when I was presenting at an Indigenous language conference in California. The room of 150 or so people was evenly divided among federal and non-federal tribal members. All were racially identifiable as Indian without exception and had lived lives very similar to one another in the state in terms of historical realities. One gentleman, a member of a federal tribe, in the most well-meaning of ways told the audience, "Even you who are not from a federally recognized tribe should be proud of being Indian." There is no question he meant this sincerely, but there was also no question that he doesn't understand that we don't need his approval or acknowledgement and that such a statement is demeaning to many. This same feeling would overcome me during meetings and conferences with the various Indian Freedmen organizations in Oklahoma. There always seemed to be somebody who was enrolled with one of the federal tribes who would attempt to almost "coach" the Freedmen population on what to say or how to act, while telling them they were "worthy" of recognition. It simply sounded condescending, and numerous

Indian Freedmen spoke to me about this over this years, while also telling me that they couldn't afford to lose any allies no matter how paternalistic they sounded, and thus, they just keep allowing them to speak.

The complexity and strange bedfellows continues to grow. Some in the white American population have bemoaned the more recent "darkening" of their country through intermarriage and immigration. Those fleeing from the American reality have begun "white flight" equivalent to that which occurred during the 1960s as white city citizens across the nation fled to newly formed suburbs and private school systems. But this new white flight is the territory of people of minimal Indian ancestry who are now using Indian legal protections and the before-mentioned nouveau ideas of sovereignty as a literal wall for the exclusion of people of color within their midst. Indian Country, it seems, is the only segment of America that is actually becoming whiter with the passage of time. While the mainstream becomes increasingly brown, many tribes have taken to the philosophy of hyperdescent for enrollment. The more heads, the more federal dollars. This shift occurred primarily in the late 1970s and early 1980s prior to tribes realizing that gaming revenues were on the horizon. The floodgates opened either through tribal constitutional amendments lowering the blood quantum requirement of various tribes or by what some feel is a lessening of racial animosity toward Indians since some tribes always had descendant status as the sole marker for enrollment, but certainly didn't have the takers for growing their rolls at the time.

"Indian" was slowly losing its negative connotation for those of minimal ancestry and enrolling in some tribes was as easy as having a singular documented ancestor on a base roll from many generations prior. Had the leaders of these tribes known at the time of the transition that gaming was on the horizon and that it could become an even bigger cash cow than massive tribal populations driving funding, they may have reconsidered. But as we know hindsight is always 20/20.

These newly arrived white people would become the catalyst for great economic and social change in many tribes. With them came previous generational white access to education and political structures. Brown tribes, with little to no access, would now be forced to compete with them for federal grants and programs. Soon, the white people would become political candidates in the tribes and justify this by harkening back to romanticized images of individuals such as one-eighth blood degree and former Cherokee chief John Ross—an image now used to "legitimize the authenticity" of tribal citizens ranging into the 1/8,192 blood degree range. Over one hundred years ago, during the time of the Dawes enrollment, people claiming as little as 1/256 Indian ancestry were placed on tribal rolls throughout eastern Oklahoma, while some with half Indian ancestry and half Black ancestry were placed on Freedmen rolls, with their Indian blood degree magically disappearing in the process: 255/256 white and they were in, while half Black and they were out. It is not an argument of whether or not they should keep those white people while attempting to eliminate those of Black ancestry; it is the fact that the tribe and federal regulatory body who have such individuals, are the primary groups attempting to police the identity of others. And unlike John Ross, most have not been connected to a tribal identity for generations. The epicenter of this phenomena is certainly not emanating from the eastern and southern areas of the United States, but rather from eastern Oklahoma and the Cherokee Nation of Oklahoma's power positions within the halls of the Department of the Interior, Bureau of Indian Affairs, and Bureau of Indian Education.

In my work as an educator in Oklahoma, I am reminded of this day in and day out, whether on the job or out in the community. On a day our family was eating at a restaurant in Shawnee, Oklahoma, the waiter asked us what country we were from, as we were speaking a language he did not recognize. I told him we were from the United States and so he inquired further. I explained to him that we were speaking Choctaw and immediately his eyes lit up and he walked off. He came back with his CDIB card in hand and told us that he was Choctaw. We are still not sure why he had his CDIB or why he felt the need to hand it to me. On the card was seemingly the heritage he seemed so very proud of. It had a blood degree of 1/128 listed. I told him that we could teach him some Choctaw and he immediately responded that he wouldn't be able to learn that because he could barely speak English. He then chuckled of course. No one at our table was chuckling. Then followed the usual "proof" of his Indianness, which he offered up by telling us that he receives the tribal newspaper (as does everyone on the roll) and that "the Indians," as he said, helped pay for him to go to college. That is how detached some of these people are. They say things like "the Indians" when referring to the tribe. They divorce themselves completely from the Indian people whom they benefit from. Even so, I have empathy for him, as I am certainly no example of "authentic" Indianness myself, having grown up in South Florida, far distanced from both Indian Country and its arch-nemesis, white mainstream America. This empathy is never shown by those who police Indian identity nationally. One of the most disgraceful examples of this was when a group calling itself the Cherokee Task Force, which I renamed the Cherokee Task Farce, presented at the annual Indian conference held in safe confines on the campus of Northeastern State University in the Cherokee Nation Capital of Tahlequah, Oklahoma. The year was 2008. During this conference, primarily white racial phenotype Cherokee citizen elected leaders and tribal employees gave themselves "faux Indian names" and proceeded to make fun of people who were not from "federally recognized" tribes, to the great pleasure of the gathered crowd. The level of immaturity it takes to display such disdain is indicative of what so many in Indian Country have to battle every day. Such antics have also served as poison in the well, as many years later, those who participated in such events and their outlying supporters have seen themselves stricken by lost elections, dissolved marriages, legal challenges, and solid overall levels of loss. The very organization itself was also disbanded due to internal problems, though shadow groups have appeared since. These people replace themselves quickly. The hard work of working with Indigenous students in inner-city schools, combating the epidemic of sexual violence toward Indian women, revitalizing traditional languages, and many more issues would simply take too much effort for them to engage in. And this is not the typical redirection to take eyes off an issue, this is simply a statement of the facts. Real, substantive issues demand real focus and work that is beyond the average "keyboard" warrior to undertake. What so many of these identity police do not understand is that every time they condemn any person or tribe without federal status as a fraud, wannabe, and charlatan, they continue a pattern that disenfranchises historic "non-federal" tribal communities and individuals. Their "harmless" retweets, message board postings, and the like only serve to further discard human beings, as the general public has no baseline from which to understand the complexity of these issues and to know of the primary racial ancestry of the nearly four hundred thousand enrolled citizens of the Cherokee Nation of Oklahoma. Our MOWA Choctaw community, for instance, has over thirty federal tribes married into our community and has numerous community residents who are enrolled with the Cherokee Nation of Oklahoma, none of whom would fall into the "white" category. Having lived and worked in Tahlequah and having our oldest child as a former student at the Cherokee Immersion School, we know all too well the difference between what is being marketed and what is the reality. I can't say how many times an identifiable Cherokee from Oklahoma has lamented how their tribe has been hijacked by white people. However, such comments cannot be made public for fear of job loss and ostracization.

On the flip side of the before-mentioned waiter, who has no ill intent toward others, are those like him in terms of ancestry who engage the culture and then go all evangelical in their pursuit of their minimal heritage. Soon they become the "authorities" on Indian culture and begin building walls against others who they do not feel are "Indian enough." It is always one extreme to the next with these people. These individuals will go so far as to attempt to take white families with minimal Indian ancestry and persuade them to claim their family as Indian in their entirety to get more dollars and representation for the tribe. It is like these white families are slot machines unto themselves. This couldn't be better explained than in the solicitation of a former Cherokee Nation of Oklahoma tribal council member.

> Based on my understanding of the Census, I am asking all Cherokee Nation citizens to list themselves as "Cherokee Nation." If you are married to a non-Cherokee and you live in the Cherokee Nation, the Cherokee citizen should list themselves as head of the household. If you are more than one ethnicity, claim only Cherokee Nation. . . . For example, a mixed-blood Cherokee woman is married to a non-Indian with four children in the household. The Cherokee woman lists herself as head of household and "Cherokee Nation," only. The husband is listed as his ethnicity and the children listed as "Cherokee Nation," only. The Census would then count the entire household of six as Cherokee, Cherokee Nation citizens. . . . Otherwise, the entire household can be listed as non-Cherokee when the data is analyzed or made to be not Indian enough if listed as mixed-blood. To me, you are either a Cherokee citizen or you are not. We do not fund partial Cherokees. By ensuring all of our citizens are properly counted as Cherokee Nation citizens, we bring more money to Rogers County and Oklahoma. The Tribe needs you to stand up and be counted.[11]

This shape-shifting in order to create a comfortable space for racially white majority populations in some of these tribes has been highly effective. Indian when it benefits, but definitely racially white when anti-Brown or Black racism rears its head has become the norm, not the exception. In fact, many of these tribal members are the very ones who lead the racist agendas. While large corporate federal tribes reap the financial rewards of these primarily racially white populations, they also spearhead the wave of questioning "non-federal" Indigenous people, whether by intention or not. When one of these assaultive individuals is challenged on their minor ancestry, the mapped-out story of how their ancestor, for fear of having their allotment lands having ward status due to them being half or more by blood, claimed to be one-quarter or one-eighth or less explains why their blood quantum is lower than it should be. Or they say that only one side of their family was enrolled, but really both sides are Indian. Of course, the second someone who is not enrolled claims that their family was living in Texas or Arkansas during the enrollment period or has another plausible story, they are immediately condemned as frauds. This is never a two-way street, especially for Indian Freedmen, many of whom have clear and honest oral traditions, as well as documented proof, of by-blood Indian ancestors who were erased by being placed on the Freedmen rolls.

Federally recognized as "real Indian" has become one of Indian Country's greatest lies and indoctrination tools thanks to the massive power exhibited by bureaucrats and economically powerful tribes. As a racially and phenotypically white person myself, who is an enrolled tribal member of a historic "non-federal" tribe with few white-phenotype tribal members, I could never understand from even very early on what gave these people descended from federal tribes the nerve to sweep into tribal communities they were rarely raised in and with whom they have little, if any, cultural connection and act as though they are the leaders. Nothing smacks of white privilege more than this. But when the majority of the federal tribe who elects them is racially white, it is clear how such individuals consistently get elected.

Invariably, these individuals have become the policing agents of Indian Country due to their own lack of the very "authentic" Indian identity they claim others do not possess. I call this Indian identity insecurity. The Oklahoma art law previously mentioned is a case in point to what a Choctaw Nation of Oklahoma citizen and employee, whose tribe along with the Cherokee Nation of Oklahoma supported this law, said to me. Her response in hearing about it was, "This is complete hypocrisy." She recognized that while Yuchi/Euchee, Nanticoke, MOWA Choctaw, Mattaponi, and other historic "non-federal" tribes who generationally attended Indian boarding schools or live on some of the nation's oldest reservations, or both, would have been prosecuted as non-Indian impostors under this frivolous law, this new concept of "real" Indian artist would have had the opposite effect by promoting a mistruth in advertising agenda. The mistruth is the notion that some federal tribal member with a blood quantum of 1/1,024 or whatever is a legitimate Indian artist, while a Mattaponi, living on one of the two oldest Indians reservations in America, is not. Most collectors of Indian art would strongly beg to differ on this, but again it is a discussion that has no ending.

Hypocrisy doesn't begin to explain it. Why must so many pay for other's identity insecurities?

Another person whom I typically stand on opposite ends of the spectrum with recently told me that they get it. They understand that my stance has always been the proverbial "why does the baby have to be thrown out with the bathwater" whenever it comes to Indian identity. In the federal lobby's rush to destroy those whom they feel are fraudulent (i.e., part Black in some instances), they simply draw a line in the sand that "federally recognized" is the gold standard, when not only is it not the gold standard, but it even legally promotes further Indian Country's increasing white privilege.

In recent years, the politicians and some tribes in Oklahoma have paraded around the academic success of Indian students in the state in comparison to their peers in other Indian inhabited states. However, they have forgotten to mention that the majority of the students in the state with CDIB cards are of primarily white ancestry. Tribes like the Ponca, Kiowa, Comanche, Sac & Fox, Absentee Shawnee, and others with primarily racially Indian identifiable populations don't add up to even half the number of the Cherokee Nation of Oklahoma citizens in terms of total enrollment. The same goes for Indian Health Service statistics, which do not differentiate between racially Indian people and white card carriers. The Indian health statistics we are seeing coming out of eastern Oklahoma are simply not realistic. Racially white people being counted as racially Indian for the purpose of Indian health reporting is simply inaccurate and damaging in relation to finding and resolving issues inherent in the health disparities impacting actual racially Indian people in America.

I would say to be a person of color, one must be a . . . drum roll, please . . . an actual person of color. I would never insult the very community of color that I grew up in or the majority of members of my father's tribe, both which accept me fully, by attempting to claim their racial identity as a person of color. My not being a person of color does not serve to excommunicate me from my tribal community. It doesn't impact my enrollment. It doesn't stop me from participating in the social, cultural, and spiritual life of our tribe or community of upbringing. Why are so many trying so hard to legitimate themselves within Indian Country instead of just owning their whiteness—owning their reality? Isn't it much less stressful to simply be who one is? I was raised completely distant from a white American cultural context, but even so I still have no problem owning my whiteness in America. When I walk on to the street as a six-foot-four, 225-pound, heterosexual, white-phenotype male, I am white coded and white privileged. Even though I wasn't raised within the cultural consciousness of a white American community, I still get that I am white coded and privileged and a recipient of such positionality. How is it that since I have been owning it all of these years, despite not growing up in white America, that so many now legally in Indian Country who look white and were raised in the white world cannot own it?

White privilege and the accompanying Indian identity insecurities that infect its practitioners drive domestic violence rates in Indian Country and produce the trolling nature of internet policing that has become so prevalent. White privilege is what disallows most adopted children and "half" brothers and sisters from having full status within the tribes of their "adoptive" and "step" (neither term having historical merit in an Indian context) parent's upbringing, by erasing historic and valued concepts of what makes one a true member of an Indian community. It is replacement theory to believe that minor lineal descent can overpower cultural, social, and familial connection, that CDIB cards can replace real lived history, or that a CDIB erases the white upbringing of the now technically legal "Indian" who possesses it. There is nothing worse than watching the creation of a delusion represented as historical fact.

And, frankly, most of the white card-carrying members of tribes are clueless about the whitening and displacement of nonwhite—and Black—Indigenous peoples. The majority of these members just want their free health care, some scholarship dollars, the ability to express a little pride, and also to continue in the white privilege they have always possessed without being pushed into the fray. Every day, in my capacity as an educator here in Oklahoma, I am directly witness to this. They don't want or even know of these types of arguments. For better or worse, that is just how it is. For the white ones who want to become uber-Indians, well, that is an extreme experienced among enrolled and nonenrolled, federally recognized, state recognized, nonrecognized, and in all socioeconomic quadrants. Extremists are extremists. Those intent on stopping them should not put "non-federal" Indians in positions of collateral damage.

Anyway, who really costs Indian Country more, the self-identified "Indian" dancing at powwows and telling "traditional" stories, while being unable to access any tribal dollars, or the white redneck with a Confederate flag T-shirt on (yes, I have seen multiples of these guys receiving services at Indian Health Service clinics here in Oklahoma) who is using thousands of dollars of federal tribal funding yearly, while identifiable tribal community coffers are bare? Who knows? I guess it all comes down to perspective.

The imposition and internalization of white privilege in Indian Country has severed Indian Country's intellectual capital and further marginalized already struggling communities and members of our families. One Oklahoma tribe that hosted a community Christmas party we attended with our kids made note on their advertising flyer that "only children enrolled in federally-recognized tribes" would be provided toys at the event. Merry Christmas?

The backward thinking of all of this and its accompanying stories is never ending. For me, it is not necessarily who one is born of, but rather who one is born for, that truly matters. I see members of my own tribe and other tribes who have adopted children from other tribal communities. Many of those children are culturally grounded and supported fully within their "adoptive" family's tribe. They identify as members of the tribe. They are community members of the tribe regardless of their biological parentage. They were born for those people, those communities and those tribal nations. And besides, I don't live in other people's bedrooms. Because one's dad showed up on the birth certificate or a Census record lists him as "head of household" doesn't necessarily support or deny the reality of one's biological heritage. Many a man has been "erroneously" placed on a birth certificate over the generations for a multitude of reasons. Life is complex. Life is messy. But the raising of a child and connecting that child to those who can love and comfort them is beautiful.

If the worst thing one ever gets called in their life is a wannabe, then they should count themselves lucky and blessed. If people can't attack them for neglecting their kids, disrespecting their wife or husband, abandoning their community, and so forth, then that person is doing pretty well.

When did it become so very bad in Indian Country that legitimate Indian communities and people are having to be legally purged in order to chase down guys claiming to be "Medicine Men" and selling sweat lodge ceremonies? When did it get so bad that tribal communities and people who have been acknowledged as Indian for centuries must be made to grovel at the feet of those whose own federal tribal enrollment has only recently come to pass after magically finding a trace of Indian ancestry on a federal roll?

This is where we find ourselves in Indian Country: trying to "out-Indian" one another. We are dividing and cutting our families up into pieces. David Cornsilk, a Cherokee Nation of Oklahoma citizen who spoke openly about his identity insecurities during his upbringing as a white-phenotype, green-eyed son of a white woman and primarily Cherokee by blood father in a *New*

York Times article titled "One Drop of Blood," has been at the forefront of racial identity policing of historic "non-federal" tribes and their members, while also being a staunch advocate of the recent return of the Cherokee Freedmen to the Cherokee Nation of Oklahoma. Again, it is all so very complex, as is the next quote from the writings of Cornsilk, which contradicts his purported support of Black people: "As I have found in my travels among the groups claiming to be tribes in Louisiana, if you mix blacks with whites over enough generations, the descendants can look like Indians."[12]

Speechless. Life is complex. Life is messy. Cornsilk has been criticized so frequently in response to his constant attacks on others that I am sure he has built up a complete immunity to any negative comments directed at him. Even getting punched in the face by Tahlequah, Oklahoma, artist Murv Jacob, who passed away in February 2019, didn't faze him, despite his trip to the hospital. In fact, he posited that he was proud to take a punch in the mouth if it stopped "wannabeism" from continuing. Wannabes where I grew up were men who couldn't handle themselves in the streets. Murv Jacob was no wannabe, so I am not too sure what Cornsilk was insinuating. Cornsilk and people like him have created sizeable echo chamber communities that enable each other, and echo chambers are virtually impossible to deconstruct.

Members of some Louisiana tribes, whom Cornsilk portrays as Black or mulatto, have a far different take on their own identity. Former tribal council member and vice chairman Michael Dardar of the United Houma Nation in Louisiana sent a letter to the Cherokee Nation of Oklahoma council and administration in September 2006 concerning their tribe's attacks on historic "non-federal" tribes that stated in part, "I see these guys all the time in their suits and ties, looking and sounding like all the other right-wing political hacks out there. Having grown up in the bayou country of Louisiana I've learned that if it flies, swims and quacks like a duck it usually is one. I've grown really tired of these 'experts' exclaiming the importance of their federally-recognized Indianness and pushing an agenda that runs counter to genuine indigenous sovereignty and self-determination."[13]

Dove Verret, an elder of the United Houma Nation in Louisiana, remarked:

> When we was growing up, no one ever heard of federal recognition. Hell, we hardly ever saw a white or black person. Then some white people in Washington, DC, some even claiming to be Indian, told us that we weren't a tribe. Can you imagine, white people telling a bunch of brown

Indians who can barely speak English that they aren't a tribe? I tried to explain to my elders that the white people said that we weren't Houma. They had a hard time understanding what I was telling them. Some still don't understand what the Indian Affairs meant by that statement. Then I told them what it meant was that we wouldn't be getting any help for health care, education, or housing. They all laughed and said, "We never have before. That is how the whites are."[14]

The then chief of the MOWA Band of Choctaw Indians, Wilford Taylor, whose tribe Cornsilk, like R. Lee Fleming, feels is Black or mulatto, reiterates this point in a letter sent on September 8, 2006, to the Cherokee Nation of Oklahoma chief and council regarding their constant attacks on the identity of others and their anti-Blackness.

> I was educated at Bacone College [Indian school in Oklahoma] many years ago. I count numerous Cherokees as friends from my time spent there. Upon more recent visits, individuals that I had known as white while living in Oklahoma have suddenly become "Cherokee." The individuals seem to be in the majority amongst your tribal enrollment. Our people on the other hand, are not white, and have never been white. We have experienced extreme prejudice here in Alabama due to our marginal position in southern society. This bigotry and racism brought against our people continues to this day. This is something the majority of your population has never encountered.[15]

Indian Country's white "CDIB carrying" academic elite and primarily racially white tribal leaders—such as Kerry Holton, former Delaware Nation of Oklahoma chairman, whose never-ending attacks on historic "non-federal" tribes with mixed-Black or perceived mixed-Black ancestry is highly suspect due to his own seven-eighths white ancestry, upbringing in Georgia, and marriage to a self-identified "little redneck from Smyrna"—directly contributes to the failing march against oppression and colonialism where individuals such as himself position themselves as leaders "in the struggle." Their white privilege has become the stairway to their towers and bully pulpits. They readily attack those who are not enrolled with federal tribes as being somehow deficient from them, as if to somehow state that their own minor Indian ancestry as defined on highly contestable century-plus-old federal Indian rolls, holds more intrinsic value than the oral traditions, localized tribal rolls, and at times Indian and non-Indian community recognition as Indian of their nonenrolled contemporaries.

While this all began with the federal government, it is perpetuated by academics who draw purposeful conclusions that allow them to exist in a bubble of comfort that they have built for one another. They herald the joint anticolonial work they engage in with their Black academic colleagues, but forget to inform these Black colleagues that they stand against or are apathetic toward historic "non-federal" tribes of mixed-Black or perceived mixed-Black ancestry, and also that they believe tribal sovereignty trumps concerns over Indian Freedmen removals, for example. They won't think about questioning someone such as academic Sonia Sanchez on her claims to Indian lineage, but have no problem disparaging those who can't strike back. In her poem "Present" she describes her connection to her Black and American Indian heritages, yet in the academy I have seen no takers attempting to "enlighten" or shame her familial conclusions. When, as a college student in the early 1990s, I was able to hear her speak and listen to her claim her Indigenous roots native to North America, I heard not a peep from those gathered. Yet in the same state of Alabama where her roots spring forth, the MOWA Choctaw are disparaged. While the audience cheers for this mindful poet, some deride her reservation-based neighbors. I don't hear the naysayers publicly shaming Boston Celtics star basketball player Kyrie Irving when the Standing Rock Sioux tribe welcomed him home in August of 2018 or when Kareem Abdul-Jabbar claims to have Cherokee ancestry. In fact, they are some of the first to get in line for autographs. It seems fame can become an exception to prejudice. If that is the exception, then it magnifies the contradiction in identity policing even further. It is clear that Kyrie's mother was adopted off the reservation as a child and that he has every right to be a member of his tribe. Kareem has no such concrete connection, yet I believe them both and not because of a genealogy chart being produced, notarized, and "certified." Kareem's work empowering Indian youth and spending time in reservation communities speaks to his sincerity. Kyrie's more recent engagement with issues such as the pipelines devouring sacred lands, or any lands for that matter, speaks also to his desire to be home and his willingness to put in the work. Should we dismiss those who engage ethically and who have the platform to genuinely affect change for the better?

Where are these big talkers of settler colonialism rhetoric when they have to speak against their own tribe's transgressions toward historic "non-federal" tribes of mixed-Black or perceived mixed-Black ancestry? Where is the outrage they so easily produce in talks concerning colonialism? In more recent times such individuals have even banded together to attack the identities of other white-phenotype Indian academics in a tour-de-force that I refer to as a tour-de-farce. How is it that people bathed in phenotype white privilege and at times suburban or middle- and upper-middle-class comforts feel they can treat others in this fashion? Do they think that having a couple identifiable Indians on their team somehow gives their words legitimacy?

In 2016 I continued putting together a comparison list of federally recognized and historic "non-federally" recognized tribes in the eastern and southern regions of the United States. These tribes, which government and academic contributors had "vetted," provide us with a legal reality put into place by generations of social prohibition to tribes that are perceived to have or do have some Black ancestry. This is of course not a complete list of the historic "non-federal" tribes, and those who do not appear here should not be assumed or perceived as not existing.

In 2016, the federal tribes included the Alabama-Coushatta Tribe of Texas, Akwesasne Mohawk, Aroostook Band of Micmacs, Catawba Indian Nation, Cayuga Nation, Chitimacha Tribe of Louisiana, Coushatta Tribe of Louisiana, Eastern Band of Cherokee Indians, Houlton Band of Maliseet Indians, Jena Band of Choctaw Indians, Kickapoo Tribe of Texas, Mashantucket Pequot Tribal Nation, Mashpee Wampanoag Tribe, Miccosukee Tribe of Indians of Florida, Mississippi Band of Choctaw Indians, Mohegan Tribe, Narragansett Indian Tribe, Oneida Indian Nation, Onondaga Nation, Pamunkey, Passamaquoddy Tribe–Indian Township, Passamaquoddy Tribe–Pleasant Point, Penobscot Indian Nation, Poarch Band of Creek Indians, Seminole Tribe of Florida, Seneca Nation of Indians, Shinnecock Indian Nation, St. Regis Mohawk Tribe, Tigua Tribe of Texas, Tunica-Biloxi Tribe of Louisiana, and Wampanoag Tribe of Gay Head (Aquinnah).

The historic "non-federal" tribes listed included the Bayou Lacombe Choctaw, Chickahominy, Chickahominy Indians Eastern Division, Choctaw-Apache of Ebarb, Clifton Choctaw, Eastern Pequot, Haliwa-Saponi, Herring Pond Wampanoag, Lenape Tribe of Delaware, Live Oak Choctaw, Lumbee, Mattaponi, Meherrin, MOWA Band of Choctaw Indians, Monacan, Nansemond, Nanticoke, Nanticoke Lenni-Lenape Nation, Nipmuc, Paugusett (Golden Hill), Pocasset Wampanoag, Ramapough, Rappahannock, Schaghticoke, Tuscarora (North Carolina), United Houma Nation, Unkechaug Nation, Upper Mattaponi, and Waccamaw Siouan.

Of twenty-nine federal tribes listed in the East and South, only six are those that media and publications have painted as having some Black ancestry. The remaining twenty-three have been designated as Indian, Indian-white, or white in media or publications. Some of the federal tribes listed did not reside on reservations until after receiving federal recognition and then taking land into federal trust. Some of the federal tribes did not have a single member who attended an Indian boarding school, unlike many of the "non-federal" tribes. And, yes, this matters greatly to the "powers that be" as Indian boarding school attendance has now been enshrined in the new federal recognition regulations and many academics, including all those mentioned previously, have used attendance at such schools as authenticators.

Of the six federally recognized tribes as of 2016 that were perceived to have some Black ancestry, all have only been recognized since the 1980s, with the most recent not being acknowledged until 2011. All of these tribes were aggressively fought against prior to and during their federal petitions and their perceived and real Black ancestry was brought forth consistently by their opponents. Luckily for the Mashantucket Pequot, Narragansett, Tunica-Biloxi, and Wampanoag Tribe of Gay Head (Aquinnah), they were able to gain recognition just prior to the advent of Indian gaming, which politicized Indian Country and became a primary wall against the recognition of various tribes due to already recognized tribes and their desire to maintain gaming monopolies in their regions. For the Mashpee Wampanoag and Shinnecock, their paths to federal recognition became highly problematic and both had to partner with massive gaming companies and take on millions of dollars in legal promises to these companies, which financed their federal petitions. The vitriol associated with the six tribes in terms of their Black identification was highly visible through the writings of anthropologists, BIA officials, academics, federal tribes, their non-Indian neighbors, and others—all attacks that their white-Indian tribal contemporaries were not inundated with.

For instance, the Mashantucket Pequot received congressional recognition in 1980, long before the advent of Indian gaming. They presented their petition to the US Congress only with white-phenotype members of the tribe at hearings. Only after federal recognition were the majority of tribal members, who are of Black phenotype, brought forth in the media. The tribe has been relentlessly attacked ever since in all forms of publications including a *New York Times* bestseller. The Mashpee Wampanoag did not receive federal recognition until 2007 and only after twenty-plus years of petitioning. During this time, continuous racial assaults were levied against them in the media and in publications. It took over $20 million in gaming backer funds to lobby Washington and pay for the petition, which comprised hundreds of thousands of pages of materials. The Narragansett received federal recognition in the 1980s prior to the advent of gaming. Their tribe was continuously attacked racially in the media and in various publications then and to some extent now. The Shinnecock did not receive federal recognition until 2011 and only after a federal lawsuit forced the Office of Federal Acknowledgment to recognize the tribe. The tribe spent over $30 million in gaming backer funds to complete their petition. The Tunica-Biloxi were recognized in 1981 prior to the advent of gaming. They ensured that primarily Indian and mixed white tribal members were at the forefront of their recognition proceedings. This enabled recognition, though there exist many tribal members of Black descent within the tribe. After recognition these individuals were able to "be seen" as it were. The Tunica-Biloxi have been steadfast supporters of historic "non-federal" tribes that are still seeking federal recognition. The Wampanoag Tribe of Gay Head (Aquinnah) endured much of the same pressures as the Mashpee Wampanoag, but they were able to get through the process in the 1980s prior to the advent of gaming.

The only other federal tribes in the eastern and southern regions of the United States to have been federally recognized post 1990 through to 2017 were the white-phenotype-identified Mohegan (1994), Jena Band of Choctaw Indians (1995), and Pamunkey (2016). The final two both had social prohibitions on intermarriage with Black people, while possessing no such prohibitions on intermarriage with whites. The Pamunkey went even further in this social norm by forbidding such unions legally within their tribal constitution. Unlike the Mashpee and Shinnecock, these three tribes did not need to spend millions in gaming industry backed funds to accomplish their results, as their identity being mixed-white kept them out of the Black racialization microscope. Although it could be argued that, like other Virginia tribes, the Pamunkey were lumped into the "questioning gaze of Blackness" that frequented the others from time to time.

Of thirty historic "non-federal" tribes (and there are some others) listed in the East and South pre-2018, though most are recognized by the state governments where their tribal lands exist, all have been typecast as having Black ancestry. Of these, nine tribes reside on recognized Indian reservations whose establishment predates many other more westerly tribe's reservations by generations if not hundreds of years, thirteen attended all-Indian boarding schools along with members of federal tribes, and others attended local Indian schools due to being prohibited from attending area white or Black educational systems. This stands in sharp contrast to some currently federally recognized tribes in the East and South that have no history of Indian boarding school attendance, have never lived on a reservation until land was placed in trust for them after federal recognition, and who generationally attended white schools. But that was up until 2017. The year 2018 ushered in one of Indian Country's greatest "surprises" and one that was foreshadowed many years prior.

In 2001, during my time as previously mentioned as a full-time student at Haskell Indian Nations University, I began a documentation effort titled Haskell Endangered Legacy Project after listening to a federal tribal leader's presentation at the college making comments that amounted to his belief that tribes not recognized by the federal government were illegitimate and worse. Little did he know the history of the very school he was speaking in. And, as previously mentioned, over the course of the semester I spent a solid amount of time researching the archives held by the university. Coupled with my own tribe's articles and yearbooks from various Indian boarding schools, I was fortunate to build a large repository of the actual history of the Indian boarding schools in the central, eastern, and southern regions of the United States and the attendance at them by members of historic "non-federal" tribes (not recognized during the time of their attendance) from the eastern and southern regions of the United States. There were other attending "non-federal" boarding school tribes from outside of this region, as well as other boarding schools, of course, but I focused my work in this smaller scope due to time constraints and a desire to do as thorough a job as my own effort would allow.

By 2002, after reviewing all relevant documents I could put my hands and eyes on, I produced my first list of these tribes, which included Abenaki (Vermont), Alabama-Coushatta Tribe of Texas (Texas), Mashpee Wampanoag Tribe (Massachusetts), Narragansett Indian Tribe (Rhode Island), Shinnecock Indian Nation (New York), Tunica-Biloxi Tribe of Louisiana (Louisiana), Wampanoag Tribe of Gay Head (Massachusetts), Chickahominy (Virginia), Chickahominy Indians Eastern Division (Virginia), Eastern Pequot (Connecticut), Haliwa-Saponi (North Carolina), Lumbee (North Carolina), Mattaponi (Virginia), Monacan (Virginia), MOWA Band of Choctaw Indians (Alabama), Nanticoke (affiliated with the Nanticoke Lenni-Lenape Nation and Lenape Tribe of Delaware) (Delaware and New Jersey), Pamunkey (Virginia), Rappahannock (Virginia), United Houma Nation (Louisiana), Upper Mattaponi (Virginia), and Yuchi Tribe of Oklahoma (Oklahoma). To this list could also be added the Unkechaug Nation of Long Island, New York, which I believe were misidentified in some boarding school records as Shinnecock.

By the time the list was produced, the Alabama-Coushatta Tribe, Narragansett Indian Tribe, Tunica-Biloxi Tribe of Louisiana, and Wampanoag Tribe of

Gay Head (Aquinnah) had already been recognized and the Alabama-Coushatta had their recognition restored after having it abolished during the termination period. Since 2002, of the seventeen remaining Indian boarding school attending tribes, nine have since obtained federal recognition, with one of the nine then having it revoked (Eastern Pequot). These include the Mashpee Wampanoag, Shinnecock, and Pamunkey. In 2018, federal recognition decisions enshrined by Congress, not the Office of Federal Acknowledgment, added the former boarding school tribes Upper Mattaponi, Chickahominy, Chickahominy Indians Eastern Division, Monacan, and Rappahannock to the federal register. Oh, what a year 2018 was for former "non-recognized" boarding school tribes in the eastern and southern region of the United States who have generationally had to endure racial remarks targeting communities of Indigenous people who are perceived by outsiders as having some Black racial ancestry. In 2002, I made a clear remark via articles and public presentations that those tribes who attended the Indian boarding schools should logically be federally recognized and in the end would be federally recognized. The hecklers, keyboard "warriors," and behind-the-scenes "activists" came up in full force over these many years to discredit this history through highly prejudicial racial attacks on both the tribes and myself in an effort to dismiss a reality that was no longer fashionable in a time of "federal recognition" and "sovereignty" as the mainstays of "legitimate" Indian identity. The powers that be even went so far as to create a rule specifically barring me from presenting at the federal recognition hearings in 2014, despite my having previously done so in the previous year's hearings in the very same location. After being invited by former assistant secretary of Indian affairs Kevin Washburn to present these boarding school attendance findings to a large number of his leadership team along with my friend and Upper Mattaponi chief Ken Adams at his offices in Washington, DC, we were assured by those gathered that this history would be supported in the new federal recognition regulations published on June 29, 2015. The final rule only went so far as to state that "the Department has concluded that boarding school records can be highly relevant when corroborated by other evidence."[16] At least it had been enshrined on some level. In a telephone conversation between me and former assistant secretary Washburn after he ended his tenure and had returned to academia, he explained to me that he had done all he could under the political conditions that were present. The area I highlighted was a compromise after some powerful gaming tribes objected to it for fear of tribes being recognized in their regional areas who they felt would be in competition for their financial resources and others who made remarks stating that just because people from a particular community generationally attended Indian boarding schools doesn't mean they are Indian. Yes, it became that bizarre. It is the same old story time and time again. What more evidence could be needed of tribal existence and federal relationship than a tribe consistently listed in Indian boarding school records and whose very blood quantum and whose school staff and funding was supplied and staffed by the BIA and the Bureau of Indian Education (BIE)?

After years of presenting this documentation at Indian symposiums, university conferences, alumni association meetings, tribal gatherings, BIA/BIE/ Department of Interior meetings and in front of both highly receptive and highly confrontational tribal councils, the Native American Rights Fund, on my behalf, researched the issue and met with governmental officials about their findings. These findings came on the heels of a recent fourteen-panel exhibition of mine staged by the Haskell Cultural Center on the campus of Haskell Indian Nations University that illustrated the pages of boarding school yearbooks, boarding school newspapers, and other governmental documents showing the true and complete history of the boarding schools, which did not revision their histories in relation to "non-federal" tribal attendance. These findings followed a formal apology written years earlier on January 6, 2009 by former BIE executive and Cherokee Nation of Oklahoma citizen Stephanie Birdwell, whose office initially stated that no such persons had ever attended their federal Indian schools. The language reads, "the Haskell Endangered Legacy Project (H.E.L.P.) consortium's support of Haskell alumni promotes a valuable effort in showcasing the rich history that the respective 'non-federally' recognized tribal communities have played in the Haskell legacy."[17]

The National Congress of American Indians and its member tribes strongly condemned the removal of these tribes from Haskell in Resolution #PDX-11-016 (Oct. 30–Nov. 4, 2011). The resolution, "Support the Return of Former Attendance Documented 'Non-federal' Boarding School Tribes to Admission at Haskell Indian Nations University in Lawrence, Kansas," reads:

> WHEREAS, there currently exist twenty "non-federally recognized" tribes in the United States which had their citizens, over several generations, attend Indian boarding schools such as Haskell, Chilocco, Bacone, Carlisle, Choctaw Central, Cherokee, and Hampton; and

> WHEREAS, citizens of these same tribes, even alumni seeking to enroll in additional classes, are no longer allowed admittance to Haskell Indian Nations University; and

WHEREAS, their removal from their own Alma-mater is an issue of historical and cultural revisionism on the part of the Bureau of Indian Affairs; and

WHEREAS, the facts clearly demonstrate attendance of these "non-federally recognized" tribes for over one hundred years at boarding schools administered and funded by the OIA/BIA; and

WHEREAS, the NCAI is tasked with protecting the rights and legacies of all historic tribal communities; and

WHEREAS, the NCAI realizes that the attempt to undermine the histories of over 700 former "non-federally recognized" tribal citizens through disallowing access to Haskell for themselves and their descendants is unethical.[18]

The resolution came after numerous reputable academic press outlets published our writings on the subject area and a large number of both scholarly and editorialized articles had engaged the issue on both the internet and in print.

The Native American Rights Fund (NARF) found after thoroughly examining the issue and meeting with representatives from the BIA, that former assistant secretary of Indian affairs and Cherokee Nation citizen Ross Swimmer's memorandum, which expelled historic "non-federal" generationally attending Indian boarding school tribes from Haskell in particular despite them all having one-fourth or more Indian blood quantums listed by the BIA/BIE, was unlawful. NARF's final communication on the matter was sent to me on May 23, 2016. It reads, "It appears to NARF that when the Bureau changed HINU's [Haskell Indian Nation University] admissions policy in the late 1980s, the agency did not follow procedures that are required under the APA [Administrative Procedure Act] when a federal agency makes a rule change or decision of this type."[19]

Upon receiving this final communication from NARF, which goes even further about the improprieties, there was nothing else for me to do in this arena, despite the Bureau of Indian Education and Haskell Indian Nations University administration's refusal to follow the law and readmit those tribes that previously had attended. In 2018, the then president of Haskell Indian Nations University who stood against the re-inclusion of the historic "non-federal" tribes who previously attended Haskell, Dr. Venida Chenault, was removed from her post as president. Her replacement, Dr. Daniel Wildcat, a former professor of mine during my time as a Haskell student, made a public request during Haskell's language conference in June 2019 to apologize to alumni and family who have been harmed during this unfortunate episode.

With that, most of the goals related to this issue have been accomplished. Nearly 50 percent of those tribes on the original 2002 list have received federal recognition due to their people's diligence and strength over many years of standing up despite attack. Ironically, the two historic "non-federal" tribes with the largest Indian boarding school attendance, the Yuchi in Oklahoma and MOWA Choctaw in Alabama, were both rejected by the Office of Federal Acknowledgment. The OFA stated that boarding school records had mysteriously been "received out of time," as were the recordings of fluent tribal language speakers from both communities, and therefore they were not eligible for consideration during the initial or appeal processes of their federal recognition petitions. R. Lee Fleming, whose own mother attended Indian boarding schools with members of the Yuchi in the 1930s, had even determined their tribe to be null and void. Both tribes, under the new regulations, which disallow any tribes previously denied any further opportunity to petition, must now navigate the congressional route again, with hopes of results much more akin to the tribes in Virginia recently than with past "failures."

The end result is that all the parties involved in the suppression of these tribes' histories lied repeatedly. It is truly unfortunate that such unbelievable lengths had to be taken in order to ensure that such a simple truth was told and that such a vital legacy was not consumed by hate.

I personally want to thank all of those, including the media sites in Indian Country, who had the strength to print my articles and who have supported or at least allowed a platform for these efforts during the last two plus decades. May the remaining 50 percent of these tribes, as well as others not mentioned, obtain the federal recognition (equity) due them in the decade to come.

White America and its corresponding government agencies no longer need to police the boundaries of Indian identity as they have for generations. They have no need to inject racial dogma into the legal and social systems impacting and guiding Indian Country. Some white "Indian" CDIB carrying academics, their white "Indian" colleagues in the Bureau of Indian Affairs, Bureau of Indian Education, and Department of the Interior, as well as white "Indian" tribal leaders and "white" Indian journalists and their nameless supporters ravaging the internet have taken up the boundary policing of identity for them. They are effectively continuing the work of such eugenics luminaries as the previously mentioned Walter Plecker and R. Lee Fleming, and they are doing an incredibly effective job. Steve Russell, a former staff editorialist for Indian Country Today Media Network, had an oft used phrase, "The test of being Indian is not who you claim, but who claims you," in relation to the identity policing he did in his own pieces. Russell, a former Texas judge of one-eighth Cherokee ancestry, with his remaining seven-eighths ancestry being white, forgets one truly important qualifier in his remarks. That qualifier is how one determines the value of those doing the identity policing, not the Indian claimant. In his analogy, a membership department in a corporate-like setting representing nearly four hundred thousand tribal citizens is somehow viewed as a legitimate identity definer. Many in Indian Country's traditional and identifiable community would argue against that strongly, including some within the identifiable Cherokee communities which dot northeastern Oklahoma. Who claims you to many in these communities is based on a very real sense of socialization, cultural upbringing, collectivity, and other factors that can never be determined in a corporate membership/citizenship sense. As he has dealt with legalities, not social realities, in his professional life, however, it is easy to see why he and others like him would agree with a legal definition as a primary exemplifier of belonging. But for me and many others, such a definition simply holds little truth.

The "Cherokee Issue," and not the one about people claiming Cherokee ancestry but rather the one concerning the Cherokee Nation of Oklahoma and Eastern Band of Cherokee Indians attempting to belittle tribes of perceived or real mixed-Black ancestry, needs to be fully addressed. For years the Eastern Band of Cherokee Indians have directed slanderous lobbying efforts against the Lumbee Nation and others and used highly paid lobbyists and lawyers such as Wilson Pipestem (an Indian from Oklahoma) to thwart their federal recognition efforts. They have resorted to racialized name calling as a tactic of oppression throughout these misguided yet "successful" efforts. They have mirrored the actions of Cherokee Nation of Oklahoma leadership in this regard. But after their own consistent inner-community turmoils, embezzlements, falling-outs, and more, people are beginning to see them more readily for what they have become. The election of sensible, nonpolarized and nonprejudicial leadership, one would hope, is a possible way forward for them.

Who left Lumbee Indian Cynthia Hunt, a member of a tribe whose people attended Carlisle Indian Industrial School and who have endured nonstop racial prejudice for generations, stranded out in no-man's land? Who took MOWA Choctaw elder Gallasneed Weaver, who attended two Indian boarding schools (including one in Oklahoma) and was listed as Choctaw by the federal government in the 1950s, and made him in to a nonentity? Who made Nanticoke Don Ahshapanek, an alumni of Haskell Institute and former Haskell professor and BIA employee, a person of legal dismissal? Leaving me with two more questions: Who presented these identity police, many of whom in the mainstream would simply be referred to as racists, with the power to decide? And, finally, why does anyone continue to accept this?

Lumbee, MOWA Choctaw, Nanticoke, Houma, Ramapough, Haliwa-Saponi, and others have always been Indian Country and will always be Indian Country. None of these tribes or any individual affiliated with these tribes are "leaving" Indian Country to appease some internet troll or gaming lobby. And what about the people with sincere engagements with Indian Country professing a family history of Indian ancestry, no matter how minor, being run off like they are the world's worst offenders for not producing a card? If a white person searching ancestry.com and finding a singular ancestor on a long ago taken Indian roll can now prance around Indian Country with a CDIB (and that happens regularly), while claiming "authenticity," then certainly a member of a tribe without CDIB s and whose families generationally attended Indian boarding schools, who are racially discriminated against as brown people, who live their community and traditions and who have always been, should not even be considered for questioning. The first example is what can be referred to as going from social fiction to legal reality and the second is social reality to legal fiction. That is the current state of tribal identity in Indian Country. Twenty years from now the pendulum will swing. Social reality can never be outdone by legal fictions.

And as for me . . . know this: There has never been a time in my life where I have contested another person's or tribe's identity or behaviors unless it was in direct response to an attack on others that was deserving of response due to misnomers and bullying. If a person doesn't like or agree with the Choctaw, Cherokee, and non-Indian ancestries that derive in me, and through me, via my MOWA Choctaw family, if they don't like the Scottish-Canadian lineage given to me by my mother, if they don't like my European surname Sunray and want to make it out to be a faux Indian name, if they don't like my published works that have appeared for over two decades, if they think my people were "mistakenly" sent to Indian boarding schools, if they believe for one second that their criticisms have even the slightest debilitating impact on my connection to community, self-worth, marriage, identity, employment, the respect my children have for me, or any other possible life scenario or situation, all I can say is don't make me laugh. As our elders, those struggling with health issues, as well as those who lack concrete access points to better funding for their higher education goals or careers are left out of the Indian Health Service (IHS), the Tribal Employment Rights Ordinance (TERO), and every other "federally recognized" Indian "benefit" in the acronym alphabet soup, there is, however, nothing to laugh about. This is a disgrace formed through a lens of marginalization and childishly belittling others that simply should no longer have a place in the Indigenous world. For some the removal or lack of access to equitable sources of support is truly a life-or-death matter. And it needs to be taken seriously and with a genuine heart.

Whether it is not acknowledging historic "non-federal" tribes who attended the Indian boarding schools, disenrolling tribal members/citizens, or never reinstating some terminated tribes to federal status, it is all the same ethical failing predicated by racism, money, and insecurity. Professor David Wilkins (Lumbee), whose tribe attended Indian boarding schools such as Carlisle and whose people have endured many racial identity attacks, has called for collectivity and accountability: "It is time for those who have averted their eyes from the plight of the dismembered to show courage and act for the good of all Native nations."[20]

Despite knowing that the current ravages of racism and identity politics in Indian Country will in some form never have an end, we must always remind ourselves that cultures of disposability have been cyclical throughout history, and akin to eras of the past informed by insecurities, much of this too shall pass.

Notes

Epigraph: This is a common saying that circulated in the 1980s when I was young.

1 *Florida Travel and Life* magazine (March/April 2012), 27.

2 Peter T. White, "Coca: An Ancient Herb Turns Deadly," *National Geographic* 175, no. 1 (January 1989), 3.

3 Mikaela M. Adams, *Who Belongs? Race, Resources and Tribal Citizenship in the Native South* (Oxford: Oxford University Press, 2016), 163.

4 Keneisha M. Green, "Who's Who: Describing the Discrepancy between the Methods of Defining African Americans and Native Americans," *American Indian Law Review* 31, no. 1 (2006): 93–110.

5 Dr. Don Rankin, letter to Chief Wilford Taylor, July 13, 1998.

6 Kevin Gover, April 21, 2004 testimony before the Senate Committee on Indian Affairs on proposed Senate Bill 297.

7 George Skibine, letter to Dr. Lebaron Byrd, September 21, 2010.

8 Terry Anderson and Kirke Kickingbird, "An Historical Perspective on the Issue of Federal Recognition and Non-recognition" (Washington, DC: Institute for the Development of Indian Law, 1978), 17.

9 Ben Fenwick, "Oklahoma Cherokee Chief Calls Abramoff Accusations 'Desperate,'" *Oklahoma Gazette*, April 12, 2007, https://www.okgazette.com /oklahoma/oklahoma-cherokee-chief-calls-abramoff-accusations-desperate /Content?oid=2967702.

10 Brian Klopotek, "Dangerous Decolonizing: Indians and Blacks and the Legacy of Jim Crow," in *Decolonizing Native Histories*, ed. Florencia E. Mallon (Durham, NC: Duke University Press, 2011), 180.

11 Cherokee Chat, "2010 US Census by Cara Cowan-Watts, Cherokee Nation Tribal Councilor District 7, Will Rogers," *Claremore Daily Progress*, June 16, 2009.

12 David Cornsilk posting on John's Place blog (cornsilks.com), April 29, 2008.

13 Michael Dardar, letter to Cherokee Nation of Oklahoma Council and Administration, September 2006.

14 Morning Dove Verret (enrolled United Houma Nation tribal citizen), interview conducted January 20, 2006.

15 Chief Wilford Taylor, letter to Cherokee Nation of Oklahoma Chief and Council, September 8, 2006.

16 Revisions to Regulations on Federal Acknowledgment of Indian Tribes (25 CFR 83 or Part 83), 39.

17 BIE deputy director Stephanie Birdwell, letter to Cedric Sunray (Haskell Endangered Legacy Project—H.E.L.P.), January 6, 2009.

18 National Congress of American Indians Resolution #PDX-11-016, October 30–November 4, 2011.

19 NARF staff attorney Joel West Williams, letter to Cedric Sunray, May 23, 2016.

20 David Wilkins, "Tribal Leaders Can't Stay Silent on Disenrollment," Indianz. Com, April 6, 2015, https://www.indianz.com/News/2015/016996.asp.

CHAPTER TWELVE

Marcus Briggs-Cloud

Ugh! Maskoke People and Our Pervasive Anti-Black Racism . . . Let the Language Teach Us!

The colonial Gregorian calendar month of January was coming to a close and Black History Month was soon to commence. A leader of the Muscogee Freedmen Association sent a request to the college where I was teaching Maskoke language saying that he would like to present a guest lecture during the month of February. Provoked by some unclaimed fear among my colleagues, I was summoned to an office meeting by two other language instructors to conspire a way of prohibiting the lecture. "We can't mislead our students," exclaimed one. Confused, I interjected to inquire about what would be misleading to our students. My young mind was "informed" that the Freedmen—persons of African descent who entered Maskoke society as refugees from white slave masters, or in many cases were the slaves of Maskoke persons who were emancipated and made citizens of the Muscogee Nation per the Treaty of 1866, but were later disenrolled by the Muscogee Nation in 1979—and their descendants are *not* Maskoke People and should not be permitted to make a presentation at the college. Knowing that some Maskoke persons, in some choice moments, uphold arbitrarily determined narrow definitions of what constitutes and authenticates a Maskoke person, and furthermore being cognizant that some persons extend those identity signifiers (such as requiring one to know their clan or tribal town affiliations) over Freedmen descendants in asymmetrical ways dissimilarly extended over persons of European phenotypes who identify as Maskoke, I simply stated that Freedmen and their descendants have lived with our People, intermarried with our People, and spoken our language, and some were, until recently, practitioners of our ceremonial lifeways. My thoughts were cut off by a perplexing testimonial from another individual, saying "Well, my grandfather owned some . . . and he said they are nothing but 'n-words', so that's how our people felt about 'em." Seeking to redirect an uncomfortable and racist conversation, I urged "*este-cate em 'ponvkv mahayvlket ont owēkv, nak-etemvponicēyat 'ste-cate em 'ponvkv temponahoyvkēs*" (we are Maskoke language teachers, so let's talk about this in our language).

The conversation persisted in English.

The anecdote above ultimately demonstrates that the concept of "ownership" is challenging to articulate in the Maskoke language. Racism imbued in the English-speaking worldview is not similarly translatable into Maskoke. Ancient grammatical structures, handed down in the language's entirety by our ancestors, restrict the ability to host such a conversation of ownership. In this chapter, I argue that linguistic critical analysis of Maskoke language yields a genuine epistemological glimpse into our ancestors' traditional worldview such that prevalent attitudes of anti-Blackness, experienced in Maskoke communities today, prove to be incompatible with and contradictory to our cultural traditions. Settler colonialism, and its physical counterpart of displacement, has bred fragmented cosmologies among Maskoke People, especially ones inextricably tied to bioregional ecologies. Disseminated dialectics concerning decolonization paradigms often emerge exclusively in academic race theory discourses where intellectuals seek to interrogate colonial impacts on identity and subsequently seek to reimagine and redefine Indigenous identity markers. Ironically, however, these conversations are attempts at responding to assimilation, yet are inadvertently steered by Western intellectual traditions. Typically therein, grassroots attributes of indigeneity defined by traditional Indigenous practitioners themselves, contained namely within language and traditional ontological frameworks, go unnoticed.

I posit here the need for a Maskoke language of blackness as an integral cosmological component of Maskoke medicine traditions, conducive to restoring wellness and balance in Maskoke communities. I attempt to show that anti-Black racism is inherently antagonistic to both traditional Maskoke medicine and collective healing processes that are needed in Maskoke communities today.

I have previously argued that Indigenous relationships to land were deeply altered by adoption of settler-colonial ideology that views land as a commodity.[1] This phenomenon is, in part, derived from the introduction of Western Christian ontological hierarchies in which humanity sits at the top of the scale and assumes dominion over all other elements of the natural world. We Maskoke Peoples are no exception to this attitude, thereby forfeiting our indigeneity. Nonetheless, we still have readily available access to the most authentic decolonization mechanism—that is, language. Critical grammatical analysis of language, especially morphological and etymological analyses, reveals how our ancestors perceived the world around them prior to the colonial disruption of spiritual evolutionary processes within their respective geographic residential spaces.

The late scholar Vine Deloria Jr. elaborated on the notion of spatiality.[2] In the Maskoke context his definition can be understood by saying that community evolves (a) in accordance with the sacred, (b) in localized geographic spaces, and (c) within multiple forms, including elements of the natural world. Traditions enter Maskoke society through introductions by certain respected individuals who bear revelations, sometimes obtained in altered states of consciousness, which may ensue from rituals such as fasting. They may deliver prophetic visions or propose integration of a new ritual or component of an existing ritual. Thereupon, the community must collectively accept and implement such a practice or concept into the society. In other words, perceptions and practices related to the Earth, for instance, ownership thereof, do not change overnight. They are a result of communally informed and discernment-driven decision making processes.

The grammatical structure of Maskoke is therefore also a product of a cultural evolutionary history that coincides with the evolving spiritual dynamics of the community in a particular space. This linguistic transformative process also takes place in a coevolutionary manner within localized ecosystems into which Maskoke People are integrated. Quintessential exemplifications of this are best found in worldwide lexicons that illustrate onomatopoeia derived from species mimicry. For example, the Maskoke word for a whip-poor-will is *cokpelapela*, which is a syllabic reproduction of the bird's call. Looking beyond mere linguistic ecological parroting, the aforesaid linguistic evolution can be illustrated through analysis of etymological correspondences between the Maskoke words *vhakv*, interpreted as "law," and *vhake,* referring to a copy or imitation of something. These two words descend from the same source—that is, the natural order. Possessing only one different letter (the final letter), both terms are ecological in origin. Maskoke "law" derives from replicating phenomena in the natural order within the contiguous Maskoke bioregion. The word *hake,* in its autonomy, conjures an active verb mode of mirroring another entity, whereas uttering its nominalized form *hakv* converts the meaning to elucidate a societally solidified perception of the biogeographical ecosystem. The first letter "*v*" serves as a locative prefix marker, placing the noun vertically in attachment to another entity. Thus, in this case, abidance to the *vhakv* (law) means to attach Maskoke People to the bioregional natural order through obligatory observance and imitation of local nonhuman ecology. Maskoke People then implement and promulgate, in worldview and praxis, cultural regulations based on the observed natural order. Albeit human arbitrary constructions to accommodate Western scientific pursuits, ecosystems regulate themselves extraordinarily, even down to micronutrient inputs and outputs. Therefore, when not subject to anthropogenic harm, ecosystems maintain balance—which is the ultimate goal of Maskoke society. In regard to upholding Maskoke *vhakv*, language revitalization practitioner and food sovereignty activist Ben Yahola states that fulfillment of *vhakv* is to be found "in the natural world, where there is no domination of one over another." *Vhakv*, then, the agent that enforces egalitarian ideology within Maskoke society, is patterned after Maskoke Peoples' understanding of balance and equity within the natural order.

Just as I attempted above to demonstrate the coevolution between language, the Maskoke worldview, and the natural order, linguistic critical analysis exercises are essential to imprinting ancient Maskoke philosophies as instinctual guides to ethical orientation. Settler colonialism, in the form of the forced removal of Maskoke People from our traditional homelands, has profoundly hindered the culturally occurring processes of communal spiritual evolution on the large scale. Nevertheless, current critical analysis exercises can be continually revisited because the basic morphological structure of the language remains unaltered.

We now turn back to the language in order to extrapolate epistemological inferences about how Maskoke People thought about land in antiquity. Here we will examine pronoun applications. In the Maskoke language, there are two forms of possessive pronouns: those applicable to either alienable or inalienable nouns. Inalienable nouns in Maskoke society are constituted only by one's body parts and one's relatives. Pronoun prefixes *Cv, Ce, E* and *Pu* are used to state *my, yours, the third person's,* and the collective *our* body part or relative, whereas all other nouns are made possessive by applying pronouns *Vm, Cem, Em,* and *Pum.* For example, to express "my grandmother" and "my ear," one says "*Cv pose*" and "*Cv hvcko.*" To say "my clothes" and "my ball" one says "*Vm accvke*" and "*Vm pokko.*" In Maskoke society it is socially inappropriate to tease or disrespect alienable nouns; one can only tease their relatives and/or body parts.

Established social ethical boundaries are defined through a mediated/ unmediated relationship dichotomy. Relationships between humans and alienable nouns are mediated. Because kinship is defined by clan affiliation (which is matrilineally inherited), inalienable kinship is defined, when subject to strict traditional cultural laws, solely in terms of maternal relatives. According to the late Maskoke spiritual leader Sam Proctor, the tradition he was reared in teaches that crossing an ethical boundary by spouting pejorative or disrespectful language about another clan is a major offense, and warrants the insulted clan to take any possession, as a form of recompense, from the insulter's clan.[3] Conversely to alienable noun relationship structures, relationships between inalienable nouns are unmediated; between inalienable nouns (namely kin), there exists a kind of intimacy wherein being part of the same circle privileges an individual to interact freely with respect to another individual of that same group.

When we look at the possessive pronoun used to state "my land" or "my earth," we cannot be grammatically appropriate uttering it as "*Cv ekvnv*"; rather, it must be invoked as "*Vm ekvnv*." By observing the pronoun additive alone, we can infer that within a Maskoke cultural context, the Earth is an alienable entity and therefore is subject to a cultural boundary wherein relationships to the Earth are mediated. This realization (and such is the case for any relationship between humans and other alienable nouns) reveals an inherent ethical prohibition on teasing and disrespecting the Earth. The combination of linguistic analysis and sociocultural protocols reveals here the irrefutably unethical nature of exploiting and commodifying the Earth.

Furthermore, the ability to tease inalienable nouns also implies a socially constructed sense of ownership. In the case of *Ekvnv*, it is impossible, however, to extract a concept of ownership since the term cannot be articulated as "*Cv ekvnv*." The fact that Earth is an alienable noun in Maskoke society demands a mediated relationship, wherein one cannot forego respect for her autonomy and must therefore maintain a relative distance from her, just as one would conduct themselves in relationship to any other alienable noun. We may not know precisely the ancestral Maskoke ontological or teleological intentions or implications of precluding ownership over the Earth, but we can speculate that because the Earth has personhood, specifically of female gender, ownership thereof is not possible.

A logical consequence of this critical analysis exercise is that the concept of land ownership resonates as counterintuitive to Maskoke language speakers through the inability to attach the pronoun prefix *Cv* to the noun *Ekvnv*. Likewise, aside from relatives and body parts, ownership over non-kin human beings is outside the scope of Maskoke philosophy. Hence, the individual who insisted (in English) that his grandfather owned slaves was unable to express that concept in the Maskoke language. The above mentioned anti-Black (racist) individuals were able to extend subjugating sentiments toward Freedmen and their descendants because they had reduced Blackness to a state of genealogical property by extension of reproducing their Maskoke forbearers' slavery practice ideologies. Use of English by Maskoke Peoples inadvertently leads to subconscious adoption of the English worldview in praxis. This is evident in relationships to land and people, whereby assuming ownership over land and people becomes explicable by speaking it, which in turn leads to doing it. Conversely, Maskoke language constrains the ability to speak it, and subsequently to do it. Whereas the language teachers who embrace anti-Black racism might engage ceremonial or church related matters in the Maskoke language, conversations about slavery and anti-Blackness inevitably devolve into English chatter.

This may be explained simply by the fact that Maskoke language does not possess an equivalent for the English term "slave," as the concept is not a part of the traditional Maskoke worldview. The English word is defined as "one who is the legal property of another and is forced to obey them."[4] The closest Maskoke approximations for the English term "slave" are *Vm vtotkv* (*vm votkvlke*—group plural), meaning "my worker" and *Vm este-svlvfke*, which is colloquially understood as my prisoner. Here again, from critical analysis of pronoun additive functions, we find the inability to convey ownership over another human being. Again, use of "my" represented by "*Vm*" does not carry the same implication of possession as "my" captured in the pronoun prefix "*Cv*." That point slightly qualified, within the confines of the worldview embedded in the language, the only acceptable scenario of "enslavement" therefore refers to an inalienable noun, that is, kinfolk. It would, however, be counterproductive to enslave a relative as Maskoke People are encouraged to support their own clan members in order to gain positive recognition from the larger society based on the character attitudes and ethics displayed by members of their clan. Needless to say, the terms *Vm vtotkv* and *Vm este-svlvfke* cannot be upheld as substitutions for the English term "slave," with all of its institutional connotative baggage.

In the Maskoke translation of the Greek biblical scriptures, there are three different translations of "slave" and "slavery" offered where the Greek passages call for them.[5] The group plural term connoting my workers, *vm vtotkvlke*, is utilized several times to refer to slaves. A more frequent word denoting the act of slavery is *svlvfketv*, commonly understood as arresting or imprisoning an individual. I propose two possible origins of the latter term.

The first possibility is that *svlvfketv* is derived from the root infinitive verb form *lvffetv*, meaning to cut or carve. Historically, *este-cate em vhakv*

(Maskoke cultural laws) dictated that an individual's defiant behavior in opposition to cultural laws, derived from the natural order, could be punished by severing one's ear or the tip of one's nose. Considering the absence of institutionalized incarceration within the confines of a concentrated space, public shaming as a consequence of a Maskoke individual's unacceptable conduct was considered appropriate disciplinary action; the ancient word that describes such action is *svlvfketv*. Upon the introduction of conventional arrest and imprisonment within a Western European disciplinary framework, the Maskoke term *svlvfketv* was carried over but eventually lost its culturally contextual significance. Thus, by the time institutionalized slavery discourses entered Maskoke society, the term *svlvfketv* was reified to signify European slavery practices, particularly among mixed-blood Maskoke persons situated along ideological borderlands of cultural assimilation and Indigenous preservation and resistance.

The alternative explanation of *svlvfketv*'s origin may simply be that it is borrowed from the English word "slave," and modified in Maskoke pronunciation; broken down into syllables, *sv-lvf-ke* (suh-luhf-ghee), it follows the typical Maskoke language consonant-vowel (or vowel consonant) sequential pattern, and reflects typical Maskoke adaptations from English words in an effort to avoid a consonant cluster (three or more consonants together), a tendency in English that is phonemically impossible to iterate in Maskoke. The *ke* on the end of *svlvfke* may be demonstrative of a historically common (and still practiced by Maskoke speaking persons in the Brighton Seminole community in Florida) suffix application to English nouns that end in consonant sounds. Maskoke grammar requires that nouns end in vowel sounds in order to attach either a subject marker "t" or an object marker "n" for the purposes of crafting intelligible thoughts in appropriate syntax. If this theory (*svlfvke* being a Maskoke variation of the English word "slave") is correct, it becomes even clearer that the concept of slavery was historically foreign to Maskoke ideology and thus solicited importation from English. This simple linguistic borrowing act not only introduced an English word but also enabled the intrusive manifestation of an entire English ethos of racial subjugation.

The third term that attempts to portray this concept of slave is found in the book of Revelations 19:18, "*pucase ocakat*," literally stating "those who have a master." Problematically, however, the term *pucase* was co-opted from its fundamental Maskoke cosmological definition in an attempt to identify a comparable portrayal of the European concept of "master." *Pucase* reflects *Pucasv* (the gerund form), which is one of the four fundamental extensions of *Epohfvnkv*, a non-anthropomorphized entity that may be seen as a sacred, everlasting overseer. More specifically, *pucasv* is the manifestation of *Epohfvnkv* in the form of fire and sun, and is seen as an authoritative spiritual energy, hence the attempt to qualify *Pucase* as a substitutive word, tasked to communicate the master/slave dichotomy. Moreover, an accurate conveyance of the slave concept in all Maskoke biblical translations is ultimately contingent upon positioning the master/slave dualism in a sentence. Therefore, without both terms present in binary form, the singular standing one renders it inexplicable, in that neither term emerged from an authentic Maskoke vernacular and cultural context; rather, the definitions are forcibly warped to approximate the English equivalent.

It is important here to point out that Maskoke language bearers have long struggled to find comparable vocabulary to express institutionalized servitude and ownership of an individual or society. In order to accurately employ the Western understanding of "slave," one is forced to insert the English word midstream in a Maskoke sentence. Thus, to conceive of and enact ownership over another individual, and harbor feelings of anti-Black racism, is abhorrent to traditional Maskoke philosophy and reflects excess subscription to Eurocentric worldview language practices.

Within Maskoke society, the permissible infiltration of anti-Blackness and attempts at insisting on ownership over human bodies can be traced to the hegemonic introduction of institutionalized, slave-trade capitalism. This process, however, proliferated under the cultural imperialist disempowerment of women. Again, Maskoke egalitarianism emerged from mimicry of ecological balance, also shaping the oration of cosmological worldview and stories from which prescribed gender roles are directed. We find this in the story of the corn woman, a female who is the sole progenitor of maize. The most sacred food in Maskoke society is corn, a gift for which profound sacrificial thanks is given during annual renewal ceremonies called *Posketv*. Revealed in the corn woman story, this sacred food having been left to the People by a female, the descendant Maskoke agriculturalist caretakers of this crop innately became females. These responsibilities also inherently bestowed great importance on the value of women as caretakers of something sacred. Settler colonialism deeply severed this connection.

In his letters, Benjamin Hawkins, the Indian agent to the Maskoke People (1796–1806), made several references to his frustrations with Maskoke women, saying "a man who keeps an Indian woman is the slave of her family and a slave to her whims and caprices." This prevented Hawkins from controlling his subagents who partnered with Maskoke women and in turn prohibited "any people in this department from having Indian wives." Finally, Hawkins reported to President Thomas Jefferson concerning Maskoke People, remarking that "the husband is a tenant at will only so far as the occupancy of the premises of the women."[6]

Hawkins assumed authority to dismantle traditional gender structures within Maskoke society, thereby removing women from agricultural responsibilities and domesticating them in a manner identical to European lifeways. Hawkins's successful hegemonic patriarchal campaign stripped women of their vital role, not only in perpetuating survival through cultivation of food sustenance but also in cultivating the source of Maskoke spirituality. Under the new patriarchy paradigm, mixed-blood Maskoke persons began to view society through a European lens of productivity. Ecofeminist and environmental activist Vandana Shiva writes, "Productivity, viewed from the perspective of survival, differs sharply from the dominant view of the productivity of labour as defined for processes of capital accumulation. 'Productive' man, producing commodities, using some of nature's wealth and women's work as raw material and dispensing with the rest as waste, becomes the only legitimate category of work, wealth and production. Nature and women working to produce and reproduce life are declared 'unproductive.'"[7] Prior to the domestication of women, even though men had, for nearly a century, accumulated material goods for their respective Maskoke *etvlwv* (an autonomous nation aligned with other *etvlwv* that were politically organized as a confederacy) through exploitation of deer in the deerskin trade with Europeans, women maintained their respected status because of the collective Maskoke value for traditional religion, which in part revolved around agriculture. By the late 1800s, however, Maskoke women were disempowered and oppressed in their domesticated state, perceived as unproductive in relation to capital accumulation, and Maskoke men, dependent on European consumerist ethics, had to find a means to generate productivity. These individuals' European kin (typically through intermarriage between Indigenous women and European "Indian countrymen") and other commerce allies ensured that Africans were readily available for servitude. Granted, African slaves may not have been treated by Maskoke owners in the same way they were treated by European slave owners, but the sedimentation of Eurocentric ideology and customs promoted ownership of bodies, and anti-Black, racist attitudes grew and were internalized and normalized among Maskoke People.

Drawing on language analysis once more, as long as she can remember from her youth, Rev. Dr. Rosemary McCombs Maxey, Maskoke scholar and language instructor, recites typical congregation discussions about inviting local African American Baptists to her own Tuskegee Maskoke Baptist Church's special gatherings in Eufaula, Oklahoma. Upon the suggestion of one congregation member that invitations be extended to the African American community, the following conversation (italicized) regularly transpired undergoing these spoken formalities:

> Ste-lvste weaksomecvlke em pohatten pun yvhikaket mekusapen nvkvft-vkes kicvntot em ohakvsvmkaken em pohatten pun mekusapet yvhika-kemvts; "*este-lvste pun yicvhana?*" *kicet vpohet onomat,* "***estet omis onkv emetetektvnkuset omes.*** *em pohatteyvres*" makakvtes.[8]

> The Maskoke Baptist would inquire about who will be on the program so they decided to invite the Black Baptist church to come and sing and pray; they agreed and came and sang and prayed. "*Are black people going to come,*" one asked? "***Well, they are human beings, so they are certainly welcome.*** *So we will ask them,*" they said.

Although the English interpretation of the bold print resonates less intensely and conspicuously with respect to the profound depth of inclusivity embedded in the Maskoke idiomatic expression "*estet omis onkv emetetektvnkuset omes*" (well, they are human beings, so they are certainly welcome), this repeated custom of forging such a particular dialogue verbally bolstered a concerted resistance to the embracing of anti-Black, racist tendencies that already permeated neighboring Maskoke communities.

Conversely, during his travels among Maskoke People W. O. Tuggle reported a story, twice orated to him, about a Dr. Buckner (a European man) who attended a large Maskoke Church gathering in 1849, in which we find a less than positive representation of how Maskoke People positioned their relationship to Blackness:

> When Dr. Buckner first came he attended a big meeting. The best young men in the Nation were there. One day they were sitting near the arbor before preaching began when a lady rode up on a very fine horse. She was closely veiled and was dressed very finely. It was before the war when there was a plenty of money. To the astonishment of Dr. Buckner none of the young men offered to assist the lady in dismounting. He determined to rebuke them quietly, & set them an example of politeness to ladies. He approached the lady while all the crowd was looking at him. He very politely requested the privilege of assisting her. She graciously consented, & he aided her in dismounting, took her horse and hitched him to a limb.

Then he turned to escort her to the arbor. The lady lifted her veil & behold she was black as a crow. It was in the days of slavery & the doctor himself owned slaves and you can imagine the roar of laughter that greeted him as he discovered his mistake.[9]

In Tuggle's other account of this narrative, he remarks that the Indian boys "roared and it was a standing joke for years."[10]

We must rescue ourselves from racist inclinations by reclaiming healthy language surrounding our interactions with Blackness, which is language not contingent upon importation of colloquial English expressions that only generate dehumanizing behaviors. The juxtaposition of Tuggle's anecdote and Rev. Dr. McCombs Maxey's recollections from Tuskegee Church highlights that although Maskoke language speakers cannot talk about ownership of an alienable noun, and therefore struggle to participate fully within European capitalist hegemonic structures of anti-Black racism (first introduced to us through institutionalized slavery practices), we are not altogether exempt from creating ways of performing our colonizer's anti-Black racist behavior and adapting some of their derogatory language practices.

Because postcolonial Maskoke language speakers are still prone to anti-Black racist language and the correlating attitudes that such language evokes, I maintain that until we come to understand the profound integral role of blackness in its medicinal and cosmological entirety, we should, in a spirit of decolonization and resistance, actively draw on the Maskoke virtues *eyasketv* (humility) and *kvncvpkv* (meekness) to reiterate, in the same manner as the Tuskegee Church congregation did, appropriate ways of referencing Blackness as our equal. Humility and meekness make us vulnerable to recognize the ways in which we perform our colonizer's worldview. Retaining and revitalizing Maskoke sociolinguistic idioms that bear humility, meekness, and notably inclusivity, those like "*estet omis onkv emetetektvnkuset omes*" are imperative to mending our interactions with blackness from a grassroots perspective. This will help us avoid borrowing mainstream non-Maskoke discourse guides that prevent us from dismantling pervasive anti-Blackness in Maskoke society.

How then can we further develop a language of Blackness that corresponds to authentic forms of Maskoke identity and reaffirms the integral role of Blackness in Maskoke society? One may ponder Blackness embodied in human form as intrinsic within precolonial Maskoke society; however, the cosmological worldview inscribed in Maskoke ceremonial traditions, as well as the canon of origin stories, disperses cognizance of Blackness and

Black bodies as integral to human history and functionality. In other words, with respect to Black bodies, when Africans were forcibly removed from their homeland to this Turtle Island, Maskoke People may have laid eyes on human Blackness incarnate for the first time, but it was certainly not the first introduction to knowledge of Black bodies inhabiting land on the other side of the ocean—as relayed to holy persons through dreams, which were subsequently disseminated to the public. Familiarity with Black bodies inhabiting the Earth, initially revealed to respected spiritual leaders, was woven into the Maskoke cosmological knowledge repertoire and at some point in antiquity was incorporated into traditional medicine practices and philosophy in the agential form of blackness.

Respecting the esoteric knowledge of Maskoke cosmology and medicine traditions, it would be unethical to expound on the subject here; so, for our purposes, it is sufficient to state that one aspect of Maskoke medicine draws on a cosmological energy from the number four: four cardinal directions and four races of people, and so forth. Among the four colors represented in the aforementioned cosmological philosophies and depictions is *lvste* (black). The invocation of blackness is a required agential holistic element in the achievement of medicinal efficacy within Maskoke society. Regardless of the context, marginalizing or disparaging the energy of blackness equals suppression of a vital property of any medicine person's power. Thus, when a Maskoke person speaks poorly of Black people, blackness is compromised and its contribution to medicinal power is weakened. That is not to be confused with some notion that Black human populations are reduced to or exclusively associated with a mythic, medicinal identity; it does, however, mean that Maskoke People should be reminded of the cosmological balance when encountering blackness in any form, including Black human bodies.

The quest for balance in Maskoke society gets problematized and compromised by the fact that many do not value traditional medicine and cosmology. Some have abandoned traditionalism through various ideological conversions, such as the adoption of fundamentalist Christianity, whereas others are less acquainted with traditional medicine because of various other by-products of settler-colonial assimilation. One major contributor to this distancing from medicine is geographic displacement. The diaspora of Maskoke Peoples under forced Indian removal policies was a traumatic experience. Mention of it today still evokes rage, confusion, and overwhelming sadness. Therefore, wounded people lacking confidence in traditional medicine might say "if we can't have our land back (meaning ecological landscape and stories tied to ancestral space that are equally essential to the efficacy of

Maskoke medicine are now inaccessible) to restore our traditional cosmology, which includes blackness, then why even seek balance with blackness today?" Nonetheless, many who do find themselves afflicted by sickness and despair continue to utilize traditional medicines, thereby becoming forever dependent on an "energy of blackness," deployed in medicine formulas for its healing properties.

Even in moments of tragedy, blackness is a necessary and potent element in conjunction with Maskoke ceremonial performance. This is evident in the story of the Snake Clan camp where Jim Jumper, son of a Black mother and Maskoke/Seminole father (perceived by some as solely Black because Maskoke People are matrilineal, but others recognized his adoption into the "little black snake clan"), reportedly enraged over being denied permission to marry a Maskoke woman, entered the camp and murdered all those present. This traumatic event, which occurred in the Snake Clan camp in 1889, was remedied by medicine man Charlie Osceola, who doctored the area survivors who escaped to hiding places or moved to a temporary camp.[11] Charlie Osceola's medicine cleansing of the village site guaranteed the wellness of those survivors, but his ritual ultimately relied on the energy of blackness to ensure that his medicine was efficacious. This ironic and seemingly contradictory scenario of relying on blackness to mend infliction caused by blackness perfectly represents the immensely valued Maskoke concept of duality (complementary antitheses). Had Charlie Osceola been a proponent of anti-Black racism, his medicine, dependent on blackness, would not have worked well enough for the Snake Clan to resume residence in their camp.

Perpetrating acts of anti-Black racism in the form of lateral oppression only reinforces settler colonialism. This, too, compromises the necessity for Blackness to be wholly Maskoke. To loosely avoid an identity politics discourse, I will not suggest who is and who is not authentically Maskoke or who is more assimilated than who, but rather point out that ethnohistorical documents show us that the majority of Maskoke slave owners were of European admixture, and therefore likely had a masterful command of the English language, enabling them to adequately "justify" and articulate a logic of slavery practices, as well as to use colloquial idioms that reinscribe structural racism. In his book *A New Order of Things*, Claudio Saunt discusses how wealthy Maskoke People acted as agents of racial segregation, in that they established their own slave plantations and even participated in returning fugitive slaves to their "owners."[12]

In light of my previous critical linguistic analysis exercises, I argue that monolingual Maskoke speakers find it challenging to engage in conversations about conventional slave ownership practices. For example, Alexander McGillivray, a debatably wealthy Maskoke person from *Tvlse Etvlwv*, was a proponent of Maskoke People owning slaves. An arguably self-appointed organizer and unifier of the Creek confederacy (autonomous Maskoke nations politically aggregated in response to settler-colonial encroachment on their territory and cultural lifeways), McGillivray was educated in Charleston, South Carolina, learned Latin and Greek, and later worked as an apprentice at a counting house in Savannah, Georgia. Because his depleted Maskoke language skills disengaged any potential captive audience during political consultation, he employed his sister Sophia McGillivray Durant, an eloquent Maskoke speaker who was reportedly the reason so many *Mekkvlke* (chiefs) regularly attended meetings; they indulged in her aesthetic oratory. Contrary to her brother's sentiments regarding her slaves, Sophia regarded them as members of her family and would not separate from them, despite pressures from Alexander, on account of her financial debt. Alexander writes in numerous letters of his sister's affinity with and concern for the Africans. Unlike her brother, Sophia's Maskoke language abilities were superior to her English language skills.

There are, of course, exceptions to this argument. In the piercing example of another Maskoke speaker resorting to English to convey depreciatory attitudes toward Black persons, Susie Ross Martin, the granddaughter of the prominent Yargee, son of the Mekko (chief) of *Tokvpvcce Etvlwv* (often considered the capital of the preremoval Maskoke confederacy), reported in a 1937 interview, "My grandfather Yargee was one of the largest slave owners among the Muskogees. As his rule was never to sell or part with a slave, he became one of the largest slave owner[s] among his tribe. . . . As he was a full-blood and his wife a half-breed, little or no English was spoken in the home. My mother said the only English words she heard her father speak were 'damn nigger' when his personal servant failed to do as she was told."[13]

Recognizing the case of Yargee as a caveat to my argument is an anomaly on account of his socioeconomic status among Maskoke People even prior to Maskoke Peoples' displacement from Alabama. Accordingly, he became a devout Christian (perhaps indicative of placing less value in an energy of blackness as medicine)[14] and unambiguously traded traditional Maskoke communal wealth systems and egalitarianism (which are prescribed and enforced by *etvlwv* law) for Western ideology and the practice of individualism and capital accumulation. We can therefore surmise that he was less invested in a resistance to settler colonialism than other Maskoke People of his time. Nonetheless, Susie Ross Martin's recollection of her grandfather is noteworthy, because recognizing that there is no Maskoke language equivalent for the disparaging English vernacular above, Yargee was forced to express disdain, in his desired sharp and scornful manner, toward the Black woman's work ethic by interpolating the particular pejorative English idiom amid Maskoke prose.

Fluency, coupled with active resistance to settler colonialism (which includes reverence for traditional medicine), appears to be the combination that positions one against sinking into anti-Black racist behavior. In addition to being constrained by the Maskoke lexicon's absence of pejorative idiomatic expressions toward Blackness in institutionalized ways, and the grammatical inability to convey ownership over human bodies, Maskoke language speakers devoted to the defense of their right to remain culturally Maskoke have no intrinsic social or economic advantageous incentive to involve themselves in structural racism. The following three anecdotes highlight two contexts wherein language speakers and traditional religious practitioners, committed to settler-colonial resistance, demonstrate the inclusivity of blackness.

In September 1849, after having been displaced from traditional homelands westward to Indian Territory (what became the colonial state of Oklahoma in 1907), Maskoke/Seminole leaders Kowakkuce, George Cloud, Pasokv Yvholv, and fifteen others sought to extend a voice on behalf of Black Maskoke/Seminoles in response to military demands that they relinquish their arms, a request that came from mixed-blood, English-speaking Maskoke leaders.[15] It was observed that Kowakkuce regularly made political and encouragement speeches to his people, exclusively in his own language. He utilized a Black Seminole, John Horse, as his interpreter. Notably, it was monolingual Maskoke/Seminole speakers who insisted that Black Seminoles needed arms to hunt to feed their families.[16]

Moreover, the leader Kowakkuce, frustrated by a deflating spirit of resistance among Maskoke/Seminole Peoples, led a faction into Mexico. Since Kowakkuce and his group of traditionalists had a history of rejecting the enslavement of Black peoples, as many others around them had, large numbers of Black Seminoles accompanied Kowakkuce in the exodus to Mexico. Oral tradition tells us that Kowakkuce was an initiated *Eposkvlke*, a well-trained *heles-hayv* (maker of medicine). I propose here the idea that his insight regarding the power of blackness in his medicine deterred the infiltration of anti-Black racism within his resistance faction. Furthermore, the aforementioned interpreter John Horse was also reported to have been a doctor of traditional medicine. He was noted for concocting medicines when persons of the community were ill and preparing emetics to purge spiritual sickness from patients; he was also recognized as having doctored with a buffalo horn. Both of these practices are common in Maskoke medicine traditions. Whereas purging traditions and buffalo horn doctoring require rigorous and proper regimented teachings to become a practitioner, John Horse would have learned these remedies in esoteric spaces reserved for medicinal spiritual knowledge transmission. There, blackness is present in diverse form, in the agential energy of blackness as well as in the biological phenotype, contributing to the power of the medicine.

Another anecdote in which Black peoples are present in medicinal spaces took place at *Ekvnvcakv* (Holy Earth/Ground). Following the Shawnee leader Tecumseh's visit to *Tokvpvcce Etvlwv* to recruit Maskoke Peoples to his resistance movement, Maskoke People formed their own resistance movement, known as the Redsticks, in solidarity with Shawnee prophecies that claimed resistance would lead to the disappearance of Europeans. Many *heleshayvlke* (makers of medicine) congregated at the site of *Ekvnvcakv* where their medicine fashioned a spiritual buffer around the territory to repel the negativity of the colonizer. This space, it was acclaimed, was one of several actions in which Black persons who resided among Maskoke People participated. The deaths of twelve Africans were included, *not* listed separately, in the report of Redstick fatalities from the US regiment's attack at *Ekvnvcakv* on December 23, 1813.[17] Blackness, both in its cosmological energy and its biological phenotypical presence, was summoned to the community of medicine, the backbone of Maskoke resistance and endeavor to defend Maskoke indigeneity. The Redstick ideology is often perceived as paramount in Maskoke traditionalism and it was a movement altogether inclusive of Blackness. Thus, anti-Black racism today exhibits one's immaturity in, ignorance, incomprehension, or mere misunderstanding of traditional Maskoke cultural knowledge.

Today, Maskoke persons sometimes employ blackness as a pejorative. In so doing, we beckon upon ourselves a disservice by weakening our own medicine. Granted, not all Maskoke People are makers of medicine (medicine proper), but our Maskoke identity is undoubtedly contingent upon the utilization of traditional medicine, and therefore dependent on blackness. Maskoke People, by internalizing jargon that accompanies structural anti-Black racist practices, only fuel the settler-colonial apparatus, in which Eurocentric ideological converts are harvested through linguistic imperialism. If more Maskoke People were committed to the task of healthy sociocultural language revitalization, which unequivocally requires critical grammatical analysis exercises to expose traditional epistemological worldviews, we would begin to see conversations about Blackness inadvertently change. As a language speaker who views my monolingual ancestors, committed to settler-colonial resistance, as dignified archetypes, I place more credibility in their example and interactions with the cosmological energy of blackness as medicine than in the example of bilingual, ideological racists who have discursively infected our communities with their settler-colonial negativity. Indeed, we are sick enough; now is the time for remedy.

Notes

1 Marcus Briggs-Cloud, "The United States as Imperial Peace: Decolonization and Indigenous Peoples," *Journal of Race, Ethnicity, and Religion* 1, no. 5 (2010).

2 Vine Deloria, *God Is Red: A Native View of Religion* (Golden, CO: Fulcrum Publishing, 2003).

3 Sam Proctor, personal interview, August 20, 1999.

4 "slave, n." *OED Online*, June 2004, Oxford University Press (accessed February 30, 2015).

5 Galatians 4:3; Galatians 4:25; Galatians 5:1; 1 Timothy 6:1; Hebrews 2:15; Revelation 18:13; Revelation 6:15; Revelation 19:18; Acts 7:9; Romans 8:15; Ephesians 6:5.

6 Benjamin Hawkins and Stephan Beauregard Weeks, *Letters of Benjamin Hawkins 1796–1806*, Morning News, Georgia Historical Society, 1916.

7 Vandana Shiva, *Staying Alive: Women, Ecology and Development* (London: Zed Books, 1988), 43.

8 Interview with Rev. Dr. Rosemary McCombs Maxey, February 4, 2015.

9 William Orrie Tuggle, *Shem, Ham & Japheth: The papers of WO Tuggle, comprising his Indian diary, sketches & observations, myths & Washington journal in the territory & at the capital, 1879–1882*, ed. Eugene Garcia and Dorothy B. Hatfield (Athens: University of Georgia Press, 1973), 137.

10 Tuggle, *Shem, Ham & Japheth*, 94.

11 Betty Mae Jumper and Patsy West, *A Seminole Legend: The Life of Betty Mae Tiger Jumper* (Gainesville: University Press of Florida, 2001), 16.

12 Claudio Saunt, *A New Order of Things: Property, Power, and the Transformation of the Creek Indians: 1733–1816* (Cambridge: Cambridge University Press, 1999).

13 Interview of Susie Ross Martin, "Indian-Pioneer History," Works Progress Administration, Western History Collection, University of Oklahoma, Norman, Oklahoma, microfiche 7256.

14 This is due to theological rhetoric of the time (and still commonly heard) that sets up traditional Maskoke/Christian dualistic frameworks, wherein one is told they must subscribe to a single religious practice. During such polarizing

discourses, many Maskoke Christians historically (and currently) turned away from traditional medicines for which formulas, relying on an energy of blackness, are required recitations.

15 Kenneth Wiggins Porter, *The Black Seminoles: History of a Freedom-Seeking People*, ed. Alcione M. Amos and Thomas P. Senter (Gainesville: University Press of Florida, 1996), 127.

16 Porter, *Black Seminoles*, 218.

17 Gregory A. Waselkov, *A Conquering Spirit: Fort Mims and the Redstick War of 1813–1814* (Tuscaloosa: University of Alabama Press, 2009), 165.

CHAPTER THIRTEEN

Hotvlkuce Harjo

Mississippian Black Metal Grl on a Friday Night (2018) with Artist's Statement

Traditional tattooing with Mvskoke (Creek), Southeastern, and Mississippian cultures was an integral part of identity construction prior to European contact. One of the main tools of annihilation was Christianity, which was forcibly adopted early on within Mvskoke and Southeastern history postcontact. Much of our knowledge of traditional tattooing was lost or demonized under the Christian faith. When the colonists arrived, the diseases they carried traveled farther and faster than they did. By the time Europeans started dictating their accounts of the Indigenous peoples, over 80 percent of people from various tribes had died from these unknown illnesses for which there was no cure. The colonists were then only interacting with the survivors of these illnesses, so thousands of years of knowledge vanished as suddenly as the diseases came. Due to this significant loss in people and knowledge, along with the violence of forced relocation, no extensive ethnographic recordings were taken of practices such as traditional tattooing. While there are some portraits drawn of Mvskoke people, interviews and photographs are rare if existent at all. This Southeastern history is the basis from which my artwork is built and extends. I always wondered why tattoos enthralled me so much, even at such a young age. I grew up seeing my grandfather's tattoos and only understood them as a part of his skin. Through my research, I have come to appreciate my yearning for these markings and their deeply rooted connection to the identity of my people.

This piece, entitled *Mississippian Black Metal Grl on a Friday Night*, reimagines the visual language seen on shell gorgets and other pieces from the Mississippian era. I utilize the tattoo marking of the lines on the fingers and the face tattoos. I also take influence from the black metal music scene, which also uses facial markings although in a completely unrelated sense.

Black metal, as well as rock music as a whole, has been a place of refuge for many Native generations due to its existence going against nonnormative systems—making it synonymous with Indigenous lives. This piece also addresses the gender discrepancy in the research around traditional tattooing, especially since those who practiced this are no longer here. When research is conducted under heteropatriarchal systems, gendered labels and roles are attached to these images of my ancestors. Here, I utilize the phrase "warrior imagery," a literal truth that the tattoos are battle-related, but more importantly to recognize and pay respect to the feminine/matriarchal structure of Southeastern tribes that was ignored in early research of this region. *Mississippian Black Metal Grl on a Friday Night* is how I imagine our feminine people looking today, doing something as simple as going to a show on a Friday night. For this piece, I used a technique of pencil line drawings, India ink, and Micron pens. In some limited editions, there are gold or copper embellishments. These small embellishments are included to enhance the experience of the viewer and to activate the space that the piece may inhabit.

13.1 *Mississippian Black Metal Grl on a Friday Night* (2018)

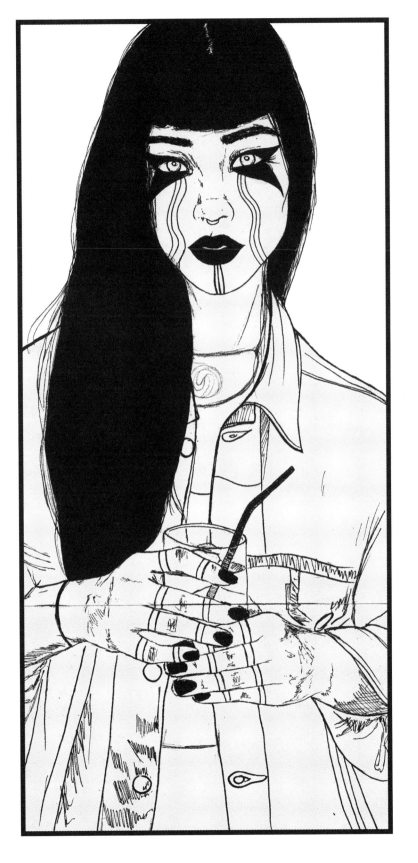

BOUNDLESS KINSHIP

Part IV

CHAPTER FOURTEEN

Jenell Navarro & Kimberly Robertson

The Countdown Remix

Why Two Native Feminists Ride with Queen Bey

We don't all think alike, do feminism alike, get crunk alike, or approach this work alike. . . . Some of us have chosen to focus on raising crunk, politically aware, radical babies. Some of us get crunk while changing the landscape of our disciplines in the academic institutions where many of us work. Some of us get crunk through our commitment to organizing. Some of us get crunk by working to preserve community institutions that share our radical vision of the future. Some of us get crunk by working with girls and young women, helping them hone a feminist sensibility that will serve them equally well on the block and in the boardroom. —Brittney C. Cooper, Susana M. Morris, and Robin M. Boylorn, *The Crunk Feminist Collection*

We are living in a time when the most vulnerable die (this includes many, many life-forms), a worldwide experience that affects our vital relations with life itself. There is a struggle against the capitalization, the commoditization of life even as it is happening. And because I am a scholar, and in particular an Indigenous scholar, I *must* act in the present to establish links; I am inhabited by the ghosts of my dead and my devoured and subjectively I cannot ignore them, nor will they be ignored. —Dian Million, "There Is a River in Me: Theory from Life"

Laying Our Cards on the Table

On February 12, 2016, approximately one week after Beyoncé broke the internet with the release of the song and video "Formation" and her accompanying Super Bowl halftime performance, Jessica Marie Johnson wrote a blog titled "Doing and Being Intellectual History: #Formation as Curated by Black Women."[1] In her post, she implicitly admonishes anyone and everyone with "Formation" on their lips to "hold up" and respect a Black feminist and radical womxn of color politics of citation, which she describes as "one that acknowledges ways Black women's intellectual production has been and continues to be rendered invisible, exploited, or devalued, then both centers the intellectual artifacts created by Black women and privileges Black women as producers and creators with the sole and extraordinary right to determine their encounters with institutions and bodies of thought outside their own circle."[2] In the case of "Formation," she suggests, this means centering the voices of Black women from New Orleans, from Louisiana, from the South, and from beyond the South, and in that very order. The rich range of responses to "Formation" Johnson curates at the end of her post models the practice she describes and encourages the reader to pause and critically reflect upon the position their own voice has in the conversation.

Three months later, when Beyoncé again took the world by storm—this time with the release of her album titled *Lemonade*—Johnson teamed up with Janell Hobson to curate a second resource list.[3] This list also includes a plethora of voices and organizes them according to their proximity to the content of the visual album: "Within each section, black women/femme creators are centered. New Orleans-based folks to the front, creators from the South second, authors from beyond the U.S. South as third. Posts that are not by black women and femme writers conclude this list."[4]

We hear Johnson and Hobson loud and clear and fully support the ordering of their citational politics. The important labor of sifting through the role Beyoncé and her work play in the lives of Black women belongs to Black women. And, as Johnson and Hobson so poignantly illustrate through their curation of resources, that work is being done.[5] We do not intend to "Nativesplain" our way into those conversations. We recognize and respect the political, intellectual, and methodological project to center Black women and Black femmes, and it is our intention to come correct and build upon Native and Black feminist relationality in our writing of this chapter. As professors in the disciplines of ethnic studies, American Indian studies, and women's, gender, and sexuality studies who teach courses on feminist, antioppressive, and decolonial methodologies, we are regularly engaged in conversations regarding the ethical and political implications of our own and others' research interests/decisions. We are exceedingly familiar with the ways in which "scholarship," indeed the very construction of knowledge itself, creates and maintains the violence of colonialism, racism, sexism, and the like. We fully understand that "when we choose a research focus, we must ask not only whose story it has the potential to tell, but also whose story it will hide, why, for whom, and with what consequence."[6]

Thus, we come to this chapter as allies/comrades/accomplices, indeed as *relatives*, as we will explain more fully in a later section, with two primary aims: (1) to bear witness to the productive work and art of Beyoncé as one gesture toward Black and Indigenous womxn affirming and seeing one another since the structure of settler colonialism has been staged to disrupt any such coalition, and (2) to operationalize a Native feminist radical kinship practice that builds upon the radical womxn of color feminist methodology and coalitional politics from which our feminist consciousnesses emerged. And, while we recognize the critiques of Beyoncé in terms of her capitalistic position, we also think that she does not necessarily have to deploy any revolutionary politics to make more money.[7] So, the fact that she does pay such close attention to the diversity of Black womxn and femmes in her work and to a growing feminist posture throughout her career, we believe, is witness worthy. Moreover, as non-Black women writing this chapter we choose to center our critical lens on relationality, rather than critiquing Beyoncé for her capital status.

More pointedly, we come to this chapter as Native feminists invested in critiques of settler colonialism that have regulated both Indigenous and Black life. And although we recognize that the regulatory regimes of dispossession and slavery are *not* one and the same, we know full well that the persistence of settler colonialism actively pursues the elimination of both communities. For example, Native and Black communities are subject to the greatest disproportionate rates of police killings in the US, the womxn in our communities not exempt. As Kelly Hayes recently wrote about the police murders of Black and Native women, "Korryn Gaines and Loreal Tsingine were both executed for refusing to lay their bodies at the feet of slave catchers and Indian Killers."[8] Indeed, Leanne Simpson reminds us, "policing in Turtle Island was born of the need to suppress and oppress black and indigenous resistance to colonialism and slavery."[9]

Indigenous and Black communities are (and have been) disproportionately targeted by other forms of state violence as well, including, but not limited to, forced sterilization and reproductive violences, the dissolution of family and community through the theft of children, dispossession and displacement, as well as environmental violences. Black and Indigenous peoples have resisted these atrocities individually and *collectively*. In fact, although the historical and ongoing collaborations between Black and

Indigenous peoples are frequently marginalized (which is in itself a product of settler colonization), there is a long history of alliance between Black and Native peoples that remains present and, as this collection demonstrates, is increasingly necessary today.[10] With this chapter, we aim to continue the important work that has already been done to build bridges between Native and Black communities, Native and Black studies, and Native and Black activism as interventions in settler colonial bullshit, in addition to honoring and regarding both Black and Native life.

Finally, in our focus upon the work Beyoncé has produced we hope to uphold homegrown feminisms that are constant works of progress.[11] While both of us currently hold academic positions at public universities in the state of California, we are both also deeply entrenched and committed to communities outside of the academy. Indeed, our locations "on the block and in the [academic] boardroom" inform our intentional mapping of our Native feminist identities as homegrown, imperfect, and constantly in the making.[12] And again, our own understanding of and entry into feminism comes from a radical womxn of color genealogy, born both in and out of academic space. This is a genealogy that has always centered the creative and innovative forms of resistance in the lives of womxn of color. So, we write this chapter in reverence to the aunties who have worked tirelessly to establish that the arts serve as a particularly well-suited method for critique, relief/release, and resistance (including but not limited to Audre Lorde, Gloria Anzaldúa, Paula Gunn Allen, Zainab Amadahy, Linda Hogan, Dian Million, and Deborah Miranda). It is our conviction that Beyoncé's work operationalizes this method at our current political moment, and we believe it should be applauded as such. In response to Beyoncé's plea in *Lemonade*, "Why can't you see me? Why can't you see me?," we answer back, "We see you, Bey!," and offer, here, a short list of reasons why we, as two Native feminists, ride with the Queen.

Reason #5: Police Violence and Settler Demands for Death

We're going to stand up as a community and fight against anyone who believes that murder or violent action by those who are sworn to protect us should consistently go unpunished.
—Beyoncé, Statement on Police Violence (2016)

As released by the Lakota People's Law Project in the *Native Lives Matter* report (2015), Native Americans are the racial group with the highest disproportionate rate of being killed by police in the United States, followed by African Americans.[13] We contend that the ceaseless settler colonial practices of policing, surveillance, and suppression of Native and Black bodies are often pronounced and operative in settler logics of elimination as a medium of continued control and dehumanization.[14] In fact, the settler logic of elimination has been persistently implemented against both Indigenous and Black communities. While the distinct histories of dispossession and slavery cannot be conflated, and while significant work has been done by scholars such as Tiffany Lethabo King to uphold these specificities within the structures/strictures of the settler state, death remains a settler requirement for Indigenous and Black peoples.[15] Because of this persistent settler desire and practice, we stand with Beyoncé because she has utilized her public platform to denounce police violence. While her statement on police violence was released in July 2016 after the police murdered Philando Castile (and the ruling in this case proved once again the settler structure of injustice since officer Jeronimo Yanez was found "not guilty") and Alton Sterling, Beyoncé has offered other critiques on militarized police earlier in her canon. For example, the music video for "Superpower" (2013) displays Beyoncé's superpower to gather, conjure, and create movement against the police.[16] In the video she calls forward a love revolution to centralize Black life when she creatively resurrects a Black man in the middle of the video and then leads everyone out of a sterile, concrete space to resist a militarized police lineup. We read such representations as intentional utterances of life and lifeways juxtaposed to the settler demands for death.

Importantly, the structure of Black death (physically, socially, psychologically) has been and continues to be predictable, rather than surprising, within the rubric of settler colonialism. As Joy James and João Costa Vargas have adeptly asked, "What happens when instead of becoming enraged and shocked every time a Black person is killed in the United States, we recognize Black death as a predictable and constitutive aspect of this democracy? What will happen then if instead of demanding justice we recognize (or at least consider) that the very notion of justice . . . produces and requires Black exclusion and death as normative?"[17] Moreover, Christina Sharpe plots the ways that Black women artists rupture the imminence of Black death through material culture and aesthetics by asserting that Black people live in the wake of slavery; in the afterlives of slavery; or in the afterlives of property. This state of being is marked by "quotidian disasters" or "quotidian atrocities."[18] We too believe, as Sharpe has stated, that it is oftentimes the artists who awaken our consciousness, what Sharpe calls "wake work" or what in popular language is often referred to as being/staying "woke." The question we seek to answer is where can we locate and witness "wake work" in Beyoncé's cultural labor?

One point of evidence is the portrayal of Black diversity in Beyoncé's work that can be read as a multiplicity of life/lives celebrated against the outright violent state attempts to squeeze out those lives. For example, the video for "No Angel" (2014) depicts the varied Black aesthetics and styles from Houston as a redesigned framing of "Black Is Beautiful."[19] The video celebrates Black aesthetics as thriving and innovative in its illustrations of Black styles as pleasures that are community grown. This is evidenced in the selections of lowriders, clothing, hair, and tattoos as they are framed within the falsetto poetics and lyricism produced by Beyoncé in a true Prince-like style. "No Angel" represents Blackness in this Texas scene as having its own experiential knowledge(s) on issues of death, where those in the video memorialize family members and loved ones who have been stolen by death's "angel." These community members attend to the "defense of the dead" as an observance of both Black life and death, as an insistence upon Black sociality. As Sharpe asks: "What does it mean to defend the dead? To tend to the Black dead and dying: to tend to the Black person, to Black people, always living in the push toward our death? It means work."[20] And, as a method to move beyond the violence of writing Black being or Black death as a theoretical abstraction, we draw on these specificities of Beyoncé's work to concretize examples of unapologetic Black existence and insistence. Arguably, Beyoncé's *work* is nowhere more pronounced than in her internet-breaking and visually stunning production of "Formation."

The display of Black New Orleans beauty and diversity in "Formation" shows Black life as unyielding to the conditions and violent structures of settler colonialism. As Zandria Robinson has stated, "Formation" offers "a blackness that slays through dreams, work, ownership, legacy, and the audacity of bodies that dare move and live in the face of death."[21] Additionally, Robinson frames this illustrious Black posture as "black southern ecstasy" that is simultaneously "rigorous and delightful."[22] Given the settler desire and requirement for controlled Black bodies, "Formation" aligns those who are deeply marked for suppression and elimination, and refuses to accept these parameters of a half-life or no-life. Instead, the many Black bodies that represent NOLA (New Orleans, Louisiana) full life in "Formation" dance in, through, and against an invasive settler society where even a young Black boy battles a militarized police lineup with his body talk. This refusal of monolithic Blackness in "Formation" is ultimately an oppositional posture and gaze that demands the settler state and its agents "stop shooting us."[23]

Because we too denounce police killings, and all forms of police violence used as a weapon against Native and Black bodies, we respect the work Beyoncé has done to call attention to these ongoing forms of settler colonial violence and echo the demand to "stand up . . . and fight against anyone who believes that murder or violent action by those who are sworn to protect us should go consistently unpunished."[24] We believe it is time to legalize being Black and legalize being Indigenous.

Reason #4: Insurgent Mothering as Engaged Futurity

Your mother is a woman and women like her cannot be contained.
—Beyoncé, *Lemonade* (2016)

On February 1, 2017 Beyoncé released her epic photo shoot titled *I Have Three Hearts*.[25] This photographic series announced her pregnancy with twins and staged a beautiful sequencing of images where she underscored life in a multivalent format. Life was depicted by her own body full of love and adorned with living flowers and color. The viewers were reminded of her capacity to be a life giver not only in the images of her pregnant belly but also in the title of bearing three hearts. In her earlier documentary, *Life Is But a Dream* (2013), she spoke about her loss with a miscarriage, and that commentary was positioned within a frame of delayed life—or life being just a "dream." Yet, Beyoncé did celebrate the arrival of Blue Ivy in 2012 and subsequently gave life to her fifth and sixth solo albums, *Beyoncé* (2013) and *Lemonade* (2016). In 2017, she reminded the world once again of her capacity to bear life when her twins, Rumi and Sir, were born. Scholars such as Robin D. G. Kelley and Fred Moten have reminded us that not only do Black lives matter, but Black *life* matters, meaning there is an immediate insurgency evident in the sociality of Black life.[26] In a settler nation where Black life has been scripted by war, terror, and death it is even more significant to underscore the presence, resurgence, and future of Black life. And, within the structure of settler colonialism, where Blackness and Black life have been marked with ongoing slavery, violence, and expendability, it is necessary to assert a celebratory affective disposition around Black life, which is what Beyoncé does with all three of her children.

Furthermore, one reading of the *I Have Three Hearts* photographs consists of the felt theoretical position embedded in the images. For example, many of the photographs are staged with bright orange, yellow, and pink flowers portraying the vibrancy of a life with "three hearts," and many of these same photos seem to be curated with a sacred posture depicting Black life revered. Yet opinion pieces berated Beyoncé for her pregnant body, stating that "having a baby isn't a miracle and doesn't make you a goddess."[27] The settler logic deployed against Beyoncé for her blissful disposition on her life-giving capacity was "Beyoncé has never known when to draw the line between what she should share with her husband and what she should share with an audience—see her chair-straddling, tush-wiggling routine from 2014, for instance."[28] This berated view of Black life is a redesign of the racist refusal for the existence of Black life couched in a white feminism that says motherhood should not be elevated and Blackness should not be respected.

Beyoncé's unabashed insistence on the visibility of her reproductive labor—in the face of white, liberal deployments against Black life and in service of the settler longing and devotion to interrupt Black family formation and decimate Black generational joy—extends a revolutionary mothering practice that is rooted in queer and women of color feminist traditions. Not unlike the work of Black feminist foremothers such as Hortense Spillers, June Jordan, Patricia Hill Collins, and Audre Lorde, Beyoncé's labor to make visible her motherwerk/work refuses the white supremacist effort to restrict the practice of mothering and the status of motherhood to straight, cisgendered, middle-to-upper class, white women.[29] Her 2017 Grammy performance (which included her sister, her mother, and Blue Ivy—three generations of Black women), as well as her inclusion of Blue's great-grandmother's voice on *Lemonade*, can also be read as homages to insurgent mothering, a reconceptualization of mothering that "leads to considering survival as a form of self-love, and as a service and gift to others whose lives would be incalculably diminished without us."[30]

As Native mothers who also work diligently to articulate and make visible an insurgent mothering practice that acknowledges the violent ways in which the politics of motherhood have been deployed against Native women as well, we want to name and witness the significance of Beyoncé's reproductive labor.[31] As Leanne Simpson argues, "Black and indigenous children have been stolen from their families throughout colonial history through the institutions of slavery, and in Canada the residential schools and the child welfare system. We are interconnected through systems of oppression that would prefer us not to exist unless it can exploit us as commodities for labor."[32] In opposition to settlers' comments on Beyoncé's pregnant body and against the ongoing assault on Black and Native families, we assert that Beyoncé's embodiment of Black life as Black presence and futurity, in her photographic series and in her musical canon, threaten the settler nation's narration and insistence upon Black death in productive and beautiful ways. To see her smiling and filled with joy about the potentiality of bringing Black life into the world is a type of insurgency because Black joy, as well as Native joy, reminds settlers that the genocidal hopes of settler colonizers are unrealized; settler colonialism is an incomplete project. And, as insurgent mothers ourselves, we ride with Bey because we too invest joy and happiness in the next generation. We also believe that Native futurity and Black futurity are co-constitutive, meaning because we have hope in the insurgent possibilities of our children to engage in the work of decolonization, we simultaneously have hope in the futures of Black children to do the same.

Reason #3: Deuces Up to Cisheteropatriarchy

Grandmother, the alchemist, you spun gold out of this hard life. Conjured beauty from the things left behind. Found healing where it did not live. Discovered the antidote in your own kitchen. Broke the curse with your two hands.
—Beyoncé, *Lemonade* (2016)

The sexual and gendered violence perpetrated against both Native and Black womxn persists as an integral component of settler colonialism. The disproportionate rates at which these womxn experience sexual and gendered violence is a direct continuation of the settler structure of cisheteropatriarchal domination. However, Black and Native artists persistently engage these historical and current conditions through their art forms, and Beyoncé has done this work, too. For instance, in "Sorry" Beyoncé presents us with a productive and strategic apathy—a decidedly femme apathy that takes over the plantation home and the historic site of the bus in order to position resurgent Black (femme-identifying and femme-identified) life amid violent and oppressive spaces.[33] Bey and her female-presenting dance crew claim the bus through a synchronized choreography and a resistant display of Yoruba rootedness. While the initial dance motions inside the bus are seamless, once they step outside of the bus they freestyle dance and Bey herself dances on top of the bus, illustrating a resilient posture of disdain in all her twerking beauty. The dancers are then shown in split scenes in and out of the bus where they move wherever they like with immense delight. Even the bus comes to life as the shackles of segregation are thrown off of it and the bus adorns itself with Yoruba body paint (the sacred art of the Ori) and a destination sign that reads "Boy Bye." Bey and her dancers throw their deuces up to leave behind lives marked with loss, grief, and violence. They also throw up a big "fuck you" with their middle fingers to the settler practices and logics of elimination and sexual and gendered violence. These dancers are not just here to survive, they are here to thrive. Because of this, the "boy" being dismissed here is the cisheteropatriarchal order that designed and implemented the violent conditions of Black life in spaces such as the bus and plantation home.

The seizing of the plantation home highlights the persistent work that must be engaged to intervene in the settler state's ongoings of slavery, sexual assault, and rape. The scenes of Serena Williams inside the plantation home are some of the most potent as she twerks all over the grand entry space and up and down the halls, engaging in body talk that is against the white supremacist persistent critiques of her body as "manly" and less than human. She moves how and where she likes as an engaged refusal to feel shame. This movement, much like the dance talk produced by the young black boy against the police in "Formation," is a localized mode of real talk.

The "wake work" (Sharpe) Beyoncé does in *Lemonade* also includes a critique of privileging forms of sexual and gendered violence against cisgendered women of color at the expense of forms of sexual and gendered violence that are aimed at queer, trans, and nonbinary peoples of color. This is especially underscored throughout the audio text. For example, we *hear* real talk in the voices of Big Freedia and Messy Mya in the video production of "Formation," and this inclusion of gender queer voices alerts listeners to the "absent presence" of queer of color visibility.[34] The "absent presence" is found in the fact that Big Freedia's voice is heard in many audio clips of the song, yet Big Freedia's gender queer body is not depicted.[35] Since we do not know the reason that Beyoncé, a cisgender Black woman, did not include the established visibility of Big Freedia's body in "Formation," we underscore the necessity to move beyond spectrality—meaning that Big Freedia's voice haunts all viewers of "Formation" and, therefore, should require us to assess violence against queer, trans, and nonbinary people of color just like the video obviously asks us to stop killing Black men and boys. As Jennifer DeClue notes, "'Formation' calls up the unresolved social violence, the murders of transwomen, transmen, and trans people of color in epidemic proportions, as well as the threat of violence and the nonlethal assaults that trans people have to contend with in their daily lives."[36] Beyoncé's stance would have been clearer regarding violence against trans and queer people of color if their bodies had been rendered visible, but affirmations of this work remain with the audio inclusion. As the Crunk Feminist Collective has asserted in their mission statement, there are modes of Black southern feminist expression that are "bound up with a proclivity for the percussive, as we divorce ourselves from 'correct' or hegemonic ways of being in favor of following the rhythm of our own heartbeats."[37] The voices of Big Freedia and Messy Mya certainly are percussive, if you will, in "Formation." Also, in "Sorry," Williams's movements pay no heed to being mindful of hegemonic, or cisheteropatriarchal, expectations of respectability—another nod to being percussive and insurgent in one's own right. Instead, the subtextual assertion is that respectability is a settler construct made by, for, and about white people. It exists to make Blackness and Indigeneity palatable and tolerable to whites. And, even when communities of color engage the offending disposition of respectability, it has not kept us safe. So, yeah, "Boy Bye."

Finally, we also affirm Beyoncé's challenges to the structure of heteropatriarchy as a cisgender Black woman. Here it is clear that her representations of her own sexuality and gender have continued to grow just like her displays of feminism have strengthened over the years. In fact, as Marquis Bey argues, "Beyoncé . . . is unsettling her place in the Black normal."[38] Her audio and visual representations have shifted drastically across her career, and her latest works push beyond the "borders of Black normality—a necessarily fugitive and insurgent practice" where she is "actualizing a Black (ab)normal posture [as] an immersion in fugitivity and an immersion in the nonnormativity of queerness."[39] For example, in her older collaborative work with Jay-Z, in songs like the couple's 2002 hit "'03 Bonnie and Clyde" she did not take center stage or challenge his male privilege.[40] However, over fifteen years later Queen Bey's homegrown feminism really shows up in the couple's latest album "EVERYTHING IS LOVE." In "LOVEHAPPY" we hear Beyoncé continue to keep accountability at the forefront. She tells Jay-Z on this track that "you fucked up the first stone, we had to get remarried" and "we keepin' it real with these people, right?"[41] These lines call heteropatriarchy into question and challenge the structural forms of male privilege that usually keep cisgender women of color silent/invisible. Additionally, their epic hit "APESHIT" illustrates that she does not play a shadow role to Jay-Z.[42] In fact, she delivers all the verses and the chorus to the song, barring the one verse he delivers at three minutes and fifteen seconds into the track. She is the primary agent, with her Black insurgent posture, which calls the listeners/viewers in to watch a scathing critique of colonial abuse of African art and culture. It is her freeform dancing in the video and her gaze of colonial refusal that delivers psychic and corporeal liberation from the colonized space of the Louvre where the video is filmed. Indeed, Beyoncé even delivers the final gaze into the camera at the end of video—a gaze that vibrates with energy and resistance far greater than the Mona Lisa could have ever offered, illustrating that she is not codified through Jay-Z's maleness or the Mona Lisa's whiteness.

Reason #2: Radical Kinship

The nail technician pushes my cuticles back, turns my hand over, stretches the skin on my palm and says, "I see your daughters and their daughters."
—Beyoncé, *Lemonade* (2016)

We posit and employ the term "radical kinship" to describe a Native feminist practice of relationality rooted in Indigenous knowledges, radical womxn of color coalitional politics, and practices of decolonial futurity and decolonial/transformative love. Our development and use of this concept is informed by Zainab Amadahy's conceptualization of a "relationship framework"—the Indigenous understanding that "by virtue of being human we are members of a community of living, non-living (in the scientific definition), once-living, and soon-to-be-living entities" on planet Earth and beyond, and the acknowledgment that "what we think, say and do impacts, directly and indirectly, everything and everyone else—and these in turn affect us."[43] Not only does radical kinship serve as one of our reasons for writing this chapter, again as an effort to witness Beyoncé's entrance into the "Black feminist cypher" and as an intentional effort to engage with, hold space for, and support this work, but we believe a relationship framework of this very sort also undergirds Beyoncé's wake work.

One of the most obvious examples of Beyoncé's deployment of radical kinship is the multi/inter-*generational* representation of Black family and community in *Lemonade* (2016). For instance, in the video portion of "Hold Up" multiple generations of NOLA folks dance, play, and laugh in the streets, including children who dance/play in the water from a purposely busted fire hydrant, elders who have come out of the neighborhood barbershops and salons to join in the festivities, and even a young Black man who rides a quad wearing a shirt that reads "In Memory of When I Gave a Fuck."[44] The album particularly highlights generations of Black women holding and making space together. In fact, the title of the album itself takes direction and guidance from one of Beyoncé's revered elders, Hattie White, Jay-Z's grandmother. Hattie White sets the tone for the affective and relational shift of the album when she is heard reciting a speech from her ninetieth birthday celebration, saying, "I had my ups and downs, but I always find the inner strength to pull myself up. I was served lemons, but I made lemonade."[45] Here, it is perhaps most telling that these words come from a Black female elder because she has the experiential knowledge of what it means to make something from nothing—to be a grandmother alchemist in the face of white settler supremacy.[46] This alchemy is part and parcel of a radical kinship structure because it is the women who have gone before us that carve out paths of possibility since they directly or indirectly guide later generations on *how* to be free. Radical kinship, therefore, is a commitment to collective freedom, collective determination, and collective conjuring so that Black and Indigenous freedom does not "rot in hell."[47]

Beyoncé again posits the significance of multi-/intergenerational (and homegrown) feminist knowledge as she recites a recipe for making lemonade between the songs "Freedom" and "All Night" on the *Lemonade* album: "Take one pint of water / add half pound of sugar, the juice of eight lemons, the zest of half lemon / pour the water from one jug, then to the other several times / strain through a clean napkin" (2016). Once Beyoncé lays out the delight of this southern recipe she attributes it to her grandmother, a woman, she adds, who "broke the curse with her own two hands." Then, Bey reminds us of the importance of Black women's knowledge and how that knowledge is transmitted to future generations as she explains, "You passed these instructions down to your daughter who then passed it down to her daughter."[48] The visual presence of Beyoncé's own daughter and other young Black girls in the film/album suggests that Beyoncé, at least in part, makes *Lemonade* (pulls joy out of the depths of sadness) for future generations of Black women. In this way, Beyoncé deploys radical kinship to generate a community held in love and oriented toward future generations so that Black peoples do not have to live in isolation and where knowledge is shared to move through historical grief/trauma with one another.

The radical kinship imperative to (re)indigenize concepts of relationality between humans and nonhumans also emerges in *Lemonade*.[49] From the moment the visual album begins, with the opening refrains of the song "Pray You Catch Me," the viewer is made aware of the significant role the Louisiana landscape plays in the story *Lemonade* tells. With reverence and grace, the camera pans across tall grasses swaying in the winds and whispering the memories and the secrets they bear. Grand sprawling oak trees, with lush shawls of Spanish moss draped across their shoulders, stand tall and secure in the knowledges they carry. "What are you hiding?" Beyoncé asks protective palm leaves as they shield the face of a woman who slowly rocks back and forth in a rocking chair on the front porch of a slave cabin. It is absolutely clear that the flora and fauna of the Southeast are not a mere backdrop for Beyoncé's visual album. These nonhuman actors play leading roles, and their agency and power are represented in all their glory.

Another of the most fierce human and nonhuman interactions in *Lemonade* is seen in the video portion of "Love Drought."[50] Here, Beyoncé leads a line of Black women into a body of water where they all in unison raise their arms toward the sky relative. This scene is certainly influenced by Julie Dash's incredible film *Daughters of the Dust* (1991), but it also operates to memorialize African resistance to slavery. The scene is staged to recall Igbo Landing (sometimes called Ebos Landing), a site in Georgia where in 1803 a ship full of Igbo peoples refused to live a life enslaved. The Igbo people in the ship had survived the Middle Passage, were sold into slavery in Savannah, Georgia, and then they were reloaded into a smaller boat that was destined for St. Simon's Island. Directly off the coast of the island, the Igbos staged a revolt and threw the slave captors overboard where they drowned in the water. Once the boat hit the island, the Igbos ran into the marsh and together they marched into the water with raised arms and drowned themselves—a collective suicide.[51] As they let the water encompass their bodies, it has been said in Black folklore that these Igbo people were "water walkers" or "flyers" and their spirits/bodies flew back home to Africa in an act of spiritual resistance where they were reunited with their kin. The water in this historic scene is the relative that rescues these individuals and recounts the narrative of their resistance to remind all of those who still live in the ongoings of the settler state and slavery that our nonhuman kin are sometimes the family members with the greatest fugitive stance for resistance.[52]

In another moving example, midway through "Pray You Catch Me," Beyoncé is transported from the living and breathing Louisiana fields to a cold and desolate urban setting.[53] In a move eerily reminiscent of a suicide jump, she perches tenuously on the top of a tall building and then leans slightly forward, allowing her body to begin plummeting toward the asphalted and concreted streets below her. At the very last moment, however, a body of water miraculously appears to break her fall and provide the protection needed to rescue her. An infinite number of tiny bubbles gently cradle her body as she becomes submerged. The camera pans out and we see that

Beyoncé is now in an underwater house and larger bubbles move in and out of her nostrils, demonstrating that water *is* life, literally, as she swims throughout the rooms. Not unlike the way a soon-to-be-born child's life is nurtured through the amniotic fluids inside its mother's body, the water in this scene nurtures Beyoncé, until she is ready, at the very moment "Pray You Catch Me" transitions into "Hold Up," to be powerfully redelivered to the world. In this scene, as glorious and fierce as the sun itself, enveloped in a flouncy, golden dress that literally breathes in unison with every barefooted step she takes, Beyoncé throws open the doors of a huge stone building and the waters that rush out from behind her, breaking down the long stone stairway before her, escort her out of the building. The smile that begins to creep across Beyoncé's face in the next few refrains of the song, as she strides increasingly confidently and joyously down the now alive New Orleans streets, is the first smile we see in the visual album. We read Beyoncé's joy in this moment as joy brought about by the life-giving possibility of radical kinship—a practice of relationality that resists the settler drive for death and isolation, that strengthens our inner and spiritual lives, that permits us to live ethically with *all* our kin, and that affords us the opportunity to feel a little bit of whoop ass in the middle of our daily hustle.

Reason #1: Transformative Love

So, how are we supposed to lead our children to the future? What do
we do? How do we lead them? Love. L-O-V-E, love.
—*Lemonade* (2016)

Near the end of the *Lemonade* film Beyoncé states "if we're going to heal, let it be glorious." In this call to healing there is a shedding of shame, which could be read as individual or collective. The collective reading challenges the desires of the settler state to keep Black and Indigenous peoples in a constant state of pain. Here, one way to refuse the current ongoings of settler colonization, and its persistent attempts to eliminate Black and Indigenous happiness, is to live gloriously. The embodiment of Black and Indigenous joy is that process where one makes lemonade out of sour lemons and drinks it with a smile. It is that aforementioned process of conjuring—making something out of nothing, or very little. It is what Zandria Robinson has termed a "Black girl alchemist journey" in writing about *Lemonade,* and it is what many have called "Black girl magic."[54] In Robinson's reading of *Lemonade,* Beyoncé presents us with a methodology for understanding Black women's alchemy. She argues, "Part of black women's magic, born of necessity, has been the ability to dissemble: to perform an outward forthrightness while protecting our inner, private lives and obscuring our full selves."[55] This is embodied collective preservation, which also relies heavily upon what we described as radical kinship. It is that ability to love one's self and one's chosen inner circle with a fierce and glorious posture bent upon healing, even though the settler state continues attempts at making our world hell. It is the way in which Black and Indigenous womxn and femmes have consistently found the strength to pull better worlds into existence. This challenge to the settler state perhaps causes the greatest settler anxiety because we demonstrate a profound ability to bring just futures into the present by gloriously loving *all* elements of creation.

In 2011 Beyoncé released her studio album *4*, which included the song "Love on Top."[56] That song, a stylistic tribute to the Jackson 5, New Edition, and other "boy bands," narrated a beautiful emotional release of finally having one's love put on top. This song underscored the notion that transformative love, love that has capacious expansion, is worthwhile work. It is an earlier juxtaposed layer to "you ain't lovin' hard enough" as stated in *Lemonade*. In fact, if we are going to heal and have that healing be glorious, we believe the core of the work must be mounted by love. The kind of love that we, two Native feminists, are invested in is a decolonial love.[57] For us, decolonial love is a love that is committed to the utter disordering of settler colonialism in all its violent forms. As a result, it is a love with a posture of strength, resiliency, and strategy to love one's Indigenous or Black self, or both, against the grain of settler imposed self-doubt and decreased self-worth. However, this type of radical self-love must extend to all our relations. It is one that can script relations with humans and nonhumans in beautiful and meaningful ways, where we see our full selves at present and in present-futures.

A demonstration of this type of transformative love incites Indigenous and Black peoples to put love on top. This is evidenced in the sonic architecture of "Love on Top," where Beyoncé recorded each verse of the song in a higher octave, giving the listener a sense of urgency and excitement to put love on top. Moreover, the opening line, "Honey, honey, I can see the stars all the way from here," places love and futurity side by side, reclaiming, as Bey will do in *Lemonade,* that the only way to lead Black and Indigenous children into the future is through love. This sense of futurity is what Reynaldo Anderson and Charles E. Jones have termed "Astro-Blackness." They state that Astro-Blackness is a form of Afrofuturity where "a person's black state of consciousness [is] released from the confining and crippling slave or colonial mentality, [and] becomes aware of the multitude and varied possibilities and probabilities within the universe."[58] Furthermore, this type of futurity has been well theorized by Laura Harjo in her articulation of "Mvskoke futurity" as a practice of "jumping scale." Specifically, Harjo argues, "Spiraling through time and space, Mvskoke space and place is in a dialectic conversation, with new ways of understanding, old ways of understanding, and impactful ways of understanding."[59] Thus, we understand Beyoncé's "see[ing] the stars all the way from here" in "Love on Top" as a homegrown feminist futurity where the stars no longer look lonesome, in that Maya Angelou sense.[60] Instead, they are full and bright as they lead us in upholding our full human dignity because they too are our relatives. We ride with the Queen in this regard because we too believe all of our relations are connected to the entire biosphere. We too look to our star relatives, our ancestors, to guide us in gloriously healing. We hope you will, too.

Notes

1 Beyoncé, "Formation," track 12 on *Lemonade*, Parkwood and Columbia, 2016; and Jessica Marie Johnson, "Doing and Being Intellectual History. #Formation as Curated by Black Women," *Black Perspectives*, February 12, 2016, http://www.aaihs.org/doing-and-being-intellectual/.

2 Johnson notes that these institutions include academia, the mainstream media, and law enforcement vis-à-vis the surveillance of social media platforms and the internet more broadly.

3 Beyoncé, *Lemonade*, Parkwood and Columbia, 2016.

4 Janell Hobson, "#Lemonade: A Black Feminist Resource List," *Black Perspectives*, May 12, 2016, http://www.aaihs.org/lemonade-a-black-feminist-resource-list/.

5 The robust range of scholarship centered around Beyoncé (critical Beyoncé studies, if you will) interrogates Beyoncé from a number of theoretical/political perspectives (e.g., feminist, antiracist, anticapitalist) and engages virtually every aspect of "the Beyoncé effect." Accordingly, the responses to her work range significantly, from some embracing her fully to others eschewing her work entirely. In addition to the Johnson and Hobson resource lists, see Adrienne Trier-Bieniek, ed., *The Beyoncé Effect: Essays on Sexuality, Race, and Feminism* (Jefferson, NC: Mcfarland and Company, 2016); Emma Silvers, "Six Beyoncé Pieces by Women of Color That You Should Read Right Now," KQED Arts, February 8, 2016, https://www.kqed.org/pop/20366/six-beyonce-pieces -by-women-of-color-that-you-should-read-right-now; and LaSha, "bell hooks vs. Beyoncé: What This Feminist Scholarly Critique Gets Wrong about 'Lemonade' and Liberation," *Salon*, May 18, 2016, https://www.salon.com/2016 /05/17/bell_hooks_vs_beyonce_what_the_feminist_scholarly_critique_gets _wrong_about_lemonade_and_liberation/.

6   Susan Strega and Leslie Brown, *Research as Resistance: Revisiting Critical, Indigenous, and Anti-Oppressive Approaches*, 2nd ed. (Toronto: Canadian Scholars' Press, 2015), 6.

7   We also see that in many cases Beyoncé utilizes her capital as a platform to lift up other Black artists or Black folx who have not received the opportunities they deserve, and therefore, she (re)distributes some capital to Black communities. For example, Beyoncé has a commitment to women of color musicians and dancers that work closely with her and travel with her, including her backup singers and all-female band, Sugar Mama (The Mamas). She has also intentionally recorded songs from songwriters who deserve more attention. For example, Vincent Berry II was homeless and struggling to make a career out of his artistry before he shared a production credit on the *Lemonade* album with Beyoncé for writing "Sandcastles." His life changed forever after that moment. Moreover, the September 2018 issue of *Vogue* with Beyoncé on the cover is another keen example. Beyoncé insisted on choosing a Black photographer for the shoot, resulting in Tyler Mitchell, a twenty-three-year-old photographer, being the first African American to shoot a cover issue for the magazine in its 126-year old history. There are also the examples of Beyoncé creating social and political capital for Black women with the founding of her Formation Scholars program—a program that funds one woman at four different historically Black colleges and universities per year. And, we respect her efforts to help alleviate some suffering caused by recent hurricane activity in Houston, Puerto Rico, Mexico, and the Caribbean by giving all proceeds from her single release of "Mi Gente" in 2017 to a relief fund for these areas.

8   Kelly Hayes, "On Korryn Gaines, Loreal Tsingine, and Refusing to Surrender," BDG, August 3, 2016, https://www.bgdblog.org/2016/08/gaines-tsingine/.

9   Leanne Simpson, "An Indigenous View on #BlackLivesMatter," Yes! Solutions Journal, December 5, 2014, http://www.yesmagazine.org/peace-justice/indigenous-view-black-lives-matter-leanne-simpson.

10 For deeper studies on Black and Native alliances and histories, see Gerald Horne, *The Apocalypse of Settler Colonialism: The Roots of Slavery, White Supremacy, and Capitalism in 17th Century North America and the Caribbean* (New York: Monthly Review Press, 2018); Tiya Miles, *Ties That Bind: The Story of an Afro-Cherokee Family in Slavery and Freedom* (Berkeley: University of California Press, 2005); and William Katz, *Black Indians: A Hidden Heritage,* repr. ed. (New York: Atheneum Books, 2012).

11 See Brittney Cooper, *Eloquent Rage: A Black Feminist Discovers Her Superpower* (New York: St. Martin's, 2018). In this seminal work Cooper similarly witnesses Beyoncé as an example of what we are describing as "homegrown" feminism. Cooper argues that, in fact, it is Beyoncé's messy and complicated *and public* engagement with feminism that makes her indispensable to feminism in general and Black feminism in particular. She states, "After Beyoncé, feminism was no longer something reserved for Black girls with college degrees and PhDs. Suddenly feminism wasn't just the province of Black girls

who'd read bell hooks. Armed with feminist narratives in the digital age, this Black girl who'd built a singing career instead of going to college could be a feminist, too" (*Eloquent Rage*, 30).

12 Brittney C. Cooper, Susana M. Morris, and Robin M. Boylorn, eds., *The Crunk Feminist Collection* (New York City: Feminist Press at CUNY, 2017).

13 Lakota People's Law Project, *Native Lives Matter,* February 2015, https://s3-us -west-1.amazonaws.com/lakota-peoples-law/uploads/Native-Lives-Matter -PDF.pdf.

14 The "logic of elimination" is a phrase coined by Patrick Wolfe to underscore the inherent eliminatory aspect of settler colonialism. See Patrick Wolfe, "Settler Colonialism and the Elimination of the Native," *Journal of Genocide Research* 8, no. 4 (2006): 387–409.

15 Tiffany Jeannette King, "In the Clearing: Black Female Bodies, Space, and Settler Colonial Landscapes," PhD diss., University of Maryland, College Park, 2013.

16 Beyoncé, "Superpower," track 12 on *Beyoncé* [self-titled album]. Parkwood and Columbia, 2013.

17 Joy James and João Costa Vargas, "Refusing Blackness-as-Victimization: Trayvon Martin and the Black Cyborgs," in *Pursuing Trayvon: Historical Contexts and Contemporary Manifestations of Racial Dynamics*, ed. George Yancy and Janine Jones (Lanham, MD: Lexington Books, 2012), 193.

18 Christina Sharpe, *In the Wake: On Blackness and Being* (Durham, NC: Duke University Press, 2016), 14–15.

19 Beyoncé, "No Angel," track 5 on *Beyoncé* [self-titled album]. Parkwood and Columbia, 2013.

20 Sharpe, *In The Wake*, 10.

21 Zandria Robinson, "We Slay, Part I," New South Negress, February 7, 2016, http://newsouthnegress.com/southernslayings/.

22 Robinson, "We Slay," 2016.

23 "Stop Shooting Us" is the phrase spray painted on a concrete wall in the "Formation" music video.

24 Beyoncé, "Statement on Police Violence," 2016.

25 Beyoncé, "I Have Three Hearts," 2017, https://www.beyonce.com/tag/i-have -three-hearts/. The title of the photographic series is taken from a poem by Warsan Shire that is also titled "I Have Three Hearts." The poem was written by Shire in 2017 and was displayed on Beyoncé's website in part with the photographs. Beyoncé is a noted fan of Shire's poetry as it is also highly featured on the *Lemonade* album.

26 Fred Moten and Robin D. G. Kelley, "*Do* Black Lives Matter?" Conversation sponsored by Critical Resistance, Bethany Baptist Church, Oakland, CA, December 13, 2014, https://vimeo.com/116111740.

27 Naomi Schaefer Riley, "Having a Baby Isn't a Miracle and Doesn't Make You a Goddess," *New York Post*, February 18, 2017, http://nypost.com/2017/02/18 /having-a-baby-isnt-a-miracle-and-doesnt-make-you-a-goddess/.

28 Schaefer Riley, "Having a Baby."

29 For a discussion of the genealogy, development, and scope of "revolutionary mothering," see Alexis Pauline Gumbs, China Marten, and Mai'a Williams, eds., *Revolutionary Mothering: Love on the Front Lines* (Oakland: PM Press, 2016).

30 Loretta Ross, preface to *Revolutionary Mothering: Love on the Front Lines*, ed. Alexis Pauline Gumbs, China Martens, and Mai'a Williams (Oakland: PM Press, 2016), xviii.

31 For discussions of Indigenous mothering, see Jeannette Corbiere Lavell and D. Memee Lavell-Harvard, *Until Our Hearts Are on the Ground: Aboriginal Mothering, Oppression, Resistance and Rebirth* (Ontario: Demeter Press, 2006); and Dawn Memee Lavell-Harvard and Kim Anderson, *Mothers of the Nations: Indigenous Mothering as Global Resistance, Reclaiming and Recovery* (Ontario: Demeter Press, 2014).

32 Simpson, "An Indigenous View on #BlackLivesMatter."

33 Beyoncé, "Sorry," track 4 on *Lemonade*, Parkwood and Columbia, 2016.

34 Jennifer DeClue, "To Visualize the Queen Diva! Toward a Black Feminist Trans Inclusivity in Beyoncé's 'Formation,' *TSQ: Trans Studies Quarterly* 4, no. 2 (2017): 219.

35 Declue, "To Visualize the Queen," 221.

36 Declue, "To Visualize the Queen," 221.

37 Cooper et al., *Crunk Feminist Collection*, xviii.

38 Marquis Bey, "Beyoncé's Black (Ab)Normal: Baaad Insurgency and the Queerness of Slaying," *Black Camera* 9, no. 1 (2017): 165.

39 Bey, "Beyoncé's Black (Ab)Normal," 165. Bey reads queerness as a subversive, nonnormative relation to power.

40 Jay-Z and Beyoncé, "'03 Bonnie and Clyde," track 4 on disc 1 of *The Blueprint 2: The Gift & The Curse*, 2002.

41 The Carters, "LOVEHAPPY," track 9 on *EVERYTHING IS LOVE*, Parkwood and Roc Nation, 2018.

42 The Carters, "APESHIT," track 2 on *EVERYTHING IS LOVE*, Parkwood and Roc Nation, 2018.

43 Zainab Amadahy, "Community, 'Relationship Framework' and Implications for Activism," rabble.ca, July 13, 2010, http://rabble.ca/news/2010/07/community-%E2%80%98relationship-framework%E2%80%99-and-implications-activism.

44 Beyoncé, "Hold Up," track 2 on *Lemonade*, Parkwood and Columbia, 2016.

45 Beyoncé, "Freedom," track 10 on *Lemonade*, Parkwood and Columbia, 2016.

46 Patricia Hill Collins, *Black Feminist Thought: Knowledge, Consciousness, and Politics of Empowerment* (New York: Routledge, 1990). In this seminal work, Hill Collins posits "lived experience" as key to a Black feminist epistemology *and* key to Black women's survival.

47 Beyoncé, "Freedom," 2016.

48 Beyoncé, *Lemonade*, 2016.

49 For examples of Indigenous feminist scholarship that interrogate human/nonhuman relations through Indigenous epistemologies, see Melissa Nelson,

"Getting Dirty: The Eco-Eroticism of Women in Indigenous Oral Litera-tures," in *Critically Sovereign: Indigenous Gender, Sexuality, and Feminist Studies*, ed. Joanne Barker (Durham, NC: Duke University Press, 2017): 229–60; Kim Tallbear, "Dear Indigenous Studies, It's Not Me, It's You: Why I Left and What Needs to Change," in *Critical Indigenous Studies*, ed. Aileen Moreton-Robison (Tucson: University of Arizona Press, 2016); and Jenell Navarro, "Solarize-ing Native Hip-Hop: Native Feminist Land Ethics and Cultural Resistance," *Decolonization: Indigeneity, Education & Society* 3, no. 1 (2014): 101–18.

50 Beyoncé, "Love Drought," track 7 on *Lemonade*, Parkwood and Columbia, 2016.

51 Terri L. Snyder, "Suicide, Slavery, and Memory in North America," *Journal of American History* 97, no. 1 (2010): 39–62.

52 During the nineteenth century there were many other instances of individu-als or groups of Black people who took some form of hope from the Igbo nar-rative and also chose suicide rather than slavery. See Snyder, "Suicide, Slavery, and Memory in North America," and, the interviews collected in the Georgia Writers' Project, *Drums and Shadows: Survival Stories among the Georgia Coastal Negroes* (Athens: University of Georgia Press, 1986).

53 Beyoncé, "Pray You Catch Me," track 1 on *Lemonade*, Parkwood and Colum-bia, 2016.

54 Zandria Robinson, "How Beyoncé's 'Lemonade' Exposes the Inner Lives of Black Women," *Rolling Stone*, April 28, 2016, http://www.rollingstone.com /music/news/how-beyonces-lemonade-exposes-inner-lives-of-black-women -20160428.

55 Robinson, "How Beyoncé's 'Lemonade.'"

56 Beyoncé, "Love On Top" track 8 on *4*, Columbia, 2011.

57 The term "decolonial love" was first deployed by Junot Díaz in an interview with the *Boston Globe* titled "The Search for Decolonial Love" on June 26, 2012. In this interview Díaz ponders the possibility of disrupting settler colonialism through relational love and self-love, stating that the only kind of love that could liberate from the legacy of colonial violence was *decolonial love*. He goes on to pose the question: "Is it possible to love one's broken-by-the-coloniality-of-power self in another broken-by-the-coloniality-of-power person?" After Díaz introduces this term and practice/process, Indigenous feminists further the implications and potentialities of decolonial love. For examples of such work, see Leanne Simpson, *Islands of Decolonial Love* (Win-nipeg: Arbeiter Ring Publishers, 2013); Karyn Recollet, "Glyphing Decolonial Love through Urban Flash Mobbing and *Walking with Our Sisters*," *Curricu-lum Inquiry* 45, no. 1 (2015): 129–45; and Gwendolyn Benaway, "Decolonial Love: A How-To Guide," Working It Out Together, accessed February 7, 2020, http://workingitouttogether.com/content/decolonial-love-a-how-to-guide/.

58 Reynaldo Anderson and Charles E. Jones, *Afrofuturism 2.0: The Rise of Astro-Blackness* (Lanham, MD: Lexington Books, 2016), vii.

59 Laura Harjo, *Spiral to the Stars: Mvskoke Tools of Futurity* (Tucson: University of Arizona Press, 2019).

60 See Maya Angelou, *Even the Stars Look Lonesome* (New York: Bantam, 1997).

References

Amadahy, Zainab. 2010. "Community, 'Relationship Framework' and Implications for Activism." rabble.ca, July 13. http://rabble.ca/news/2010/07 /community-%E2%80%98relationship-framework%E2%80%99-and -implications-activism.

Anderson, Reynaldo, and Charles E. Jones. 2016. *Afrofuturism 2.0: The Rise of Astro-Blackness*. Lanham, MD: Lexington Books.

Bey, Marquis. 2017. "Beyoncé's Black (Ab)Normal: Baaad Insurgency and the Queerness of Slaying." *Black Camera* 9, no. 1: 164–78.

Beyoncé. 2011. "Love On Top." Track 8 on *4*. Columbia.

Beyoncé. 2013. "No Angel." Track 5 on *Beyoncé* [self-titled album]. Parkwood and Columbia.

Beyoncé. 2013. "Superpower." Track 12 on *Beyoncé* [self-titled album]. Parkwood and Columbia.

Beyoncé. 2016. "Formation." Track 12 on *Lemonade*. Parkwood and Columbia.

Beyoncé. 2016. "Freedom." Track 10 on *Lemonade*. Parkwood and Columbia.

Beyoncé. 2016. "Hold Up." Track 2 on *Lemonade*. Parkwood and Columbia.

Beyoncé. 2016. "Pray You Catch Me." Track 1 on *Lemonade*. Parkwood and Columbia.

Beyoncé. 2016. "Sorry." Track 4 on *Lemonade*. Parkwood and Columbia.

Beyoncé. 2016. "Statement on Police Violence." July 27. https://www.beyonce.com /freedom/.

The Carters. 2018. "APESHIT." Track 2 on *EVERYTHING IS LOVE*. Parkwood and Roc Nation.

The Carters. 2018. "LOVEHAPPY." Track 9 on *EVERYTHING IS LOVE*. Parkwood and Roc Nation.

Cooper, Brittney C., Susana M. Morris, and Robin M. Boylorn, eds. 2017. *The Crunk Feminist Collection*. New York: Feminist Press at CUNY.

DeClue, Jennifer. 2017. "To Visualize the Queen Diva! Toward a Black Feminist Trans Inclusivity in Beyoncé's 'Formation.'" *TSQ: Trans Studies Quarterly* 4, no. 2: 219–25.

Gumbs, Alexis Pauline, China Martens, and Mai'a Williams. 2016. *Revolutionary Mothering: Love on the Front Lines*. Oakland: PM Press.

Harjo, Laura. 2019. *Spiral to the Stars: Mvskoke Tools of Futurity*. Tucson: University of Arizona Press,.

Hayes, Kelly. 2016. "On Korryn Gaines, Loreal Tsingine, and Refusing to Surrender." BDG, August 3. https://www.bgdblog.org/2016/08/gaines-tsingine/.

James, Joy, and João Costa Vargas. 2012. "Refusing Blackness-as-Victimization: Trayvon Martin and the Black Cyborgs." In *Pursuing Trayvon: Historical Contexts and Contemporary Manifestations of Racial Dynamics*, edited by George Yancy and Janine Jones, 193–205. Lanham, MD: Lexington Books.

Lakota People's Law Project. 2015. *Native Lives Matter.* February. https://s3-us -west-1.amazonaws.com/lakota-peoples-law/uploads/Native-Lives-Matter -PDF.pdf.

Million, Dian. 2014. "There Is a River in Me: Theory from Life." In *Theorizing Native Studies*, edited by Audra Simpson and Andrea Smith, 31–42. Durham, NC: Duke University Press.

Moten, Fred, and Robin D. G. Kelley. 2014. "*Do* Black Lives Matter?" Conversation sponsored by *Critical Resistance*. Bethany Baptist Church, Oakland, CA, December 13. https://vimeo.com/116111740.

Robinson, Zandria. 2016. "We Slay, Part I." New South Negress, February 7. http://newsouthnegress.com/southernslayings/.

Robinson, Zandria. 2016. "How Beyoncé's 'Lemonade' Exposes the Inner Lives of Black Women." *Rolling Stone*, April 28. http://www.rollingstone.com/music /news/how-beyonces-lemonade-exposes-inner-lives-of-black-women -20160428.

Sharpe, Christina. 2016. *In the Wake: On Blackness and Being.* Durham, NC: Duke University Press.

Simpson, Leanne. 2014. "An Indigenous View on #BlackLivesMatter." Yes! Solutions Journal, December 5. http://www.yesmagazine.org/peace-justice /indigenous-view-black-lives-matter-leanne-simpson.

Snyder, Terri L. 2010. "Suicide, Slavery, and Memory in North America." *Journal of American History* 97, no. 1: 39–62.

Strega, Susan, and Leslie Brown. 2015. *Research as Resistance: Revisiting Critical, Indigenous, and Anti-Oppressive Approaches.* 2nd ed. Toronto: Canadian Scholars' Press.

Wolfe, Patrick. 2006. "Settler Colonialism and the Elimination of the Native." *Journal of Genocide Research* 8, no. 4: 387–409.

CHAPTER FIFTEEN

Kimberly Robertson

Slay Serigraph with Artist's Statement

15.1 Kimberly Robertson

20″ × 26″ serigraph on archival quality fine art paper
Edition of 43
Released in 2017
Printed by Dewey Tafoya
Published at Self Help Graphics & Art
Signed and numbered by Kimberly Robertson

Informed by Black, Indigenous, and Women of Color feminisms, this print pays homage to the women-identified warriors who lead the resistance against the settler colonial, white-supremacist, capitalist, and heteropatri-archal bullshit that permeates our lives and affects our abilities to live in relationship—with one another, with the earth, with our ancestors, and with our futures.

CHAPTER SIXTEEN

Jenell Navarro & Kimberly Robertson

Mass Incarceration since 1492

Located in California (on Northern Chumash and Tongva land), we work with a number of Native feminist activists, scholars, artists, and community members dedicated to addressing the settler colonial and heteropatriarchal violences that plague Indigenous communities. We address these issues to remedy them and operationalize the decolonial worlds we desire to live in. As a way to engage our local communities and beyond on important Indigenous issues, we often use art as a vehicle of disruption. In December 2017 we collaborated with JusticeLA to bring attention to the disproportionate and unjust practices of locking up Indigenous peoples in jail or prison. We specifically focused on some of these practices that take place in Los Angeles, California—a city that incarcerates more people than any other location in the United States.[1]

The project was initiated by JusticeLA when they put out a call to Los Angeles area artists to decorate and place jailbeds across Los Angeles County on Christmas Eve 2017 to call attention to the county's decision to expand the world's largest jail system with a $3.5 billion investment. In the end, over fifty jailbeds were designed and dropped across the county, and all of them focused on the problems of mass incarceration and its attendant violence.

Our bunk, titled *Mass Incarceration since 1492*, was specifically dedicated to Indigenous people who have been incarcerated. It also was meant to serve the Los Angeles Indian community and beyond as a love letter to incarcerated Indigenous people to say we see you and we hear you. This is important because as Kelly Lytle Hernández states, "Mass incarceration is mass elimination."[2] We know that the settler state continues to seek the elimination of Indigenous folks as it swallows up more land, poisons more waterways, and marks our people for extermination. We see this so clearly in the tactics of policing and incarceration. For example, the 2015 Lakota People's Law Project report titled *Native Lives Matter* details, in no uncertain terms, that Indigenous people are killed by the police at the highest rates and continue to face anomalous rates of incarceration, all the while being absent from public discourses on these issues. In fact, the report states that "American Indians suffer the most adverse effects of a criminal justice system which consistently reifies itself as structurally unjust."[3] And important to this conversation is the fact that Native peoples, including many of us who worked on this bed, are constantly aware of how our loved ones are stolen away from our lives and locked up as a means for the state to dissolve our cultures, our kinship structures, and our political wherewithal. As Luana Ross states in *Inventing the Savage: The Social Construction of Native American Criminality*, "It is common for Native people either to have been incarcerated or to have relatives who have been imprisoned. Because we are a colonized people, the experiences of imprisonment are, unfortunately, exceedingly familiar. Native Americans disappear into Euro-American institutions of confinement at alarming rates. People from my reservation simply appeared to vanish and magically return."[4] Therefore, because these injustices are ongoing, we wanted to bring this issue to the forefront in the city of Los Angeles since the county has not been willing to divest from these inhumane practices.

In addition, we were motivated to design this bed for incarcerated or formerly incarcerated Native peoples because the structure of settler colonialism continues to divide the communities that are most likely to be subject to the violence of jailing and incarceration. Namely, Native and Black communities are both targeted to be locked away at extremely high rates since settlers, and the settler state, predicate their existence in these lands on slavery and land dispossession. While the forms of settler surveillance, suppression, and violence against Native and Black communities are distinct and cannot be conflated, we do not believe viable routes to prison abolition are possible without considering the needs of both Native and Black peoples. It was our hope that this jailbed, in combination with the many others created and dropped with JusticeLA, would begin some constitutive conversations that move in these directions.

The artistic design of our jailbed was carefully thought out to educate those who viewed it and, hopefully, incite action on their part to change the violent system of carcerality. We beaded the posts of the bed in the colors of the four directions as a call to ceremony. Within the beadwork we also added turquoise as a representation of strength, and we created white lines of beads to make sure any spirits or thoughts within the beaded patterns had a safe and sacred way out of the bunk. For many Indigenous people, beadwork is a form of healing and medicine, so we offered the beadwork to all our relations who have suffered at the hands of an unjust carceral system in these lands for centuries. The top bunk of the bed was dedicated to our incarcerated brothers and the bottom bunk of the bed to our incarcerated sisters—both bunks were dedicated to all our womxn relatives who identify as brothers and men who identify as sisters. We were also constantly thinking of the excessive violence the state delivers upon our Two-Spirit relatives and our Indigenous youth and, therefore, both bunks are for them as well. Between the two bunks we hung abalone shells as gifts to our California Indian relatives, and around the bottom bunk we created a shawl with fringe to wrap everyone in love and protection (see figures 16.1–16.4).

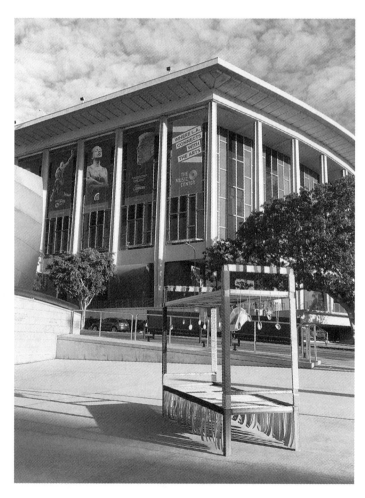

16.1 *Mass Incarceration since 1492* jailbed. Downtown Los Angeles, 2017.

16.2 *Mass Incarceration since 1492* jailbed. Downtown Los Angeles, 2017.

Attached to the bed were many copies of an accompanying zine—a DIY self-publication booklet. That zine, also titled *Mass Incarceration since 1492*, was yet another educational tool that we utilized to disseminate information about the structural violence of incarceration against Indigenous peoples. Specifically, the zine narrated Indigenous incarceration over centuries of persistent settler colonialism by providing statistical details about this issue, but more importantly, by humanizing this dialogue with family photos and anecdotal stories about those we have lost due to this unnecessary violence.[5]

We decided to drop the bed in downtown Los Angeles in front of the Walt Disney Concert Hall. This location was a strategic choice because it is within close proximity to the site where Indigenous people, especially Tongva and Tatavium people, were sold as slaves in the city well into the 1850s. Many people incorrectly assume the inhumane practice of slavery was not happening in California in the mid-nineteenth century, so we wanted to draw attention to this history. As journalist Robert Petersen writes, "The present-day location of the human auction is Main Street between Temple and Aliso Streets in downtown, where the United States Courthouse now stands. It is ironic that such a great injustice occurred at a place where Angelenos now go to seek justice. In fact, over the past few decades, Native American groups have staged several different protests at the federal courthouse in an effort to seek justice, on the very site where, a century earlier, their forefathers

16.3 *Mass Incarceration since 1492* jailbed. Downtown Los Angeles, 2017. Top bunk of the jailbed.

MASS
INCARCERATION
SINCE 1492
The first peoples of these lands have always been imprisoned as a form of social control: military forts, the CA mission system, boarding schools, reservations...
Native Americans per capita in state and federal prison is 38% above the national average.
Colonization began by marking CA Indian bodies for genocide and has continued by criminalizing our very existence.
Native Americans are the racial group most likely to be killed by law enforcement.

[and foremothers] were auctioned off like cattle."[6] It is also important to note that not only were Indigenous people sold on the slave auction block in downtown Los Angeles as what can only be described as a "spectacle" that took place every Monday morning in the mid-nineteenth century, but the entire city was built upon the exploitation of these same people.[7] Namely, Tongva people were regularly jailed because if they were labeled "criminal" they could then be sentenced to a chain gang and forced to work in slave conditions. Again, as Petersen reports,

> this process was not undertaken in the shadows—out of the reach of law enforcement—because auctioning off Native people was totally legal in 1850s California. The ironically named California Act for the Govern-

ment and Protection of Indians of 1850 allowed any white person to post bail for a convicted Indian and then require the Native person to work for the white man until the fine was discharged. Historian Robert Heizer called this legislative act "a thinly disguised substitute for slavery." Imitating the state legislature, the Los Angeles City Council passed its own ordinance in 1850 which allowed prisoners to be "auctioned off to the highest bidder for private service."[8]

Given the fact that this history of Los Angeles has been rendered largely invisible, we created the jailbed with the aim of educating residents and visitors to these unceded Tongva lands.

Furthermore, we see incarceration as an extension of the settler desire to control, suppress, and surveil Indigenous people. These efforts are structural,

MY CRIME?
Being An American Indian Woman
– *Stormy Ogden*

Native men are admitted to prison at 4 times the rate of white men.

Native women are admitted to prison at 6 times the rate of white women.

Native American youth are 30% more likely than whites to be referred to juvenile court than have charges dropped.

Native youth are 1% of the national youth population, yet 70% of Native Youth are committed to the Federal Bureau of Prisons.

16.4 *Mass Incarceration since 1492* jailbed. Downtown Los Angeles, 2017. Bottom bunk of the jailbed.

along with being insatiable, since they are evidenced in the ways the settler state has always sought to contain us. This containment is highly motivated by both race and gender, hence the high rates of confinement for Native and Black peoples and the womxn in our communities. For example, our auntie (chosen kinship) Stormy Ogden has written specifically about the personal and structural atrocities of US incarceration. In her article "Ex-Prisoner Pomo Woman Speaks Out," she argues that the settler state has sought social control over Indigenous people for centuries by locking us up in military forts, missions, reservations, and boarding schools.[9] This means carcerality has *always* been a tactic of settler colonizers in these lands, no one in our communities is safe from this violence, and it continues to this day in the re-design of the jail and prison system. So, Indigenous people have faced mass incarceration since 1492. Enough already.

Notes

1 Kelly Lytle Hernández, *City of Inmates: Conquest, Rebellion, and the Rise of Human Caging in Los Angeles, 1771–1965* (Chapel Hill: University of North Carolina Press, 2017).

2 Hernández, *City of Inmates*, 1.

3 Lakota People's Law Project, *Native Lives Matter*, 2015, 1. https://s3-us-west-1 .amazonaws.com/lakota-peoples-law/uploads/Native-Lives-Matter-PDF.pdf.

4 Luana Ross, *Inventing the Savage: The Social Construction of Native American Criminality* (Austin: University of Texas Press, 1998), 1.

5 For a free digital copy of the accompanying zine, please email one of the authors.

6 Robert Petersen, "Los Angeles' 1850s Slave Market Is Now the Site of a Federal Courthouse," *Los Angeles Times*, September 2, 2016.

7 Hernández, *City of Inmates*, 38.

8 Petersen, "Los Angeles' 1850s Slave Market Is Now the Site of a Federal Courthouse."

9 Stormy Ogden, "Ex-Prisoner Pomo Woman Speaks Out," *Social Justice* 31, no. 4 (2004): 63–69.

References

Hernández, Kelly Lytle. 2017. *City of Inmates: Conquest, Rebellion, and the Rise of Human Caging in Los Angeles, 1771–1965*. Chapel Hill: University of North Carolina Press.

Lakota People's Law Project. 2015. *Native Lives Matter*. https://s3-us-west-1 .amazonaws.com/lakota-peoples-law/uploads/Native-Lives-Matter-PDF .pdf.

Ogden, Stormy. 2004. "Ex-Prisoner Pomo Woman Speaks Out." *Social Justice* 31, no. 4: 63–69.

Petersen, Robert. 2016. "Los Angeles' 1850s Slave Market Is Now the Site of a Federal Courthouse." *Los Angeles Times*, September 2.

Ross, Luana. 1998. *Inventing the Savage: The Social Construction of Native American Criminality.* Austin: University of Texas Press.

Se'mana Thompson

"Liberation,"
Cover of *Queer Indigenous Girl*, Volume 4

17.1 "Liberation," Cover of *Queer Indigenous Girl*, Volume 4

& "Roots,"
Cover of *Black Indigenous Boy*, Volume 2

17.2 "Roots," Cover of *Black Indigenous Boy*, Volume 2

Lindsay Nixon

Visual Cultures
of Indigenous Futurism

Indigenous Artists and the Dystopian Now

Armed with spirit and the teachings of our ancestors, all our relations behind us, we are living the Indigenous future. We are the descendants of a future imaginary that has already passed; the outcome of the intentions, resistance, and survivance of our ancestors. Simultaneously in the future and the past, we are living in the "dystopian now," as Molly Swain of the podcast *Métis in Space* has named it.[1] Indigenous peoples are using our own technological traditions—our worldviews, our languages, our stories, and our kinship—as guiding principles in imagining possible futures for ourselves and our communities. As Erica Lee has described, "In knowing the histories of our relations and of this land, we find the knowledge to recreate all that our worlds would've been if not for the interruption of colonization."[2]

Indigenous artists on Turtle Island have engaged with tropes of science fiction in their artwork: alien figures straight out of Space Invaders, post-apocalyptic landscapes that bear an eerie resemblance to contemporary landscapes devastated by resource extraction, and unidentified flying objects that mark first contact with otherworldly beings. Speculative visualities are used to project Indigenous life into the future imaginary, subverting the death imaginary ascribed to Indigenous bodies within settler colonial discourse. As Andrea Smith has written, the death imaginary purports that Indigenous peoples must always be disappearing in order to legitimize settler occupation and the Canadian state.[3] Settler art, in its imagining of Indigenous disappearance, its representation of the romanticized but dying homogenized Indigenous peoples of Turtle Island,[4] offers a location for Indigenous artists to contest colonial representations in art with their own futuristic imaginings and art practices—art practices that weave together tradition and technology, fusing them together into a future present.

The future imaginary and its catalogue of science fictive imageries affords Indigenous artists a creative space to respond to the dystopian now, grounding their survivance in contextual and relational practices. Indigenous artists have no problem portraying possible undesirable futures wherein colonial capitalist greed has resulted in the subjugation of life within all creation, because these narratives are evocative of our known realities. We have realized the apocalypse now, and we are living in a dystopian settler-occupied oligarchy fueled by resource extraction and environmental contamination, completely alternative to our traditional ways of being and knowing.

Despite dystopic realities, the possibilities of love and kinship as survivance in the face of ecological disaster are a visceral narrative for Indigenous peoples. Indigenous women, and gender variant and sexually diverse Indigenous peoples, have consistently employed kinship and love within their communities in order to positively transform contemporary colonial realities for their kin. Lou Cornum has considered the advanced technologies of kinship that Indigenous peoples possess for intergalactic engagement, offering us the concept of kinship as technology: "The Indian in space seeks to feel at home, to understand her perceived strangeness by asking: why can't indigenous peoples also project ourselves among the stars? Might our collective visions of the cosmos forge better relationships here on earth and in the present than colonial visions of the final frontier?"[5] My own cultural knowledge of Cree-Saulteaux-Métis kinship[6] grounds my analysis of Indigenous artists who, in the face of misrepresentation and erasure within settler art, imagine and create themselves into being using speculative visualities—a body of work I have found particularly evocative and transformative to my own imaginings of the Indigenous future.

Indigenous Technologies

In their depictions of the future imaginary, contemporary Indigenous artists on Turtle Island have tended toward a contextual ideology of survivance—as Gerald Vizenor termed it—by using their philosophies of love and kinship to give voice to resistance.[7] In her work *Islands of Decolonial Love* Leanne Simpson traces this decolonial ethic of love, each "island" a song or story addressing the complexity of interactions between animate beings in the contact zone. Simpson is describing sâkihitowask (love medicine)[8]—or future love—a better, prosperous, and kinder future for all life within the galaxies.[9]

Masculinist political and philosophical thinkers may deem love as too emotional and embodied, *feminine* if you will, and thereby outside the realm of formal thought and action. In doing so, masculinist Indigenous thinkers unwittingly uphold Western thought's dichotomization of mind and body, and its hierarchicalization of mind over body as reification of patriarchal inequities associating the logical mind with masculinity, and the inferior and passive body with femininity.[10] Marxists would perhaps argue against corrupt forms of love they perceive as sentimental bourgeoisie platitudes, like those described by Michael Hardt and Antonio Negri, which situate love as a biopolitical moment born from our capitalistic tendencies, and one that is constrained by acts of obligation, to boot.[11] Decolonial scholars too might denounce love, mistakenly associating its ethic with neoliberal state-led and settler-led attempts to reconcile relations with Indigenous peoples.[12] I'm interested in what is lost in such analyses, namely a central focus on Indigenous ways of being and knowing, like kinship, as well as the essential roles of Indigenous women, and Indigenous gender variant and sexually diverse peoples, in guiding our communities toward a truly emancipatory future.

I want to be careful here when teetering on the language of reconciliation, as I know it's a contentious one. I am not describing a politics of recognition led by settlers or by the state, but rather an ethical concept I experience within all facets of Indigenous life: being through kinship. I am perplexed by decolonial thought that hierarchically dichotomizes land work and relational work, favoring decolonization scholarship over reconciliatory action. Such rhetoric tends toward infantilizing those Indigenous peoples who exercise agency in their interactions with the state, including elders. While decolonial scholars consistently give lip service to centering Indigenous thought, they ultimately still envision Indigenous futurities as linked to scholarly permissible conceptions of decolonization. What does this mean when Indigenous peoples from within my own community don't identify with the exclusionary academic discourse of decolonization, and center the language of reconciliation in their own attempts to heal community?

Like my kin before me, I would argue that the project of Indigenous survivance is nothing, is inanimate, without an ethics of love and kinship as a guiding principle. True deliverance from settler colonial occupation finds its foundation in Indigenous knowledges that understand land, love, and life as one and the same. It was Patricia Monture-Angus who described the concept of "justice as healing," which among many other principles, values, and aspects of care entails a recentering of women within all political realms of Indigenous community, and establishing meaningful external relations with settler communities in harm reductive ways.[13] I'm also reminded of Leanne Simpson's evocation of Monture-Angus in *Dancing on Our Turtle's Back*, reinforcing that "self-determination and sovereignty begin at home," and that healing our communities through cultural reawakening begins with how we treat ourselves, then spirals outward to our own communities, and extends even further still—outward into our relationships with external communities.[14]

It doesn't surprise me that Indigenous women like Erica Lee, Christi Belcourt, Chelsea Vowel, and Maria Campbell are leading conversations around reconciliation, because the language of reconciliation bears resemblance to the language of kinship and, therefore, the relational work they already do within community—an often invisibilized labor—is work based in restoring relationships between one another that have been eroded by colonialism. It is work that understands theory as conceptual and grounds itself in reducing the harmful effects of colonial violence on our bodies, minds, and spirits. While Eve Tuck necessarily reminded us that decolonization is not a metaphor,[15] the Indigenous peoples in my community also recognize the dire need to support one another's survivance, right here, right now. I'm not interested in debating the correct usage of colonial terminologies that we then describe through European and Euro-American linguistics, which limit our ability to describe Indigenous concepts and their complex meanings. What does drive my work is our mutual survivance as a people, and the sâkihitowask necessary to heal our communities into the Indigenous future.

As someone who has consistently received teachings from nôhkomak (grandmothers) and nisikosak (aunties) around relationality and kinship, I can see how the language of reconciliation parallels an ethic of love and kinship. While I may prefer to call a political act of love decolonial love or even a return to kinship, I also want to honor the truth of my kin who choose to describe such work as reconciliation. In the midst of the dystopian now—an apocalypse come to life for Indigenous peoples—we cannot wait for some faraway time when the land has been returned to heal the embodied effects of colonialism that are literally killing us every day. We must liberate both land and life by actively honoring our responsibilities to kinship in this moment, fostering good relations within all creation in our intentions and actions. Contemporary Indigenous artists on Turtle Island speak these ideologies of kinship in their work, using its advanced technologies in conjunction with speculative visual cultures to project their communities into the future imaginary.

Visual Cultures of Indigenous Futurism

Access to art historical methodologies and museum studies within academic art history departments has exposed me to the cultural life of my relations both north and south of the medicine line, including some work as old as 100 AD. However, as a Cree-Saulteaux-Métis person, I also recognize the complexity of my relationship to archival and museum practices on Turtle Island. I'm hesitant to call nonconsensually and invasively unearthed cultural objects "artifacts" or "art," descriptors allocated to them by settler appropriators and grave robbers. To see the cultural objects of my ancestors displayed behind glass cases in sterile museums, void of the life and meaning they held within community, feels like another facet of the death imaginary ascribed to Indigenous communities within the arts. Nevertheless, access to the cultural objects of my ancestors has been visceral and has afforded me representations of Indigenous knowledges, experiences, stories, and life unadulterated by the gaze of the settler academy. As Sara Ahmed would say, these are representations free of translation by the "stranger."[16]

Inuit art offers a particularly interesting location for the future imaginary because of the proximity to first contact moments with settler society. For some Inuit, close encounters with an alien culture, outside of anything within the worlds they have ever known, have happened within their lifetime. Inuit artists have depicted their early interactions with settlers in speculative ways using futuristic imaginative concepts: a future imagery in the present. One jarring example is Ovilu Tunnillie's green stone carving *This Has Touched My Life*, a representation of the artist's experience of being removed from her home and taken to an infirmary in the South, her first time away from her home in the North. The nurses who are escorting Tunnillie in the carving are wearing veiled hats but, in Tunnillie's depiction, the hats look like space helmets.

Pudlo Pudlat is often revered for being the first Inuk to feature Western technology in his work; his lithograph *Aeroplane* even appeared on a Canadian postage stamp. The irony, of course, is that the Baffin Island Inuk artist's usage of speculative visualities actually critically engages with destructive colonial technologies rather than condoning them. In Pudlat's lithograph *Imposed Migration*, he depicts an otherworldly flying object: a UFO, if you will. The UFO is cabled to a variety of northern animals: a walrus, a bear, and a buffalo, and is lifting them off the ground, transplanting them to new territories. The absurdity is transparent. To remove kin from their home territories is to separate them from their context, to remove their very essence and connection to the land. Here Pudlat openly denounces the colonial project of forced removal and migration inflicted on Inuit communities in the North.

Ligwilda'xw Kwakwaka'wakw artist Sonny Assu has also engaged with diasporic Indigenous identities using tropes of futurity. In his series *Interventions on the Imaginary*, Assu adds digitally created alien-like figures to settler depictions of Indigenous peoples at early contact. In doing so, Assu reappropriates the visuals of the settler art he has selected, contesting the romanticized and orientalized representation of Indigenous peoples as what some have called "the imaginary Indian" of the colonial art period.[17] *They're Coming! Quick! I have a better hiding place for you. Dorvan V, you'll love it* depicts an alien force entering a precolonial Indigenous community, as if to remove or exile the Indigenous population, beaming them up into an otherworldly "space invader" object. Assu depicts Indigenous peoples in migration, within a so-called Fourth World, living in diasporas within their own territories. These figures have been forced off of their home territories, their bodies propelled through occupied space by an alien force, whose gaze they attempt to hide from.

Within the artworks discussed, Assu, Pudlat, and Tunnillie all deal with themes of displacement, relating these experiences to dislocation from kin and kinship. At the center of these removals from community and disruptions of Indigenous ways of life is a distrust of the ominous alien force that seeks to either abduct or annihilate them. Rather than the otherworldly aliens from space depicted in the artwork, the artists are exposing their experiences of the settler-colonial project that seeks to displace and remove them from the land. This dislocation from their communities, from kinship ways, is a fracture to their very identities as Indigenous peoples. Dystopian science fictive futures are reconciled by love and kinship, and Indigenous futures become a location for survivance through self-representation. Art is both the means to project Indigenous life into the stars and the space canoe we use to paddle through these imagined galaxies, and a medicinal practice, healing our spirits, minds, and bodies as we move into possible futures.

Erin Marie Konsmo explores expressions of kinship and the dystopian now in several of her works. While I'm crediting Konsmo for her work, Konsmo herself has been hesitant to describe her work using individualistic pronouns, viewing her art as coming from community rather than solely from herself. Art is a part of all Indigenous life and art practice should, too, be based in principles of kinship. In 2016 I had the opportunity to attend the vernissage for Dayna Danger's and Cecilia Kavara Verran's exhibit *Disrupt Archive*, curated by Heather Igloliorte at La Centrale Galerie Powerhouse in Montreal. During the artist talk, Igloliorte noted that it is often claimed Indigenous languages don't have a word for art. The nehiyaw language, for instance, does not have a word that translates exactly into English as "art" or "artist." Instead, as Igloliorte explained to the audience, "art" is a part of everything we do in community, a part of all language, and cannot be reduced to a singular concept.

Konsmo's artwork *Discovery Is Toxic: Indigenous Women on the Frontline of Environmental and Reproductive Justice* depicts an Indigenous figure scaled to fit into the landscape, as if the figure were itself a part of the land. Indigenous bodies are interrupted by settler colonial occupation, ships that bring with them a toxic commerce and colonizing religion—what the Native Youth Sexual Health Network has called environmental violence.[18] A gas mask hangs from around the figure's neck, because settler occupation is unnatural and has resulted in the subjugation of all Indigenous life, including land. The result is a postapocalyptic environmental wasteland made of our territories and the embodied complexities of ecological warfare, including within the reproductive life of our communities. As the title suggests, it is kinship that frees the land and our bodies from the dystopian now. Indigenous women, and sexually diverse and gender variant Indigenous peoples, are resituating themselves as leaders of community, resisting settler colonial occupation and environmental violence, and resisting occupation on the land through kinship and love.

Contemporary Indigenous artists on Turtle Island convey kinship in their artworks to envisage survivance outside of cissexist and heteronormative relations. Accounting for the intricate and multiple ways we interact as interconnected communities puts us in a position to consider the location, or lack thereof, of gender variant and sexually diverse Indigenous peoples within conceptions of Indigenous survivance and peoplehood. It was Billy-Ray Belcourt who questioned which of our peoples are actually represented in the Indigenous future, borrowing from Gayatri Spivak to ask: "Can the other of Native Studies speak?"[19]

Dayna Danger's *Masks* series, which I first saw at *Disrupt Archive*, asks that Indigenous communities consider how our own sexualities and genders factor into our future imaginaries—what Qwo-Li Driskill, Daniel Heath Justice, Deborah Miranda, and Lisa Tatonetti have called a sovereign erotic.[20] Danger asks: What space exists for our gender variant and sexually diverse Indigenous communities, for our own ways of loving, in the future imaginary? *Masks* is composed of a series of photographs featuring Indigenous peoples wearing black leather BDSM fetish masks adorned with rows upon rows of black matte and glossy beads. One mask prominently featured a labrys, a symbol associated with lesbian feminism or radical feminism. Danger produced the masks with the help of Indigenous relations from among her community. Hours of painstaking care and love were put into the masks, just as would be put into any beading project. The image of beading entire masks of leather evokes the blood drawn from needle injuries, the sweat of such laborious and love-filled work, and the tears integrated into the work itself, the emotions and relationships associated with the making of these objects.

During her artist's talk, Danger said she was hesitant to describe the gender or sexuality of the people in her *Masks* series, arguing that they had their own culturally specific ways of describing those elements of themselves. The Indigenous peoples in Danger's series are presented as fluid, androgynous, and limitless not only in gender but in spirit and body as well. Danger reminds us that Indigenous futures must include a return to our traditional ways of understanding gender: outside of the colonial gender binary, returning balance between the genders through kinship and love. Danger proposes a restoration of gender variant life within Indigenous community, actively remembering our traditions of gender fluidity and sexual diversity, in order to create a future imaginary that is responsive and respectful to the multiplicity of ways Indigenous peoples express their genders and sexualities.

Indigenous peoples' sexualities are frequently equated to histories of sexual violence, commodified and institutionalized by settlers seeking to dominate, discipline, and control Indigenous bodies. Danger's use of the leather BDSM mask references the kink community as a space to explore complicated dynamics of sexuality, gender, and power in a consensual and feminist manner. Danger engages with her own medicine, beading, in order to mark kink as a space for healing colonial trauma. There is no shame in this action. Here the models' gender expressions and sensual lives are integral to their resurgent identities as Indigenous peoples.

Every day, Indigenous peoples are restoring their beings, bodies, genders, sexualities, and reproductive lives from colonial institutions through play, self-representation, and sexual self-determination. Enacting kinship in their art, the Indigenous artists discussed here embody the past and future in their present representations, projecting decolonial love and kinship ways into the cosmos. The future imaginary becomes a realm within which Indigenous artists express disconnection from kinship and land, a medicinal space to imagine new futures for Indigenous life.

Notes

Note: This article was originally featured in GUTS as a part of the spring 2016 Futures issue, http://gutsmagazine.ca/visual-cultures/, (c) 2016, GUTS magazine. Reprinted by permission.

1 Molly Swain and Chelsea Vowel, "World-Building in the Dystopian Now: Imagining and Podcasting Indigenous Futures," presentation at the Future of First Nations, Inuit, and Métis Broadcasting: Conversation and Convergence, Edmonton, AB, April 21, 2017.

2 Erica Violet Lee, "Reconciling in the Apocalypse," *Canadian Centre for Policy Alternatives*, March 1, 2016, https://www.policyalternatives.ca/publications /monitor/reconciling-apocalypse.

3 Andrea Smith, "Heteropatriarchy and the Three Pillars of White Supremacy: Rethinking Women of Color Organizing," in *Color of Violence: The Incite! Anthology*, ed. Incite! Women of Color Against Violence (Cambridge: South End Press, 2006), 68.

4 Daniel Francis, *The Imaginary Indian: The Image of the Indian in Canadian Culture* (Vancouver: Arsenal Pulp Press, 2012).

5 Lou Cornum, "The Space NDN's Star Map," *The New Inquiry*, January 26, 2015, https://thenewinquiry.com/the-space-ndns-star-map/.

6 Robert Alexander Innes, *Elder Brother and the Law of the People: Contemporary Kinship and Cowessess First Nation* (Winnipeg: University of Manitoba Press, 2013).

7 Gerald Vizenor, *Manifest Manners: Postindian Warriors of Survivance* (Lebanon, NH: University Press of New England, 2000).

8 Arok Wolvengrey, "love medicine," *Online Cree Dictionary*, http://www .creedictionary.com/.

9 Leanne Simpson, *Islands of Decolonial Love* (Winnipeg: Arp Books, 2013).

10 Elizabeth Grosz, *Volatile Bodies: Toward a Corporeal Feminism* (Bloomington: Indiana University Press, 1994), xii.

11 Michael Hardt and Antonio Negri, "De Singularitate 1: Of Love Possessed," in *Commonwealth* (Cambridge: Belknap Press of Harvard University Press, 2009).

12 Glen Coulthard, "Subjects of Empire: Indigenous Peoples and the 'Politics of Recognition' in Canada," *Contemporary Political Theory* 6, no. 6 (2007): 438.

13 Patricia Monture-Angus, *Thunder in My Soul: A Mohawk Woman Speaks* (Black Point, NS: Fernwood Publishing, 1995), 219.

14 Patricia Monture-Angus, *Journeying Forward: Dreaming First Nations Independence* (Halifax, NS: Fernwood Books, 1999), 8; as cited by Leanne Simpson, *Dancing on Our Turtle's Back* (Winnipeg: Arp Books, 2011), 144.

15 Eve Tuck and K. Wayne Yang, "Decolonization Is Not a Metaphor," *Decolonization: Indigeneity, Education & Society* 1, no. 1 (2012).

16 Sara Ahmed, *Strange Encounters: Embodied Others in Postcoloniality* (Abingdon, UK: Routledge, 2000).

17 Francis, *Imaginary Indian*.

18 Women's Earth Alliance and Native Youth Sexual Health Network, VIOLENCE ON THE LAND, VIOLENCE ON OUR BODIES: Building an Indigenous Response to Environmental Violence, 2016, http://landbodydefense.org/uploads/files /VLVBReportToolkit2016.pdf.

19 Billy-Ray Belcourt, "Can the Other of Native Studies Speak?," *Decolonization: Indigeneity, Education and Society*, February 1, 2016, https://decolonization .wordpress.com/2016/02/01/can-the-other-of-native-studies-speak/.

20 Qwo-Li Driskill, Daniel Heath Justice, Deborah A. Miranda, and Lisa Tatonetti, *Sovereign Erotics: A Collection of Two-Spirit Literature* (Tucson: University of Arizona Press, 2011).

References

Ahmed, Sara. 2000. *Strange Encounters: Embodied Others in Postcoloniality*. Abingdon, UK: Routledge.

Belcourt, Billy-Ray. 2016. "Can the Other of Native Studies Speak?" *Decolonization: Indigeneity, Education and Society*, February 1, https://decolonization .wordpress.com/2016/02/01/can-the-other-of-native-studies-speak/.

Cornum, Lou. 2015. "The Space NDN's Star Map." *The New Inquiry*, January 26, https://thenewinquiry.com/the-space-ndns-star-map/.

Coulthard, Glen. 2007. "Subjects of Empire: Indigenous Peoples and the 'Politics of Recognition' in Canada." *Contemporary Political Theory* 6, no. 6: 437–60.

Driskill, Qwo-Li, Daniel Heath Justice, Deborah A. Miranda, and Lisa Tatonetti. 2011. *Sovereign Erotics: A Collection of Two-Spirit Literature*. Tucson: University of Arizona Press.

Francis, Daniel. 2012. *The Imaginary Indian: The Image of the Indian in Canadian Culture*. Vancouver: Arsenal Pulp Press.

Grosz, Elizabeth. 1994. *Introduction to Volatile Bodies: Toward a Corporeal Feminism*. Bloomington: Indiana University Press.

Hardt, Michael, and Antonio Negri. 2009. "De Singularitate 1: Of Love Possessed." In *Commonwealth*, 179–189. Cambridge: Belknap Press of Harvard University Press.

Innes, Robert Alexander. 2013. *Elder Brother and the Law of the People: Contemporary Kinship and Cowessess First Nation*. Winnipeg: University of Manitoba Press.

Lee, Erica Violet. 2016. "Reconciling in the Apocalypse." Canadian Centre for Policy Alternatives, March 1, https://www.policyalternatives.ca/publications /monitor/reconciling-apocalypse.

Monture-Angus, Patricia. 1995. *Thunder in My Soul: A Mohawk Woman Speaks*. Black Point: Fernwood Publishing.

Monture-Angus, Patricia. 1999. *Journeying Forward: Dreaming First Nations Independence*. Halifax: Fernwood Books.

Simpson, Leanne. 2011. *Dancing on Our Turtle's Back*. Winnipeg: Arp Books.

Simpson, Leanne. 2013. *Islands of Decolonial Love*. Winnipeg: Arp Books.

Smith, Andrea. 2006. "Heteropatriarchy and the Three Pillars of White Supremacy: Rethinking Women of Color Organizing." In *Color of Violence: The Incite! Anthology*, edited by Incite! Women of Color Against Violence, 1–6. Cambridge: South End Press.

Swain, Molly, and Chelsea Vowel. 2017. "World-Building in the Dystopian Now: Imagining and Podcasting Indigenous Futures." Presentation at the Future of First Nations, Inuit, and Métis Broadcasting: Conversation and Convergence, Edmonton, AB, April 21.

Tuck, Eve, and K. Wayne Yang. 2012. "Decolonization Is Not a Metaphor." *Decolonization: Indigeneity, Education & Society* 1, no. 1: 1–40.

Vizenor, Gerald. 2000. *Manifest Manners: Postindian Warriors of Survivance*. Lebanon, NH: University Press of New England.

Wolvengrey, Arok. "Love medicine." Online Cree Dictionary, http://www.creedictionary.com/.

Women's Earth Alliance and Native Youth Sexual Health Network. 2016. VIO-LENCE ON THE LAND, VIOLENCE ON OUR BODIES: Building an Indigenous Response to Environmental Violence. http://landbodydefense.org/uploads/files/VLVBReportToolkit2016.pdf.

CHAPTER NINETEEN

Rinaldo Walcott

Diaspora, Transnationalism, and the Decolonial Project

Leaving? To leave? Left? Language can be deceptive. The moment when they "left" the Old World and entered the New. Forced to leave? To "leave" one would have to have a destination in mind. Of course, one could rush out the door with no destination in mind, but to "rush" or "to leave" would suggest some self-possession; rushing would suggest a purpose, a purpose with some urgency, some reason. Their "taking"? Taking, taking too might suggest a benevolence so, no, it was not taking. So, having not "left," having no "destination," having no "self-possession," no purpose and no urgency, their departure was unexpected; and in the way that some unexpected events can be horrific. What language would describe that loss of bearings or the sudden awful liability of one's own body? The hitting or the whipping or the driving, which was shocking, the dragging and the bruising it involved, the epidemic of sickness with life which would become hereditary? And the antipathy that would shadow all subsequent events.[1]

Migration. Can it be called migration? There is a sense of return in migrations—sense of continuities, remembered homes—as with birds or butterflies or deer or fish. Those returns that are lodged indelibly, unconsciously, instinctively in the mind. But migrations suggest intentions or purposes. Some choice and, if not choice, decisions. And if not decisions, options, albeit difficult ones. But the sense of return in the Door of No Return is one of irrecoverable losses of those very things that make returning possible. A place to return to, a way of being, familiar sights and sounds, familiar smells, a welcome perhaps, but a place, welcome or not.[2]

Words like origins and beginnings are held with suspicion and skepticism in our postmodern and deconstructed poststructural era. The aftermath of the "theory wars," with their frontal assault on the slightest appearance of anything that appeared to offer a grand or universalizing narrative, remains with us still, even if claims of "theory's demise" now abound. However, the impact of those debates continues to wreak havoc on any claim that seeks to offer what appears to be a foundational narrative of any kind, thus guaranteeing the continuing insidious influences of "theory."[3] In the realm of diaspora studies and, in particular, Black diaspora studies, "origins" and "beginnings" have been largely assumed rather than given careful and sustained thought about what they might mean. Indeed, the debate has been characterized more by what is meant by the term "diaspora" than, for example, why diaspora in the first instance (after all, it could have been something else).[4] And even when the move has been to the "uses of diaspora," a certain shortfall remains evident in the conversation. Thus, what we end up getting is a debate that has largely focused on what is a diaspora and who is or might be missing from it as opposed to what diaspora forces us to contend with historically and in the present moment.[5]

I hope to offer a slight revision and thus to intervene in the conversation from a different place, opening up the dialogue in a manner that stakes a claim for a more rigorous and meaningful Black diaspora studies that takes anti-Blackness as central to the colonial project and its aftermath. Such a shift, in my view, has to take 1492 and transatlantic slavery as central, if not foundational, to Black diaspora studies. A serious and rigorous engagement with 1492 and transatlantic slavery keeps important elements of the Black diaspora story in play, forcing understandings of contemporary movements in light of the historical tremors of European expansion.[6] Such a position brings Indigenous populations to the debate not as a surprise but rather as a fundamental force in the reordering of knowledges that European Enlightenment and domination unleashed on a host of other cultures and nations in what we now call the Americas, and then extends outward globally. Thus, the profound impact of the remaking of the globe on European terms comes into clearer view. Such a claim is one that will take seriously what Walter Mignolo, drawing on Frantz Fanon and Sylvia Wynter, has recently termed the "geopolitics of economy." By this, Mignolo is keen to distinguish the geopolitics of economy from political economy, which, in his view, a view I have come to share, "can only tell part of the story, the story of Western capitalism as seen by its own agents and intellectuals." The claim made by Mignolo is one that neither denies nor diminishes political economy as a major part of the story; rather, it understands political economy as only part of the story.[7] Indeed, the critique that I shall proffer later in this chapter concerning the limits of settler colonialism's discourse is in part my discomfort with the waning of a radical critique of capitalism among some of its articulators.

It is my contention that Black diasporic studies only matter to the extent that such inquiries tell the alternate and much more disturbing story of global capitalism's apparent triumph and concurrently the attempts to resist it and undo its impacts in the past, present, and future. Instead, what is at stake is an analysis that tells the tale of the cost of European expansion as more than a story of economics (an idea that does not really exist in such fashion in some precontact cultures). I have written elsewhere that diaspora discourse matters because such discourses are the B-side to the celebratory narratives of globalization (especially in the academy).[8] In this view, diaspora narratives temper and offer other indices of globalization's history and its impact, as well as its present, so that modernity's vicious charms may be unmasked and the consequences laid bare. Diaspora then is about the historical unfolding of Europe's run at global domination but also about the continuous refusal of that domination by various global forces since its inception. Significantly, diaspora is about the making of meaningful lives within the context of Euro-Western Enlightenment and modernity—both as products of it and crucially as resignifiers, inventors, and originators of what can only be described as discrepant modernities for those who have borne the brunt of Europe's expansionist practices.[9]

My comments are deeply influenced by the methods of Stuart Hall's "Cultural Studies and Its Theoretical Legacies." While Hall's essay is not a direct engagement with diaspora studies, it is instructive about the politics of intellectual work and the demand that intellectual work should be about something. Hall's argument is made in regard to his own partial accounting of the history of cultural studies as a formation and an intervention into the work that scholarship, at least radical or progressive scholarship, seeks to do in the world. I take that demand quite seriously in what follows for Black diaspora studies as well. I, too, believe that a Black diaspora studies is about a particular and specific intellectual politics, which is meant to do something in the world. Part of its intellectual politics demands that we take certain kinds of knowledge seriously in diaspora studies in a way that such knowledge matters beyond the institutional confines of universities, their programs, our conferences, and our publications. I am also fully aware of the academy's attempt to matter without at all appearing to do so. But that is the university in its most conservative functional guise.[10]

Black diaspora studies thus engages with the ways in which, as Lisa Brock, Robin D. G. Kelly, and Karen Sotiropoulos put it, it "serve[s] as both a political term with which to emphasize unifying experiences of African peoples dispersed by the slave trade and as an analytical term that enabled scholars to talk about Black communities across national boundaries."[11] In this way, diaspora as a conceptual turn is meant to do something. What that something is may still be up for grabs politically since politics is never a settled terrain or proposition. What is clear to me, however, is that diaspora cannot be adequately deployed as a term that means all kinds of movement across borders as has partly become evident in much scholarship and institutional posturing today (an issue I'll return to later). Indeed, there is something at stake in calling or naming a particular group a diaspora. A more historically rigorous definition is required as the word "diaspora" gets invoked and attached to all kinds of contemporary movements. The politics of diaspora should seek to impact the Euro-Western worldly organization of our globe, and if we take that as a political position then what might be at stake in Black diaspora studies comes further to the fore.

Black diaspora as a concise conceptual and political term allows us to begin to appreciate the enormity of the dispersal of those now known as Africans at a moment in European expansion and the tragic and complicated legacy of their brutal dispersal.[12] But a Black diaspora studies does not begin and end there. The dispersal that is in part set in motion by the genocide and near genocide of the Indigenous populations of the Americas has inaugurated the longest continual colonial resistance in recent human history. Any Black diaspora studies that does not take seriously the genocide and near genocide of Indigenous populations of the Americas alongside the commencement of African transatlantic slavery is in my view a diaspora studies not worth having at all. At the same time, any conceptual and discursive rendering of settler colonialism that does not seriously grapple with the far-reaching brutality of the invention of Black beings is also a politics not worth having. Thus, my ideas and work are also deeply influenced by Wynter's numerous essays on the European invention and proliferation of a "new world" that European Enlightenment expansion ushered in for all of us. Central to the idea of the "new world" is an understanding of the geopolitics of economy and the geopolitics of modernity's imaginary sphere that has followed in the wake of Europe's expansion into worlds it previously had not known—those worlds we have come to call in such fashion the Americas. Part of the story is how discourses of coloniality have come to mark even the ways in which we have dealt with these conceptual and material turns so that terms like "diaspora" can sometimes come to conceal crucial and important links and contexts for the materiality that diaspora also seeks to capture in its conceptual and political range. In this instance, the disappearance of Indigenous peoples from the diaspora conversation is a case in point. Partially understanding slavery in relation to Indigenous genocide and ongoing colonization means that more is at stake in the conception of diaspora that I attempt to work with. Part of the "more" that is at stake is a radical engagement with the category of the human, and thus with an order of knowledge and worldview that is complicated by the creative conditions of a Black discrepant modernity produced in the Americas from the myriad encounters of worldviews brutally cohering together in contradiction and mutuality to produce a different people continually since 1492. Indeed, the politically contentious phrase "new world" does hold both a negative and positive possibility and potentiality.[13]

Thus, transatlantic slavery is more than a political economy phenomena or history of early capitalist accumulation, it is a seismic human cultural shift in economy, thought, and culture and in human alterability.[14] Transatlantic slavery, along with the brutal theft of Indigenous territories, is the engine that has driven capitalism and its various global incarnations for the last five hundred years plus, as well as European and indeed global thought.[15] Such a claim is immediately evident to most, but its deployment always seems to lodge the story only at the juncture of political economy as though that is the beginning and the end. Instead, we need to think about transatlantic slavery and Indigenous colonization as a cultural revolution that is still unfolding in ways that remain deeply traumatic but that now are also complicatedly implicating and entangling, which makes the pinpointing of victims and victimizers much more difficult to demarcate.[16] Recognizing the complications and "the intervention of history," as Hall puts it, can help us to better work with the still unfolding impact of Indigenous colonization and transatlantic slavery. Following Wynter we might understand 1492 and transatlantic slavery as ushering in new forms of human and social life in which the European comes to name and order the world on the terms of their cosmo-political, religio-social worldview—or, more plainly, European cultural foundations of their knowledge systems.

Thus, in my view, Black diaspora studies is implicated in the unraveling of this "new world view," which, as Mignolo states, involves the "control of money, and control of meaning and being," which are "parallel processes" in Europe's reordering of the globe on its Judeo-Christian philosophical terms.[17] From this perspective Black diaspora studies is concerned with the remaking and the resignifying of the category of the human beyond the boundaries imposed on it in a post-1492 and after worldview for which revisions have been made through and by a host of various political and cultural struggles.[18] The fundamental question and concern of Black diaspora studies it seems to me is to make sense of, to analyze, what the events of 1492 and their aftermath set into motion, and how various configurations of peoples have dealt with these events in myriad ways for which the language of resistance and domination is now wholly inadequate, but still sometimes partially useful.

Thus, it remains an enigma to me why so much of the Black diaspora debate has not seriously asked the question of why "diaspora"? In many respects, this is a question that concerns the politics of history and the ways in which such politics and histories can be mobilized for global justice. In this regard, historians of Atlantic history seem to have reached a crucially important place in their debates—the recognition of how the global impact of the European expansion has reshaped the globe on Euro-Western terms.[19] The ideas birthed in the context of the Atlantic world have been central to the ways in which European coloniality spread its global reach and thus the ways in which many other diasporas have come into being. Peter Linebaugh and Marcus Rediker's rather useful metaphor of the "many-headed hydra" is apt for thinking the historical and contemporary peregrinations of Euro-Western reordering of the globe post-1492. In this regard, capitalism as an organizing structure and new emergent ideas about humanness emerge as the most salient examples of that reshaping, and Atlantic historians have been front and center in demonstrating the global historical reach and impact of both economy and culture—in fact, of how the two might indeed be one.

Instead, much of the noise in Black diaspora studies has been about what some see as too central a focus on the Atlantic world, in essence a juggling for comparative equality of seas. Since the two decades after the publication of Paul Gilroy's *The Black Atlantic,* the desire to displace the Atlantic as foundational to Black diaspora studies has been a constant in the debate. It seems to me that there is a fundamental misunderstanding at work in the debate. To insist upon the world-changing impact of the ongoing colonization of the Americas and transatlantic slavery as central to Black diaspora studies is neither to argue for exceptionalism nor to produce a singular grand narrative of modernity's birth, since, as Sibylle Fischer writes, "heterogeneity is a congenital condition of modernity." Fischer further argues: "If we do not take into account to what extent modernity is a product of the New World, to what extent the colonial experience shaped modernity—in Europe and elsewhere—politically, economically, and aesthetically, and to what extent modernity is a heterogeneous, internally diverse, even contradictory phenomenon that constituted and revolutionized itself in the process of transculturation, then, obviously, talk of modernity is just a reinstantiation of a Eurocentric particularism parading as universalism."[20] I find in Fischer an important point of departure for thinking about 1492 and transatlantic slavery in the context of debates concerning diaspora, transnationalism, and settler colonialism. The departure concerns itself with the ways in which the Atlantic zone functions to put in place the mechanisms for the production of the resources (material, intellectual, and otherwise) for Europe to make its global play. Thus, a position like Fischer's runs counter to the kind of critique that has for so long been the mainstay of Black diaspora studies and the Atlantic refusal.

Take, for example, Paul Zeleza's critique of Paul Gilroy in which he suggests that "the studies of diaspora agency and originality" are valorized. Zeleza correctly acknowledges that Gilroy's version is only one part of a complicated and entangled context that comes to be read as the whole. Zeleza faults "cosmopolitan intellectuals" for peddling such analyses, not mentioning that he too might be read within that group, as he reports that he travels with a Canadian passport, resides in the US, and travels to Africa often, making him a member of what he terms the "new or contemporary African diaspora."[21] But even more important, it might have been useful to Zeleza's critique of Gilroy if he could have at least positioned Africans' complicated complicity with the production of the "new world" as Saidiya Hartman's *Lose Your Mother: A Journey along the Atlantic Slave Route* has so retraumatizingly and brilliantly done. As I have stated before, not all movement across borders makes a diaspora, and while it is politically useful to make crucial distinctions about forms of migration, the Black being out of which the ideas of anti-Blackness are invented against have no easy shores to return to.

It seems to me that part of what it means to speak of a Black diaspora is to account for the ways in which the possibility of return to an imaged or real homeland is always foreclosed and profoundly impossible. The impossibility is conditioned by the brutal dispersal, along with the severe cultural interruptions and the intervention of history that brought new attachments, subjectivities, and identifications into being or formation. Thus, not all contemporary continental African migration might or can count as diasporic even though a certain political logic requires it to be so given the all-encompassing logics and practices of anti-Black formations in the West. There is a qualitative difference between the now clear impossibility of return for, say, many Somalis and that of, let's say, some South Africans. Such claims are difficult evaluative ones to make, but taken within a rubric of cultural identity and the very materiality of the nation-state as a point of return makes the evaluation a useful one even if it still does have some unresolved fault lines in its conceptuality. The primary issue to consider nonetheless is how the *longue durée* of Euro-Western domination has impacted the complicated postcolonial politics set in motion through the events of the last five hundred plus years, which continues to produce new subjects for the Black diaspora out of a post-1492 and postcolonial Africa. Our debates have failed to adequately think those moments and conditions.

I would suggest that much of the energy spent on trying to displace the Atlantic Black diaspora is wrongheaded and could be better deployed engaging the foundational conditions, which make the Atlantic the paradigmatic example—and not the exceptional case. In this regard, too, we must not be sidetracked by linguistic differences. I am not suggesting that language and regions (obviously) are not important to these concerns, but what I am trying to stress is that the Atlantic region, with its history of territorial theft, transatlantic slavery, and genocide, is the *incubator* of a set of conditions that we have inherited as a global situation organized on the basis of Euro-Western traditions of thought and the human, from which we must figure out how to extricate ourselves. A sober conversation about what that extrication means will account for political economy, cultural borrowing, sharing, and mixing, and their outcomes and impacts—contradictory, antagonistic, and otherwise—and our entangled histories of power, knowledge, and land.

The difficulty of this project belies the political stakes involved. In particular, the Americas and the African continent offer different and difficult focal points in this debate. Africa remains a difficult and troubling place of Black diaspora identification. The story of Africa is a complex one for "new world" Black peoples who make use of Africa as well as make "Africa" in numerous and many different ways.[22] The making of reparation with Africa and the "new world" is of particular importance here too. As Jamaica Kincaid has presciently written about Caribbean peoples, they are a people who must make themselves native to a place they are not from. In the idea is the genocide of the Taíno, the near genocide of the Caribs, and the brutal evidence of transatlantic slavery. Stacking Kincaid's claim next to the announcement by the Nigerian minister of culture apologizing for slavery complicates the picture. The public relations impact of such a story simultaneously limns the rupture and desire for a "new world" reconnection with Africa at the same time that it reinstates the foundational importance of transatlantic slavery to a Black global body politic. But in the statement's discursive effect is the recognition of the ongoing tremors of transatlantic slavery on the continent and in the diaspora. All of this occurs in a context when yet another revival of Indigenous resistance to the colonial condition is taking place in various spheres across the Americas from North to South.

The consequences for diaspora studies of not taking 1492 and transatlantic slavery seriously are many. But since I have been mainly interested in addressing this argument to the institutional imperatives of producing knowledge in the university, I will conclude there. Everywhere these days there are diaspora programs, centers, conferences, and seminars springing up. In part, many of these circumstances are fueled by the older and newer migratory populations forced, planned, and unplanned. In fact, if the post-1492 world bequeathed us anything it has been the massive shifts in population around the globe in its aftermath, the first such movement being transatlantic slavery and continuing since.

What I fault most in the debate on Black diaspora conceptuality is its reluctance to grapple with the central claim of the European Enlightenment and modernity—to make a better human—a human that is fundamentally always positioned against Black being and indeed is dependent upon logics of anti-Blackness that produce Black beings as nonhuman. Grappling with that claim would prove useful and powerful for Black diaspora studies because it is in fact the various ways in which deployments of Western conceptions of the human function that continue to be the basis from which diasporic sensibilities, consciousness, and a potential politics might arise. In the case of "new world Blacks" the impossibility of any return imagined or real (even when individuals and groups physically return) means that the break that transatlantic slavery produced for some people who identify with Africa is an identification that can only be sutured through various and different kinds of performances of politics that place Africa within their discursive reach and imagination.[23]

Derek Walcott's divided tongue best captures the actual place of Africa when he asked rhetorically "choose between my English tongue and the Africa that I love," but he also furnishes that divided tongue, come self, with an insistence on a hopeful self who has "no nation but the imagination," allowing for a world citizenship that entangles, implicates, and complicates anew by refusing one of modernity's central inventions—the nation-state.

By so doing Walcott offers a useful lens from which to make reparation with the ongoing traumas of a world reconfigured on the basis of Euro-Western terms. Walcott seizes the moment to reside in the interstices of a creole and thus evolving sensibility and reality, what we might call a new indigenism, or he at least points to indigeneity not as identity but as process.

A radical Black diaspora studies should engage conversations concerning the Atlantic region seriously, because the social and cultural revisions of the last five hundred years have produced asymmetrical positions that allow for a kind of "racial contract" based on class and gender in which some Black people enter a revised Euro-Western body politic.[24] The same cannot be said for the large masses of Indigenous peoples whom many still like to think of as extinct and or in the past, especially in parts of the Caribbean. Black diaspora politics might be about something—about how land, power, and knowledge have come together to enact and unfold one of the longest unbroken colonial periods in human history. It might help to provide a better explanation of the past and the ways in which current conceptions of the present find their sustenance in the past—ideologically and otherwise.

It is nonetheless my argument that Black diaspora studies takes us a long way toward refusing and offering better analyses of institutional and corporate multiculturalisms that mobilize difference as a commodity for corporate munificence. Additionally, it is a buttress against a postcolonial studies, a transnational and a globalization studies that refuses to complicate the tensions between old and new colonialisms and the ways in which empire in its old and new forms might be situated in a discontinuous continuum of Euro-Western ethno-domination. Significantly, diaspora sensibilities allow us to confront and engage the difficult and violent politics of modernity's invention of the nation-state and its inability to produce a space for the full expression of human possibility. Instead, the nation-state provides ethno-cultural identities as the basis of an imagined care for the self that always seems to fall short of full human status and expression. Such insights position the North Atlantic academy in a sphere of power for which our studies should attempt to mean something. It means not letting the university off the hook as a crucial link in global capitalism's domination in Euro-Western guise, because ideas have been the central ingredient in the geopolitics of the globe in the past five hundred years. In my view a Black diaspora studies that begins with the European attempt to conquer the Americas and the inauguration of transatlantic slavery limits nothing, but it opens up all the avenues for a more honest global conversation to occur about what that expansion set in motion. Furthermore, such Black diaspora studies should not step away from the difficult debate of making life in a place where the ethics of arrival can be fashioned through the brutal thefts of Euro-Western dominance and Indigenous claims to restore their stewardship of the lands. That is, how might Black diaspora studies, taking as central the transatlantic slavery invention of Black beings, engage the further dynamics of Black ontologies in the Americas?

Settler Colonialism's Limit, Its Complicity

It is precisely when Black ontologies are taken into consideration that the language of settler colonialism might reach certain limits where its usefulness wanes. In particular, if it is agreed that Black peoples come into the world in part as an outcome of European colonial expansion and that the invention of Black peoples both aids the practice of settler colonial societies and simultaneously undermines it by producing new indigenisms of the West, then further complication arise for our studies and politics. The invention of Black peoples troubles understandings of land, place, indigeneity, and belonging, because the brutal rupture that produces Blackness breaks bodies and identities—indeed personhood—from all those claims now used to mark resistance to modernity's unequal distribution of its various accumulations. In this sense, it might be more precise to think of indigeneity as more a process than an identity, and I would further suggest that to invoke it as identity is to accede to Europe's Enlightenment and modernist anthropological project of categorizing humans on its terms and logics. Indeed, peoples became Indigenous in the midst of the colonial project. Such logics allow European modernity to fetishize its category-making schemas of marking, naming, placing, and knowing.

Indeed, some contemporary arguments concerning the ongoing colonization of Indigenous people in North America do not adequately account for the ways in which a sustained and ongoing critique of capitalism is required. Such a critique would recognize the nonhuman status of the Black and the ways in which Black peoples' legacy as a commodity continues to haunt our barely human status in the present. By bypassing such an engagement, those arguments and discourses find themselves embedded in anti-Black thought and logics. As commodities—that is, Black peoples—of the colonial project, they/we always remain outside modernity's various inventions, especially those of the human (gender, sexuality, disability, queer, trans, and so forth), but always overdetermined by racialogical thinking. I must point out that I am not attempting to produce a negative dialectic of oppression in which

Black people might be marked as the most oppressed, nor am I attempting to produce some kind of oppression exceptionalism or sweepstakes. Rather, my aim is to point to the profound ways in which Black personhood is directly implicated in what Wynter calls genres of the human—that is, their ongoing production and Blackness's ongoing devaluation under such terms. Let me be clear, then, in each instance a normative Black politics struggles to be seen within these genres, genres that can never seem to contain Blackness in any way that recognizes Black being and thus constantly point to the anti-Black foundations of contemporary identity making.[25]

As Wynter has pointed out, our environmental destruction began with Columbus's voyages to the Americas and the removal of Africans from that continent and accelerated with the Industrial Revolution, which is often marked as being from 1750 to 1850. She suggests that a certain kind of bovarism—that is, the idea of great achievement—has profoundly hindered our more mutual possibilities, especially in the West.[26] It is also precisely within that period that the invention of Black *nonpersonhood* comes into being in multiple and conflicting ways. This invention was indeed necessary in that "eventful moment" because it helped to inaugurate the terms of freedom and unfreedom that remain with us today.[27] It is precisely by reading Black nonpersonhood alongside the complicated dynamics of Indigenous colonization that a more fruitful conversation about our contemporary moment might be had. For example, in the contemporary Canadian context the almost universal silence on Indigenous Conservatives (such as Leona Aglukkaq, Patrick Brazeau, Shawn Atleo, and others) in the then Harper government and extragovernmental organizations is a case in point. Very little attention has been critically paid to these individual "ethnic" neoliberals in debates on settler colonialism.[28]

So, for example, if we return to contemporary debates concerning settler colonialism, in its critical articulation its utterances would have to engage the conditions and ideas of the plantation, the reservation, and the ghetto, revealing their euphemisms and most importantly their material practices and realities as the logics and practices of anti-Blackness and therefore coloniality. Thus, a set of relational logics requires us to take seriously that the colonial project is a project skilled at producing what can too easily appear to be nonrelational dynamics. "Priority neighborhoods" have nothing to do with *banlieus*, and none of them have anything to do with European colonial practices in the past and the present-continuing and definitely nothing to do with reservations. Such pedagogies of coloniality require us to reside in notions of the human that have as their foundation global anti-Black logics, for it is upon the body of the Black being that coloniality configured and practiced its most significant antihuman projects of management and reordering. Zainab Amadahy and Bonita Lawrence write: "From Indigenous perspectives, the true horror of slavery was that it has created generations of 'de-culturalized' Africans, denied knowledge of language, clan, family, and land base, denied even knowledge of who their nations are."[29] Such thought fails to comprehend the inventive being of Blackness as only possible in the context of the terrible upheavals this chapter has been addressing and that simultaneously rely on an anthropologic discourse of origins lost. Consequently, the Black body is not the most abject body in a war of abjection and oppression, but the Black body is the template of how to produce abjection of/for the other.

Such social and political configurations require us to contend with the ways in which the seductions of capitalism in late modernity do not merely simply and easily replicate colonialism's "Red, White, and Black" past.[30] After all, a Black man has been in the White House and in the Canadian nation-state some Indigenous people were in Stephen Harper's government of austerity. Nonetheless, those bodies are engaged in a project for which the trajectory is one of our collective death. One cannot stress enough capitalism's founding in death and its constant and continuous trajectory toward death as enacted on Indigenous and Black bodies.

At the same time, given the intimate crossing of Blackness and capitalism, "Black freedom" as an "authentic" possibility inaugurates a challenge to the imagination to produce new modes of living that might be in accord with some of the most radical global "Indigenous" calls for a different kind of world. It is precisely in the moment that Black personhood can be accorded its full human status that new indigenisms enter the world, I would argue. A radical recognition that new indigenisms are possible is a significant move away from Euro-Western foundational understandings of the globe.

Toward the, or a, Decolonial Project

In my view, then, a *pure decolonial project* attempts to unmoor the silences that condition our contemporary moment by risking identity in favor of a politics of thought. By "politics of thought" I mean to signal the ways in which coloniality's most profound operations work at the level of what it means to know and how knowing places some bodies out of place. The demand here is to think new possibilities for human life beyond capitalist modernity. In a postcommunist world and a neoliberal globe, thinking, articulating, and moving toward different and new modes of human life is our present challenge. As a *pure decolonial project* unmasks, unearths, repositions, rereads, reworks, and remakes, it also works to produce new modes of relational logics and conditions in which the intimacies that European colonial expansion produced for us might be refashioned.[31]

These new modes call for moving beyond and may be even against the "romance stories" of a linear and progressive liberation, especially for those who have been formerly colonized, into the bounty of rights and freedoms. To refuse such a "romance story" is not to deny history, but rather to account for the ways in which history might offer us a better calculation of how to alter the human yet again in our time. Such an alter-native will require the production of "new indigenisms" of our globe, and those new indigenisms will require of us conversations, debates, politics, and maybe even policies that are centered in the "catastrophic culture" that has brought us together. Such a catastrophe also produced and continues to produce profound human possibilities, practices, and potentialities, as Kamau Brathwaite points out. If neoliberalism does anything, it attempts to interrupt human creativity and imagination. A *pure decolonial* project works the ruins of catastrophe to produce more hopeful tales of our present human intimacies and to allow the opportunity to reimagine the self anew again.

Notes

1   Dionne Brand, *Map to the Door of No Return: Notes to Belonging* (New York: Random House, 2001), 21.
2   Brand, *Map*, 24.
3   By theory I mean that body of abstracted knowledge of the post-1968 cultural debate and turn in the academy influenced by a retreat from Marxism and an announcement of a New Left; a body of knowledge largely but not exclusively European in its influences and references but mostly characterized by its valorization in the Euro-American academy as the site of the most serious and engaging mode of thought.
4   Pan-Africanism, internationalism, and various kinds of other political ideologies could also have been useful terms for thinking and mobilizing transnational Black identifications. The specificity of why diaspora is the chosen term is not as well thought out in the literature as it might appear.
5   Diaspora as a concept has been made use of in more utilitarian fashion even by those who have sought to think with it in ways that produce ruptures for various taken-for-granted Black formations. Here, I am thinking of Paul Gilroy's *The Black Atlantic: Modernity and Double Consciousness* (Cambridge: Harvard University Press, 1993) and *Against Race: Imagining Political Culture*

beyond the Color Line (Cambridge: Harvard University Press, 2000), which offer his most sustained discussion of what and how he makes use of the term. I am also thinking of Brent Edwards, "The Uses of Diaspora," *Social Text* 19, no. 1(2001): 45–73, and *The Practice of Diaspora: Literature, Translation, and the Rise of Black Internationalism* (Cambridge: Harvard University Press, 2003).

6 See the following works by Sylvia Wynter: "1492: A New World View," in *Race, Discourse, and the Origin of the Americas*, ed. Vera Hyatt and Rex Nettleford (Washington, DC: Smithsonian Institute, 1995), 5–57; "The Pope Must Have Been Drunk, the King of Castile a Madman: Culture as Actuality, and the Caribbean Rethinking Modernity," in *The Reordering of Culture: Latin America, the Caribbean and Canada (In the Hood)*, ed. Alvina Ruprecht and Cecilia Taiana (Ottawa: Carleton University Press, 1995), 17–42; "Columbus, the Ocean Blue, and Fables That Stir the Mind: To Reinvent the Study of Letters," in *Poetics in the Americas: Race, Founding and Textuality*, ed. Bainard Cowain and Jefferson Humphries (Baton Rouge: Louisiana State University, 1997), 141–64; and "On How We Mistook the Map for the Territory, and Re-Imprisoned Ourselves in Our Unbearable Wrongness of Being, of Désêtre: Black Studies toward the Human Project," in *Not Only the Master's Tools: African-American Studies in Theory and Practice*, ed. Lewis R. Gordon and Jane Anna Gordon (Boulder: Paradigm Publishers, 2006), 107–72, throughout which Wynter has engaged the fundamental philosophical implications of the reordering of the globe on Europe's terms. See also Peter Hulme, *Colonial Encounters: Europe and the Native Caribbean, 1492–1797* (London: Routledge, 1986), in which he demonstrates how various ideas came into being as a way to manage Europe's encounter with the Indigenous Indies; and see, most recently, Walter Mignolo, *The Idea of Latin America* (Oxford: Blackwell Publishing, 2005), in which he argues and reanimates the conversation about the invention of the Americas by dissecting the idea of Latin America.

7 Mignolo, *Idea*, 153.

8 See Rinaldo Walcott, "Salted Cod . . . : Black Canada and Diasporic Sensibilities," in *Reading the Image: Poetics of the Black Diaspora*, curator Andrea Fatona (Chatham: Thames Art Gallery, 2006).

9 I am using the term "Euro-Western" to signal the ethno-centered organization of what we have come to call the West. It is a term meant not only to signal Europe but also those satellite settler colonies like the US, Canada, Australia, and so forth, which understand themselves to be Euro-Western in founding and organization. However, as much of my argument suggests or implies, the West itself is now so complicated that it would be a conceptual problem to take "new world" Black people out of it. Thus, Euro-Western works here to anchor the particular discourses that I am addressing to a Europe that, at a certain historical moment, understood itself as a mono-ethnic region insofar as its expansionist project was concerned.

10 Bill Readings, *The University in Ruins* (Cambridge: Harvard University Press, 1996), offers a critique of cultural studies institutions and remains relevant for these concerns.

11 Lisa Brock, Robin D. G. Kelly, and Karen Sotiropoulos, "Editors' Introduction," *Radical History Review*, no. 87 (2003): 1–3.

12 I use the term "Black diaspora" as opposed to African diaspora or Afrodiaspora because for me the impossibility and the complicatedness of any return to an imaged or lost homeland called Africa complicates the ethno-distinctiveness of the latter terms. I understand the instability of the invented, always uncertain marker, Black as holding many possibilities for reparations within the new world where Blackness in its most potent forms was invented. For further discussion, see Rinaldo Walcott, "Pedagogy and Trauma: The Middle Passage, Slavery, and the Problem of Creolization," in *Between Hope and Despair: Pedagogy and the Representation of Historical Trauma*, ed. Roger I. Simon, Sharon Rosenberg, and Claudia Eppert (Lanham, MD: Rowman and Littlefield, 2000), 135–52.

13 This is why the debate on reparations in the US and elsewhere has been such an impoverished one. The inability to think both the genocide of Indigenous populations alongside ongoing colonization means that any meaningful debate on reparations for transatlantic slavery proceeds on the terms of European conceptions of the world. And, in such a worldview, reparations for those crimes only become thinkable in the aftermath of World War II and the Universal Declaration of Human Rights. Thus, any conversation about reparations must take seriously the issues of land, power, and coloniality/colonialism as a central aspect of its purview.

14 In particular I am thinking of the many new world religions and spiritualities, which have ushered in numerous cosmologies of the world. These practices, ideas, and beliefs have come out of the brutal encounters of European expansion, but reading them only with a context of brutality would not adequately account for the collective appeal, meaning, and power they hold today.

15 See Eric Williams, *Capitalism and Slavery* (London: Andre Deutsch, 1964); Walter Rodney, *How Europe Underdeveloped Africa* (Washington, DC: Howard University Press, 1982); and, more recently, Sakia Sassen, *Territory, Authority, Rights: From Medieval to Global Assemblages* (Princeton: Princeton University Press, 2006), in particular, chapter 3, "Assembling National Political Economies Centered on Imperial Geographies," 74–140.

16 I am thinking of recent elections in Latin America; Indigenous resistance in North America (most recently Six Nations/Caledonia in what we call Canada); and the immigrant/migrant movement in what we call the US.

17 Mignolo, *Idea*, 153.

18 National independence movements, the US civil rights movement, Indigenous movements, and various kinds of land reclamation movements have all forced revisions of the category of the human, making it more expansive. We also must see feminist and queer movements within a similar light—a resignifying and expanding of the terms of humanhood.

19 See, for example, Afua Cooper, *The Hanging of Angélique: The Untold Story of Canadian Slavery and the Burning of Old Montréal* (Toronto: Harper Collins, 2006); Peter Linebaugh and Marcus Rediker, *The Many-Headed Hydra: Sailors, Slaves, Commoners, and the Hidden History of the Revolutionary Atlantic* (Boston: Beacon Press, 2000); Simon Schama, *Rough Crossings: Britain, the Slaves, and the American Revolution* (Toronto: Viking Canada, 2005); and, Ronald Segal, *The Black Diaspora: Five Centuries of the Black Experience outside of Africa* (New York: Farrar, Straus and Giroux, 1995).

20 Sibylle Fischer, *Modernity Disavowed: Haiti and the Cultures of Slavery in the Age of Revolution* (Durham, NC: Duke University Press, 2004), 22–24.

21 Paul Zeleza, "Rewriting the African Diaspora: Beyond the Black Atlantic," *African Affairs* 104, no. 414, (2005): 35, 38.

22 Again, it is crucial to keep in mind the ways in which various new world religions call on "Africa"; but also the ways in which various new world protest movements have made use of Africa as mostly a concern about this continent; thus, Africa means and comes into play meaning many different things, some of which are in accord with the continent itself but much of which is not.

23 I am thinking here of the existence of the Kriolles in Sierra Leone, of Liberia, and movements/religions like Rastafari.

24 I borrow the term "racial contract" from Charles Wright Mills.

25 Here my thinking is very much influenced by Lindon Barrett, *Blackness and Value: Seeing Double* (New York: Cambridge University Press, 1999).

26 See Katherine McKittrick and Sylvia Wynter, an interview in *Sylvia Wynter: On Being Human as Praxis* (Durham, NC: Duke University Press, 2015).

27 I borrow the phrase from Geoffrey Hartman.

28 See, for example, Bonita Lawrence and Enakshi Dua, "Decolonizing Antiracism," *Social Justice* 32, no. 4 (2005): 120–43; and, Zainab Amahady and Bonita Lawrence, "Indigenous Peoples and Black People in Canada: Settlers or Allies?," in *Breaching the Colonial Contract: Anti-Colonialism in the US and Canada*, ed. Arlo Kempf (New York: Springer, 2009), 105–36.

29 Amahady and Lawrence, "Indigenous Peoples," 127.

30 See Wynter, "1492," and Frank B. Wilderson III, *Red, White & Black: Cinema and the Structure of U.S. Antagonisms* (Durham, NC: Duke University Press, 2010).

31 Kamau Brathwaite articulates what he calls "the literature of catastrophe" in *Middle Passages: A Lecture*, an audio CD (Toronto: Sandberry Press, 2006), as the by-product of European colonial expansion. Brathwaite points out that this catastrophe of colonialism produces death, racism, environmental degradation, and so on but it also produces jazz, Caribbean, African American, and Indigenous literatures, and other cultural forms and practices that have reshaped the globe and human life. I adapt his term to articulate a culture of catastrophe, which draws on his insights.

References

Amahady, Zainab, and Bonita Lawrence, 2009. "Indigenous Peoples and Black People in Canada: Settlers or Allies?" In *Breaching the Colonial Contract: Anti-Colonialism in the US and Canada,* edited by Arlo Kempf, 105–36. New York: Springer, 2009.

Barrett, Lindon. 1999. *Blackness and Value: Seeing Double.* New York: Cambridge University Press.

Brathwaite, Kamau. 2006. *Middle Passages: A Lecture.* Audio CD. Toronto: Sandberry Press.

Brock, Lisa, Robin D. G. Kelly, and Karen Sotiropoulos. 2003. "Editors' Introduction." *Radical History Review,* no. 87: 1–3.

Cohen, Robin. 1997. *Global Diasporas: An Introduction.* Seattle: University of Washington Press.

Cooper, Afua. 2006. *The Hanging of Angélique: The Untold Story of Canadian Slavery and the Burning of Old Montréal.* Toronto: Harper Collins.

Edwards, Brent Hayes. 2001. "The Uses of Diaspora." *Social Text* (19, no.1): 45–73.

Edwards, Brent Hayes. 2003. *The Practice of Diaspora: Literature, Translation, and the Rise of Black Internationalism.* Cambridge: Harvard University Press.

Fischer, Sibylle. 2004. *Modernity Disavowed: Haiti and the Cultures of Slavery in the Age of Revolution.* Durham, NC: Duke University Press.

Gilroy, Paul. 1993. *The Black Atlantic: Modernity and Double Consciousness.* Cambridge: Harvard University Press.

Gilroy, Paul. 2000. *Against Race: Imagining Political Culture beyond the Color Line.* Cambridge: Harvard University Press.

Hall, Stuart. 1992. "Cultural Studies and Its Theoretical Legacies." In *Cultural Studies,* edited by Lawrence Grossberg, Cary Nelson, and Paula Treichler. New York: Routledge.

Hall, Stuart. 2000. "Cultural Identity and Diaspora." In *Diaspora and Visual Culture: Representing Africans and Jews,* edited by Nicholas Mirzoeff. London: Routledge.

Hulme, Peter. 1986. *Colonial Encounters: Europe and the Native Caribbean 1492–1797.* London: Routledge.

Kincaid, Jamaica. 1992. "In the Garden: Flowers of Evil." *New Yorker,* October 5, 154–59.

Lawrence, Bonita, and Enakshi Dua. 2005. "Decolonizing Antiracism." *Social Justice* 32, no. 4 (2005): 120–43.

Linebaugh, Peter, and Marcus Rediker. 2000. *The Many-Headed Hydra: Sailors, Slaves, Commoners, and the Hidden History of the Revolutionary Atlantic.* Boston: Beacon Press.

Mignolo, Walter. 2005. *The Idea of Latin America.* Oxford: Blackwell.

Mills, Charles Wright. 1997. *The Racial Contract.* Ithaca: Cornell University Press.

Readings, Bill. 1996. *The University in Ruins.* Cambridge: Harvard University Press.

Rodney, Walter. 1982. *How Europe Underdeveloped Africa*. Washington, DC: Howard University Press.

Sassen, Saskia. 2006. *Territory, Authority, Rights: From Medieval to Global Assemblages*. Princeton: Princeton University Press.

Schama, Simon. 2005. *Rough Crossings: Britain, the Slaves, and the American Revolution*. Toronto: Viking Canada.

Segal, Ronald. 1995. *The Black Diaspora: Five Centuries of the Black Experience outside of Africa*. New York: Farrar, Straus and Giroux.

Walcott, Derek. 1986. *Collected Poems: 1948–1984*. New York: Farrar, Straus and Giroux.

Walcott, Rinaldo. 2000. "Pedagogy and Trauma: The Middle Passage, Slavery, and the Problem of Creolization." In *Between Hope and Despair: Pedagogy and the Representation of Historical Trauma*, edited by Roger I. Simon, Sharon Rosenberg, and Claudia Eppert. Lanham, MD: Rowman and Littlefield.

Walcott, Rinaldo. 2006. "Salted Cod . . . : Black Canada and Diasporic Sensibilities." *Reading the Image: Poetics of the Black Diaspora*. Curator Andrea Fatona. Chatham: Thames Art Gallery.

Wilderson, Frank B., III. 2010. *Red, White & Black: Cinema and the Structure of U.S. Antagonisms*. Durham, NC: Duke University Press.

Williams, Eric. 1964. *Capitalism and Slavery*. London: Andre Deutsch.

Wynter, Sylvia. 1995. "1492: A New World View." In *Race, Discourse, and the Origin of the Americas*, edited by Vera Hyatt and Rex Nettleford, 5–57. Washington, DC: Smithsonian Institute.

Wynter, Sylvia. 1995. "The Pope Must Have Been Drunk, the King of Castile a Madman: Culture as Actuality, and the Caribbean Rethinking Modernity." In *The Reordering of Culture: Latin America, the Caribbean and Canada (In the Hood)*, edited by Alvina Ruprecht and Cecilia Taiana, 17–42. Ottawa: Carleton University Press.

Wynter, Sylvia. 1997. "Columbus, the Ocean Blue, and Fables That Stir the Mind: To Reinvent the Study of Letters." In *Poetics in the Americas: Race, Founding, and Textuality*, edited by Bainard Cowain and Jefferson Humphries, 141–64. Baton Rouge: Louisiana State University.

Wynter, Sylvia. 2006. "On How We Mistook the Map for the Territory, and Re-Imprisoned Ourselves in Our Unbearable Wrongness of Being, of Désêtre: Black Studies toward the Human Project." In *Not Only the Master's Tools: African-American Studies in Theory and Practice*, edited by Lewis R. Gordon and Jane Anna Gordon, 107–72. Boulder, CO: Paradigm Publishers.

Zeleza, Paul. 2005. "Rewriting the African Diaspora: Beyond the Black Atlantic." *African Affairs* 104, no. 414: 35–68.

CHAPTER TWENTY

Chris Finley

Building Maroon Intellectual Communities

The coalition emerges out of your recognition that it's fucked up for you, in the same way that we've recognized that it's fucked up for us. I don't need your help. I just need you to recognize that this shit is killing you, too, however much more softly, you stupid mother-fucker, you know? —Fred Moten, *The Undercommons*

In April 2015, I attended a colloquium at the University of California at Riverside about settler colonialism and anti-Blackness, which is where many of the chapters in this anthology were first presented. I did not like a lot of what was said in Riverside because I could only compare what I heard with what I already knew and felt was true in relation to Indigenous studies. I also was not presenting a paper so I did not feel vulnerable or invested like other attendees of the colloquium. In other words, I liked the ideas of the scholars I was already familiar with but did not understand a lot of what was happening and, unfortunately, thought I did know. Then Denise Ferreira da Silva, who went toward the end of the day, started out her presentation by saying, "I hear a lot of people here today saying the same things." And, frankly, this blew my mind because that is not what I had heard or what I had witnessed. What I had been hearing was a lot of people talking over each other and not to each other. She went on to present a great paper, but I was trying to wrap my head around her first statement. I have a great deal of respect for Denise, and I have never stopped thinking about this idea that Black and Native people may be saying the same things, but with my Native studies and ethnic studies institutionalization all I can hear is difference when discussing settler colonialism and anti-Blackness. My reading of Denise's idea of sameness shall haunt this entire chapter. I will be critiquing my interpretation of native studies and ethnic studies and my own defense of Indigenous difference in order to try to theorize a method of discussing anti-Blackness and settler colonialism without reifying whether settler colonialism or anti-Blackness is worse or which analytic came first or is more significant. We all need to find a way to start working together within the academic industrial complex and let ethnic differences define us.

Without Black studies, there would be no Native studies. I owe a debt to Black theory, history, and the long history of Black intellectualism within the academic industrial complex. Currently, the analytic of settler colonialism is seen as sexy. This has not meant that nonnative people are suddenly recognizing native nation's sovereignty or the fraught relationship natives and non-natives have to the settler colonial nation. Many natives and nonnatives did support the encampment and the efforts of the water protectors in the No Dakota Access Pipeline movement that began in April 2016 and ended when the federal government burned down the encampment in February 2017. Some Black activists complained about the amount of resources native people received and the anti-Black racism that happened at the encampment. I'm not trying to support anti-Black racism in native communities, but why should native and other communities of color keep trying to pretend we are pure and are beyond supporting white supremacy? How can we build movements together that understand that we all have a lot to learn about each other and that we are going to make mistakes with each other? How can people of color get along in the academic industrial complex when discipline, history, possession, and scarcity define the institutionalization of ethnic studies?

This article uses Denise Ferreira da Silva's *Towards a Global Idea of Race* (2007) to discuss how struggles in ethnic studies to be a universal subject through being affected negatively by other affectable subjects is another struggle for postmodern subjectivity that actually doesn't benefit people of color as a whole. As Denise argues, striving to be a universal subject as an affectable subject will not make people of color less killable. We cannot pass into transparency even if we show how much more another affectable subject is. Being most uniquely affected by white supremacy through Enlightenment thinking, whether it is through being negatively affected by settler colonialism or slavery, does not ultimately lead to Black and Native people having a productive conversation with one another, because all we can do is talk about how anti-Black natives are because a few of our nations were slave-owning nations or how Black people are settlers. Simply name calling, naming this history of affectability, or "proving" through statistics which community is most damaged has not yet brought our communities together.[1]

In using the language of the academy, we are calling each other out without the respect we owe to each other. In other words, few of us are saying anything new or revolutionary because enlightenment provides us with the tools to critique and compare, but not to love and understand each other. The language of the academy is violent and institutionalized: you often need a degree and years of reading academic and political writing to even understand what we are trying to say to each other. Sometimes we don't even know what we are trying to say to each other.

Within the traditional framework of ethnic studies, Indigenous peoples can only be victims of settler colonial violence, which makes them disappeared or silenced in present discussions, or Indigenous peoples are the perpetrators of violence against Black people. In earlier ethnic studies models, there was an attempt made by communities of color to show how our oppressions overlapped and to try and organize from this place of shared oppression.[2] This did not work too well for too long because it isn't long before our messed up ideas about one another or ourselves float to the surface and we say and do something stupid. We should expect that we will not be perfect with one another. We should embrace failure in the attempt toward intimacy. After all, isn't working together a move toward intimacy? Hasn't this always been a bit icky, scary, and awkward? Why do we expect each other to be perfectly formed political subjects when we have all been institutionalized to think badly of each other and ourselves? One of my dear friends, political organizer Lee Ann Wang, theorizes that we need to prepare for things to go wrong as part of political organizing campaigns. None of us is completely right or good, so why do we act like political organizing is a sacred space where only whole, righteous subjects roam? We are all broken and cannot possibly have read everything, so we will be wrong sometimes. We live in a rape culture. None of us gets to be free of this even as we work toward critiquing heteropatriarchy and white supremacy. Living among humans and in the world is a true act of courage because, even with those working toward social justice, institutionalization and violence exist. We are all in this world, which is full of violence. This is not an excuse for bad behavior but an acknowledgment of the fact that we can try our best but still fall short of being perfect subjects. The call-out culture has only made the gap between the good and the wrong deeper and wider. We need to celebrate moments of truth and solidarity too.

Settler colonial studies and Native studies are not the same fields of study. We in Native studies know this and many people in Native studies use settler colonialism as an analytic and not strictly as an identity category to "rub up on and against." Not everyone in ethnic studies and beyond understands the critical distinctions between these fields of study, yet some scholars choose to discuss settler colonialism without or with very little mention of Native communities in the present moment or use analytics in the field of Native studies. This chapter would like to interrogate the trend of some work in ethnic and American studies that discusses settler colonialism or puts it in the title of an article or book, yet fails to discuss Native peoples or Native studies. Once again, Native peoples, Native studies, and Native land claims get engulfed, erased, and ignored by settlers and settler colonialism even though the author's intention may be to do the opposite work. But not everyone has read Eve Tuck and K. Wayne Yang's "Decolonization Is Not a Metaphor".[3] I do not say this to argue for the inclusion of Indigenous peoples, but I am making this claim and argument to ask for relationality, which is much deeper and decolonial than simple inclusion. I am asking for the recognition and political and social engagement with aboriginal life, which includes the intellectual work, lands, and nations of Indigenous peoples. I also have been thinking about how Indigenous peoples, or specifically myself, are also invested in settler colonialism (damage, recognition by settlers, focus on the loss). Just confessing our fucked experiences or our trauma is not enough.[4] As affectable subjects,[5] we are expected to confess how much we have been hurt by settler colonialism and loss. Native feminism, at its best, *theorizes* loss, rape, and land theft instead of simply *confessing* this as part of our identity and experience under the regime of settler colonialism.

Importantly, I am not making an argument to police and uphold ethnic studies scholarship segregation but want to produce work that actually brings us all closer together. I am deeply invested in talking and working with other people of color from lots of different communities. In other words, I do not want to participate in essentialist arguments, or epistemological arguments where we have to decide whether slavery and anti-Blackness, settler colonialism, land claims, or immigration is more significant or what came first. The battle for innocence and victimhood are the gold medals to be won in the oppression Olympics to represent and recognize ourselves as proper innocent (not intersectional) victims.[6]

There was a beautiful moment at the first critical ethnic studies conference in Riverside, California in 2011 when scholars of color started taking Native studies and Native peoples seriously. For me, this hope came from the sheer number of panels and plenary sessions discussing settler colonialism as an analytic and the fact there were Native studies scholars on almost every plenary session. Since Critical Ethnic Studies Association 2011, there has been some serious engagement with Native studies, and some Native studies scholarship has gained attention outside of Native studies. This is exciting. At the same time this is occurring, there also has been even more engagement with the analytic of settler colonialism, yet not more interest in Native studies or Native peoples or the idea that decolonization means giving the land back to Indigenous peoples. There is this idea in ethnic studies that you can just read an article or a book and then be fluent in the field of Native studies, Black studies, Asian studies, Arab American studies, Latin@ studies, and be "in conversation" with this field of study. Or since you are discussing a situation where Black and Asian people cooperated or struggled against each other, that your project is Asian American and Black studies. We must refuse this type of ethnographic entrapment and actually try to enter into study with each other. How do we have actual respect for each other and not just respect for our disciplines? I'm not trying to call people out or shame anyone, but I actually want to start having some real conversations. Because, if you haven't noticed, the wheels are coming off the tracks. And, frankly, why am I am using a train metaphor when this shit was one of the major technologies used to try and annihilate Native peoples? Also, we can think of the labor that Chinese, Mexicans, and Black people put into building this shit. And where is this wealth? Not in our hands. We must start thinking more about how shit we do affects other oppressed communities negatively and positively. We need to keep talking about imperialism.

The questions are really these: Where do you live? If you live in Canada or the United States, you are living on stolen Indian land. Does this scare the shit out of you? It really should, because it is really scary. And also, if the only tool Native studies has is to call you out as a settler, then we are really failing in Native studies. In other words, we should not just have a critique where you fall into an either with us (Indigenous) or against us (settler) identity. How can we complicate this binary? What responsibilities should you possess as a settler toward Indigenous peoples?

As Mia Mingus says, "In order to have accountability you must be in a relationship with that person." In academia, citation is a form of relationship, but not really. We like to pretend that the person we are citing thinks the same thing forever or that they might change. As an Indigenous person, I am asking those who want to study settler colonialism to have a relationship with Indigenous peoples and intellectualism and not with settlers and settler colonialism. Like Indigenous peoples, you also do have a relationship with settler colonialism where it might benefit you and also might deeply hurt you both in the present and historically. So what about the future?

The problem of affectability is the problem of particularity. Denise makes it impossible to strive for universalism, but I am advocating for letting go of our particular wounds or a comparison of them. Only under the regime of universal reason would anything like this make any sort of sense.

When discussing the relationship between anti-Blackness and settler colonialism, we need to remember the alienating forces of white supremacy, capitalism, universalism, and heteropatriarchy. There is a way where we are always trying to think of these situations as separate. And they are separate but they are also similar. They cannot exist without each other, but under capitalism and the thought labor produced in the academic industrial complex through ethnic studies, we must always think of these systems as separate. We also try to understand and compute the misery inherent in these systems and make a judgment whether genocide or slavery was worst. Of course, we rarely discuss the overlap where Indigenous people were enslaved or how Black people were violently displaced from different indigenous communities in Africa. A lot of the violence focuses on how our communities hurt each other, but problems arise when white supremacy falls out of this conversation. I'm not saying this because I love to talk about whiteness, but we need to recognize how white supremacy and universalism sets us in opposition and competition with each other for the saddest stories. For nonnatives, settler colonialism only seems to be sexy without the subject of the native. Living and breathing Native communities complicate the Black and white story of the formation of the United States. Instead of trying to argue for the primal scene of oppression that started the movement of rape, land theft, ecological exploitation, imperial expansion, genocide, and slavery from Europe to Africa and the Americas, can we let go of the question "Did it start with colonialism or anti-Blackness?" and start to ask, How do Black and Native communities continue to hurt each other in the present? What are we actually fighting for? Can we form maroon communities? What kind of political commitment and relationship would we need to make to each other to build a relationality that does not rely on competition for institutional resources or recognition?

I don't want to be all alone. I don't want to be the most oppressed scholar in the academy. It is lonely at the bottom of the heap. I want to be with other people. I want to talk with other people. This is why Stefano Harney and Fred Moten's theorization of the undercommons is so important, because there is no word at the door that must be known to enter. You just come on in no matter how much or how little you possess. I began this article with a quote from *The Undercommons* because I became a revolutionary when I was a teenager and read *The Autobiography of Malcolm X, Zami: A New Spelling of My Name, Roots, Beloved,* and read about the Black Panthers. I had access to Black scholars and authors before I ever heard of Charles Eastman, Zitkala-Ša, Vine Deloria Jr., or Paula Gunn Allen. I knew that white supremacy was not experienced by Black and Native people in the same way, but I could see the failure of the promise of equality of the civil rights movement and poverty reflected in my own life. And I could hear some of the "same things" Denise may have been talking about in her opening summary of the anti-Blackness and settler colonialism conference that twenty-five years later I have been institutionalized to recognize as differences and territory to be battled over in ethnic studies.

So what if we give up and stop fighting and embrace a maroon identity? Careers may be lost and the race for the bottom of racial hierarchy will no longer be relevant. We will have to keep reminding each other about this new strategy because it will not be easy. Competition is a large part of the academic industrial complex and also how I've built my own oppressed persona. Letting go of ideas that have been supported by schools, popular culture, laws, and so forth will not just change because we say so, but at least I hope this chapter creates a desire for an identity formation that works for togetherness and love. The maroon identity is full of mistakes and failures. It is not for individualism but a hope to start hearing more similarities in our stories than differences. Being a maroon is a call to the past when Black and Native people took care of each other; instead of trying to pull each other down to pull ourselves up. We have survived over five hundred years of slavery and colonialism, yet many of us have moved far away from even a hope of togetherness. I'm talking about a deep way of being together. A place where we see the brokenness as a method of relatedness instead of seeking wholeness through comparison and loss. In a maroon community, we theorize love and failure. We try for ideals that could not exist in a "free" world because freedom always comes at the price of building a wall to keep somebody out, killing for peace, and incarcerating and capturing people for profit and safety. This is the "recognition that it's fucked up for you, in the same way it's fucked up for us." The maroon community does not try to save or help one another in a colonial patriarchal way, because we have begun to recognize this modern project of identity and freedom isn't really working for many of us.

Notes

Epigraph: Stefano Harney and Fred Moten, *The Undercommons: Fugitive Planning and Black Study* (New York: Minor Compositions, 2013), 140–41.

1 Eve Tuck, "Suspending Damage: A Letter to Communities," *Harvard Educational Review* 79, no. 3 (September 2009): 409–28.

2 Andrea Smith, "Heteropatriarchy and the Three Pillars of White Supremacy: Rethinking Women of Color Organizing," in *Color of Violence: The Incite Anthology*, ed. INCITE! Women of Color Against Violence (Boston: South End Press, 2006).

3 Eve Tuck and K. Wayne Yang, "Decolonization Is Not a Metaphor," in *Decolonization: Indigeneity, Education & Society* 1, no. 1 (2012): 1–40.

4 Dian Million's *Therapeutic Nations: Healing in an Age of Indigenous Human Rights* (Tucson: University of Arizona Press, 2013).

5 Again, I am referring to Denise Ferreira da Silva's excellent and important work *Towards a Global Idea of Race* (Minneapolis: University of Minnesota Press, 2007). She argues that within the regime of Enlightenment thinking and science people of color can never be transparent universal subjects, and this places us on the horizon of death instead of the horizon of life. This makes affectable subjects, ruled by external forces and our animal instincts instead of an interior and rational mind.

6 Smith, "Heteropatriarchy and the Three Pillars of White Supremacy."

Contributors

Maile Arvin is Assistant Professor of Gender Studies and History at the University of Utah. She is the author of *Possessing Polynesians: The Science of Settler Colonial Whiteness in Hawai'i and Oceania* (Duke University Press, 2019).

Marcus Briggs-Cloud (Maskoke) is the son of the Wind Clan and grandson of the Bird Clan. He is a scholar, environmental and language preservationist, and educator with degrees from the University of Oklahoma and Harvard Divinity School.

J. Kameron Carter is Professor of Religious Studies at Indiana University. His first book is *Race: A Theological Account* (Oxford University Press, 2008). He edited a collection of essays, "Religion and the Future of Blackness," a 2013 special issue of *South Atlantic Quarterly*. He is finishing a book called "Black Rapture: A Poetics of the Sacred."

Ashon Crawley is Associate Professor of Religious Studies and African American and African Studies at the University of Virginia. Crawley's research and teaching experiences are in the areas of Black studies, performance theory and sound studies, philosophy and theology, and Black feminist and queer theories. Crawley's book *Blackpentecostal Breath: The Aesthetics of Possibility* (Fordham University Press, 2016) engages a wide range of critical paradigms from Black studies, queer theory, and sound studies to theology, continental philosophy, and performance studies to theorize the ways in which alternative or "otherwise" modes of existence can serve as disruptions against the marginalization of and violence against minoritarian lifeworlds and possibilities for flourishing.

Denise Ferreira da Silva is Associate Professor and Director of the Institute for Gender, Race, Sexuality, and Social Justice at the University of British Columbia. She is the author of *Toward a Global Idea of Race* (University of Minnesota Press, 2007) and the principal editor for the Routledge/Cavendish book series Law, Race, and the Postcolonial.

Chris Finley is Assistant Professor of American Studies and Ethnicity at the University of Southern California. She is the coeditor of *Queer Indigenous Studies* (University of Arizona Press, 2019). In her research, writing, and teaching, Finley critiques how dominant US popular culture sexualizes Native bodies as culturally and, therefore, racially unable to conform to white heteroreproductive norms.

Hotvlkuce Harjo is a Mvskoke (Creek) visual artist with a concentration in photography, both digital and film (4×5 large format), ink illustration, and a growing emphasis on video art, sound art, jewelry, and creative coding. Their work explores themes of contemporary representations of Indigeneity along with alternative forms of womxnhood and femininity. More recently, they investigate a resurgence in Mvskoke traditional tattooing through southeastern/Mississippian imagery. Common motifs and discourses that inform their articulation of visual language are connected to women + gender studies, queer theory, Indigenous feminism, disability studies, and Mvskoke epistemology. They are currently based in Albuquerque, New Mexico.

Sandra Harvey is Assistant Professor of African American Studies at UC Irvine. She researches the production of race and gender through surveillance technologies originating in colonialism and chattel slavery. Her book project, "Passing for Free, Passing for Sovereign: Blackness and the Formation of the Nation," traces narratives of race/gender passing within science, settler colonial law, conceptual art, and Enlightenment philosophy. The work asks after the assumptions about Blackness that emerge in the passing regime and how these might influence contemporary notions of freedom, sovereignty, the nation, and the citizen.

Chad Benito Infante is a postdoctoral fellow and Assistant Professor of African American and Native American literature in the English department at the University of Maryland, College Park. Infante earned his doctorate in English from Northwestern University in 2018. Originally from Jamaica, his research focuses on Black and Indigenous US and Caribbean literatures, gender, sexuality, critical theory, and political philosophy. He is currently working on a book manuscript that studies representations of murder, revenge, and vengeance in Black and Indigenous literature and art in the twentieth century as a philosophical response to a history of colonial violence.

Tiffany Lethabo King is Assistant Professor of Women's, Gender, and Sexuality Studies and affiliate faculty in the Department of African American Studies at Georgia State University. Her book *The Black Shoals: Offshore Formations of Black and Native Studies* (Duke University Press, 2019) focuses on when, where, and how Black studies and Native studies have been in dialogue with one another.

Jenell Navarro is Associate Professor of Ethnic Studies at California Polytechnic State University, San Luis Obispo. Her work focuses on Native hip-hop and Native feminisms such as her articles "Solarize-ing Native Hip-Hop: Native Feminist Land Ethics and Cultural Resistance" in *Decolonization: Indigeneity, Education & Society* and "WORD: Hip-Hop, Language, and Indigeneity in the Americas" in *Critical Sociology*.

Lindsay Nixon is a Cree-Métis-Saulteaux curator and editor. They are a doctoral student at McGill University in Art History working within the area of Indigenous feminism in contemporary art. They currently hold the position of Editor-at-Large for *Canadian Art*. Their writing has appeared in *The Walrus*, *Malahat Review*, *Room*, GUTS, *Mice*, *esse*, the *Inuit Art Quarterly*, *Teen Vogue*, and other publications. Their memoir, titled *nîtisânak*, was published with Metonymy Press (2018).

Kimberly Robertson (Mvskoke) is an activist, artist, scholar, teacher, and mother who hustles to fulfill the dreams of her ancestors and to build a world in which her daughters can thrive. She works diligently to employ Indigenous feminist theories, practices, and methodologies in her personal, political, intellectual, and professional endeavors. She is an Assistant Professor of Women's, Gender, and Sexuality Studies at California State University, Los Angeles. Her scholarship focuses on Native feminisms and antiviolence work. Some of her recent articles are "The 'Law and Order' of Violence against Native Women: A Native Feminist Analysis of the Tribal Law and Order Act" in *Decolonization: Indigeneity, Education & Society* and "Leading with Our Hearts: Anti-Violence Action and Beadwork Circles as Colonial Resistance" in *Keetsahnak: Our Missing and Murdered Indigenous Sisters* (University of Alberta Press, 2018).

Jared Sexton teaches African American studies at the University of California, Irvine. He is the author of *Amalgamation Schemes: Antiblackness and the Critique of Multiracialism*, *Black Masculinity and the Cinema of Policing*, and *Black Men, Black Feminism: Lucifer's Nocturne*.

Andrea Smith is Professor of Ethnic Studies at UC Riverside. She is the author of *Unreconciled: From Racial Reconciliation to Racial Justice in Christian Evangelicalism* (Duke University Press, 2019); *Conquest: Sexual Violence and American Indian Genocide* (Duke University Press, 2015); and *Native Americans and the Christian Right: The Gendered Politics of Unlikely Alliances* (Duke University Press, 2008). She is also coeditor of *Theorizing Native Studies* (Duke University Press, 2014) and *Native Studies Keywords* (University of Arizona Press, 2015).

Cedric Sunray is a teacher and advocate for historic "non-federal" tribes across the country with a primary focus on those living in the eastern and southern regions of the United States. He focuses on those "non-federal" tribes who generationally attended the federal, and closely related, mission Indian boarding school systems. He is a founder of helphaskell.com.

Se'mana Thompson is an Akimel Otham artist and scholar and the current curator of *The People's Zine Library*, a zine library by and for Black, Indigenous, and People of Color. They are editor of the zines *queer indigenous girl*, *Decolonizing P@renting*, and *Black Indigenous Boy*, and their art has been featured in the *Deaf Poets Society* and reviewed in *Canadian Art*.

Rinaldo Walcott is Director of the Women and Gender Studies Institute at The University of Toronto. He is the author of *Black Like Who: Writing Black Canada*

(Insomniac Press, 1997, with a second revised edition in 2003); he is also the editor of *Rude: Contemporary Black Canadian Cultural Criticism* (Insomniac, 2000); and the coeditor with Roy Moodley of *Counseling Across and Beyond Cultures: Exploring the Work of Clemmont E. Vontress in Clinical Practice* (University of Toronto Press, 2010).

Frank B. Wilderson III is an award-winning writer, activist, and critical theorist who spent five and a half years in South Africa, where he was one of two Americans who held an elected office in the African National Congress during the country's transition from apartheid. He also worked clandestinely as a member of the ANC's armed wing, Umkhonto We Sizwe. He has worked as a dramaturge for Lincoln Center Theater and the Market Theater in Johannesburg. He is the recipient of the National Endowment for the Arts Fellowship, the Alexander von Humboldt Fellowship for Experienced Researchers, and the American Book Award as well as other literary awards and honors. His books include *Incognegro* (Duke University Press, 2015) and *Red, White & Black: Cinema and the Structure of U.S. Antagonisms* (Duke University Press, 2010).

Index

Page numbers in italics refer to illustrations.

Arvin, Maile, 6, 18, 121; on settler colonialism, 88
Assu, Sonny, 337
Atkins, J. D. C., 120
Atleo, Shawn, 354
authenticity, 216, 223; and identity policing, 288; and Indianness, 251–52, 273; and "non-federal" tribes, 249; and race, 216, 224, 227; and tribal enrollment, 270

Bacone College, 240
Baker, Courtney, 140–41
Baldwin, James, 17, 149; on cool fratricide, 133–34, 151n2
Bambara, Toni Cade, 176
Baraka, Amiri, 159–60
bare life, 112n15; and universalism, 84
Bataille, Georges, 164–68, 171; on the monstrous, 173; on sacrifice, 184; on untouchables, 167
beadwork, 323–24
Belcourt, Billy-Ray, 338
Belcourt, Christi, 335
Bell, John Stewart, 42
Benjamin, Walter, 48–49; on violence, 203n95
Bergson, Henri, 48–49
Berry, Vincent, II, 314n7
Betty's Case, 198n49
Bey, Marquis, 307
Beyoncé, 19, 166; and capitalism, 299, 314n7; cultural labor of, 302–3, 314n7; feminism, engagement with, 314n11; heteropatriarchy, critique of, 307–8; I Have Three Hearts (photo shoot), 303–4, 315n25; "Love on Top," 312–13; and mothering practice, 304–5; "No Angel," 302; police violence, condemnation of, 300–303; and radical kinship, 308–11; scholarship on, 313n5. See also Lemonade (Beyoncé visual album)
Big Freedia, 306–7
Birdwell, Stephanie, 266
Black bodies: as abject, 154n57; and anti-Blackness, 14–15, 137, 141; and Black studies, 56; and criminality, 141; female, 141–42, 153n39; and law, 137; and settler colonialism, 229, 302; and sexual violence, 137–38; territoriality of, 141–42

Black death: and settler colonialism, 301–2, 305; and whiteness, 57; and white supremacy, 78
Black diaspora: and impossibility of return, 349–50
Black diaspora studies, 344, 356nn4–5; and anti-Blackness, 344; the Atlantic, centrality of, 348–52; and Black studies, 5; and colonialism, 5; and enslavement, 5; and globalization, 345; and the human, 347–48; and Indigenous genocide, 346; and Indigenous studies, 20–21; and transatlantic slavery, 344–52
Black feminism, 297–98; and Afropessimism, 61; and relationality, 298–300
blacklight, 44
Black Lives Matter, 77, 81
black metal, 291–92
Blackness, 12; and abjection, 65–66, 78, 134, 151n2; and citizenship, 224; and conquest, 78, 83; disavowal of, 95; ecstatics of, 178; and the flesh, 31–33, 85–86; and humanness, 29, 85–86, 153n44, 351, 354; and identity formation, 354; and Indianness, 134, 245–46; Indian rejection of, 239, 242; and indigeneity, 17, 33, 353; and land, 353; as lapsarian condition, 177; and modernity, 34, 83, 84; in Maskoke cosmology, 283–84, 286, 287–89; and Native Hawaiianness, 216–17; and Nativeness, 134–35, 150, 224, 230; and Native peoples, 16, 119–21, 125–28; and "non-federal" tribes, 260–63; and ontology, 16; as property, 17, 278; queerness of, 159; and race, 233n17; and recognition, 245–46, 261–63; and the sacred, 163–64, 169; and settler colonialism, 82; and slavery, 225; and sociality, 226–28; and sovereignty, 224–25; and subjectivity, 66, 68; and surveillance, 224–25; and tribal enrollment, 242; and violence, 62. See also anti-Blackness
Black people: abjection of, 13; as property, 124; surveillance of, 18; as "unthought of sovereignty," 125
Black Power movement, 3
Black Seminoles, 287
Black studies: and African diaspora studies, 5; and Black bodies, 56; and conquest,

16; diasporic approach to, 12; and ethnic studies, 2–4; and gender, 61; genealogy of, 3–5; humanism, critique of, 83; and Native studies, 2–3, 6, 22n8, 300, 363; outside of US, 4–5, 72; racial slavery in, 108; suffering, centrality of, 14–15

Black women, 229; invisibility of, 298

blood: and belonging, 221–24; and law, 229; and race, 226

blood quantum, 153n46, 241; and allotment, 354; and Cherokee Nation, 248; and Choctaw enrollment, 226–27, 231n4; and citizenship, 218–19; and Indianness, 251; and tribal identification, 249

Bloomfield, Mandy, 183–84

Boughman, Mary, 220–21, 223–25, 228–30

Boylorn, Robin M., 297

Brady, Jean, 78

Brand, Dionne, 13

Brathwaite, Kamau, 356, 359n31

Brazeau, Patrick, 354

Briggs-Cloud, Marcus, 6, 12, 15, 18–19

Brock, Lisa, 346

Brookings, Polly, 220–21, 223–24, 226–28, 230

Brown, Antonio, 22n10

Brown, Sharon Scholars, 243

Brown v. Board of Education, 126

Butler, Judith, 62

Byrd, Jodi A., 87, 139, 140, 229

Caillois, Roger, 164, 165–66

call-out culture, 364

Campbell, Maria, 335

Camus, Albert, 151n2

capitalism, 367; and Beyoncé, 299, 314n7; and death, 355; and the human, 348; and interanimation, 159; and the public interest, 39; and slavery, 104; and whiteness, 121

Carnell, Yvette, 22n10

Carruthers, Charlene, 11

Carter, J. Kameron, 8, 17, 138

Castile, Philando, 56, 195, 301

Cavanaugh, Edward, 80, 89

Cervenak, Sarah Jane, 174

Chenault, Venida, 267

Cherokee Freedmen: expulsion of, 246–47; re-enrollment of, 247, 258

Choctaw Nation: Black citizenship in, 222–25; Black enrollment in, 219–21; and blood quantum, 226–27, 231n4; citizenship in, 231n4, 231n8; Freedmen, enrollment of, 224–25, 232nn10–11; tribal rolls of, 231n4. *See also* MOWA Band of Choctaw Indians

Churchill, Ward, 67–71, 89

citizenship: and Blackness, 224; and blood quantum, 218–19; in Choctaw nation, 231n4, 231n8; and enrollment, 219–21; and marriage, 229; and Native peoples, 105, 273; and race, 221; and slavery, 105–6; and whiteness, 273

civil rights, 7, 111n11, 368; and anti-Blackness, 122

Clooney, George, 214

Cloud, George, 287

coalitional politics, 65, 150, 362

Coleman, Arica L., 154n46

Collins, Patricia Hill, 304

colonialism: and African diaspora studies, 5; as conquest, 89; and diaspora, 348; and land, 125; and modernity, 349; and Native American studies, 91n12; and racial difference, 97; racial logic of, 96–97, 111n7; racism of, 95; resistance to, 351; versus settler colonialism, 96–97, 122, 124; and slavery, 109; violence of, 298

coloniality, 4; and anti-Blackness, 354–55

colonial unknown, 78–79

colonization, 124–25; afterlife of, 7; and genocide, 358n13; and land, theft of, 119. *See also* decolonization

colorblindness, 95

Columbus, Christopher: and Black death, 78; Christian humanism of, 85; and slavery, 79

community, 151; evolution of, 275

conquest: and Blackness, 78, 83; and colonialism, 89; discourse of, 84, 86, 91n13; and the flesh, 43; and genocide, 85, 140; and the human, 70, 85; and law, 136; and Native studies, 16; and settlement, 91n13; and slavery, 80, 85; and subjectivity, 70; violence of, 78–79, 83–85, 91n13; and white settler colonial studies, 80, 89–90

Continental theory: and liberal humanism, 87–88

Cook-Lynn, Elizabeth, 2

cool fratricide, 133–35, 141, 150–51, 151n2, 155n64; in "Tony's Story," 148
Cooper, Brittney, 297, 314n11
Cornsilk, David, 257–59
Cornum, Lou, 333
cosmology, Maskoke: Blackness in, 283–84, 286, 287–89
Coulthard, Glen Sean, 10, 111n9; on capitalism, 121; on genocide, 123
Crawley, Ashon, 6, 13–15, 17; on disappearance, 128; on otherwise worlds, 158, 159
Critical Ethnic Studies Association: inaugural conference, 366
Critical Resistance, 59–60
critical theory, 344; as masculinist space, 61
crunk, 297
Crunk Feminist Collective, 307
Curtis Act, 221

Danger, Dayna, 338–39
Daniel, Peter, 124
Dardar, Michael, 258
Darwin, Charles, 87
Daughters of the Dust (film), 310
Dawes Allotment Act, 120–21, 221
DeClue, Jennifer, 306
decolonial love, 312, 317n57
decolonization, 2–4, 13; and anti-Blackness, 119; discourse of, 334; and land, 128, 366; and language, 275; and love, 333–35; Native, 10, 230; and settler colonialism, 100; and settler decolonization, 97–99, 111n6; and sovereignty, 95; and suffering, 49n9
Deleuze, Gilles, 42, 88, 93n33; nonrepresentation, theory of, 58
Deloria, Philip, 148
Deloria, Vine, Jr., 67, 69, 89, 368; on spatiality, 275
Derbecker, Andrea, 123
Descartes, René, 178
Descendants, The (film), 213–14, 217
Descendants, The (Hemmings novel), 213, 216
determinacy, 44–45, 47
Díaz, Junot, 317n52
difference, cultural: and political-symbolic violence, 39–40; and protest, 40–41
Diouf, Sylviane, 35–36

disappearance, 128; as deferred genocide, 126; logic of, 123
disenrollment: of Indian Freedmen, 237, 246–47, 273
displacement: of Black Indians, 256; in Inuit art, 337; of Maskoke People, 284–85, 286, 287; and settler colonialism, 274, 276; violence of, 222
dispossession, 66; and land, 102; politics of, 65; and slavery, 299, 301, 323; trauma of, 139
Douglass, Patrice, 56
Dred Scott v. Sandford, 124, 126
Driskill, Qwo-Li, 338
Du Bois, W. E. B., 178, 195
Durant, Sophia McGillivray, 286
Durkheim, Émile, 164, 168

Easley-Houser, Arika, 3
Eastman, Charles, 368
ecstasy, 165–66, 169–70
Einstein, Albert, 42
Eliade, Mircea, 173
Enlightenment: and the human, 351; and reason, 44
ethnicity, 227, 232n17
ethnic studies: and Black studies, 2–4; Indigenous peoples in, 364; and Native studies, 2; and settler colonial discourse, 81
eugenics, 221, 269
excess: and the flesh, 33; as metaphor, 32
explication, 177–78, 180–82

Fanon, Frantz, 97, 344; on decolonization, 13; on recognition, politics of, 111n9
Farley, Anthony, 137
femininity, 334
feminism, 61; and Beyoncé, 314n11; Black, 297–300; epistemology of, 87; Native, 298–300, 365; radical womxn of color, 298, 299–300, 308; white, 304
Ferreira da Silva, Denise, 6, 15, 17, 35, 362; on death, 363; on disappearance, 128; on nullification, 165; on poethics, 169; on universal subject, 363, 367–68, 369n5
Filiyah, John, 228
Finley, Chris, 8, 15, 21
Fischer, Sibylle, 348–49

National Coalition of Blacks for Reparations in America, 22n10

Native American studies, 91n12. *See also* Native studies

Native feminism, 300, 365

Nativeness: and abjection, 65, 146–47; as atemporal ethnicity, 233n17; and Blackness, 134–35, 150, 224, 230. *See also* Indianness; indigeneity

Native peoples: and anti-Blackness, 55; and Blackness, 125–26; and citizenship, 105; coalitional politics of, 65; as "disappearing," 10–11, 119–20, 332–33, 364; and labor, 120–21; as "natural resources," 119–20; and whiteness, 119–21; whiteness and Blackness, disappearance into, 16, 119–21, 125–28

Native studies, 17; and anti-Blackness, 67; and Black diasporic studies, 20–21; Black-Native solidarity in, 101–3; and Black studies, 2–3, 6, 22n8, 300, 363; colonialism, critique of, 96; and conquest, 16; development of, 95–96; emancipation, narrative of, 111n10; and ethnic studies, 2; genealogy of, 2; and racism, 105; and resistance, 100, 102; settler colonialism in, 102–8, 366; and settler colonial studies, 365; and sovereignty, 2; and violence, 69–70

Navarro, Jenell, 8, 12, 19–20

Negri, Antonio, 334

Negrophobia: and sovereignty, 107

neocolonialism, 98

neoliberalism, 354, 356

Nichols, Robert, 121

Nixon, Lindsay, 8, 12, 20

"non-federal" tribes: and authenticity, 249; and Blackness, 260–63; at Haskell, 267–68; identity policing of, 252–54, 258; and Oklahoma art law, 247, 254–55; recognition of, 264–69

Obama, Barack, 176

Ogden, Stormy, 328

Olson, Joel, 71

one-drop rule, 153n46

ontology: and anti-Blackness, 203n107; Black, 86; of Blackness, 16, 52, 86; of indigeneity, 16; Indigenous, 99; Native, 86; otherwise, 13; and political theology, 192; and relation-ality, 12; settler, 86; of sovereignty, 168; and Western Christianity, 274

Ortiz, Simon, 136

Osburn, Katherine, 232n8

Osceola, Charlie, 285

Otherwise Worlds conference, 5–7, 53–54, 362

Otto, Rudolf, 160

Pacific Islanders: as property, 215

Pan-Africanism, 356n4

Pancoast, Henry, 126

Pateman, Carole, 81, 91n13

Patterson, Orlando, 225

Peltier, Leonard, 65

Petersen, Robert, 325–27

Philip, M. NourbeSe, 159; poetics of, 174, 182–85, 188, 192–94; on the shaman, 203n95; *Zong!*, 161, 182–94. See also *Zong!* (Philip poem)

Pipestem, Wilson, 269

Pistoletto, Michelangelo, 42

Plecker, Walter, 245, 269

Plessy v. Ferguson, 126

poethics, 15, 40–41, 48–49, 169; of the sacred, 170

police killings, 299, 300–303; of Indigenous people, 323

political theology, 163, 170–77; as cosmology of settlement, 173; as discourse of Being, 170–71; and ontology, 192; and the sacred, 171

Polynesians: as "almost white," 214; as possessions of whiteness, 214, 215

Porete, Marguerite, 178

pornotroping, 62–63

postcolonial studies, 352

postracialism, 95; and Charlottesville white nationalist rally, 176

"Power" (Lorde poem), 134–38, 140–44, 149–50; retributive murder in, 140–44; universality in, 137

prison abolition, 58–59, 64–65, 323

prison industrial complex, 59

Proctor, Sam, 277

property: anticolonial, 40; Black people as, 124; Indigenous, 38–39; land as, 119

protest: and cultural difference, 40–41

psychoanalysis: as anti-Black, 68
Pudlat, Pudlo, 336–37
Pugliese, Joseph, 119

queerness, 307; of Blackness, 149
queers of color: visibility of, 306–7

race: and authenticity, 216, 224, 227; and
    Blackness, 233n17; and blood, 226; and
    citizenship, 221; and colonialism, 95–97,
    111n7; and ethnicity, 232n17; and sover-
    eignty, 221, 225–26; and tribal enrollment,
    221
racism: anti-Black, 101, 244, 253; anti-Brown,
    253; and Native studies, 105; violence of,
    298
radical kinship, 308–12
radical womxn of color feminism, 298,
    299–300, 308
Rankin, Don, 243
Rankine, Claudia, 159
rationality: political, 162, 171–73; theological,
    162, 173
reason: post-Enlightenment, 44
recognition: and anti-Black racism, 244; and
    Black abolition, 10; of Black Choctaws,
    224–25; and Blackness, 245–46, 261–63;
    and blood quantum, 266; and boarding
    school attendance, 262, 263–68; and Indig-
    enous decolonization, 10; and language,
    227; and proximity to whiteness, 245–46;
    and settler colonialism, 33–34
reconciliation, 98, 334–35; politics of, 334
Rediker, Marcus, 348
redress, 149; and Black-Native relations, 7;
    politics of, 65
Red Star, Wendy, 12
Red, White, and Black (Wilderson), 15, 16,
    106–8; Black and Indigenous flesh in,
    63–64; Indigenous thought in, 54; ontology
    in, 52
relationality, 1–2, 14, 61; and anti-Blackness,
    69; between genocide and anti-Blackness,
    1–2; between Native and Black feminists,
    298–300; non-human, 12; and ontology, 12;
    and suffering, 33; and violence, 33
religion: and law, 184, 191; and the state,
    162–63

reparations, 22n10, 358n13; to colonialism,
    351; kinship as, 333, 338; and US settler
    colonialism, 7
resistance: land-based, 102; and Native stud-
    ies, 100, 102
respectability, 236; as settler construct, 307
resurgence, 100, 106; and settler decoloniza-
    tion, 99
retribution: in "Tony's Story," 147
Richman, Michèle, 166, 167
Rifkin, Mark, 33–34, 112n14
Riley, Alexander, 168
Robertson, Kimberly, 8, 12, 19–20
Robinson, Cedric, 171–72, 181
Robinson, Zandria, 302, 311–12
Rodriguez, Dylan, 123
Ross, John, 250–51
Ross, Luana, 323
Russell, Steve, 269

sacred, the: ambivalence of, 164–70; and
    Blackness, 163–64, 169; and Black studies,
    167–68; etymology of, 168; malpractice
    of, 163–64, 169, 171, 174–75, 184; and mo-
    dernity, 176, 195; poethics of, 170, 171–75,
    177–82; and political theology, 171; and the
    profane, 159–60, 165–70, 184; and sover-
    eignty, 171, 181
Sanchez, Sonia, 260
Saranillio, Dean, 216
Sartre, Jean-Paul, 97
Saunt, Claudio, 285
Schmitt, Carl, 170
Schurz, Carl, 125–26
Scott, Darieck, 147–48
Scott, Walter, 27
separability, 40, 42–44, 47–49, 50n11
settler colonialism: and allotment, 220–21;
    as analytic, 365; and anti-Blackness, 5–6,
    12, 18, 22n8, 111n6, 285, 362–63, 367–68;
    and antiracism, 99–100, 121; and the black
    body, 229, 302; and Black death, 301–2, 305;
    and Blackness, 82; and the body, 14–15, 229,
    302; versus colonialism, 96–97, 122, 124;
    and conquest, 80–81; and containment,
    327–28; and death, 13, 301, 305, 311, 332; and
    decolonization, 100; and displacement,
    274, 276; and ethnic studies, 81; and gender,

settler colonialism (cont.)
145–46; genealogy of, 88; and genocide, 82,
88, 103, 107, 145, 299, 305; and humanism,
82; and land, 81–83, 122, 274, 338; limits
of discourse, 345, 353; and modernity, 94;
and murder, 149–50; and Native American
studies, 91n12; and Native studies, 102–8,
366; in the Pacific, 215; and policing, 301;
and property, 215; and racial difference, 97;
and racial mixture, 216; and recognition,
33–34; resistance to, 287; and slavery, 82,
102, 105; as structure, 80; and surveillance,
301; violence of, 6, 145, 305, 322; and the
white body, 147; and whiteness, 213, 215–16;
and white supremacy, 215
settler colonialism, Asian, 216
settler colonial studies: and Black studies,
78–80; colonial studies, critique of, 108;
and genocide, 80; and Native studies, 365;
origins of, 80. *See also* settler colonialism;
white settler colonial studies
Settler Colonial Studies (journal), 80, 96,
110n6
settler decolonization: and Indigenous
resurgence, 99; and sovereignty, 111n6; and
violence, 97, 98
Sexton, Jared, 4–5, 6, 16; on abolition, 58–60;
on colonization, 124–25; on Indigenous
liberation, 122–23; Native studies, critique
of, 17; on Native subjectivity, 55–56, 67; on
settler colonialism, 65; on the "unthought"
of sovereignty, 118–19; Wilderson, as corrective to, 64; on Zapatistas, 49n9
sexual violence, 305; and the Black body,
137–38; and Indigenous sexuality, 339; in
"Power," 135, 137–38
Sharpe, Christina, 10
Shaw, Lemuel, 198n49
Shire, Warsan, 315n25
Shiva, Vandana, 281
Silko, Leslie Marmon, 67, 69–70, 89; "Tony's
Story," 134–35
Simons, Booker T., 219
Simons, Donnie, 218–19, 221
Simpson, Audra, 145
Simpson, Leanne Betasamosake, 19, 33, 299,
304, 333–35
Skibine, George, 244

slave labor: and exchange value, 45; as surplus
value, 46
slavery: afterlife of, 7, 59, 225, 301; and Black
diaspora studies, 344–52; and Blackness,
225; and Black studies, 108; and Black
women's bodies, 229; and capitalism, 104;
and citizenship, 105–6; and colonialism,
109; and conquest, 85; and consent, 62; and
dispossession, 299, 301, 323; and the flesh,
43; and free will, 199n49; and gender, 144;
and genocide, 106; and genocide, Indigenous, 134; and global capital, 43, 347; Indians, enslavement by, 4, 101, 273–74, 278–82,
285–87; Indians, enslavement of, 325–26;
and indigeneity, loss of, 101–2; and kinship,
225; and labor, 16, 106; and law, 136; logic
of, 104–5, 112n14; and Maskoke language,
278–80, 287; and modernity, 94, 109; and
murder, 149–50; and property, 199n49;
and resurgence, 108; and settler colonialism, 82, 102, 105; and sovereignty, 106; and
subjectivity, 69; and tribal enrollment, 227;
violence of, 16, 144; and the white body, 147
Slay (Robertson serigraph), *320*
Smith, Andrea, 6, 12, 15, 91n12, 111n11; on the
death imaginary, 332; on land, 17; on slavery, 16, 104–6, 112n14; on white supremacy,
103–4
Smith, Chad "Corntassel," 247
Smith, Tracy K., 195
social death, 52, 89
sociality, 17–19; and Blackness, 226–28; and
the festival, 166; otherwise, 36
sociality, Black, 302
Soldier, Layli Long, 174
solidarity: Black-Native, 100–103; rejection
of, 2
Somerville, Alice Te Punga, 215
Sotiropoulos, Karen, 346
sovereignty, 4, 7; and anti-Blackness, 55; and
Blackness, 224–25; and Black survival,
67; and decolonization, 95; and federal
recognition, 258–59, 265; and Freedmen removal, 260; and genocide, 123; and home,
335; and identity policing, 248; and land,
100; and Native claim to land, 118; and Native studies, 2; and Native women's bodies,
229–30; ontology of, 168; and race, 221,

225–26; and the sacred, 171, 181; and settler ontology, 89; as temporary, 127
Sparks, John, 246
Spillers, Hortense, 14, 304; on the Black body, 142; on Blackness, 169; on conquest, 85; on ethnicity, 227, 232n17; on the flesh, 15, 28, 29, 31–32, 43, 62, 86, 144; and the human, 84–85; on the monstrous, 173; on Moynihan Report, 232n17; and relationality, 61
spirit possession: and ecstasy, 166; in *Zong!*, 193
Spivak, Gayatri, 338
state violence: and forced sterilization, 299
Sterling, Alton, 56, 301
Stevenson, Winona, 2
Stitt, Kevin, 271
subjectivity, 184; and agency, 5; Western, 178
subjectivity, Black, 66, 68; and Native genocide, 68
subjectivity, Native, 5, 63; and anti-Blackness, 53
suffering: and Afro-pessimism, 57; in Black studies, 14–15; and decolonization, 49n9; and genocide, 65; grammar of, 15, 65, 72; logic of, 34–35; and sovereignty, 65
suffering, Black, 67–68
Sunray, Cedric, 8, 12
surveillance: and Blackness, 224–25; of Black people, 18; and settler colonialism, 301
Swain, Molly, 332
Swimmer, Ross, 267
syncretism, 150, 155n66

TallBear, Kim, 127
Tatonetti, Lisa, 338
tattooing, 291–92; and gender, 292; traditional, 19
Taylor, Wilford, 259
Tecumseh, 288
Terada, Rei, 171–73
Thompson, Se'mana, 8, 20
"Tony's Story" (Silko short story), 134–36, 138–40, 144–50; cool fratricide in, 148; masculinity in, 146
Torre, Manuel, 202n83
Trask, Haunani-Kay, 69–70, 89; on genocide, 88–89; on settler colonialism, 88–89
Tribe Called Red, A, 12

Trump, Donald, 176, 271
Tsingine, Loreal, 299
Tuck, Eve, 335, 365
Tuggle, W. O., 282–83
Tunnillie, Ovilu, 336, 337

undercommons, 158, 192, 368
universalism, 349; and bare life, 84; and biopolitics, 84; and humanism, 87; and whiteness, 140–41, 148, 367

Vargas, João Costa, 301
Veracini, Lorenzo, 80, 89, 96–97, 124
Verran, Cecilia Kavara, 338
Verret, Dove, 258–59
Vicente Vásquez, Saúl, 38
Viera, Mario Pete, Jr., 240
violence, 203n95; and anti-Blackness, 6, 10, 139–40; and Blackness, 62; of colonialism, 298; of conquest, 78–79, 83–85, 91n13; of displacement, 222; and excess, 33; of genocide, 16, 140; and Indianness, 147; metaphysical, 150; of Middle Passage, 185; of modernity, 36, 185; and Native studies, 69–70; quotidian nature of, 27–28; of racism, 298; and relation, 33; retributive, 133–34, 140–44, 150–51; and settler colonialism, 6, 145, 305, 322; of sexism, 298; and sexuality, 62; and slavery, 62, 222; and sovereignty, 222; and surveillance, 28; against transwomen of color, 35; and whiteness, 149; and white supremacy, 78
Vizenor, Gerald, 333
Vowel, Chelsea, 335

Walcott, Derek, 351–52
Walcott, Rinaldo, 5, 6, 20–21
Wang, Lee Ann, 364
Warren, Calvin, 203n107
Washburn, Kevin, 265
Waziyatawin, 100
Weaver, Gallasneed, 270
Webber, Andrew Lloyd, 188
Weheliye, Alexander, 14, 83–84; on the flesh, 36; on genocide, 84; on Spillers, 28, 30, 34; on Wynter, 28, 30, 34
White, Hattie, 309
white feminism: and motherhood, 304

whiteness: and Black death, 57; and blood quantum, 154n46; and capitalism, 121; and Indianness, 241, 245–46; and indigeneity, 18, 105, 121, 123; and law, 142, 147; and logic of disappearance, 123; metaphysics of, 146; and modernity, 86; and Native citizenship, 273; and Native peoples, 118; Native proximity to, 105, 121, 123, 216, 245–46; and Pacific Islanders, 215; and Polynesia, 18, 216; and property, 17, 215; and recognition, 245–46; as religion, 190, 195; retributive violence against, 134; and settler colonialism, 213, 215–16; and universalism, 140–41, 148, 367; vengeance against, 17; and violence, 149

white privilege: and federal recognition, 255; in Indian Country, 254–63; of mixed-race Indians, 241, 243, 252; among Natives, 236, 247–49

white settler colonial studies, 16, 22n8, 82; and anti-Blackness, 22n8; and colonial unknown, 79; and conquest, 80, 89–90; emergence of, 4; and land, 79; and settler colonialism, 22n8; and settler subjectivity, 79. *See also* settler colonialism; settler colonial studies

white supremacy, 364; and anti-Blackness, 95; and Black death, 78; and Black-Native relations, 9; and Black women's bodies, 229; and humanity, 128; and settler colonialism, 215; and sovereignty, 126; and universalism, 367; and violence, 78

Wildcat, Daniel, 267–68

Wilderson, Frank B., 4–5, 12, 15, 18; Afropessimism of, 89; on community, 151; on the flesh, 86; on genocide, 107, 123, 134; Indigenous ontology, critique of, 66; Native studies, critique of, 17; on settler colonialism, 107–8, 123; on slavery and labor, 118, 120; on subjectivity, 84, 128

Williams, Delores, 34–35

Williams, Phillip B., 169–70

Williams, Robert A., 87, 126

Williams, Serena, 306, 307

Winner, Lauren, 188

"Woke Up This Morning" (song), 30, 32–33, 36

Wolfe, Patrick, 68, 70, 80–81; on land, 82–83; on logic of elimination, 315n14

Woodson, Carter G., 3

Worcester v. Georgia, 127

Wright, Michelle, 11

Wynter, Sylvia, 5, 14, 344; on conquest, 85; on the "new world," 346; on slavery, 347; on universalism, 87; on western Man, 29, 31–32, 84, 87, 354

Yahola, Ben, 276

Yancey, Daunasia, 78

Yanez, Jeronimo, 301

Yang, K. Wayne, 365

Yargee, 286–87

Yelle, Robert, 168

Yvholv, Pasokv, 287

Zapatistas, 38, 40, 47–48, 49n9; and "cultural difference," 44

Zeleza, Paul, 349

zines: *Black Indigenous Boy, 331; Mass Incarceration since 1492, 325; Queer Indigenous Girl, 330*

Zitkala-Sa, 368

Zong! (Philip poem), 161, *187*; Christian ritual in, 185–86, 188–93; as malpractice, 182, 183–85, 188; and the sacred, 164, 184; and the sacred otherwise, 194; spirit possession in, 193. *See also* Philip, M. NourbeSe